Book of Ages

Book of Ages

The Life and Opinions of Jane Franklin

Jill Lepore

ALFRED A. KNOPF | NEW YORK | 2013

THIS IS A BORZOI BOOK
PUBLISHED BY ALFRED A. KNOPF

www.aaknopf.com

Knopf, Borzoi Books, and the colophon are registered trademarks of Random House, Inc.

Library of Congress Cataloging-in-Publication Data
Lepore, Jill, [date]
Book of ages : the life and opinions of Jane Franklin / Jill Lepore.—First Edition.
pages cm.
Includes bibliographical references.
ISBN 978-0-307-95834-1
1. Mecom, Jane, 1712–1794.   2. Franklin, Benjamin, 1706–1790.   3. Women—United States—Social conditions—18th century.   4. Boston (Mass.)—Biography.   I. Title.
E302.6.F8L427 2013
973.3092—dc23
[B]   2013001012

Front-of-jacket portrait of Jane Flagg Greene (Jane Franklin's granddaughter) by Joseph Badger, oil on canvas, 1765, Thayer Memorial Library, Lancaster, Massachusetts
Jacket design by Kelly Blair

Appendix G, "A Map of Jane's Boston," adapted by Robert Bull, from *Jane Mecom* by Carl Van Doren (New York: Viking, 1950)

Manufactured in the United States of America

First Edition

In memory
of my father
and of my mother
their youngest daughter
places this stone

One Half of the World

does not know

how the other Half lives.

BENJAMIN FRANKLIN,
Poor Richard's Almanack

Contents

Preface

Benjamin Franklin's sister Jane thought of her brother as her "Second Self."[1] He was the youngest of ten sons; she was the youngest of seven daughters. Benny and Jenny, they were called, when they were little. No two people in their family were more alike.

Their lives could hardly have been more different. He ran away from home when he was seventeen. She never left. He taught himself to write with wit and force and style; she never learned how to spell. The day he turned twenty-one, he wrote her a letter—she was fourteen—beginning a correspondence that would last until his death sixty-three years later. He became a printer, a philosopher, and a statesman. She became a wife, a mother, and a widow. He signed the Declaration of Independence, the Treaty of Paris, and the Constitution. She strained to form the letters of her name. He loved no one longer. She loved no one better. He wrote more letters to her than he wrote to anyone. All her life, she wrote back: letter after letter filled with news and recipes and gossip and, when she was truly, sorely vexed, and only then, with her blistering opinions about politics.

He wrote the story of his life, a well-turned tale about a boy who runs away from poverty and obscurity in cramped, pious Boston and leaves all that behind—leaves home behind, leaves his sister behind, leaves the past behind—to become an enlightened, independent man of the world: a free man. It is one of the most important autobiographies ever written. It is also an allegory about America: the story of a man as the story of a nation.

In that story, he left her out. Never once did he so much as mention her name. All the same, little of what Benjamin Franklin wrote—not the Silence Dogood essays, not *Poor Richard's Almanack*, not *The Way to Wealth*, not the autobiography—can be understood without her. This book, a history of the life and opinions of Jane Franklin, contains with it a wholly new reading of the life and opinions of her brother. But more, it tells her story. Like his, her life is an allegory: it explains what it means to write history not from what survives but from what is lost. "One Half of the World does not know how the other Half lives," Franklin once wrote. His sister is his other Half.

She never wrote the story of her life. This would scarcely have occurred to her.[2] But she did once write a book. She stitched four sheets of foolscap between two covers to make sixteen pages. On its first page, she wrote,

Jane Franklin Born on March 27 1712

She called it her Book of Ages.[3] It is a record of the births and deaths of her children, a litany of grief.

I once held it in my hands. It was so small, so fragile, so plain, her handwriting so tiny and cramped. Sixteen pages and, as I turned them, I discovered that she had left the last pages blank. Had she nothing more to say?

Virginia Woolf once asked, "What would have happened had Shakespeare had a wonderfully gifted sister, called Judith"? Woolf gave herself permission to invent this Judith Shakespeare—"Let me imagine, since facts are so hard to come by"—and conjured a girl as brilliant and daring as her brother:

> She was as adventurous, as imaginative, as agog to see the world as he was. But she was not sent to school. She had no chance of learning grammar and logic, let alone of reading Horace and Virgil. She picked up a book now and then, one of her brother's perhaps, and read a few pages. But then her parents came in and told her to mend the stockings or mind the stew and not moon about with books and papers.

What, Woolf wondered, would have been Judith Shakespeare's fate?

> Before she was out of her teens, she was to be betrothed to the son of a neighbouring wool-stapler. She cried out that marriage was hateful to her, and for that she was severely beaten by her father. Then he ceased

to scold her. He begged her instead not to hurt him, not to shame him in this matter of her marriage. He would give her a chain of beads or a fine petticoat, he said; and there were tears in his eyes. How could she disobey him? How could she break his heart?

Judith Shakespeare did break her father's heart: she ran away. "The force of her own gift alone drove her to it," Woolf wrote. "She made up a small parcel of her belongings, let herself down by a rope one summer's night and took the road to London. She was not seventeen." In London, she was seduced by an actor, after which "she found herself with child by that gentleman and so—who shall measure the heat and violence of the poet's heart when caught and tangled in a woman's body?—killed herself one winter's night."[4]

Judith Shakespeare is a figment of Virginia Woolf's imagination, a heroine trapped, skirts aflutter, in a modern, manly idea of the self, and of the author as solitary and unencumbered: a free man. No American writer did more to mold that idea of authorship than Benjamin Franklin. Judith Shakespeare could not reconcile a life of the mind with the life of a mother. Neither could Virginia Woolf.

The facts of Jane Franklin's life are hard to come by. Her obscurity is matched only by her brother's fame. If he meant to be Everyman, she is everyone else. Most of what she wrote is lost—the first letter in her hand to survive is one she wrote when she was forty-five years old—and what scant record of her life is left has been saved only because she was Benjamin Franklin's sister.

But Jane Franklin is not a figment of my imagination. She was flesh and blood and milk and tears. Her brother ran away and broke their father's heart; she would not, could not. She never gave herself that much rope. She didn't kill herself one winter's night. She never gave herself that kind of rope, either. She had too many people to look after. She never left anyone behind. She hardly ever left the house. She didn't have a room of her own until she was sixty-nine years old. "I write now in my own litle chamber . . . & nobod up in the house near me to Desturb me," she wrote, delighted.[5] She was very happy to have it, but not having that room sooner isn't why she didn't write more or better.

Whether a poet's heart beat inside her woman's body I leave it to the reader to decide, but sitting in that archive, holding those sheets of foolscap stitched together with the coarsest of threads, I began to think that Benjamin Franklin's sister had something to say after all, something true, something new. Very delicately, I once more turned the brittle pages of the Book of Ages, and in them I saw an unwritten story: a history of books and papers, a history of reading and writing, a history from reformation to revolution, a history of history. This, then, is Jane Franklin's story: a book of ages about ages of books.

PART ONE

Jane

1537–1727

CHAPTER I

Lady Jane

Lady Jane Grey, a red-haired, freckle-faced grandniece of Henry the Eighth, read, while still a girl, the Old Testament in Hebrew and Plato in Greek. She was remarkable; she was untoward. A royal tutor once found her shut in her room reading an account of Socrates's execution for heresy, "with as moch delite, as som jentleman wold read a merie tale." She was thirteen. The tutor confessed himself astonished. Why, he asked, did she closet herself in her chamber to study the philosophy of death when she might instead hunt in the park with the duke and duchess?

She looked up from her book. "They never felt, what trewe pleasure ment," she said.

This scarcely slaked him.

"And howe came you," inquired he, "to this déepe knowledge of pleasure"?

"I will tell you," she obliged: when she was in the company of other than books, she said, "that I thinke my selfe in hell."[1]

Lady Jane was a cousin of the king's son, Edward. From the age of twelve, he kept a journal, uncommonly canny, an account at once of himself and of the state; he called it his "Chronicle." He began with his birth: "The yere of our Lord 1537 was a prince born to king Harry th'eight."[2]

The chronicle of a king is a history of the world. The royal weddings alone could have filled a folio. The Church of England had separated from the Church of Rome when Edward's father divorced his wife to marry Anne Boleyn. He would have four wives more. Born, married, buried. Born, married, beheaded.

Then there were the heretics, the readers of banned books. Born, married, burned. "The secrets mysteries of the faith ought not to be explained to all men in all places," the church had decreed in 1215. "For such is the depth of divine Scripture that, not only the simple and illiterate but even the prudent and learned are not fully sufficient to try to understand it."[3] But in the 1450s, after a German blacksmith named Johannes Gutenberg cast letters of lead and antimony in his forge and, with a machine hewn of wood, pressed ink onto a page, the secret mysteries began to seep out. If a book could be made so well and copied so cheaply, might there not, one day, be mountains of books? And then, might not every man, and even every woman, down to the merest girl, read the word of God? William Tyndale, a scholar, began translating the Bible into English. "If God spare my life," he warned a clergyman, "I wvyl cause a boye that dryveth the plough shall know more of the scripture than thou doest."[4]

Tyndale went to the gallows.[5] The next year, Edward was born:

The yere of our Lord 1537 was a prince born to king Harry th'eight.

Thus begins the chronicle of a king.

But what of the king's humble subjects, the merchants and gentle ladies, the busy tradesmen and the surly apprentices, the frugal housewives and their virtuous daughters, the thieves and the rogues, the beggars and the whores? What of the plain?

Thomas Cromwell, the king's minister, ordered every parish to "kepe one boke or registre wherin ye shall write the day and yere of every weddyng christenyng and buryeng": a record of births, marriages, and deaths— a chronicle of everyone. Each book was to be kept in a coffer, fastened with two locks. Not every vicar complied.[6] Impertinent parsons kept no books at all. They could think of no purpose for which a king might make a count except to tax.

In 1547, Henry died and Edward, nine, was crowned. The boy king, he was called. A council ruling in his name strove to have every last vestige of idolatry destroyed. Vestries were ransacked, stained glass shattered, statues smashed. In their stead, on altars and in pews, went print: psalters, catechisms, books of common prayer. To read was to be saved.

Lady Jane kept reading. Her piety was daunting; her learning was said to be "almost past belief."[7] Edward fell ill; there were rumors that he had been poisoned. On his deathbed, he named as his successor Lady Jane.

When Edward died, Jane became queen. She was sixteen. Then Edward's half sister Mary, with an army behind her, seized the crown. Jane's reign lasted only nine days. She was locked in the Tower of London, and sentenced to death. Before she was executed, she sent one of her sisters a Bible. "It wil teache you to live," she told her, "and learne you to die."[8]

Far from the Tower of London, in the tiny village of Ecton, in Northampshire, in the very middle of England, there lived a blacksmith named Thomas Francklyne, a clever man, a tinkerer. When, during Mary's reign, she restored the Church of Rome, Thomas Francklyne contrived an ingenious device: with cloth tape, he fastened a Bible to the underside of a stool with a hinged seat so that he could turn it up and read his book when he would, but when anyone came to the door, he could tuck it under.[9] When Mary died in 1558, and her sister Elizabeth, a Protestant, succeeded her, Thomas Francklyne took his Bible out from under his stool and kept it out. *It wil teache you to live, and learne you to die.*

Only then did the recalcitrant rector of the village of Ecton begin, at last, to keep a parish register.[10] In it, in the year of the Lord fifteen hundred sixty-five, he recorded a baptism:

Jane, the daughter of Thomas ffrancklyne.

It sounds so plain. But, at the time, Jane wasn't just any name.

CHAPTER II

The Franklin's Tale

In the spring of 1758, Benjamin Franklin made a pilgrimage to Ecton to uncover his ancestors. Thomas Francklyne, who hid his Bible under a stool, was Jane and Benjamin Franklin's great-great-grandfather.

In Ecton, Franklin walked through a maze of stone. He sought out the villagers, the crooked and the haggard, leaning upon their canes. He stopped at the rectory to inquire after the parish register. "By which I find," he wrote, "that our poor honest Family were Inhabitants of that Village near 200 Years, as early as the Register begins."[1] *Jane, the daughter of Thomas ffrancklyne.*

In the churchyard, he trudged along narrow, grassy paths, squinting at stones, looking for the family name. "The short and simple Annals of the Poor," Thomas Gray had called gravestones, in "An Elegy Wrote in a Country Church Yard," in 1751, thinking about how "Some mute inglorious *Milton* here may rest."[2]

Jane Francklyne, born in 1565, had lived for less than a month. She left very little behind. She was buried in the Ecton churchyard, but her father would hardly have paid a carver to engrave so small a stone.[3] If not for the parish register, there would be no record that this Jane Francklyne had ever lived at all. History is what is written and can be found; what isn't saved is lost, sunken and rotted, eaten by earth.

Thomas Francklyne had four sons who lived longer than their unfortunate sister. The youngest, Henry, grew to be a pigheaded, contrary man. A blacksmith like his father, he once spent a year and a day in prison, "on suspicion of his being the author of some poetry that touched the character of some great man."[4] Silence was not Henry Francklyne's handmaiden. He named his youngest son Thomas. By now, the spelling of the family name had begun to change. Thomas Francklin minded the forge in Ecton. He forged pots and hinges and rasps and fetters, like the blacksmith in Isaiah 54:16: "Behold, I have created the smith that bloweth the coales in the fire, and that bringeth foorth an instrument for his worke."[5] He "had very little hair and used to wear a cap," one of his sons remembered. Not only a blacksmith, "he alsoe practised for diversion the trade of a Turner, a Gun-Smith, a surgeion, a scrivener, and wrote as prety a hand as ever I saw. He was a historian."[6]

Behold the historian. His hand holds a pen. His eye lingers on the past.

Thomas Francklin's wife, Jane White, loved to sing and to recite to her children the last verses of the third chapter of Malachi: "they that feared the Lord, spake often to one another, and the Lord hearkened and heard it, & a booke of remembrance was written before him, for them that feared the Lord, & that thought upon his name."[7]

The word, the name, the book: reckoning and remembrance. A history.

Thomas and Jane White Francklin didn't fasten their Bible under a stool. They inked it on plaster. On the very walls of their house, they wrote their favorite verses: "God so loved the world that he gave his only begotton Sonne: that whosoever beleeveth in him should not perish but have everlasting life. For God sent not his sonne into the world to condemne the world: but that the world through him might be saved" (John 3:16–17).[8] This, their word of gods, father and son, snaked around the walls, a foot above the floor.

Their youngest son, Josiah, was born in 1657. He became not a blacksmith but a dyer of silk and a maker of ink, and not in the sleepy village of Ecton but in the bustling town of Banbury, a Puritan town.[9] He and brother Benjamin wrote down the family recipes. How to whiten linen: "Lay it two dayes in soure Milk, closs coverd." How to dye leather blue: "Boyle in Water, Walwort berries, and Elderberries." How to make black printer's ink: "Burn Rozin in an Iron pan, hold a bag with ye Mouth downward to catch the smoak, When it is cold shake yor bag on a paper, Mix the soot Exceeding well with Linseed oyle, and then boyle it over a gentle fire, until you find it thick."[10]

And then, in 1683, Josiah Franklin left Ecton and Banbury behind to cross an ocean in search of a more bookish faith.

·　·　·

In 1758, when Jane Franklin's brother Benjamin walked through the Ecton churchyard, squinting at stones, he wasn't looking for Janes. He was looking for Franklins. At last he found one:

> *Here lyeth*
> *the Body of*
> *Thos. Franklin*[11]

This Thomas Franklin was their uncle, another of Josiah's brothers. Bred a blacksmith, "being ingenious, and encourag'd in Learning," he "became a considerable Man in the County Affairs." He was wise.[12]

In Ecton, Benjamin Franklin found the very ancestors he was looking for: they were poor; they were obscure; they were honest; they were ingenious. They were franklins.

He turned this story over in his mind, round and round, like wood on a lathe, year after year. And then, on folio sheets folded into quarters, he put it down on paper, in the form of a letter to his son. It is the most famous thing ever written by the most famous American who had ever lived. It begins,

Dear Son,

I have ever had a Pleasure in obtaining any little Anecdotes of my
Ancestors. You may remember the Enquiries I made among the
Remains of my Relations when you were with me in England; and the
Journey I took for that purpose.

He had gone to Ecton to learn about the lives of his forefathers. "Now, imagining it may be equally agreeable to you to know the Circumstances of *my* Life," he explained, "I sit down to write them for you."[13]

He never called what he was writing an "autobiography"; that word had not yet been coined. Sometimes he called it a history, sometimes a memoir, sometimes a relation, and sometimes an account. He wasn't quite sure what it was. It certainly wasn't the chronicle of a king. *The yere of our Lord 1537 was a prince born to king Harry th'eight.* It was, instead, the story of a poor boy who learns to read and comes to know as much of politics as a prince. This story was new.

He labored over it; he was a quick writer with a ready wit and tart opinions, but it took Benjamin Franklin eighteen years to write what he did of
the story of his life, and he never finished it. It ends in 1758, on the eve of
his visit to Ecton.

He never explained why he didn't finish, but he did explain why he
started: "Having emerg'd from the Poverty and Obscurity in which I was
born and bred, to a State of Affluence and some Degree of Reputation in
the World, and having gone so far thro' Life with a considerable Share of
Felicity, the conducing Means I made use of, which, with the Blessing of
God, so well succeeded, my Posterity may like to know, as they may find
some of them suitable to their own Situations, and therefore fit to be imi-
tated."[14] My story will tell you how I got here, that you might follow me. *It
wil teache you to live, and learne you to die.*

He began with his genealogy, of which he was abundantly fond. "This
obscure Family of ours," he called it.[15] He had read their short and simple annals. He had collected what he could: his grandfather's poems, his
uncle's recipes. *Mix the soot Exceeding well with Linseed oyle, and then boyle
it over a gentle fire, until you find it thick.* He asked his father about the
family name.

In Middle English, a frankeleyn is a free man, an owner of land but not
of title: neither a serf nor a peasant but not a nobleman, either. There's a
frankeleyn in *The Canterbury Tales.* He is unlettered and unschooled, but
when he tells his tale, he proves a man of truth, a man who "lernyd never
rethorik" and speaks "bare and pleyn." There are frank men in Shakespeare. Lear has a "franke heart" and Henry V urges his ministers to speak
"with franke and with uncurbed plainnesse."[16] Undisguised, ignorant of
the arts of rhetoric, guileless, *uncurbed:* by the sixteenth century, to be
frank meant to be sincere.

Jane and Benjamin Franklin's father knew none of this. "As to the original of our name," he told his son, "there is various opinions." Maybe it
meant "free," the way to "frank" a letter meant that you didn't have to
pay for postage. "Our circumstances," Josiah explained, "have been such
as that it hath hardly been worth while to concern ourselves much about
these things, any farther than to tickle the fancy a little."[17]

This, however, is exactly what tickled Benjamin Franklin's fancy. His
ancestors' poverty and obscurity only made his own rise the more extraordinary: the rougher they, the smoother he. His admirers felt the same way.

In 1853, Thomas Carlyle got his hands on an ancient Ecton tithe book; a friend had bought it for him, having found it while rummaging through a bookstall in London. "A strange old brown *ms.*, which never thought of travelling out of its native parish," Carlyle wrote, holding in his hands a record of the doings of Benjamin Franklin's forebears: a treasure, the wealth of ages. It contained, he wrote, "the very *stamp* (as it were) of their black knuckles, of their hobnailed shoes." Thomas Francklin and his sons were listed in its pages. "Here they are, their forge-hammers yet going; renting so many 'yard-lands' of Northamptonshire Church-soil, keeping so many sheep &c &c.," Carlyle wrote, "little conscious that one of the Demigods was about to proceed out of them." From hobnailed shoes to a demigod in five generations. Carlyle sent the tithe book to Boston, to Edward Everett, an American statesman, orator, and former president of Harvard. Everett had the book bound, "as if it were a very *Iliad*."[18]

Benjamin Franklin's epic, his *Iliad,* the story of his great expectations, started in that churchyard in Ecton, on the mossy face of a gravestone, on the musty pages of a parish register, in the fiery fury of a blacksmith's forge, where men who walked from one place to another hammered iron into shoes for the horses of men who rode.

In England, titles and wealth went to the eldest son: he, alone, was entitled. A franklin had no title; he had only his freedom but, still, the eldest son could expect to inherit the estate—he was entitled, at least, to that. Younger sons scrambled. And therein, Franklin thought, lay true nobility. As Poor Richard put it, *Many a Man would have been worse, if his Estate had been better.*[19]

"I am the youngest Son of the youngest Son of the youngest Son of the youngest son for five Generations," Franklin wrote, after he read the entries in that Ecton parish register, "whereby I find that had there originally been any Estate in the Family none could have stood a worse Chance for it."[20]

Who could have had a worse start?

CHAPTER III

The Tender Wombe

Benjamin Franklin was his father's youngest son, but he wasn't his youngest child. Josiah Franklin's youngest child—the youngest child of the youngest child of the youngest child of the youngest child, for five generations—was a girl.

Her story starts not with her great-great-grandfather, minding the forge in Ecton, but with her mother's mother, scrubbing and mending. In 1635, a young Englishwoman named Mary Morrill wished to go to the New World. Having no property but herself, she sold her labor to pay her way. Sailing across the ocean, she met a Norfolk man named Peter Folger. He was making a pilgrimage of faith.

They landed in Boston, a harbor and haven among rocky coasts and stony meadows and mountains steeped with thickets of pine. Puritans hoped that in this, their New England, even the savages in the very wilderness would speak Scripture. The seal of the Massachusetts Bay Colony pictured a bare Indian, with Acts 16:9 issuing out of his mouth: "COME OVER AND HELP US."

Morrill went to Salem as servant to a minister; Folger settled near Boston and worked as a weaver, miller, and shoemaker. He pocketed every penny.[1] Harvard College was founded in 1636. Three years later, Boston opened a post office, the first in the colonies: "all letters which are brought from beyond the seas, or are to bee sent thitherm are to bee brought unto."[2] New England would be a paper commonwealth. Paper flocks of paper birds would fly across the ocean. In 1639, a printing press—the first in the New World—was carried east to west over the three thousand miles of blue water, rowed up the river to Cambridge, and wheeled into a stout building in Harvard's yard, a pastureland where pigs rutted and cows lowed and the smell of hops wafted out of the brew house.

For this, their new England, there would be new books. The press's first imprint was a book of psalms, "faithfully translated into English metre." In the King James, the Twenty-second Psalm, ripe with carnal beauty, reads, "I was cast upon thee from the wombe: thou art my God from my mother's belly." Puritans sang their own song: "Unto thee from the tender-womb committed been have I: yea thou hast been my mighty-God from my mother's belly."[3] Their womb was more tender, their god mightier: the word was their faith.

To read was to be ruled. A 1642 Massachusetts law required that all children acquire the "ability to read & understand the principles of religion & the capitall lawes of this country."[4] The Bible nourished every new-weaned babe. "Whome shall he teach knowledge?" asked the twenty-eighth chapter of Isaiah: "them that are weaned from the milke, *and* drawn from the breasts." The press at Cambridge printed, in 1656, a catechism: *Spiritual Milk for Boston Babes in either England, Drawn out of the Breasts of both Testaments.*[5] The good book gave suck, its words like milk.

It took Peter Folger nine years to save the £20 he needed to pay Mary Morrill's debt and buy her freedom, but it was the best money, he said, he ever spent. They were married in 1644. They moved first to Martha's Vineyard and then to Nantucket, where, in 1648, their first son was born. Folger served as surveyor and schoolmaster, teaching not only English children but also Algonquians. On the islands, he said, "Noe English Man but myselfe could speak scarse a Word of Indian."[6]

In the colonies, it was illegal to print a Bible translated into English; the Crown held the copyright. But no law prevented a man from printing the word of God in another language. In 1663, the press in Cambridge issued *Mamusse Wunneetupanatamwe Up-Biblum God,* a translation made by John Eliot, minister of Roxbury, and his Algonquian interpreters, Indian students at Harvard. Then came Indian psalters, Indian catechisms, Indian primers, and *Nashauanittue Meninnunk wutch Mukkiesog:* spiritual milk for Indian babes.[7]

In 1665, one of Peter Folger's students, John Gibbs, spoke the name of Massasoit, the Wampanoag sachem with whom the pilgrims of Plymouth had shared a thanksgiving in 1621. "The naming of their dead *Sachims* is one ground of their warres," Roger Williams had once explained. Massasoit's son Metacom went to Nantucket to kill Gibbs. Folger calmed him. He said, "I have ever bin able to keep Peace upon the Island."[8]

Peter and Mary Folger's ninth and last child, Abiah, was born in 1667. By then, Folger had become a dissident in a land of dissenters.

The war he'd helped avert finally came in 1675, a war so bloody the land was said to look like "a burdensome, and menstruous Cloth." The fighting, one Boston poet thought, was the Indians' only chance to be "found in print," writing "in blud not ink." More than half the towns in New England were laid waste. The Indians besieged the devout in their meetinghouses. They burned their Bibles. They mocked their psalms. The press at Cambridge had printed one thousand copies of *Up-Biblum God;* by the end of the war, there was hardly a page left.

"Why should we suppose that God is not offended with us," Boston minister Increase Mather asked, "when his displeasure is written, in such visible and bloody Characters?"

History alone promised redemption. In 1676, Mather published *A Brief History of the Warr with the Indians.* From the pulpits and the printing presses, ministers cited Exodus 17:14: "And the Lord said unto Moses, write this for a memoriall in a booke."[9]

Peter Folger remonstrated. Seven months into the war, he refused to hand over a deed book needed to settle a land dispute. Found guilty of contempt of court, he was fined £20. This he refused to pay. "All of my Estate, if my Debts were payd, will not amount to halfe so much," he insisted. There being no prison on Nantucket, he was locked in a pen "where the Neighbors Hogs had layd but the night before, and in a bitter cold Frost and deepe Snow." He slept on a board; he pleaded for hay to better his bed. He stayed there for a year and a half, believing there to be no saner place than prison for a man of peace in time of war.

"The Mercy of some of these Men is Cruelty itself," he wrote. "It were better for us and the Indians also, that we had no Liberty."[10]

From his pigsty, he wrote a poem of protest. He called it "A Looking-Glass for the Times." He would hold, before his enemies, a mirror. For the slaughter, he blamed the colony's "College Men"—Harvard men:

I would not have you for to think
    that I am such a Fool,

> *To write against Learning, as such,*
> *or to cry down a School.*

Still, it would always be an error to

count School Learning best.

    Abiah was ten years old then. Every week, she visited her father in that hog shed. She watched him write a poem that he knew no one would print but that, he said, was still worth writing:

> *'Tis true, there are some times indeed*
> *of Silence to the Meek;*

But, sometimes,

there is a time to speak.[11]

She listened to her father's lessons. Speak up, he told her. Speak up.

CHAPTER IV

A Tub of Suds

Abiah Folger met her husband on a boat. In 1689, when she was twenty-one, she took a skiff from Nantucket to Falmouth and, from there, sailed to Boston. All of her brothers had stayed on the islands. Three of her sisters had married Nantucket men. But two had proved more venturesome. Bathsheba had married Joseph Pope of Salem, and Dorcas had married a man from Charlestown.[1] It was on her way to visit Dorcas that Abiah met a thirty-two-year-old widower.

Benjamin Franklin once described the man his mother met on that boat this way: "He was ingenious, could draw prettily, was skill'd a little in Music and had a clear pleasing Voice, so that when he play'd Psalm Tunes on his Violin and sung withal as he some times did in an Evening after the Business of the Day was over, it was extremely agreeable to hear. He had a mechanical Genius too, and on occasion was very handy in the Use of other Tradesmen's Tools. But his great Excellence lay in a sound Understanding, and solid Judgment."[2] Artistic, musical, mechanical, and wise, a poor man but a good man: a franklin.

Josiah Franklin, formerly of Ecton, late of Banbury, had landed in Boston in 1683, after eight weeks on the ocean, with a wife, Ann, and three children, Elizabeth, five; Samuel, two; and Hannah, a baby. He had joined the Old South Meeting House, whose pastor, Samuel Willard, had seen his last church, in the town of Groton, burned to the ground by Indians. Government, he preached, is "God's Ordinance."[3]

Josiah held prayer meetings at his house. "I was mov'd last night at Mr. Josiah Franklin's," his neighbor Samuel Sewall wrote in his diary. "I got Brother Franklin to set the Tune, which he did very well."[4] He had a beautiful voice.

He had settled in a crooked, noisy city of ten thousand souls, ruled by the king of kings. In the winter it was dark and it was cold, colder than anyone raised in England had ever known. He dyed, but, more often, he made candles, to light the night. He made soap. He tinkered. His family grew. In 1689, his wife died after being brought to bed for the seventh time. Then he, a widower with five young children—two of their children had died in infancy—sailed to Cape Cod to buy mutton fat from a sheep farmer, to make tallow for candles. On the boat ride home, he met the venturesome daughter of a dissident.

When Abiah Folger moved from Nantucket to Boston to become Josiah Franklin's wife, she brought with her a root of mint from her mother's garden and planted it in the yard of her husband's house.[5] "Let no changes change you," Peter Folger told his children.[6] Five months after the wedding, she was pregnant.

"All things within this fading world hath end," the Boston poet Anne Bradstreet wrote in "Before the Birth of one of her Children."[7] Men waged wars, but for women each birth was another battle. No woman dared imagine herself spared, not by grace, not by wealth; pain was her portion. Even if she survived childbirth, she could scarcely expect that her child would.[8] Queen Anne, who ascended to the throne in 1702, was pregnant seventeen times. Six of her pregnancies ended in miscarriage, six in stillbirth. One son and daughter, the little prince and princess of Denmark and Norway, died the day they were born. Anne Sophia, not yet one, was carried away by smallpox, along with her sister Mary, not yet two. William reached ten, only to be taken. All the king's horses and all the king's men: none could save the queen's children.

Abiah Folger Franklin fared far better than her queen. In 1703, when no one was looking, one of her toddlers fell into a tub. "Ebenezer Franklin of the South Church, a male-Infant of 16 months old, was drown'd in a Tub of Suds," Samuel Sewall wrote in his diary.[9] And Thomas, not yet three, died in 1706. But in 1712, when Abiah was pregnant again, she had given birth to nine children and seven had survived.

Her tenth would be her last.

"She suckled all her 10 Children" is nearly all that Benjamin Franklin ever wrote about his mother.[10] She stitched, prayed, read, butchered, cooked, washed, scrubbed, tended her garden, boiled soap, and dipped candles, and, on the darkest day of her life, she fished one of her sons, slippery as an eel, out of a tub of suds.[11] But it was the suckling that Franklin remembered: his mother, with a baby at her breast.

To suck was to live. "My Wife set up and he sucked the right Breast bravely, that had the best nipple," Sewall wrote in his diary, with pride and relief, after the birth of his first child. "You will *Suckle your Infant your Self* if you can; Be not such an *Ostrich* as to Decline it," Increase Mather's son Cotton preached from his pulpit at Boston's North Church.[12] Through the second summer was wisest. That meant mothers weaned their infants at somewhere between a year and sixteen months, sending them away to bleat under someone else's roof. Or they went on a "weaning journey" and left their children at home. Or they rubbed mustard or wormwood on their nipples, and everyone stayed put: at so bitter a breast, babies pouted and puckered and spat.[13]

A mother's last child she nursed the longest, to stave off getting another. "It may be my dear wife may now leave off bearing," Sewall prayed, after his wife, Hannah, gave birth for the fourteenth time, at the age of forty-four. Then she marked what she hoped would be her retirement by hosting a feast for the seventeen women who had attended her during her lyings-in. They ate meat to give thanks, and to pray that her trials were over.[14]

The Sewalls' trials had been severe. In Salem in 1692, Samuel Sewall had served as judge on a court that had sent twenty people to death, accused of witchcraft by frantic, twitchy young girls (including Bathsheba Pope, Abiah's niece). After that, four of Sewall's children died in five years. He blamed himself: he had sent innocents to their deaths; now God was taking his innocents, as punishment. From the altar at Old South, Sewall begged the pardon of God and men, the Franklins sitting, watchfully, in their pew.[15] But there could be no bargain with so hard a god. Of Samuel and Hannah Sewall's fourteen children, only five survived.

In 1712, Abiah was forty-four. The children of Josiah's first wife were grown. Elizabeth was thirty-three, and married. Samuel had become a blacksmith; he was thirty, married, and a father. Hannah had already been married, widowed, and married again. Josiah Jr., twenty-six, had run away to sea. Only the youngest, Anne, twenty-five, was still at home; before the year's end, she would be married, too. Of Abiah's own children, John, a tallow chandler and soap boiler like his father, was about to come of age:

he was nearly twenty-one. Peter was nineteen, Mary seventeen, James fourteen, Sarah twelve, Benjamin six, and Lydia three.

Josiah then bought the only house he would ever own. It cost him £320; he paid £70, ready money, and mortgaged the rest. It was a rickety, wooden two-story on Union Street, nearly next door to the Green Dragon Tavern. By the front door, he hung from an arm of iron his shop sign: a wooden ball, twelve inches in diameter, painted blue.[16]

Inside the house known as the Blue Ball, there were four rooms: two up and two down, separated by a chimney and narrow stairs. Upstairs was not so much two small rooms as one biggish one, a place to sleep and to store things, with the chimney in the middle. Downstairs, a chamber and a hall.

In the hall, Josiah hung four maps and boiled his soap and dipped his candles and kept his books.

In the chamber, Abiah gave birth for the last time, on the twenty-seventh of March, one thousand seven hundred and twelve.[17] Josiah named the baby after the Nine Days' Queen, whose throne was a prison. He named her after his mother, who raised him in a house where the word of God was inked on the very walls.

He named her Jane.

CHAPTER V

Benny and Jenny

The two eyes of man do not more resemble, nor are capable of being upon better terms with each other, than my sister and myself," Benjamin Franklin once wrote, "were it not for the partiality of our parents, who make the most injurious distinctions between us."[1] Between brothers and sisters, likeness is hidden by difference.[2]

We "had sildom any contention among us," Jane once wrote her brother, looking back at their childhood. "All was Harmony."[3]

He remembered it differently.

"I think our Family were always subject to being a little Miffy," he remarked.[4]

She took his hint.

"You Introduce your Reproof of my Miffy temper so Politely," she wrote back slyly, "won cant aVoid wishing to have conquered it as you have."[5]

He was the last of their father's sons; she was the last of his daughters. Of Josiah's ten sons, four died young and one ran away to sea. After Ebenezer drowned, no one in that house could have reached into a tub of suds without thinking of that little boy. But of his seven daughters, Josiah had lost not one; he had more daughters than he knew what to do with.

Abiah might have thought of them otherwise. Jenny was her last. Maybe she nursed her last a little longer and hugged her a little tighter. Maybe she kept her a little closer.[6]

When Jenny was born, Benny had just turned six. Their uncle Benjamin, a dyer who fancied himself a poet, sent his namesake an acrostic (with *I*, as was common, doing service for *J*):

B e to thy parents an Obedient Son;
E ach Day let Duty constantly be Done;
N ever give Way to sloth or lust or pride
I f free you'd be from Thousand Ills beside.
A bove all Ills be sure Avoide the shelfe:
M ans Danger lyes in Satan, sin and selfe.
I n vertue Learning Wisdome progress make.
N ere shrink at suffering for thy saviours sake;

F raud and all Falshood in thy Dealings Flee;
R eligious Always in thy station be;
A dore the Maker of thy Inward part:
N ow's the Accepted time, Give him thy Heart.
K eep a Good Conscience, 'tis a constant Frind;
L ike Judge and Witness This Thy Acts Attend.
I n Heart with bended knee Alone Adore
N one but the Three in One Forevermore.[7]

Let thy Child's first Lesson be Obedience, Poor Richard says, *and the second may be what thou wilt.*[8] "Families are the Nurseries of all Societies," Cotton Mather preached. "A family is a little Church, and a little Common-wealth," wrote another minister. "It is as a schoole wherein the first principles and grounds of government and subjection are learned."[9]

The first lesson of childhood was submission. The second was reading.

He "read his Bible at five years old," Jane said about her brother. As a child, she said, he "studied incessantly" and was "addicted to all kinds of reading."[10] Save London, Dublin, and Edinburgh, Boston had, for bookshops, no rivals.[11] Cotton Mather's library held seven thousand volumes: "Seldome any *new Book* of Consequence finds the way from beyond-Sea, to these Parts of *America,* but I bestow the Perusal upon it," Mather boasted.[12] But the books belonging to a poor chandler were few. Benjamin Franklin wasn't far wrong when he remembered, "My Father's little Library consisted chiefly of Books in polemic Divinity," regretting "that at a time when I had such a Thirst for Knowledge, more proper Books had not fallen in my Way." Josiah Franklin's library was scanty and narrow. An inventory taken of the Blue Ball counted only the Reverend Willard's *Complete Body of*

Divinity, a collection of 250 sermons, "2 large Bibles," "1 Concordance," and "A Parcell of small Books."[13] Sermons, many; Bibles, large; books, small.

When Benny and Jenny were very young, they dressed alike. They wore loose, long gowns with what were called "hanging sleeves," flouncy and full. At seven, boys got to wear pants. "Never had any bride that was to be drest upon her weding night more handes about her," one grandmother wrote of the day her grandson put on pants.[14] Jenny was not quite one, a toddler taking first steps, when Benny was breeched. On that day, he was given a halfpence coin. He spent it on a whistle.[15]

The year Benny put on pants he started writing poetry ("wretched Stuff," as he remembered it). "My Father discourag'd me," he wrote, "telling me Verse-makers were generally Beggars; so I escap'd being a Poet, most probably a very bad one."[16] But Josiah did send the boy's poems to Uncle Benjamin, who, in turn, sent back a poem of his own, full of admiration for the young sprite:

> *Tis time for me to Throw Asside my pen*
> *When Hanging-sleeves Read, Write, and Rhime Like Men.*
> *This Forward Spring Foretells a plenteous crop,*
> *For if the bud bear Graine what will the Top?*

Benny dressed like a man; he even rhymed like man. He was a startling, brilliant, adventurous boy. He kept pigeons; swam in the Mill Pond; flew kites; tussled with neighborhood boys; boxed; threw his best friend, John Collins, into the Charles River; and used his father's tobacco pipe to blow bubbles with soapsuds, a trick that must have enchanted his baby sister.[17] Benny was precocious, the very bud bearing grain. About that, everyone agreed. What was to be done with such a child?

Josiah inquired of his pastor, his neighbors, his brother, and his friends. "My early Readiness in learning to read," Franklin recalled, "and the Opinion of all his Friends that I should certainly make a good Scholar" convinced his father to send him to school, "intending to devote me as the Tithe of his Sons to the Service of the Church." Josiah had put his other sons to trades, but he would give one, a tenth of his sons, to the church. In 1714, when Jenny was two, Benny, at the age of eight, entered the South Grammar School, where he studied Latin and Greek.[18]

The next year, Uncle Benjamin emigrated from England and came to live at the Blue Ball. He was sixty-five, and sickly. Jenny adored him; "good old unkle Benjamin," she called him. "A good humour'd Child," he called her. He meant to stay only till he found a place of his own. His visit lasted four years. As Poor Richard says, *Fish and Visitors stink in 3 days.*[19]

About this, Uncle Benjamin wrote a poem:

> *. . . they did me kindly Treat*
> *But noe Imployment did present,*
> *Which was to me a burden great*
> *And could not be to their content.*[20]

Then sea-legged Josiah Jr. turned up, smelling of pitch and tar, after nine years at sea, during which he had sent not a letter, not a word. Of his father's seventeen children, Benjamin wrote, "I remember 13 sitting at one time at his Table." This can only have been the day, in 1715, that Josiah Jr. was there for dinner. Uncle Benjamin wrote a psalm of thanksgiving and sang it at the table:

> *Adore this God who did us Save*
> *From the much feared Watery Grave*
> *And softly Set thee on thy Land*
> *O Bless his kind and pow'rfull Hand.*[21]

But the seafaring Franklin had no taste for psalms. He disappeared, and was never heard from again.

Then Josiah pulled his son out of school. Franklin later explained that his father had become aware of "the Expense of a College Education which, having so large a Family, he could not well afford." But Josiah had known all along how much Harvard would cost. Maybe, instead, he had come to understand that his son would make a poor preacher. At dinner one night, the boy begged his father to bless the whole winter's worth of salted meat all at once, to avoid the tedium of having to say grace before every meal.

Or maybe Abiah, whose father had no use for Harvard men, steered her youngest son away from the college in Cambridge. There was also this:

Josiah had paid a considerable sum to send his son James to London to buy a printing press and type.[22]

At first he sent Benny to a much cheaper school, one run by George Brownell on Hanover Street, two blocks from the Blue Ball. But after Benny had spent a while at Brownell's, Josiah took him out of that school, too, and kept him at the shop. "I was employed in cutting Wick for the Candles, filling the Dipping Mold, and the Molds for cast Candles, attending the Shop, going of Errands," Franklin remembered. He hated it. "I dislik'd the Trade and had a strong Inclination for the Sea, but my Father declar'd against it." Something had to be done. *Virtue and a Trade are a Child's best Portion,* Poor Richard says.[23]

"*NOW* O Young People is *your chusing time,*" Benjamin Colman, the liberal pastor of Boston's Brattle Street Church, preached. "Now you commonly chuse your *Trade;* betake your selves to your business for life, show what you incline to, and how you intend to be imploy'd all your days."[24] About his son's choosing time, Josiah was painstaking. He took him for walks all over town, to "see Joiners, Bricklayers, Turners, Braziers, &c. at their Work."[25] At last, he determined to apprentice him to his nephew Samuel, a blacksmith turned cutler who plied his trade at the sign of the Razor and Crown. But when Samuel asked for money for the boy's keep—the fees a father ordinarily paid to have his son apprenticed—Josiah stormed across town and brought Benny home. Hadn't he been lodging and feeding Samuel's father, Benjamin, for years, at his own expense?

It was at this uncomfortable juncture, when Benny was eleven and Jenny was five, that Uncle Benjamin tried to find some quiet in the busy rooms of the Blue Ball. He bent his creaky self and sat down in a chair. He picked up his pen.

"A short account of the Family of Thomas Franklin of Ecton," he wrote, by way of title. Behold, the historian. He wrote about his grandfather Henry and about his father, Thomas, and about his mother, Jane, "whose name as much as his," he wrote, "I shall ever love."

He wrote about his own life, and about the births of his ten children and the deaths of nine. He lingered on the death of his wife. "In her I Lost the delight of mine Eyes, the desire of my heart, and the comfort of my life." He came, at last, to the family of his youngest brother. He listed the dates of the births of Josiah's children with Abiah.

John born . . . 7 Dec. 1690
peter . . . . 22 Nov. 1692
Mary . . . . 26 Sept 1694
James . . . . 4 feb. 1696
Sarah . . . . 9 July 1699
Ebenezer ⎱ dead 20 Sept 1701
Thomas ⎰ . . 7 Dec. 1703
Benjamin . . 6 Jan. 1706
Lidia . . . . 8 Aug 1708
Jane . . . . 27 mar 1712

And then: he put down his pen.

In 1712, the history of the Franklins of Ecton ended with the birth of a girl named Jane.[26]

CHAPTER VI

The Ladies' Library

Jane Franklin learned to read. Everyone needed to learn to read, even girls. But that didn't mean they needed to learn to read well. A taste for books could ruin a girl; when she grew up, she'd make a poor helpmeet. "I am one of those unfortunate tradesmen who are plagued with a reading wife," lamented one essayist. "My wife does hardly one earthly thing but read, read, read."[1] Reading too much spelled trouble.

"Beware the bookish woman" was an adage of the age. In 1711, in the first volume of the English gentleman's magazine the *Spectator,* Joseph Addison told the story of visiting a house and being asked to wait for the lady in her library. "The very sound of a *Lady's Library* gave me a great Curiosity to see it." The "library," he discovers, is ridiculous: beautiful, gilt-edged books, arranged not by subject or author but by size and color, set on shelves cluttered with gewgaws. When he meets the lady, he finds that she has read indiscriminately—history alongside fiction—with no capacity to tell the difference between them. He determines "to recommend such particular Books as may be proper for the Improvement of the Sex."[2] If a woman were to read, a man had to tell her what.

Three years later, Addison's partner, Richard Steele, published a three-volume anthology called *The Ladies Library,* compiled by the Reverend George Berkeley. Berkeley gathered excerpts from conduct manuals, sermons, and philosophy.[3] For a chapter called "Ignorance" he printed excerpts from *A Serious Proposal to the Ladies,* a treatise about girls' education written in 1694 by the Englishwoman of letters Mary Astell. "From our Infancy we are nurs'd up in Ignorance and Vanity," Astell complained; girls' "very Instructors are Froth and Emptiness." Women were no better educated than the beasts: "tho we Move and Speak and do many such like things, we live not the Life of a Rational Creature but only of an Animal." Reminding parents that "the Sons convey the Name to Posterity, yet certainly a great Part of the Honour of their Families depends on their Daughters," Astell pleaded with parents: Please, give your daughters learning.[4]

Jane Franklin's parents could not easily have obliged. They couldn't have sent her to school, even if they'd wanted. No public school in Boston enrolled girls. In 1706, "Mistress Mary Turfrey at the South End of Boston" announced that "If any Gentlemen desires their Daughters should be under her Education; They may please agree with her on Terms."[5] But Jane Franklin was not a gentleman's daughter. She was the daughter of a tradesman. And at George Brownell's school, as at the rare private schools to which females were admitted, those few girls who enrolled were allowed to attend only after the boys had finished for the day, and what they learned was different: boys learned to write; girls learned "English and French Quilting, Imbroidery, Florishing, Plain Work, marking in several sorts of Stitches."[6]

Everyone needed to learn to read, but there was no need for a girl to learn to write. Massachusetts's poor laws required that boys be taught to write and girls to read.[7] For most girls, book learning ended there. At home and at school, when boys were taught to write, girls learned to stitch.[8] Boys held quills; girls held needles.[9] A female writer was worse than unnatural; she was monstrous. Observed Anne Bradstreet:

> I am obnoxious to each carping tongue
> Who says my hand a needle better fits.[10]

Jane's mother could write, if not well—"Pray excuse my bad riting," Abiah Folger Franklin once begged Benjamin, in the sole letter in her hand that survives—but, after all, Abiah's father was a schoolmaster, and she had been an unusually venturesome girl.[11] In 1710, three in five women in New England could not even sign their names. Signing is mechanical. Writing—putting ideas down on paper—is something more. Most of those two in five women who could sign their names could do no more than that, at least with pen and quill.[12] Sometimes, with needles, they stitched their stories, copying lines from books onto scraps of silk, like a sampler that read:

Sarah Silsbe is my name.
I belong to the English nation.
Boston is my dwelling place.
And Christ is my salvation.

This Sarah Silsbe copied verses, too, about history:

When I am dead and laid in grave,
And all my bones are rotten.
When this you see, remember me.
And never let me be forgotten.[13]

Her needlework is her artifact. It is all that is left of her: threadbare lines.

There were exceptions. The most unnaturally accomplished girl in Boston was Jane Colman, the daughter of Benjamin Colman, the minister of the Brattle Street Church, the church Jane's uncle Benjamin belonged to. Colman was a far sight worldlier than most Massachusetts ministers, more a man of the Enlightenment than of the Reformation. He had graduated from Harvard in 1692 and three years later sailed for London. Captured by pirates, he was imprisoned in France. Ransomed, he went to England, where he stayed until 1699, and studied; he read widely; he especially admired Alexander Pope. His sermons were Addisonian.[14]

Jane Colman was born in Boston in 1708. For the first seven years of her life, she was an only child. She knew her letters by the age of two. By five she could recite the psalms. When she turned six, her father began teaching her to write; he wanted her to learn to write not only well but forcibly: manfully. By eleven, she was composing hymns: "Happy are they that walk in Wisdom's Ways, / That tread her Paths, and shine in all her Rays." At fourteen, she began keeping a diary. Her father "spar'd no Cost nor Pains in my Education," she wrote. She composed poetry for him: "An Infant Muse begs leave beneath your Feet, / To lay the first Essays of her poetic Wit."[15] She and her father began a daily correspondence.[16] "A very little Use will make you Mistress enough of the Art of decent, familiar, common Letters," her father wrote. "Practice is the best and shortest Way of learning this." On receiving her letters, he corrected them, and sent them back. He once parsed for her the different meanings of *fortune, chance,* and *providence.* But he offered, too, more capacious advice: "Write more or less according as you find your Thoughts flowing or restrained. But always remember, that it is better to be short and full of good Sense, than to draw out your Letters to an empty Length."

This continued every day until she was eighteen. "With the Advantages of my liberal Education at School and College," her father wrote her, "I have no reason to think but that your Genius in Writing would have excell'd mine."[17]

Jane Franklin never had the education Jane Colman had. Her mother taught her some. What more she learned, she learned from her brother. From childhood, she loved him tenderly. "My Affection for you has all ways been so grate I see no Room for Increec," she once wrote to him, "& you have manifested yrs to mee in such Large measure that I have no Reason to suspect Itts strength."[18]

All her life, she wrote to him the way Jane Colman wrote to her father. She wrote to him the way a student writes to a tutor. "I have such a Poor Fackulty at making Leters," she confessed, again and again.[19]

She tried to correct herself. "When I read this over I see so many buts I am ashamed," she once apologized. "Place them to the old accompt."[20]

Her brother would have none of it; he knew her pride well enough not to credit her humility. "Is there not a little Affectation in your Apology for the Incorrectness of your Writing?" he teased her. "Perhaps it is rather fishing for Commendation. You write better, in my Opinion, than most American Women."[21] This was, miserably, true.

Benjamin Franklin fought for his learning, letter by letter, book by book, candle by candle. He valued nothing more. He loved his little sister.

He taught her how to write. It was cruel, in its kindness. Because when he left, the lessons ended.

CHAPTER VII

Book'ry, Cook'ry

She learned to bake and to roast, to mend and to scrub. She learned to sew and to knit. She helped her mother tend the garden. She learned to dye.[1] She helped her father in the shop, doing the work that her brother hated, "cutting Wick for the Candles, filling the Dipping Mold, and the Molds for cast Candles."[2]

What more could she study? A Boston newspaper printed "A Dialogue between a thriving Tradesman and his Wife about the Education of Their Daughter." The wife wishes to send the girl to school. The husband refuses, telling her:

> *Prithee, good Madam, let her first be able,*
> *To read a Chapter truly, in the Bible,*
> *That she may'nt mispronounce God's People, Popel,*
> *Nor read Cunstable for Constantinople;*
> *Make her expert and ready at her Prayers,*
> *That God may keep her from the Devils Snares;*
> *Teach her what's useful, how to shun deluding,*
> *To roast, to toast, to boil and mix a Pudding.*
> *To knit, to spin, to sew, to make or mend,*
> *To scrub, to rub, to earn and not to spend,*
> *I tell thee Wife, once more, I'll have her bred*
> *To Book'ry, Cook'ry, Thimble, Needle, Thread.*[3]

That Jane Franklin learned to write as well as she did was a twist of fate: she was her brother's sister. Mostly, she learned other things. She was bred to bookery and cookery, needle and thread.

She learned how to make soap. She once wrote down the family recipe. In a wooden box with a hole bored in the bottom and set over a tub filled with bricks, soak eighteen bushels of ashes and one bushel of lime with water. Leach lye. Then, in a copper pot, boil the lye with wax—"won third mirtle wax two thirds clean tallow the Greener the wax the beter," she wrote—and keep it from boiling over "by flirting the froith with a scimer." Stir in salt. "Be carefull not to Put two much salt in it will make it Britle." Line a mold with a cloth ("not too coars") and pour in the boiling soap: "keep it smoth on the top take care to let your Frame stand on a Level let care be taken when it is in that it Is not Jogd." Let it set overnight, and in the morning cut it "with a small wier fixed to a round stick at Each End." Use a gauge to make sure each cake is of equal weight and, if not, "Pare it fitt."[4]

She lived a life of confinement. She never learned to ride. ("I hant courage to ride a hors," she once admitted.)[5] If she left the city, it was with her mother, by boat, to visit the Folgers on Nantucket, where she played with her cousin Keziah.[6] She spent her Sundays at the Old South Meeting House, listening to men's voices thundering from the pulpit. She ran errands, to the shops, to the docks, and to James's printing house, to visit her brothers. She visited her married sisters and helped care for their children, or they for her: some of her nieces and nephews were older than she was. She loved best her niece Grace.[7]

Most days she spent at home, close to the fire. She was curious, and she could be untoward. But she was dutiful. She was pared to fit.

A girl's apprenticeship was girlhood itself. A boy's apprenticeship was a trade. In 1717, when Jane was five, her brother James came back from England and set up a printing shop in Boston, "over against the Prison in Queen Street."[8] It was a godsend. Here at last was a trade for Benjamin, the bookish boy too poor to go to Harvard. In 1718, he became his brother's apprentice: a printer's devil. He moved into a room above James's shop. Benny was twelve; Jenny was six.

The best part of his apprenticeship, Franklin always said, was the chance it gave him to read. At the Blue Ball, he had only ever found in his father's library a few books he liked: Plutarch's *Lives,* "a Book of Defoe's called an Essay on Projects and another of Dr. Mather's call'd Essays to do Good." But working at a printer's shop was almost as good as working at a bookshop. "I now had Access to better Books," he remembered. "An Acquaintance with the Apprentices of Booksellers, enabled me sometimes to borrow a small one, which I was careful to return soon and clean. Often I sat up in my Room reading the greatest Part of the Night."[9]

Jane Colman read all night long, too. Her father's house was stocked with books. She read "all the *English* Poetry, and polite Pieces in Prose, printed and Manuscripts in her Father's well furnish'd Library, and much she borrow'd of her Friends and Acquaintance. She had indeed such a Thirst after Knowledge that the Leisure of the Day did not suffice, but she spent whole Nights in reading."[10]

Jane Franklin enjoyed neither the leisure of a minister's daughter nor the library of a printer's apprentice. What books she read were what books she found in the house of a poor soap boiler. "My Father's little Library consisted chiefly of Books in polemic Divinity," her brother had written. Her world of learning widened so far, and no farther.

Her brother resolved to be his own tutor. Determined to become a good writer, he trained himself by reading. The boy who wanted to become the author of his own life taught himself to write by copying the prose style he found in the *Spectator*. "I thought the Writing excellent, and wish'd if possible to imitate it," he explained. He read an essay, wrote an abstract, and then rewrote the argument from the abstract, to see if he could improve on the original. Then he rewrote the essays as poems since, he thought, "nothing acquaints a Lad so speedily with Variety of Expression, as the Necessity of finding such Words and Phrases as will suit with the Measure, Sound and Rhime of Verse, and at the same Time well express the Sentiment." He wrote rules, pledging himself to brevity ("a multitude of Words obscure the Sense"), clarity ("To write *clearly*, not only the most expressive, but the plainest Words should be chosen"), and simplicity: "If a Man would that his Writings have an Effect on the Generality of Readers, he had better imitate that Gentleman, who would use no Word in his Works that was not well understood by his Cook-maid." His cook-maid . . . or his little sister.

"Prose Writing has been of great Use to me in the Course of my Life," Franklin knew, "and was a principal Means of my Advancement." He would write his way up, and out.[11]

Reading, he grew skeptical of his family's faith. The more books he read, the less he believed the Bible. "I was scarce 15," he remembered, "when, after doubting by turns of several Points as I found them disputed in the different Books I read, I began to doubt of Revelation itself."

He discovered, too, that he liked to argue. "My indiscrete Disputations about Religion began to make me pointed at with Horror by good People, as an Infidel or Atheist." He especially liked to debate, like "University Men," with "another Bookish Lad in the Town, John Collins by Name." They once debated "the Propriety of educating the Female Sex in Learning, and their Abilities for Study." Young Collins "was of Opinion that it was improper" and that girls "were naturally unequal to it." Franklin disagreed: "I took the contrary Side, perhaps a little for Disputes sake."[12]

In crafting his argument, Franklin leaned on Defoe's *Essay on Projects,* one of the few books in his father's library that he liked. Defoe had proposed the establishment of an "Academy for Women": "I have often thought of it as one of the most barbarous Customs in the world, considering us as a Civilised and a Christian Countrey, that we deny the advantages of Learning to Women." Like Astell, Defoe regretted the frivolousness of girls' education: "Their youth is spent to teach them to Stitch and Sew, or make Bawbles. They are taught to Read indeed, and perhaps to Write their Names, or so; and that is the heighth of a Woman's Education." His Academy for Women was to embrace every subject: "To such whose Genius wou'd lead them to it, I wou'd deny no sort of Learning."[13]

But, for all his Defoe, Franklin didn't win the argument. Collins, he admitted, "was naturally more eloquent, had a ready Plenty of Words, and sometimes . . . bore me down more by his Fluency than by the Strength of his Reasons." They parted without settling the question and continued the debate by letters. "Three or four Letters of a Side had pass'd," Franklin wrote, "when my Father happen'd to find my Papers, and read them. Without entering into the Discussion, he took occasion to talk to me about the Manner of my Writing, observ'd that tho' I had the Advantage of my Antagonist in correct Spelling and pointing (which I ow'd to the Printing House) I fell far short in elegance of Expression, in Method and in Perspicuity."[14]

Spelling and pointing (punctuating) were genteel accomplishments; they date to the rise of printing. People used to spell however they pleased, even spelling their own names differently from one day to the next. Then came the printing press, and rules for printers: how to spell, how to point.

More books meant more readers; more readers meant more writers. But only the learned, only the lettered, knew how to spell.

Franklin was a better speller than his friend Collins, and he could point better, too, but Collins proved a better debater. Be more precise, Josiah urged his son. Be plainer. On the question itself, he did not venture an opinion.

While Benny was improving his writing by arguing about the education of girls, Jenny was at home, boiling soap and stitching. Quietly, with what time she could find, she did more. She once confided to her brother, "I Read as much as I Dare."[15]

CHAPTER VIII

Silence Dogood

She never put on pants. Instead, she bled and tied rags between her legs. "Menses," her doctor John Perkins wrote in his commonplace book, "begin at 9 or 10 years," adding, on another page, this warning: "Early Menstruation renders the Uteri Hard & dry; so that they ought not to prompt the early appearance by obscene books, and frequent touchings."[1] Beware the bookish girl.

In the summer of 1721, when Jane was nine and Benjamin was fifteen, their brother James began printing a newspaper, the *New-England Courant*.[2] The first newspaper in the colonies, *Publick Occurrences,* begun in Boston in 1690, had stopped printing after only one issue. To be successful, a newspaper printer usually had to have earned the favor of the government. The *Boston News-Letter*, "published by authority," started in 1704. Its printer was also the postmaster. In 1710, "An Act for establishing a General Post Office of All Her Majesties Dominions" had fixed postage rates both overseas (one shilling per letter, between London and America) and between colonial cities (fifteen pence between Boston and Philadelphia).[3] A printer who was also a postmaster had a near monopoly both on news, relayed from the magistrates who had appointed him, and on readers, who came to his print shop to pick up their mail.[4]

James Franklin was not the postmaster. His *New-England Courant* was the first unlicensed paper in the colonies. It was also, by far, the best.[5] The *Courant* contained political essays, opinion, satire, and some word of goings-on. The *Boston News-Letter* contained the shipping news, official government pronouncements, letters from Europe, and whatever news was bland enough to pass the censor.[6] James Franklin had a different editorial policy: "I hereby invite all Men, who have Leisure, Inclination and Ability, to speak their Minds with Freedom, Sense and Moderation, and their Pieces shall be welcome to a Place in my Paper."[7]

The *Courant* began printing in August 1721; that October, James Franklin joined Benjamin Colman's church, where he worshipped with his uncle Benjamin.[8] The next month, James Franklin and Cotton Mather met on the street.

"The Plain Design of your Paper," Mather told him, "is to Banter and Abuse the Ministers of God, and if you can, to defeat all the good Effects of their Ministry on the Minds of the People."[9]

Calling the *Courant* "A Wickedness never parallel'd any where upon the Face of the Earth!" Mather dubbed Jane's brother and his writers the Hell-Fire Club.[10] Increase Mather wrung his hands, too, thinking, perhaps, of how well he had suppressed the writings of heretics like Peter Folger, only to be plagued by this young shaver: "I can well remember when the Civil Government could have taken an effectual Course to suppress such a *Cursed Libel!*"[11]

But Jane's brother James, so far from backing down, printed essay upon essay about the freedom of the press.[12] "To anathematize a Printer for publishing the different Opinions of Men," he insisted, "is as injudicious as it is wicked."[13] He knew, as his grandfather had known, that there is a time for silence and, as well, a time to speak.

Not long after James Franklin started printing the *Courant,* and hired his brother Benjamin as his apprentice, another of Josiah's children left home. In 1722, Sarah Franklin married James Davenport, a baker and tavern-keeper. Of Josiah's seventeen children, only Lydia and Jane were still at the Blue Ball.[14]

At the print shop, Benny set the type and printed and delivered the *Courant,* but what he wanted to do was write. "Being still a Boy, and suspecting that my Brother would object to printing any Thing of mine in his Paper if he knew it to be mine," he later wrote, "I contriv'd to disguise my Hand, and writing an anonymous Paper I put it in at Night under the Door of the Printing-House."[15]

He gave himself a pen name: "I am courteous and affable, good humour'd (unless I am first provok'd,) and handsome, and sometimes witty, but always, Sir, Your Friend and Humble Servant, SILENCE DOGOOD."[16]

This was another sneaky assault on Cotton Mather. "Silence Dogood" mocked both Mather's *Essays to Do Good*—a book Franklin had found in his father's library—and his 1721 sermon *Silentiarius,* an elegy on "holy silence" that Mather had delivered at the funeral of his daughter, who'd died, along with her baby, in childbirth. "It must be our study," a grieving Mather had preached, "To *hold our peace* when we have *sad things* befalling of us."[17] Silence Dogood did not counsel silence; she counseled outrage.

She introduced herself by way of remarks about the art of biography:

To the Author of the New-England Courant.

SIR, [No 2]

ISTORIES of Lives are seldom entertaining, unless they contain something either admirable or exemplar: And since there is little or nothing of this Nature in my own Adventures, I will not tire your Readers with tedious Particulars of no Consequence, but will briefly, and in as few Words as possible, relate the most material Occurrences of my Life, and according to my Promise, confine all to this Letter.

A young widow with three children, Mrs. Dogood had benefited from an unusual upbringing. After her father's death, her mother, too poor to keep her, had apprenticed her to a minister, not unlike Benjamin Colman, with liberal views about female education. "He endeavour'd that I might be instructed in all that Knowledge and Learning which is necessary for our Sex, and deny'd me no Accomplishment that could possibly be attained in a Country Place; such as all Sorts of Needle-Work, Writing, Arithmetick, &c. and observing that I took a more than ordinary Delight in reading ingenious Books, he gave me the free Use of his Library, which tho' it was but small, yet it was well chose, to inform the Understanding rightly, and enable the Mind to frame great and noble Ideas." She spent much of her childhood "with the best of Company, *Books.*"[18]

When Jane Franklin was ten years old and her brother was sixteen, he broke out upon the literary stage disguised as a woman whose girlhood had been spent reading books, and who refused to keep quiet. As the sharp-tongued Widow Dogood, he took the trouble to offer "a few gentle Reproofs on those who deserve them," including Harvard students.[19] Curious about "the Education of Children," Mrs. Dogood spent an afternoon in Cambridge, which led her to reflect upon "the extream Folly of those Parents, who, blind to their Childrens Dulness, and insensible of the Solidity of their Skulls, because they think their Purses can afford it, will needs send them to the Temple of Learning, where, for want of a suitable Genius, they learn little more than how to carry themselves handsomely, and enter a Room genteely, (which might as well be acquir'd at a Dancing-School,) and from whence they return, after Abundance of Trouble and Charge, as great Blockheads as ever, only more proud and self-conceited."[20]

This was dangerous. So was much else that James Franklin printed. In the summer of 1722, James Franklin was arrested after he suggested in the pages of his newspaper that the Massachusetts government had been negligent in its efforts to capture a pirate ship.[21] While his brother was in jail, Benjamin Franklin printed, on the pages of the *Courant,* remarks about the freedom of speech.[22]

Meanwhile, he kept up his do-gooding disguise. Mrs. Dogood wrote about meeting a man who charged, "*That tho' I wrote in the Character of a Woman, he knew me to be a Man.*" This the widow denied. And then, suddenly, she fell silent.[23] But the battle between the *Courant* and the clergy raged on. In January 1723, after James printed a piece titled "Essay on Hypocrites," mocking Cotton Mather, the Massachusetts Council appointed a committee to investigate. "The Tendency of the said Paper," it reported, "is to mock Religion, and bring it into Contempt, that the Holy Scriptures are therefore profanely abused, that the Reverend and faithful Ministers of the Gospel are injuriously Reflected on, His Majesty's Government affronted, and the Peace and good Order of his Majesty's Subjects of this Province disturbed."[24] James Franklin was ordered to stop printing the *Courant.*

He first considered defying that order by changing the newspaper's name but decided, instead, to change the name of its printer. (He had been ordered to stop printing the *Courant.* No one had said that someone *else* couldn't print it.) He changed the name on the masthead to Benjamin Franklin. This introduced a complication. Franklin's apprenticeship was supposed to last until his twenty-first birthday—the day he would come of age—but, because an apprentice couldn't be the paper's printer, his brother had to cancel his indenture. Still, James had no intention of losing his apprentice: he drew up a secret contract, for the same term.[25]

At this Benjamin bridled. In the end, he decided to run away. Later, when he told the story of his life, he made James out to be a tyrant. But he also admitted that it might have been his fault: "Perhaps I was too saucy and provoking."[26]

He booked a berth on a ship headed to New York, having told the ship's captain that he was running away because he "had got a naughty Girl with Child." He paid for his passage with books.[27]

And then, he sailed away. He was seventeen. Jane was eleven.

An advertisement appeared in the *New-England Courant:*

> *James Franklin, Printer in Queen-Street,*
> *wants a likely lad for an Apprentice.*[28]

He had no use for a likely lass.

CHAPTER IX

Dear Sister

On January 6, 1727, the day Benjamin Franklin turned twenty-one, he wrote Jane Franklin a letter.[1] She was fourteen. More than three years had passed since he'd run away.

"Dear Sister," he began. "I always judged by your behaviour when a child that you would make a good, agreeable woman, and you know you were ever my peculiar favourite."

He had gotten news about her from Isaac Freeman, a ship's captain from Boston. "I hear you are grown a celebrated beauty," he wrote.

An eighteenth-century letter is a tissue of coyness and custom. Was Jane Franklin beautiful? She never sat for a portrait. She never described her appearance. She almost never described herself at all, except to remark upon her flaws, which she considered to be chiefly failings of temperament. She was, by nature, of a cheerful disposition. "I Love to hope the Best," she said.[2] Even amid setbacks, she once explained, "I am still chearful for that is my Natural Temper."[3] But she suffered from restlessness. "I believe I am as happy as it is common for a human being, what is otherways may proceed from my own Impatience," she wrote her brother.[4] "My natural temper is none of the patientest."[5] She was miffy.

It was, he once told her, as if she were made of tinder. "I think there is rather an overquantity of Touchwood in your Constitution."[6]

Maybe she was beautiful and maybe not. But she was bridling. People who are proud and impatient and flammable tend to be at their worst between the end of childhood and the beginning of adulthood. "I my self was a Queen from the Fourteenth to the Eighteenth Year of my Age," Silence Dogood had confessed.[7] Jane, at that age, must have been cheerful but restless and, like her brother, saucy and provoking.

Something Captain Freeman told Franklin must have been troubling, because he was writing Jane in order to warn her to watch out for her virtue: "Remember that modesty, as it makes the most homely virgin amiable and charming, so the want of it infallibly renders the most perfect beauty disagreeable and odious."[8] A brother urging modesty on his sister was a letter-writing convention. But, curiously, this letter came from a very passionate young man who, in the time since he had run away, had jilted a woman on one side of the ocean and been whoring on the other.

After leaving Boston, Franklin had settled in Philadelphia, a city as worldly as Boston was provincial. He lodged in the Market Street house of a man named John Read. He courted Read's daughter Deborah, and found work in the print shop of Samuel Keimer.[9]

Everywhere Franklin went, he made friends. "I began now to have some Acquaintance among the young People of the Town, that were Lovers of Reading. . . . I lived very agreeably, forgetting Boston as much as I could, and not desiring that any there should know where I resided, except my Friend Collins who was in my Secret, and kept it." Only Collins even knew where he was, until Franklin's brother-in-law Robert Homes, a ship's captain who sailed between Boston and Delaware and who had married Franklin's sister Mary, heard word of him and wrote him a letter, urging him to return to Boston.[10]

Franklin was such an extraordinary young man that William Keith, the governor of Pennsylvania, made him an extraordinary proposition: if Franklin would venture to travel to London to buy a press and type, Keith would give him letters of credit and would set him up in a print shop when he came back. But for this he first needed his father's approval. Keith gave Franklin a letter to carry to Boston. In May 1724, eight months after he left home, Franklin had turned up at the Blue Ball.

"My unexpected Appearance surpris'd the Family," Franklin wrote. "All were however very glad to see me and made me Welcome, except my Brother." James might have forgiven his former apprentice had not Franklin made matters worse. "I went to see him at his Printing-House: I was better dress'd than ever while in his Service, having a genteel new Suit from Head to foot, a Watch, and my Pockets lin'd with near Five Pounds Sterling in Silver. He receiv'd me very frankly, look'd me all over, and turn'd to his Work again." Their mother tried to effect a reconciliation, but James was so offended by his brother's behavior at the print shop—"I had insulted him in such a Manner before his People that he could never forget or forgive it"—that James would barely speak to him.

About Keith's proposal that Franklin sail to London, Josiah was dubious. "My Father receiv'd the Governor's Letter with some apparent Surprise," according to Franklin. Josiah thought that Keith must be a gentleman "of small Discretion to think of setting a Boy up in Business who wanted yet 3 Years of being at Man's Estate." He refused his support, his son "being in his Opinion too young to be trusted with the Management of a Business."[11] If Benjamin had been twenty-one—"at Man's Estate"—and not eighteen, he said, he might have felt differently.

Franklin stopped in to visit Cotton Mather: "As I was taking my Leave he accompany'd me thro' a narrow Passage at which I did not enter, and which had a Beam across it lower than my Head. He continued Talking which occasion'd me to keep my Face partly towards him as I retired, when he suddenly cry'd out, Stoop! Stoop! Not immediately understanding what he meant, I hit my Head hard against the Beam. He then added, *Let this be a Caution to you not always to hold your Head so high; Stoop, young Man, stoop—as you go through the World—and you'll miss many hard Thumps.*"[12] These young Franklins were all alike: they would not learn to stoop.

Days after he arrived, Franklin left, with no help from his father—only "some small Gifts as Tokens of his and my Mother's Love"—and little more than his father's advice to "avoid lampooning and libeling to which he thought I had too much Inclination."[13] Back in Philadelphia, Franklin "interchang'd some Promises" with Deborah Read and, soon after, sailed for London. When he arrived, he found that Keith had trifled with him. Not only had he sent him no letters of credit, he had no credit to give: "he wish'd to please everybody; and having little to give, he gave Expectations." Franklin, who could not afford a return passage across the Atlantic, found work at a printer's and forgot "by degrees my Engagements with Miss Read, to whom I never wrote more than one Letter, and that was to let her know I was not likely soon to return."[14]

In London, he amused himself. *Gulliver's Travels* was published that year; Franklin undertook his own adventures, treading streets that were trod, in those same months, by Voltaire, Newton, Defoe, Fielding, and Swift, none of whom he met, though not for lack of trying. Samuel Richardson, having recently finished his apprenticeship, had opened his own printing shop, on Fleet Street; Franklin found journeywork in the shops of one printer after another. Nights, he went to plays and trawled the city. He indulged, he admitted, in more than a few "Intrigues with low Women that fell my Way, which were attended with some Expence and great Inconvenience, besides a continual Risque to my Health by a Distemper which of all Things I dreaded, tho' by great good Luck I escaped it."[15] He did not get the pox. For all his dissolution, he impressed a great many people as being "a young Man of some Ingenuity," especially after he wrote *A Dissertation on Liberty and Necessity, Pleasure and Pain,* ridiculing the argument that evil, pain, and suffering can be taken as evidence of God's existence.[16] He had traveled a great distance from the pews at Old South.

He began to have misgivings. The whoring, the lampooning: weren't these pleasures at the cost of someone else's pain? He had been aimless, and cruel. In the summer of 1726, he sailed back to Philadelphia, determined to mark the change of situation with a reformation of morals. On board the ship, he drafted a plan of conduct, a creed, pledging to be frugal, honest, and industrious, and "to speak ill of no man."[17]

He landed in Philadelphia to find that Deborah Read had married "a worthless Fellow" named Rogers. This was a disappointment, but Franklin found other satisfactions. He set up a printing shop, on Water Street. He did, on his own, what his father had said so young a man could not. And then, on the day he turned twenty-one, he wrote a letter to his sister.

To write a letter is to reveal one's character. There were rules, conventions, forms: molds. There were also, therefore, manuals, like recipe books, and Franklin must have owned one; he was schooling himself in the art of becoming a gentleman.

The Young Secretary's Guide, published in Boston beginning in 1703, had run to six editions by 1727. It included a template for "A Brother's Letter to a Sister, enquiring of her Welfare."

"Loving Sister," it begins, "My long Absence from you, tho' I have not wanted good Conversation, has however made the Time seem tedious."[18]

Most writing manuals, including *The Young Man's Companion,* published in New York by William Bradford, and in Philadelphia by Bradford's son Andrew, included a template for "A Letter from a young Man newly out of his Time"—that is, a letter written by an apprentice who has completed his apprenticeship: on the day he turns twenty-one.[19]

On his twenty-first birthday, when Benjamin Franklin wrote a letter to Jane Franklin, telling her how much he missed her and urging her to cultivate modesty, he was adapting for his purposes a variety of forms— A Brother's Letter to a Sister, enquiring of her Welfare; A Letter from a young Man newly out of his Time. But he also made those forms his own. He wished to send her a gift. "I had almost determined on a tea table," he wrote, "but when I considered that the character of a good housewife was far preferable to that of being only a pretty gentlewoman, I concluded to send you a *spinning wheel*." This was a joke. A tea table was a preposterous extravagance, a luxury, something for fine ladies with two-foot-tall peri-wigs and whalebone bustles as wide as a two-horse cart. He wasn't about to give Jane a tea table, no matter how beautiful she was.[20] But he wasn't about to send her a spinning wheel, either.[21]

Whether a girl warranted a gift of a tea table or a spinning wheel was a measure of her virtue. The tea table was a symbol of female vanity, the spinning wheel a symbol of female chastity. "Who can find a vertuous woman?" asks Proverbs 31. "She layeth her handes to the spindle, and her handes hold the distaffe." It was more than a symbol. When Benjamin and Jane Franklin were growing up, there had been plans afoot in Boston to force poor girls to toil at spinning wheels to offset the cost of the alms-house (a building for which their father supplied the candles). In 1720, the Boston town meeting appointed a committee to "Consider abt promoting of a Spinning School."[22] It doesn't appear that any school was then built, though, since in 1725 someone signing himself "Homespun Jack" wrote a letter to James Franklin, published in the *New-England Courant,* putting forward a similar proposal:

> In many, if not most of our Country Towns, Children are taught to read by a School-Master; so that the Girls must be idle between Times of Reading, for want of a Mistress to teach them some suitable Employment. If therefore a School were set up in every Town, the Mis-tress whereof to be a good Spinner, the Girls might be very profitably employ'd in Spinning between the Hours of Reading.[23]

Spinning between the Hours of Reading: while the schoolmaster was teaching boys to write, girls had nothing to do. They might as well spin.

That was Boston. In the more lurid corners of London that Franklin had been frequenting, the battle of the furniture was smutty: the wanton tea table versus the virginal spinning wheel was a commonplace of early-eighteenth-century English satire. In Edward Ward's 1702 poem *The City Madam, and the Country Maid,* the city madam is "ripe to be undone: / Loosing at last, so little is her Care, / Her Virgin Treasure on a Founder'd Chair," and all because she does not spin: she'd been "bred, / Scarce knowing Hemp from Flax, or Yarn from Thread." By contrast, the virtuous country maid does naught *but* spin: "Her Needle, Bobbins, Knitting Pins, or Reel, / Some new Device, or the old Spinning Wheel / Are still Employ'd, and with Content Caress'd."[24] A spinster was a virgin. A 1714 pamphlet called *Adam and Eve Stript* included a chapter on "the Huswifry of the Spinning-Wheel"; it describes a spinster who "waddles, like a Duck, with her Toes inwards, in due Observance of her Mother's good Counsel, who bid her always be careful, before she was marry'd, to keep her great Toes together, lest some Clown or other should tumble in between them."[25] A spinster kept her toes together.

Franklin himself once wrote a satire about a tea table and a spinning wheel, in the guise of "Anthony Afterwit," a tradesman saddled with a wife whose vanity and taste for finery leads her to buy "a *Tea-Table* with all its Appurtenances" and who, before he can stop her, goes on to buy, on credit, a clock, a horse, and a maid. To save himself from debtors' prison, Afterwit rids himself of the maid, swaps the clock for an hourglass, trades in the horse for a milch cow, and disposes of the tea table by putting a spinning wheel in its place.[26]

And so: when Benjamin Franklin, on the day he turned twenty-one, wrote to fourteen-year-old Jane, a "celebrated beauty," that he considered sending her a tea table but then thought better of it and promised instead to send her a spinning wheel, as better befitting her, he was warning her to keep her toes together.

In writing to her, he had been free with her, but more frank he could not be. He knew their parents would read his letter, and he knew, too, that his quick-witted sister would read every word with care. "Every hint of yrs appeared of two much consequence to me to be neglected or forgoten," she once wrote him. "I all ways knew Everything you said had a meaning."[27]

He closed with an apology.

Excuse this freedom, and use the same with me.
  I am, dear Jenny, your loving brother.

B. Franklin.

J. Franklin tucked this letter away. And then, she picked up her pen.

PART TWO

her book

———————

1727–1757

Book of Ages

Her paper was made from rags, soaked and pulped and strained and dried. Her thread was made from flax, combed and spun and twisted and dyed. On a table, she laid down a sheet of foolscap and smoothed it with the palms of her hands. She creased it and folded it, and folded it again. She pressed it open. With a needle made of steel, she stitched a seam.

It made the slimmest of volumes, no thicker than a patch of burlap. She dipped the nub of a pen slit from the feather of a bird into a pot of ink boiled of oil mixed with soot.[1] And then, on the first page, she wrote three words:

The handwriting is unlike anything else she ever wrote: a lavish, calligraphic letter *B*, a graceful, slender, artful *A*. She wrote these three words, and only these three words, in a loopy and Italian round hand, known as the "Flourishing Alphabet."

She could have learned it out of a writing manual. *A very Useful Manual; or, The Young Mans Companion*, printed in London in 1681, was first advertised for sale in Boston in 1694.[2] By the middle of the eighteenth century, there were dozens of "young man's companions." In Philadelphia, her brother printed *The American Instructor; or, Young Man's Best Companion*.

It included "Directions to Beginners." How to make a pen: "before you begin to cut the Quill, scrape off the superfluous Scurf with the Back of your Pen-knife." How to hold a pen: "the Fore Finger lying straight on the Middle Finger." Then came "Instructions to write a Variety of Hands," including alphabets of "the most usual fashionable, and commendable Hands for Business."[3]

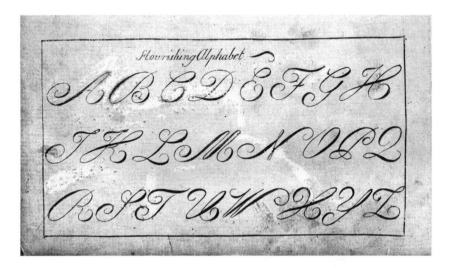

She chose her words with care. Book of Age's. There is no article; it's neither "The Book of Ages" nor "A Book of Ages." The apostrophe must have been an error; she had no idea how to punctuate, and it's not, really, age's book. At first, the meaning seems plain: this book contains a record of people's ages—it contains a list of dates, a record of births and deaths. But, looking closer, the meaning isn't plain at all. The phrase sounds common, but it's not. It's not in the Bible; it's not in Shakespeare. It's not in Milton or Bunyan. It's not in anything she ever seems to have read. It only very rarely appeared in any seventeenth- or eighteenth-century English or American book, pamphlet, broadside, song sheet, or newspaper, at least before 1791, when it turned up—as a synonym for the Bible—in a catechism: "Thus learn to read my child the word of God. It speaks by words and by deeds. It is a book of ages."[4]

Maybe the phrase came not from something she read but from something she heard: a hymn. Sometime about 1250, Thomas of Celano, an Italian monk, wrote "Dies Irae," a poem about the day when the dead shall be judged, their lives written in a book.

Liber scriptus proferetur,
In quo totum continetur,
Unde mundus judicetur.

This stanza was sometimes translated into English as:

Lo, the Book of ages spread
From which all the deeds are read
Of the living and the dead.[5]

"Dies Irae" formed part of the Roman Catholic Requiem; it is a song sung for the dead. A book of ages was a book of the dead.

Maybe there is some family story here, some family hymn about a book of ages. Jane Franklin's grandmother had loved to sing and had loved to recite Malachi to her children, telling them of how "a booke of remembrance was written." Her uncle Benjamin wrote psalms and sang them over dinner. Her father had a beautiful voice; maybe he had sung to his daughter a song he had learned from his mother, a song about a book of ages, in which all the records are written, of the living and the dead. But unless someone wrote them down, no one can know what songs anyone sang.

When Jane was a girl, whether songs ought to be written down had been much disputed. In meeting, deacons would call out songs, line by line, for the congregation to repeat; the result was something short of tuneful. In 1721, Benjamin Colman argued for singing psalms from printed books. Taking Colman's side, James Franklin printed *The Grounds and Rules of Musick Explained,*[6] and, in the *New-England Courant,* offered this squib: "I am credibly inform'd, that a certain Gentlewoman miscarry'd at the ungrateful and yelling Noise of a Deacon in reading the first Line of a Psalm; and methinks if there were no other Argument against this Practice (unless there were an absolute necessity for it) the Consideration of it's being a Procurer of Abortion, might prevail with us to lay it aside."[7]

Still, that a girl growing up in Puritan Boston in the early years of the eighteenth century could have heard an English translation of a hymn sung at a Catholic Mass is hard to believe. More likely, she simply made up "book of ages." Not a copy: an original. A Jane Franklin invention.

If the phrase was odd, the keeping of a chronicle of births and deaths was not. Genealogy was everywhere. Bibles printed genealogies tracing

Christ's ancestry back to Adam. Schoolbooks listed the kings and queens of England, back to Henry VIII.[8] Parish registers were patchy. Records kept by town clerks were spotty. There were no birth certificates. The only way to be sure who was born when was to write it down, on scraps of paper pressed between the pages of the family Bible—a book was a good place to store a piece of paper—or scribbled on its endpapers.[9] Only a book would last.

Instead of using a Bible, Jane Franklin made her own book. "Book of Age's," she wrote on the front. Then she turned the page. At the top of the next recto, in a small and unflourishing hand, she began her chronicle, a book of dates.

> *Edward Mecom Senr Born in December 1704*
> *Jane Franklin Born on March 27—1712*
> *Edward Mecom Marryed to Jane Franklin the 27th of July 1727*

The Book of Age's: *her* age.

Born, March 27, 1712; married, July 27, 1727. Fifteen years, four months. She married as a child. *I hear you are grown a celebrated beauty.* Six months after her brother wrote to her on January 6, 1727, the day he turned twenty-one, Jane Franklin was married.

The legal age for marriage in Massachusetts was sixteen. The average age was twenty-four, which, except for Jane, is also the average age at which Josiah Franklin's daughters were married.[10] So, too, his sons: Josiah's sons all married in their mid-twenties, none before twenty-two. Benjamin didn't marry until he was twenty-four. Jane's two closest sisters, Sarah and Lydia, both married when they were twenty-three. Their mother had married at twenty-two.[11]

Marrying the man she did, when she did, determined the whole course of Jane Franklin's life. Marriage determined the whole course of every woman's life.[12] Maybe, if Benjamin Franklin wrote more letters to his little sister than he wrote to anyone else, he wrote because he bore the burden of her fate. "I never can forgit that you have not only been the best of Brothers but as a Tender Father to me," she once wrote him.[13] Tender, but absent. He left her behind.

He wasn't the last to leave. Her brother James had shut down the *Courant* in June 1726 and moved to Newport, Rhode Island. Jane had had other losses since. "I fainted at Meeting and again when I came home," her uncle Benjamin wrote after collapsing during Reverend Colman's sermon at Brattle Street. In 1726, in a catalog he kept of his illnesses, he had written but a single entry: "I have been much out of order this year with the Dropsie, & faintings."[14] He died the next year, on March 27, 1727—Jane's birthday, the day she turned fifteen.

"A Person who was justly esteem'd and valu'd as a rare & exemplary Christian," his obituary read, "and tho' he courted not the Observation of Men, yet there were many that could not but take notice of, and admire the peculiar Excellencies that so visibly adorn'd him."[15] He did his good in silence. He was buried at the Granary Burying Ground.[16] Benjamin Colman preached a funeral sermon at the Brattle Street Church from Psalms 37:37.[17] The sermon Jane heard that day she never forgot. *Marke the perfect man, and behold the upright: for the end of that man is peace.*[18]

Four months later, she was married. The man she married, Edward Mecom, was not the perfect man. He was twenty-two. She never knew his birthday. (Nor, probably, did he, but he was born on December 15, 1704.) He was the son of Duncan and Mary Hoar Mecom.[19] He had an older sister, Mary; two older brothers, Hezekiah and Ebenezer; and three younger sisters, Rebecca, Elizabeth, and Ann, the youngest.[20] He was poor, he was a saddler, and he was a Scot.[21] He wore a wig and a beaver hat.[22]

Jane never once wrote anything about him expressing the least affection. She hardly ever wrote anything about him at all. She knew about the worst of marriages—"Ill be Ansurable for yr Husband that He shall not Beet you," she once wrote a friend—but she never wrote about hers.[23] She left her parents' church to marry Edward Mecom; their marriage was entered into the books in Colman's church, her uncle Benjamin's church, her brother James's church. Brattle Street was also Edward Mecom's church.[24] He led the church in singing psalms.[25] He had a beautiful voice. He once proposed opening a singing school.[26] Maybe she loved the sound of him.

If there was something at home that Jane had wanted to run from, marrying proved no escape. Edward Mecom had no place of his own. Once they were married, he simply moved in, threading himself into the lives led in the dark, tallow-lit rooms behind the door of the Blue Ball.

Jane Franklin was restless and impatient and even saucy and provoking.

The day she got married, she might also have been pregnant, which would explain why her father gave her permission to marry so unpromising a man at so unwise an age. Very many eighteenth-century brides were pregnant when they married.[27] *Neither a Fortress nor a Maidenhead will hold out long after they begin to parly,* says Poor Richard.[28] A Harvard society even debated, in 1721, "whether it be lawful to lie with one's sweetheart before marriage."[29]

But in the parish register of the Brattle Street Church, the first child recorded as having been born to Jane Franklin and Edward Mecom didn't arrive until nearly two years after their wedding.[30] If she was pregnant when she married, she either miscarried or gave birth to a baby born dead.[31] And then she might have stared out across the water in the harbor and known that she had married a wastrel for naught.

In her Book of Ages, below the record of her marriage, she added another line.

Josiah Mecom their first Born on Wednesday June the 4: 1729

She named him after her father.[32]

She was seventeen. Her belly had swelled, and burst, and then there were two. "That knot's unty'd that made us one," Anne Bradstreet wrote, about giving birth.[33] Jane Colman wrote poems about childbirth, too. Colman had married Ebezener Turell, minister of Medford.[34] Her first child was stillborn; her next lived eleven days. Pregnant for the fourth time, she wrote about her first three pregnancies—

> *Thrice in my Womb I've found the pleasing Strife,*
> *In the first Struggles of my Infant's Life*

—about the torture of each birth—

> *in Travail-Pains my Nerves are wreck'd,*
> *My Eye-balls start, my Heart-strings almost crack'd*

—and about the agony of loss—

But O how soon by Heaven I'm call'd to mourn,
While from my Womb a lifeless Babe is torn?

And then she prayed that this child might live:

To this my earnest Cry and humble Prayer,
That when the Hour arrives with painful Throws,
Which shall my Burden to the World disclose;
I may Deliverance have, and joy to see
A living Child, to Dedicate to Thee.

When that hour arrived, "No humane Help was nigh." Jane Colman endured her final trial alone. Her baby died. And then, at the age of twenty-seven, so did she. The only one of her children to survive her died the next year; he was six.

The Father's Tears over his Daughter's Remains was the title Benjamin Colman gave the funeral sermon he preached for her, a sermon he had printed as a pamphlet made to look like a gravestone.[35]

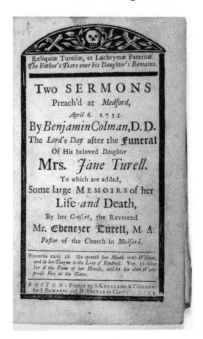

What remains of a life? "Remains" means what remains of the body after death. But remains are also what remains of a person's body of work. "Literary remains" are unpublished papers. And "remains" can also mean descendants: what remains of the family line. Benjamin Franklin wrote about his visit to Ecton as a journey to see "the Remains of my Relations."[36] Bradstreet wrote about her children as her remains: "my little babes, my dear remains." But her poems were her children, too: "Thou ill-form'd offspring of my feeble brain."[37] Bradstreet's poems were all that her children would, one day, have left of her. "If chance to thine eyes shall bring this verse," she told them, "kiss this paper."[38]

At Jane Colman Turell's funeral, her father gave out to mourners 144 pairs of mourning gloves to wear and remember her by. He paid for a tomb, carved of stone. To members of his family, he gave out mourning rings, bands of gold inscribed with his daughter's name and decorated with a tiny skeleton encased in a coffin of glass. Tokens of the dead, given to the living.[39]

After Jane Colman Turell's death, her husband published a collection of her writing, with the running head "Mrs. Turell's Remains." In it, he chose to omit all "Pieces of *Wit* and *Humour,* which if publish'd would give a brighter Idea of her to some sort of Readers," on the ground that her mind was, on the whole, of a more serious and sober cast.[40] He didn't want anyone to remember that she was funny.

All of Jane Colman Turell's papers have been lost; all of her children died. What remains of her is what her father preached and what her husband published.[41]

Jane Franklin Mecom's Book of Ages is her remains.[42] She wrote it herself.

Josiah Mecom their first Born on Wednesday June the 4: 1729

And, below this, she wrote,

and Died May the 18—1730

Her firstborn, the child of her childhood, a nursling, died two weeks shy of his first birthday. She counted the days of his life. And what of her grief?

"A Dead Child is a sight no more surprising than a broken Pitcher, or a blasted Flower," Cotton Mather preached, in a sermon called *Right Thoughts in Sad Hours*. One in four children died before the age of ten. The dead were kept at home, wrapped in linen or cerecloth—linen dipped in melted wax—while a box made of pine was built, fit to size, and painted black. Jane had no money for gloves or rings. At the tolling of a bell, pallbearers carried the coffin to the burying ground, in silence. A minister might offer a sermon the next Sunday, but no sermons were preached at the grave. Puritans banned prayers for the dead. There would be no words.[43] Nor, ministers warned, ought there to be tears. *A Token for Mourners; or, The Advice of Christ to a Distressed Mother, bewailing the Death of her Dear and Only Son*, published in Boston the year Jane buried her baby, explained "the Boundaries of Sorrow," citing Luke 7:13: "Weepe not."[44]

She washed him and kissed him and bundled him in linen and watched him being laid in the ground, the place marked with a cross made of sticks. She tried to have right thoughts. As best she could, she wept not. But she could not abide silence.

The Book of Ages is a book of remembrance. *Write this for a memoriall in a booke.* She had no portraits of her children, and no gravestones. Nothing remained of them except her memories, and four sheets of foolscap, stitched together. The remains of her remains.

The Book of Ages was her archive. *Kiss this paper.* Behold the historian.

CHAPTER XI

Poor Jane's Almanac

I am sorry to hear of Sister Macom's Loss," Franklin wrote to their sister Sarah after Jane's first baby died, "and should be mighty glad of a Line from her."[1]

He hadn't written to Jane, or maybe he had, but she hadn't written back to him, and he wished she would.

"I have wrote & spelt this very badly," she often apologized to him, "but as it is to won who I am shure will make all Reasonable allowances for me and not let any won Els see it I shall venter to send it."[2]

He worried that his sisters were embarrassed to write to him, as he was such a fine writer, and they such poor ones. He sent reassurance.

You "need be under no Apprehensions of not writing polite enough to such an unpolite Reader as I am," he insisted. "I think if Politeness is necessary to make Letters between Brothers and Sisters agreeable, there must be very little Love among 'em." And then he added, as if it were an afterthought: "I am not about to be married as you have heard."[3]

About this last, Franklin was lying. (Letters are full of lies.) He was about to be married, if without ceremony. He lied because he didn't want his sisters to know that he had fathered a bastard.

Franklin once wrote a satire of a gentleman's conduct manual, in the form of a letter advising a young man suffering from "violent natural Inclinations" but unwilling to seek marriage as a remedy for what ailed him to take only older women for mistresses. "There is no hazard of Children." Also, older women are wiser, better talkers, better at intrigue, and better at other things, too, "every Knack being by Practice capable of Improvement"; not to mention, "They are *so grateful*!!"[4]

But his dalliances had not been without consequence, even if the consequences were, for him, far different than they were for his sister. About the time Jane Franklin married Edward Mecom, Benjamin Franklin took a mistress in Philadelphia who soon gave birth to a son. They named him William. Historians don't know what year William was born. Franklin kept it a secret, and kept it well, because he hoped to make it seem as though the boy were not a bastard and, to do that, he had to hide the boy's age. Franklin never recorded his son's birth in a book of ages. William's age is exactly what Franklin needed to hide.

He also had to find a wife, quickly: a woman worthy enough to yoke himself to for life but desperate enough for a husband that she'd be willing to pretend that William was hers. Fortunately for Franklin, Deborah Read's husband, a man named Rogers, had abandoned her. There were rumors, too, that Rogers had another wife. "I pitied poor Miss Read's unfortunate Situation," Franklin wrote.[5] But, in truth, her situation was, for him, an excellent bit of luck. On September 1, 1730, Benjamin Franklin and Deborah Read Rogers set up house; there was never any wedding; theirs was a common-law marriage. They simply moved in together, and William came to live with them. Then they told everyone he was their son. If you were a man, such things could be done.

Franklin was, by now, not just any man but one of the most important men in Philadelphia. In 1727, he had founded a literary society called the Junto. In 1729, he had purchased the *Pennsylvania Gazette*. Most printers were booksellers, and stationers, too, as well as paper merchants and book publishers. In his shop, Franklin sold ink, pens, pencils, blotters, paper, and blank books. He cast type (a rare skill for a printer) and carved his own engravings. He was also an editor and, strangest of all for a printer, a writer. He admitted that much of his success was a result of his "having learnt a little to scribble," but he still liked best to sign himself "B. Franklin, Printer."[6]

The most successful printers were also postmasters; Franklin, at first, was not. Philadelphia's postmaster Andrew Bradford, who printed a rival newspaper, the *American Weekly Mercury*, forbade Franklin to distribute the *Gazette* by post, leaving him to bribe the post riders to carry his papers.[7] In the *Gazette*, Franklin fought for the liberty of the press. In a 1731 "Apology for Printers," he observed "that the Opinions of Men are almost as various as their Faces" but that "Printers are educated in the Belief, that when Men differ in Opinion, both Sides ought equally to have the Advantage of being heard by the Publick; and that when Truth and Error have fair Play, the former is always an overmatch for the latter."[8]

Franklin and his sister differed in their opinions. But what she had to say went not only unwritten but also unprinted and unsaved. In May 1731, Jane, nineteen, wrote her brother a letter. It's known that she wrote it only because he mentioned it: the letter itself is lost; all of Jane's letters from these years are lost. This might have been her first letter to him, but, more likely, she had been writing to him since 1727, or even before. It's impossible to know, because, for these years, only his letters remain.

She told him their sister Sarah had died in childbirth at the age of thirty-one.

"She was a good woman," he wrote back.[9]

She told him that their sister Mary, who had three children, was dying of breast cancer.

"I know a cancer in the breast is often thought incurable," he returned, "yet we have here in town a kind of shell made of some wood, cut at a proper time, by some man of great skill (as they say,) which has done wonders in that disease among us, being worn for some time on the breast." He promised to send some along if he could. If he did, it didn't help. Mary died later that year. She was thirty-seven.

But Jane had sent him good news, too: after the loss of her first son, she had given birth to another. She had gotten pregnant less than three months after burying baby Josiah. She recorded the birth in her Book of Ages.

Edward Mecom Born on Munday the 29 March 1731

She named the new baby after her husband. She called him Neddy.[10] She swaddled him and nursed him and hugged him close.

"I had before heard of the death of your first child," Franklin wrote her, "and am pleased that the loss is in some measure made up to you by the birth of a second."[11]

He, too, soon had a second son. Deborah Franklin gave birth to a boy on October 20, 1732. They named him Francis Folger Franklin; they called him Franky.

By the time Franky was born, Jane was seven months pregnant. She had gotten pregnant before Neddy was a year old. She named her third son after her brother.

Benjamin Mecom Born on Fryday the 29 of December 1732.

She called him Benny.[12]

She was a gentle mother and tender. When toddlers fall, she once wrote, they need you "to Kiss the Dear Lip after it was Hurt" for "the Litle Rogues all want to be Pityed by them that Loves them."[13] She was demanding. "Perhaps I am two Severe with Every won," she mused, "& I am tould with my Self two."[14] She could be hard. But she admired a woman who was "an Indulgent mother." And she could tell when a mother was "much Pleasd" with her children, "as we all are with our litle wons."[15]

She was frank in her affections. Her children were her pleasure, her little ones, her little rogues. She adored them.

The day before Jane gave birth to her third son, her brother advertised his first *Poor Richard's Almanack.*

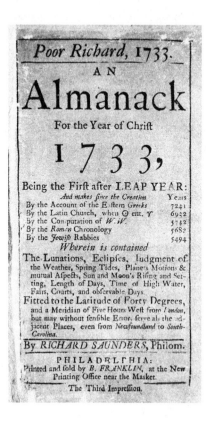

Almanacs, issued just before the New Year, were calendars—books of days—listing tides, holidays, and the phases of the moon. They sold better than everything except Bibles and were bought, as Franklin pointed out, by "the common People, who bought scarce any other Books."[16] In the middle of the eighteenth century, about fifty thousand almanacs were printed in the colonies every year, for a population of about nine hundred thousand (that is, one almanac for every eighteen people). Franklin sold about ten thousand *Poor Richard's* a year, five pence each.[17] Deborah called them *Poor Dicks*. In the shop, she could barely keep them in stock.[18]

Franklin filled the pages of his almanacs with proverbs, most of which he didn't write. "Not a tenth Part of the Wisdom was my own," he admitted.[19] The rest he found in books, mostly anthologies like Thomas Fuller's *Gnomologia: Adagies and Proverbs; Wise Sentences and Witty Sayings Ancient and Modern, Foreign and British,* a book printed in London in 1732. But Franklin was a deft editor. Where Fuller had written, "A Man in Passion rides a Horse that runs away with him," Franklin outpaced him: *A Man in a Passion rides a mad Horse.* And where Titan Leeds, author of the deathless prose in *The American Almanack,* blathered, "Many things are wanting to them that desire many things," Franklin pegged it: *If you desire many things, many things will seem but a few.*[20]

"He had wit at will," John Adams once wrote about Franklin. "He had humor that, when he pleased, was delicate and delightful. He had a satire that was good-natured or caustic, Horace or Juvenal, Swift or Rabelais, at his pleasure. He had talents for irony, allegory, and fable."[21] He also had a taste for counterfeit. He loved a pen name. He pretended that his almanacs were written by a hapless, witless, befuddled astrologer named Richard Saunders—poor Richard—who had picked up his pen because his wife, Bridget, had threatened to burn his books if he didn't earn a few more farthings and because, as Franklin wrote, "The Printer has offer'd me some considerable share of the Profits."[22]

Saunders once complained that rumors had circulated "*That there is no such a Man as I am; and have spread this Notion so thoroughly in the Country, that I have been frequently told it to my Face by those that don't know me.*" Some fiends had even suggested that Benjamin Franklin was really Poor Richard. For this, Saunders had an answer. "My Printer, to whom my Enemies are pleased to ascribe my Productions," he protested, "is as unwilling to father my Offspring as I am to lose the Credit of it."[23] Poor Richard's almanac was a bastard.

CHAPTER XII

Bookkeeping

O n March 27, 1733, Jane turned twenty-one. She had come of age. That year, her brother gave her the gift of a book: a copy of *The Ladies Library*, a duodecimo, in three volumes, the fourth edition, printed in London in 1732.[1] On the flyleaf she wrote,

The Ladies Library was a birthday present. Not a tea table, not a spinning wheel: a book, a library.

In 1731, Benjamin Franklin had founded the first lending library in America, the Library Company of Philadelphia. In April 1732, a member of the Library Company sailed to London with a list of titles to purchase. A shipment of books—fifty-six titles in 141 volumes—arrived in Philadelphia in October. Franklin printed up charge slips, for borrowers.[2]

The first box of books sent to the Library Company did not include *The Ladies Library*. But it did include booksellers' catalogs.[3] In a catalog printed in London in October 1732, *The Ladies Library* appeared on the same page as Thomas Fuller's *Gnomologia*, the source for many of Poor Richard's proverbs. In the summer of 1733, Franklin set off on a visit to Boston.[4] He knew what imported books he might try to pick up in bookshops along the way. "At the time I establish'd myself in Pennsylvania," he wrote, "there was not a good Bookseller's Shop in any of the Colonies to the Southward of Boston."[5] He likely bought *The Ladies Library* at a bookstore in Boston run by a bookseller from London who advertised that he sold "the newest and most valuable Books" for "the very lowest Prices."[6]

Then he gave it to Jane. "Given her by her Brother," she wrote on the flyleaf. And then, again, on the title page, she inscribed her name, "Jane Mecom." She once lent the second volume to Franklin's wife, writing on a blank page, "borrowed of Sister Mecom," so that there would be no misunderstanding about who owned it. When she didn't get it back, she wrote to Deborah, asking her to return it, "as it breaks the sett." She had her own ideas about lending and her own ways of keeping track of what books belonged to her. People who borrowed her books had to give them back.[7]

The year Franklin founded the Library Company, he wrote a short essay called "Observations on my Reading History in Library."[8] There was no history in *The Ladies Library*. Men who recommended books to women only rarely recommended that they read history. "They allow us Poetry, Plays, and Romances to Divert us and themselves," Mary Astell complained, "and when they would express a particular Esteem for a Woman's Sense, they recommend History." Nor did women themselves seem much interested in reading history, a preference Astell found understandable. "History can only serve us for Amusement and a Subject of Discourse," Astell remarked. "For tho' it may be of Use to the Men who govern Affairs, to know how their Fore-fathers Acted, yet what is this to us, who have nothing to do with such Business?"[9]

David Hume urged women to read history—"There is nothing which I would recommend more earnestly to my female readers than the study of history"—but he, too, found women were reticent. He illustrated this observation with a story about "a young beauty" who asked him to send her some novels to read in the country. He sent her, instead, a volume of history, Plutarch's *Lives,* "assuring her, at the same time, that there was not a word of truth in them from beginning to end." She read it avidly, "till she came to the lives of ALEXANDER and CAESAR, whose names she had heard of by accident; and then returned me the book, with many reproaches for deceiving her."[10]

The Ladies Library contains no history but plenty of advice. The first volume consists of essays on female virtues (chastity, modesty, meekness) and vices (envy and pride). The second describes women's roles: daughter, wife, mother, widow. The third offers instruction in the practices of piety: prayer, fasting, repentance.[11] A lady's learning was the study not of public affairs but of private pieties.

Franklin once explained what the Library Company of Philadelphia had meant to him. "This Library afforded me the Means of Improvement by constant Study, for which I set apart an Hour or two each Day," he wrote, "and thus repair'd in some Degree the Loss of the Learned Education my Father once intended for me."[12] Maybe he meant *The Ladies Library* to do the same for his sister. It went only so far. Still, for all its narrowness, *The Ladies Library* stated on the first page of the first volume an astonishing premise: "It is a great Injustice to shut Books of Knowledge from the Eyes of Women."[13]

When Neddy was four and Benny was two and a half, Jane took out her Book of Ages and dipped her quill in ink.

Ebenezer Mecom Born on May the 2 1735

Another boy. She named him after the brother she never met, the little boy who drowned in a tub of suds.[14]

Her days were days of flesh: the little legs and little arms, the little hands, clutched around her neck, the softness. Her days were days of toil: swaddling and nursing the baby, washing and dressing the boys, scrubbing everyone's faces, answering everyone's cries, feeding everyone's hunger, cleaning everyone's waste. She taught her children to read. She made sure they learned to write better than she did.[15]

Pigs rutted in the streets; horses clattered on the cobbles; the blood of butchered chickens dripped to the floor. The house smelled of soap and tallow and leather and smoke, and it smelled, too, of sweat. Each cord of wood had to be ported and stacked. Every bucket of water had to be hauled from one of the city's wells. Every pot of night soil had to be lugged out the door and dumped in the privy in the yard. Soap had to be boiled and linens scrubbed.

"I am in the midst of a grate wash," she once wrote, stealing a moment from the endless drudgery to sit down and write, smudging ink upon the page, a different sort of stain. Everyone was used to living in filth—what counted as dirt was different if you were richer—but there was always washing to be done, with soap made by her own hands.[16]

"READY MONEY for old RAGS, may be had of the Printer thereof," her brother advertised in the pages of the *Pennsylvania Gazette*.[17] Franklin had a hand in the establishment of eighteen American paper mills. He bought rags to turn into paper. Or, rather, Deborah did this, Franklin wrote, explaining that his wife kept busy "folding and stitching Pamphlets, tending Shop, purchasing old Linen Rags for the Paper-makers."[18] Between 1739 and 1747, Franklin sold 166,000 pounds of rags, earning more than £1,000.[19] Jane's life was cluttered with a different sort of rags: rags for washing, rags for diapering, rags for catching blood.

The house was close, hot in summer, cold in winter, and dark: windows so small, tallow so dear. With a baby in her arms, now squirming, now slumbering, she stared into kettles and vats and tubs and barrels, cooking, leaching, and washing. She stirred and she watched, shifting her weight from one foot to the other, quietly rocking, the rhythm of soothing.

"This Library afforded me the Means of Improvement by constant Study, for which I set apart an Hour or two each Day," her brother had written about his gentleman's library. For her *Ladies Library*, Jane could hardly have set apart one hour each day, nor half, nor even a quarter.

Her nights were unquiet. Her husband reached for her. Her belly swelled, and emptied, and swelled again. Her breasts filled, and emptied, and filled again. Her children waked, first one, and then another, tumbling together, like a litter. She must have had very little sleep.[20]

Her Neddy, her Benny, her Eben. They grew like flowers. She pressed them to her heart. The days passed to months, the months to years, and, in her Book of Ages, she pressed her children between the pages.

In 1736, Benjamin Franklin was elected clerk of the Pennsylvania Provincial Assembly: he was a keeper of records. That year, his son Franky died of smallpox. Franklin had a gravestone carved in marble: "The DELIGHT of all that knew him." Franklin counted the days of his son's life: four years, one month, one day. Then he had a portrait painted, oil on canvas, thirty-three inches high, as tall as the boy had been, showing him in the bloom of unblemished health: Franky, his hanging sleeves rolled up to his elbows, waving his little hand, as if in parting.[21] Franklin never recovered from this child's death. No one ever does.

"My Son Franky," he once wrote Jane, "I have seldom since seen equal'd in every thing." About him, "to this Day I cannot think of without a Sigh."[22]

He would always have that portrait. And his sister would always have her Book of Ages.

When Eben was only four months old, Jane was pregnant again.

Sarah Mecom Born on Tuesday ye 28 June 1737

Her first daughter she named her after her sister. She called her Sally.[23]

The week before Sally was born, Edward Mecom borrowed three pounds from a leather dresser named David Collson. Collson wrote out a note, which Mecom signed. It read, "I promise to pay or Cause to be paid to David Collson on Order the Sum of three pounds one Shilling & five pence on Demand for Vallow"—value.[24]

They lived in a world of paper credit.[25] The "IOU," as parlance, dates to the 1610s. The first paper money in the colonies—the first official paper money anywhere in the Western world—was printed in Boston in 1690. Debt might be a crime and, worse, a sin, Cotton Mather preached in a 1716 sermon titled *Fair Dealing between Debtor and Creditor,* but "without some *Debt,* there could be no *Trade* be carried on."[26] In Philadelphia, the first paper money wasn't printed until 1723. It was widely regarded as suspicious, until, in 1729, Franklin advocated it in a pamphlet he both wrote and printed: *A Modest Enquiry into the Nature and Necessity of a Paper-Currency.*[27] It would be good for trade, he said. In 1729, Franklin began printing forms for borrowing, slips of paper, to be filled out by hand: "Bills of Lading bound and unbound, Common Blank Bonds for Money, Bonds with Judgment, Counterbonds, Arbitration Bonds, Arbitration Bonds with Umpirage, Bail Bonds, Counterbonds to save Bail harmless, Bills of Sale, Powers of Attorney, Writs, Summons, Apprentices Indentures, Servants Indentures, Penal Bills, Promissory Notes, &c. all the Blanks in the most authentick Forms, and corrently printed." Soon he was printing money, not only for Pennsylvania but also for Delaware and New Jersey. Between

1729 and 1747, he printed 800,000 paper bills, earning about £1,000. (Eventually, he made more money printing money than he did from the *Pennsylvania Gazette* and *Poor Richard's Almanack* combined.)[28]

 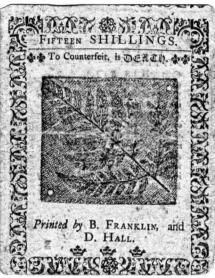

While Jane's brother printed money, her husband fell into debt. Paper money has its perils, especially in hard times. In 1712, the year Jane Franklin was born, the average daily wages of a tradesman could buy fifteen pounds of butter. In 1739, the year Edward Mecom's debts ruined him, those same wages could buy only seven pounds of butter.[29] Tradesmen and merchants kept account books, records of wages and prices, lists of credits and debts. (Sometimes, in those same books, they recorded births and deaths.)[30] Trading in paper—paper money, bills of exchange, bills of credit, and promissory notes—people tended to spend money they didn't have. The trick was to keep track. That meant knowing how to read and write and tally and having a place to store paper. That meant being a bookkeeper.[31]

In a world of paper credit, people fell into paper debt, for which they were thrown into prisons of stone. Statutes decreeing imprisonment for debt date to the thirteenth century.[32] For a long time, the colonies had been a debtors' asylum. Two out of three people who left England for America were debtors; creditors found it all but impossible to pursue debtors across the Atlantic. Defoe's fictional Moll Flanders, born in London's Newgate prison, sailed to Virginia; Roxana, another of Defoe's heroines, stayed in London and died in debtors' prison.[33] (Defoe was himself twice arrested for debt.)[34] In the seventeenth century, Virginia and North Carolina, hungry for settlers, promised five years' protection from Old World debts.[35] Connecticut and Maryland, desperate for labor, forbade the prosecution of debtors between May and October and released prisoners to plant every spring and to harvest come fall.[36]

Massachusetts was stricter. A 1641 Massachusetts law known as the "Body of Liberties" spelled out a rule of thumb: "No mans person shall be Arrested, or imprisoned upon execution or judgment for any debt or fine, If the law can finde competent meanes of satisfaction otherwise from his estaite, and if not his person may be arrested and imprisoned where he shall be kept at his owne charge, not the platife's till satisfaction be made." A man was free unless he couldn't afford to pay what he owed, and then he could be put in prison, the cost of which he had to bear.[37] The idea was that a debtor might be hiding his money and, if he wasn't, his family would pay his debts to secure his release.

A promise on paper is only as good as the man who makes it. Edward Mecom made many promises. ("He then Run in Debt, to all who would trust him," Jane once wrote, about another debtor in her family.)[38]

Edward Mecom borrowed three pounds from David Collson in June 1737. When Mecom failed to pay Collson what he owed him, Collson sought a remedy in court. The day the case was heard, Mecom neglected to show up and the court ruled in Collson's favor, adding three pounds of damages to the original debt. The judge then issued to the sheriff a writ, a set of instructions on a printed form, with blanks where the names and places and amounts were to be filled in: "We Command you to Attach the Goods or Estate of *Edward Mecom of Boston* in *Our County of Suffolk Sadler* to the Value of *Six* Pounds, and for want thereof to take the Body of the said *Edward Mecom* (if *he* may be found in your Precinct) and *him* safely keep."[39]

When you run in Debt you give to another Power over your Liberty, Poor Richard says.[40] The sheriff and his deputies were authorized to collect the six pounds Mecom owed and, failing that, "to take the Body"—*habeas corpus*—of the debtor.

On December 20, 1737, when Jane was twenty-five, at home with Neddy, six; Benny, nearly four; Eben, two; and six-month-old Sally, the

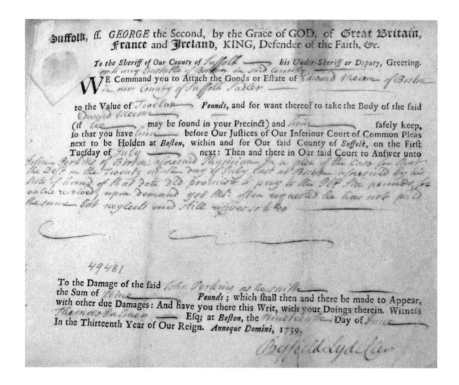

Suffolk, ff. *GEORGE* the Second, by the Grace of GOD, of *Great Britain,* *France* and *Ireland*, KING, Defender of the Faith, &c.

To the Sheriff of Our County of Suffolk ———— *his Under-Sheriff or Deputy,* Greeting.

WE Command you to Attach the Goods or Estate of Edward Mecom of Boston

to the Value of *Twelve* ———— *Pounds,* and for want thereof to take the Body of the said Edward Mecom

(if *he* ———— may be found in your Precinct) and *him* ———— safely keep, so that you have *him* ———— before Our Justices of Our Inferiour Court of Common Pleas next to be Holden at *Boston,* within and for Our said County of *Suffolk,* on the First Tuesday of *July* ———— next: Then and there in Our said Court to Answer unto

49481

To the Damage of the said John Perkins as he saith the Sum of *Nine* ———— *Pounds;* which shall then and there be made to Appear, with other due Damages: And have you there this Writ, with your Doings therein. Witness Thomas Palmer ———— Esq; at *Boston,* the *Nineteenth* Day of *June* In the Thirteenth Year of Our Reign. *Annoque Domini,* 1739.

sheriff knocked on her door. Her husband was out, or hiding. The sheriff had his orders. He was to get the money, Mecom, or six pounds' worth of goods. He seized a wooden horse, a form used for making saddles.

By the end of the month, two more men—Thomas Green, a merchant, and Thomas Price, a saddler—had sued Mecom for still more debts. Mecom's indebtedness to Price went back a decade. Mecom then filed a suit of his own, hoping to recover eleven pounds, seventeen shillings from a farmer from Watertown. While all these suits were awaiting the next meeting of the court, the Mecoms moved out of the Blue Ball. Maybe Edward thought it would be better if the sheriff didn't know where he lived.

In January 1738, Jane left home for the first time in her life. Her husband rented a house on Sudbury Street from a printer named Samuel Kneeland, who charged him £25 a year in rent. They didn't stay there long. Mecom's creditors came calling and, then, his landlord. *Creditors have better memories than debtors,* says Poor Richard.[41] Once one creditor hauled a debtor into court, his other creditors, fearing his imminent insolvency, followed suit, bringing their account books as evidence. Aside from his debts to

Colson, Green, and Price, Mecom owed Samuel Banister and Joseph Corbett nineteen pounds, seventeen shillings. Banister was a merchant and Corbett a brewer. To Edward Carter, a silk dyer, he owed twenty pounds, six pence. Each of these creditors sued Mecom, but Mecom never showed up in court. With most of these men, Mecom had business necessary to his livelihood. He had bought leather from Colson, and Price had paid him to make saddles. With others, he bought goods that had nothing to do with his trade. From Banister and Corbett, Mecom had bought a half a barrel of sage ale and two and a half barrels of small beer.

Near about that time, Franklin printed in the *Pennsylvania Gazette* a drinker's dictionary, a glossary of euphemisms for "A MAN IS DRUNK." The entries for the letter *R:*

> *He's Rocky,*
> *Raddled,*
> *Rich,*
> *Religious,*
> *Lost his Rudder,*
> *Ragged,*
> *Rais'd,*
> *Been too free with Sir Richard*
> *Like a Rat in Trouble.*[42]

Edward Mecom might well have been too free with Sir Richard. His debts for small beer and sage ale don't seem extravagant—everyone drank beer—but they're not minor, either. Maybe he had lost his rudder. Maybe he had been raddled even before he married Jane.

On June 20, 1738, eight days before Sally Mecom's first birthday, the deputy sheriff came to the house on Sudbury Street with another writ. Finding no Mecom and no money, he took a desk.[43] If Benjamin Franklin's sister wanted to write, she'd have to lean on a table.

She had more to worry about. One of her children was sick. "I hope my Sister Janey's Child is by this time recovered," Franklin wrote to his parents in April 1738. The child needed doctoring: another debt, this time to a doctor, John Perkins.

Perkins, who was born in the colonies, had once traveled to London, to "see what they had in practice new, or better than we had."[44] He was one of the ablest physicians in Boston. In his case notes, he described an epidemic that hit Boston in the middle of the 1730s. "We had a great run of the malignant sore throat," he wrote, describing an ailment that especially affected children. "Some Children were seized with a paralytic incapacity of using their Limbs, so that they would fall two or three times in walking across the floor." Perkins recommended purging.[45] It could have been any of them: Neddy, Benny, Eben, or Sally. The child recovered, and Edward Mecom signed another promissory note: "I acknowledge my self Indebted to Mr John Perkins Six pounds for Value Recd. which I Promise to pay upon Demand as Wtiness my hand this 29th Day of July 1738." Mecom never paid. Perkins sued.

By fall, Jane was pregnant again. In all the months they had been living on Sudbury Street, her husband had never paid the rent. The landlord sued on December 22, 1738, for thirty-one pounds, five shillings.

The money was short, but the children kept coming.

Peter franklin Mecom Born on ye Lords Day May the 13. 1739[46]

Keeping her own book, Jane reckoned ages. Her husband was thirty-four. She was twenty-seven. Neddy, eight; Benny, six; Eben, four; Sally, almost two. In June, when Peter Franklin was just over a month old, the sheriff knocked on the door once more, looking for Mecom, this time for failing to pay the doctor's bill. He was nowhere to be found. The sheriff left a summons. This time, he took the Mecoms' horse.[47]

"I trembled at Every knock at the Dore least it should be some officer with demands on him," Jane wrote.[48]

Very likely, Edward Mecom went to debtors' prison. In Boston, debtors were locked up in a stone jail on Queen Street, right next to the courthouse and near where, the decade before, James Franklin had opened his print shop.[49] Debtors consigned to prison often found it very difficult to get out.[50] When a man was arrested for debt, his wife and children often went to prison with him, having no place else to go.[51] Debtors in New York City's prison—where a man and his family might stay for years—established their own constitutions and courts and elected their own sheriffs, to enforce the laws.[52]

Mecom lost his lease. Jane and the children went back to the Blue Ball.[53] To get himself out of debtors' prison, Mecom must have borrowed a substantial sum of money from his father-in-law, because, by 1745, he owed Josiah Franklin twenty-three pounds, eight shillings, and two pence. He never paid him back.

Benjamin Franklin, keeping his own accounts, credited far more than he debited.[54] In 1737, he was appointed postmaster of Philadelphia, much to the advantage of his newspaper. Almost overnight, the number of advertisements in the paper doubled. He ran the post office out of his print shop.[55] "My Business was now continually augmenting, and my Circumstances growing daily easier, my Newspaper having become very profitable," he wrote. "I experienc'd the Truth of the Observation, that *after getting the first hundred Pound, it is more easy to get the second.*"[56]

He tallied his wealth. His sister tallied her children.

John Mecom Born on Tuesday March ye 31. 1741[57]

She had filled the first page of her Book of Ages. It was four days past her twenty-ninth birthday. Her father was eighty-three, her mother seventy-three. They might have paid Mecom's debts to get him out of prison, but they were hardly caring for Jane; she was caring for them. And what they paid to get her husband out of debtors' prison wouldn't pay the cost of food. What could she bring in? Other married women earned money by selling the milk in their breasts: "If any Family have Occasion for a good Wet Nurse with a good Breast of Milk, or to put out a Child to a Wet Nurse in *Boston,* may hear of one by inquiring of the printer hereof," read the usual advertisement in the back of the newspaper.[58] But Jane needed her milk for her own children.

To add to the family accounts, there wasn't much else a married woman might do, unless her husband approved. Widowed and unmarried women, who enjoyed a legal status known as *feme sole,* ran shops and taught at dame schools. But a married woman couldn't earn a shilling without her husband's permission. She could neither own property nor sign a contract. Legally, any money she earned belonged to her husband. As William Blackstone explained in his *Commentaries on the Laws of England,* "The very being or legal existence of the woman is suspended during the marriage, or at least is incorporated and consolidated into that of the husband: under whose wing, protection, and cover, she performs every thing."[59] In the eyes of the law, a married woman was *feme covert:* a woman covered by a man.

Jane began to take in boarders; the rent would belong to her husband, but she would do her best to mind it. There was little she could do, but she could do this: she knew how to take care of people living under her roof. One army captain who boarded with her on and off for thirty years never forgot her "past favors and acts of kindness."[60] She was practical and wise. She was warm. "We cannot Easely feel our Selves crowded with the company of those we Love," she liked to say.[61] She was chatty. "I very often in imagination have a fine Dish of Chat with you," her friend Caty Ray Greene once told her, missing her. She knew how to console. "If anything labors with me," Caty wrote her, "I tell you the whole."[62]

If, in these years, Jane wrote little more than cryptic entries in her Book of Ages and a handful of letters, it's not hard to imagine why.

"My mind is keept in a contineual Agitation that I Dont know how to write," she apologized.[63]

She had no time, no quiet, no solitude. But she loved to read.

"My litle wons are Interupting me Every miniut," she wrote her brother, "& I can add no more but that I wish for the comfort of a leter from you."[64] Please write.

CHAPTER XIII

Useful Knowledge

She turned the page, and began again.

Josiah Mecom Born on friday March ye 26. 1743

Another boy named after her father, who was, by now, bent and hobbled and weary.[1]

Her parents, leaning on their youngest daughter, were vexed by their youngest son. "You both seem concern'd lest I have imbib'd some erroneous Opinions," he wrote them. "I think Opinions should be judg'd of by their Influences and Effects; and if a Man holds none that tend to make him less Virtuous or more vicious, it may be concluded he holds none that are dangerous; which I hope is the Case with me."[2]

That year, in Philadelphia, Deborah Franklin gave birth to a girl. They named her Sarah; they called her Sally. She was their last.

Meanwhile, Franklin printed *A Proposal for Promoting Useful Knowledge among the British Plantations in America*. In the history of the world, even on the far side of the ocean, the time had come, he believed, for improvement. "The first Drudgery of Settling new Colonies, which confines the Attention of People to mere Necessaries, is now pretty well over," he wrote. Everywhere in America there were "Men of Speculation," conducting experiments, recording observations, making discoveries. "But as from the Extent of the Country such Persons are widely separated, and seldom can see and converse or be acquainted with each other, so that many useful Particulars remain uncommunicated, die with the Discoverers, and are lost to Mankind." He therefore proposed establishing a society "of Virtuosi or ingenious Men residing in the several Colonies, to be called *The Ameri-*

can Philosophical Society; who are to maintain a constant Correspondence." They would meet when they could but, more, they would write—letter after letter. He closed, "Benjamin Franklin, the Writer of this Proposal, offers himself to serve the Society as their Secretary, 'till they shall be provided with one more capable."[3]

The word, the book, the letter: knowledge. The American Philosophical Society was the colonies' first learned society. This was Franklin's world, the world he had escaped to, the world he was making, the world of Newton and Locke: a world that embraced a philosophy of progress based on the application of reason to nature. Freedom of opinion and the rights of man: equality and enlightenment. The light of truth, deduced. "The general spread of the light of science has already laid open to every view the palpable truth," as Thomas Jefferson put it. And that palpable truth, Jefferson believed, was this: "the mass of mankind has not been born with saddles on their backs, nor a favored few booted and spurred, ready to ride them legitimately, by the grace of God."[4] Blacksmiths who forge shoes for horses and saddlers who stitch saddles: they were not men fated, forever, to be ridden. Their children were not born with saddles on their back.

That light did not fall on Jane's world. Nor, though, was her world so very far away. The road Franklin traveled took him to her house; his letters reached her door; he sent her books. In May 1743, the month Franklin founded the American Philosophical Society, he and his son William left Philadelphia for a tour of New England, during which Franklin would inspect the post roads and spread word of his new society. In Boston, they stayed at the Blue Ball, with Jane. Franklin had not been to Boston for ten years.[5] While he was there, Archibald Spencer, a visiting Scottish empiricist, offered "a Course of Experimental Philosophy." Spencer showed Franklin his experiments with electricity. "They were imperfectly perform'd, as he was not very expert," Franklin wrote, "but being on a Subject quite new to me, they equally surpriz'd and pleas'd me."[6] He bought Spencer's apparatus. He wanted, when he returned to Philadelphia, to do some experimenting of his own. He wished to discover the secrets of nature, and of nature's God: the light of science, palpable truth. Maybe man could harness the very lightning that struck from the sky.

At the Blue Ball, William played with his cousins. He came to admire his aunt. But Franklin and his sister fought. *Talking against Religion is unchaining a Tyger,* says Poor Richard.[7] He couldn't stop himself. Neither the first nor the last man to act like a child in the house where he grew up, he was impious and irreverent. He taunted her. She was troubled. She had very little else, but she did have faith. Like her parents, she feared for his soul.

She worried that he thought that all he had to do, to achieve salvation, was do good in the world. After he left, she wrote him a letter, upbraiding him even as she apologized for her audacity. That letter is lost. In July, he wrote back:

Dearest Sister Jenny,

I took your Admonition very kindly, and was far from being offended at you for it. If I say any thing about it to you, 'tis only to rectify some wrong Opinions you seem to have entertain'd of me, and that I do only because they give you some Uneasiness, which I am unwilling to be the Occasion of. You express yourself as if you thought I was against Worshipping of God, and believed Good Works would merit Heaven; which are both Fancies of your own, I think, without Foundation. I am so far from thinking that God is not to be worshipped, that I have compos'd and wrote a whole Book of Devotions for my own Use: And I imagine there are few, if any, in the World, so weake as to imagine, that the little Good we can do here, can *merit* so vast a Reward hereafter. There are some Things in your New England Doctrines and Worship, which I do not agree with, but I do not therefore condemn them, or desire to shake your Belief or Practice of them. We may dislike things that are nevertheless right in themselves. I would only have you make me the same Allowances, and have a better Opinion both of Morality and of your Brother. Read the Pages of Mr. Edward's late Book entitled SOME THOUGHTS CONCERNING THE PRESENT REVIVAL OF RELIGION IN NE. from 367 to 375; and when you judge of others, if you can perceive the Fruit to be good, don't terrify your self that the Tree may be evil, but be assur'd it is not so; for you know who has said, *Men do not gather Grapes of Thorns or Figs of Thistles.* I have not time to add but that I shall always be Your affectionate Brother

B FRANKLIN[8]

He had taken her seriously. He loved her no matter their differences, but he would neither ignore those differences nor slight her opinions. Instead, he recommended a course of study. He pressed upon her a book.

Franklin really had written his own Book of Devotions. It ends with a prayer of thanks "For Knowledge and Literature and every useful Art."[9] He had written, too, a Book of Virtues. He had made it himself: he had folded it and stitched it. "I made a little Book in which I allotted a Page for each of the Virtues," he explained. "I rul'd each Page with red Ink, so as to have seven Columns, one for each Day of the Week, marking each Column with a Letter for the Day. I cross'd these Columns with thirteen red Lines, marking the Beginning of each Line with the first Letter of one of the Virtues, on which Line and in its proper Column I might mark by a little black Spot every Fault I found upon Examination to have been committed respecting that Virtue upon that Day."

He counted thirteen virtues: temperance, silence, order, resolution, frugality, industry, sincerity, justice, moderation, cleanliness, tranquillity, chastity, and humility. Soon the Book of Virtues was a mess. Every week he marked his faults; at the end of the week, he tried to erase them. But in the eighteenth century, writing could not be easily erased: "My little Book, which by scraping out the Marks on the Paper of old Faults to make room for new Ones in a new Course, became full of Holes." In the end, he gave up, and that was his point: no life is without blemish and, after all, "a benevolent Man should allow a few Faults in himself, to keep his Friends in Countenance."[10]

Jane's Book of Devotions was her Book of Ages. Her devotions were prayers that her children might live. And her Book of Virtues was the Bible, indelible. She explained her creed to her brother: "I profess to Govern my Life & action by the Rules laid down in the scripture."[11] The virtue she valued most was faith. It had no place on Franklin's list. She placed her trust in Providence. He placed his faith in man.

Between Providence and freedom, between faith and reason, between God and nature, Franklin was forever straddling.[12] He and his sister disagreed. He suggested that she do some reading—a hint of their relationship, from childhood. They were living in the middle of what would come to be called the Great Awakening. The greatest minister of the awakening, George Whitefield, had come to Boston. Benjamin Colman had even allowed Whitefield to preach at Brattle Street. When Colman's fellow pastor, William Cooper, died, in 1743, the vestry appointed Cooper's nineteen-year-old son, Samuel Cooper, in his place. (Samuel Cooper was Samuel Sewall's grandson; his mother, Judith, was Sewall's fourteenth child, one of the five who survived.) Young Samuel Cooper, Jane's new minister, was less orthodox and more liberal even than Colman. He preached a practical religion, a religion of love and affection, and also a religion of prosperity: wealth was no sin, so long as the wealthy remembered that it was their obligation to use their wealth to do good. Nor did poverty mean damnation, so long as the poor sought faith: "a poor and mean Condition in this Life, is often the Lot of those who are yet the Favourites of Heaven," Cooper said. With devotion came "sweet Peace."[13]

Preachers promised redemption from affliction. The standard of living, in the 1740s, was the lowest of the century. The "great Distress" in the colonies, Jonathan Edwards preached, "gives us more abundant Reason to hope that what is now seen in America, and especially in New England, may prove the Dawn of that glorious Day," that day when God would "turn the Earth into a Paradice."[14]

That, however, is not the part of Edwards's sermon that Franklin urged upon his sister. Instead, he recommended she read where Edwards had written, "It is incumbent upon God's People at this Day, to take Heed, that while they abound in external Duties of Devotion, such as Praying, Hearing, Singing, & attending religious Meetings, there be a proportionable Care to abound in moral Duties, such as Acts of Righteousness, Truth, Meekness, Forgiveness & Love towards our Neighbour; which are of much greater Importance in the Sight of God than all the Externals of his Worship." Deeds, Edwards argued, counted as much as words. Devotion, submission, obedience, resignation: these were not enough. He quoted the third chapter of First John: "Let us not love in Word, neither in Tongue, but in Deed."[15]

Dear Sister, dear Jenny. Do not wave your Bible at me: my philosophy is to do good.[16] She thought that wasn't good enough. This argument between them never ended.

CHAPTER XIV

Dear Reader

Josiah Franklin, who left the forges of Ecton to sing a new song of faith, died in Boston in January 1745. He was eighty-seven.

"Dear Sister, I love you tenderly for your care of our father in his sickness," Benjamin Franklin wrote Jane. Whenever anyone in the family was unwell, Franklin offered cures: "I apprehend I am too busy in prescribing, and meddling in the Dr's Sphere, when any of you complain of Ails in your Letters," he once apologized. He sent recipes, but it was Jane who mixed remedies, made of tartar and wormwood and turpentine.[1]

Josiah Franklin was buried at the Granary Burying Ground, just past the Common.[2] The bulk of his small estate he had left to his wife; most of the rest he had divided into ninths, to be distributed to his remains: his surviving children or their heirs. To his youngest daughter, he left nothing above this portion. But even this meager bequest was generous because when Josiah Franklin died, Edward Mecom owed his father-in-law a debt the estate would never collect.[3] To his youngest son, the person who needed it least, Josiah left, above his ninth, the extraordinary sum of £30. He had taken him out of school; he had failed him; he meant to make it up to him. Franklin would not have it; he gave the money to Jane.[4]

The spring after her father died, Jane gave birth to a daughter: a namesake.

Jane Mecom Born on Saturday April the 12. 1745[5]

Before baby Jenny was seven months old, Jane was pregnant again. This boy she named after her brother, James, who had died in Newport in 1735.

James Mecom Born on July 31. 1746

And then there were nine. Neddy, Benny, Eben, Sally, Peter, Johnny, Josiah, Jenny, and Jemmy.[6]

But the littlest, born so soon after his sister, wilted.

Died november ye 30 1746

And then there were eight.

She bundled him and kissed him and buried him. "Dost thou sit alone and mourn to think whitherto thy Hopes and Comforts are now come?" asked *A Token for Mourners*. Do not. Instead, "let the Covenant God hath made with thee, comfort thee in this thy desolate Condition."[7] Weep not.

She would have had to teach her children this lesson: how to bound sorrow, how to silence grief. In a sermon called *A Devout Contemplation on the Meaning of Divine Providence, in the Early Death of Pious and Lovely Children*, Benjamin Colman preached that parents ought to remind their children, again and again, that they could die any time. Death will knock, like a sheriff with a warrant for a debtor. "There's no locking our Doors against this Officer, when he comes to Arrest," Colman warned. But if your children are prepared to die, Colman said, "you'll have the more peace and comfort in their death, if they are *suddenly* taken from you."[8] And there was no better occasion for preparing a child to die than the death of a brother or sister. As *The New-England Primer* had it, in verses Jane might have taught her children:

> *I in the Burying Place may see*
> *Graves shorter there than I.*
> *From Death's Arrest no Age is free,*
> *Young Children too may die;*
> *My God, may such an awful Sight,*
> *Awakening be to me!*
> *Oh! That by early Grace I might*
> *For Death prepared be.*[9]

She taught her children how to die.

Death and birth: she watched both. She sat by the bedsides of friends as they delivered. Her niece and closest friend, Grace Harris (the daughter of Jane's half sister Anne Franklin Harris), had married a Boston merchant named Jonathan Williams in 1746. Jane might have been with Grace when she gave birth to a son named Josiah, in December of the next year. He either was born blind or lost his sight in infancy. When Grace delivered Josiah, Jane was seven months pregnant.[10] She prayed her child would be spared such a calamity.

Mary Mecom Born febr'y ye 29 1747/8

And then there were nine. Another girl, named after another sister. She called her Polly.[11]

In 1748, Jane turned thirty-six. She had been pregnant or nursing, almost without pause, since she was sixteen.[12]

In 1748, Benjamin Franklin turned forty-two, and retired from his printing business. He had become the largest bookseller in Philadelphia and the most important paper merchant in the colonies. He had his portrait painted by Robert Feke, standing placid and composed, wearing a brown curled wig and a black cloak trimmed with white ruffles.[13] He had done what very few eighteenth-century men ever could; the son of a chandler, the grandson of a blacksmith, he had climbed out of the trades: a franklin had become a gentleman.

He retired from business to devote himself to science. Having purchased Spencer's electrical apparatus, he had begun conducting a series of experiments with electricity. He proved that there were not two kinds of electricity but one, a single force, with two variants; these he labeled plus and minus. He demonstrated, too, what came to be called the law of conservation of charge: electricity travels but, within a closed system, is never lost or gained. In 1749, his letters describing his experiments were read at the Royal Society in London.

Everywhere, Franklin's rise as a philosopher of nature, a scientist, was celebrated as all the more extraordinary for his having begun life at a rank so low. In an age of empiricism, Franklin was, himself, a proof, a palpable truth: the light of science had penetrated even the darkness of the "Lowly Dweling we were brought up in," as Jane described it, a crowded and cramped house in a small and crooked town, an ocean away from the magnificence of London.[14] Across that distance, and into that obscurity, had shone a shaft of light.[15]

It helped the story—light into darkness—that his father had made candles and that Franklin had harnessed lightning. Eighteenth-century philosophers believed they were living in an age of enlightenment that had followed an age of darkness. Dark and light were more than metaphors. Franklin believed this to be as true of politics as it was of science. Free speech was like electricity. His reading of history had taught him that there would always be parties, discord, error, and factions, but so long as speech was free, truth would prevail: light would be cast. "By the Collision of different Sentiments," Franklin wrote, "Sparks of Truth are struck out, and political Light is obtained."[16]

No eighteenth-century philosopher united science and politics the way Franklin did. As the French statesman Anne-Robert-Jacques Turgot put it, "He seized the lightning from the skies and the scepter from the tyrants."[17] He held the light.

In 1750, when Franklin's daughter Sally was six—the age Jane had been when Franklin had moved out of the Blue Ball to begin his apprenticeship at his brother's print shop—Franklin reported to his mother that Sally "delights in her Book," adding, "Perhaps I flatter my self too much, but I have Hopes that she will prove an ingenious sensible notable and worthy Woman like her Aunt Jenney."[18] The next year, when Jane was pregnant for the twelfth time in twenty-two years, Franklin's *Experiments and Observations on Electricity* was printed in London. Later, he sent her six copies, five to distribute to men in Boston and "one for your Trouble." On its title page, she wrote, "Mrs Jane Mecom Her Book."[19]

He was its author, but it was her book. She had begun, maybe even as a girl, collecting a library of everything he ever wrote. She might have kept copies of his Silence Dogood columns. She certainly saved his letters. When he sent her books, she kept them if she could; when she couldn't keep them, she read them before she had to give them away.

"I Read it my self before I sent it," she once wrote him about a volume he had posted to her—his *Maritime Observations*, which he had asked her to send to a friend—"and found a grat deal of Pleasure in it as I do in all

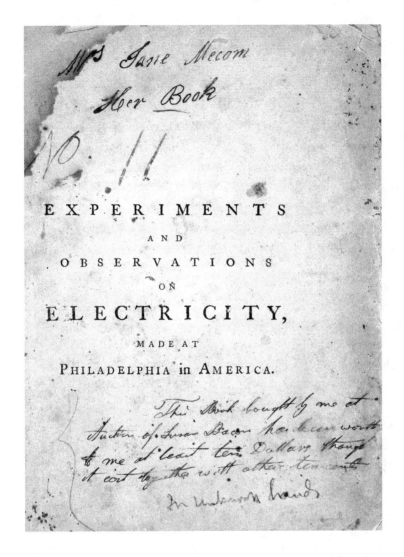

you write as far as my capasety Enables me to under stand it."[20] His books;
her capacity.

Franklin devoted himself to his experiments. But he had more plans,
too. In May 1751, he found out that the position of deputy postmaster
general of America had been vacated. "My Friends advise me to apply for
that Post," he wrote to the English naturalist Peter Collinson, suggesting
that, as postmaster, he would be able to enlarge the work of the American
Philosophical Society. But he was far from insensible of the fact that the
position carried an annual salary of £150.[21]

Jane, in Boston, nursing her ailing mother, was living off what she could make by taking in boarders. She kept close to Grace Harris Williams and her growing family. They belonged to Jane's church, too. Grace, raising blind Josiah, had another son, Jonathan Williams Jr., in 1750. She would eventually have seven sons and three daughters. Grace's husband, Jonathan Williams Sr., was a successful merchant who sold cider, vinegar, and Madeira on Cornhill. His brother was Boston's customs inspector, which gave Jonathan, as an importer, a leg up.[22] Jane's husband had no such success. Edward Mecom had announced that he intended to open a singing school in 1744 but, if it ever got under way, it didn't last. He was still making saddles, though not well, or not fast enough. Franklin ordered a horse's collar from him and was left to pester when it didn't come. "I doubt not but brother Mecom will send the collar as soon as he can conveniently," he wrote delicately.[23]

She took out her Book of Ages.

Abiah mecom born augst 1st 1751

Abiah was her last child. The year she gave birth, her brother wrote "Observations concerning the Increase of Mankind, Peopling of Countries," in which he argued that the promise of America was to be measured in its fertility:

> Marriages in America are more general, and more generally early, than in Europe. And if it is reckoned there, that there is but one Marriage per Annum among 100 Persons, perhaps we may here reckon two; and in Europe they have but 4 Births to a Marriage (many of their Marriages being late) we may here reckon 8, of which if one half grow up, and our Marriages are made, reckoning with another at 20 Years of Age, our People must at least be doubled every 20 Years.[24]

Jane had given birth to twelve children. Benjamin, with a mistress, and then with his wife, had fathered three. That made fifteen children between them, an average of almost eight. According to Franklin's calculations on population, four might grow up to have children of their own. As it turns out, he reckoned nearly right.[25]

The week Jane gave birth to Abiah, Franklin took a seat in the Pennsylvania Provincial Assembly. "I am very weeke and short bretht so that I Cant set to rite much," his eighty-four-year-old mother wrote him that October. "I am too old to rite letters. I can hardly se and am groud so deff that I can hardly hear any thing that is sed." To this letter, Jane added a postscript:

> P S Mother says she an't able and so I must tell you my self that I rejoyce with you and bles god for you in all your prosperity and doubt not but you will be grater blessings to the world as he bestows upon you grater honers.

> J M[26]

Aside from her Book of Ages, and the inscription she wrote in *The Ladies Library*, this postscript is the first writing in Jane's hand that survives, a single sentence, written—abashedly, reluctantly—when she was thirty-nine years old: a single sentence, not about herself, but about her brother's good fortune. *I bles god for you in all your prosperity.*

Ten days later, Franklin sent a reply by way of William, who traveled to Boston in his father's stead.

"My compliments to my new niece, Miss Abiah," he wrote Jane, "and pray her to accept the enclosed piece of gold, to cut her teeth." *I wish your daughter a fortune, too,* he was telling her. By winter, smallpox had hit Boston. John Perkins visited the house that February. (He also borrowed Jane's copy of *Plain Truth,* her brother's treatise on colonial defense.)[27] Abiah Franklin wrote to her son that Jane's baby had grown sick.

"The account you give of poor little Biah grieves me," he wrote back.[28]

During the outbreak, Perkins estimated that only one in eleven of his patients died.[29] Abiah Mecom was among them. By the time Franklin's letter arrived, Jane had added a line to her Book of Ages:

died april ye 23 1752

Two weeks later, Abiah Franklin followed her granddaughter and namesake to the grave. She was eighty-four. This page of Jane's Book of Ages reads like a tombstone, the engraving on a family crypt:

Father Franklin Died Jany 17 1744
my Dear mother Died May 8 1752

"I thank you for your long and continued care of her in her old age and sickness," Franklin wrote to his sister after their mother died. "Our distance made it impracticable for us to attend her, but you have supplied all."[30]

My Dear mother, Jane wrote in the Book of Ages. She loved her; she fed her; she washed her. And then, she buried her.

"I never knew either my Father or Mother to have any Sickness but that of which they dy'd," Franklin later wrote, though it was something he could hardly say with any authority: he was never there. When they were sick, it was Jane who nursed them. She named her first child after her father, and her last after her mother. Benjamin, unlike nearly all of his brothers and sisters, did not name any of his children "Josiah" or "Abiah."[31] But it was Franklin who paid for a marble tablet to be erected in Boston's Granary Burying Ground above their parents' graves, bearing an extraordinarily elaborate inscription:

JOSIAH FRANKLIN,
And,
ABIAH, *his Wife,*
Lie here interred.
They lived lovingly together in Wedlock
Fifty-five Years;
And without an Estate or any gainful
Employment,
By constant Labour, and honest Industry,
(With GOD's Blessing)
Maintained a large Family
Comfortably,
And brought up thirteen Children and
Seven Grand-children
Reputably.
From this Instance, Reader,
Be encourage to Diligence in thy Calling.
And distrust not Providence.

He was a pious and prudent Man,
She a discreet and virtuous Woman.

Their youngest Son,
In filial Regard to their memory,
Places this Stone.

This book of remembrance was a monument not to his mother and father but to Franklin himself: prodigal son, gentleman. But it was more, too. Josiah and Abiah Franklin had dozens of grandchildren, not seven. The "seven grandchildren" Franklin counted as having been "brought up" by them were Jane's children, the seven of hers raised in the Blue Ball, before Josiah Franklin's death: Neddy, Benny, Eben, Sally, Peter, Johnny, and Josiah.[32]

Reader, Be encouraged to Diligence in thy Calling. Dear Reader, dear Sister, dear Jenny. *Distrust not Providence.*

The Way to Wealth

In 1745, after Josiah Franklin died, Franklin arranged for Jane's thirteen-year-old son, Benny, the most promising of her sons, to become an apprentice to James Parker, a printer in New York. Parker was another of Franklin's projects. In 1733, when Parker, then nineteen, had run away from his own apprenticeship, Franklin had taken him in. In 1742, Franklin bought Parker a press and four hundred pounds of type, allowing him to set up his own shop in New York, in exchange for one-third of his profits.[1] Three years later, Franklin sent Parker his nephew.

"I am confident he will be kindly used there," Franklin assured his sister, "and I shall hear from him every week. You will advise him to be very cheerful, and ready to do everything he is bid, and endeavour to oblige every body, for that is the true way to get friends."[2]

"The Way to Wealth, if you desire it, is as plain as the Way to Market," Franklin wrote in an essay called "Advice to a Young Tradesman": "It depends chiefly on two Words, INDUSTRY and FRUGALITY."[3] But Benny Mecom proved neither cheerful nor obliging, neither industrious nor frugal. In 1748, both he and Jane wrote to Franklin, complaining that Parker had shown himself at best an indifferent master and at worst a cruel one. Jane wanted Franklin to get her son out of his indenture. The boy had gotten smallpox, she said, and Parker had taken poor care of him. He clothed him in rags. He beat him. He sent him on petty errands. He had treated him so badly that Benny, wretched and unloved, had run away to a privateer, only to be snatched up by Parker just before the ship set sail.

To Jane, Franklin sent reassurance bundled with remonstrance. As for the smallpox, and Benny's complaint that Parker's "negro woman," a slave, didn't bring him what he needed when he asked for it, maybe, Franklin delicately suggested, the boy might have been, "like other sick people, a little impatient, and perhaps might think a short time long." If Benny was staying out all night, Parker ought to be beating him more often, not less. "If he was my own son, I should think his master did not do his duty by him, if he omitted it, for to be sure it is the high road to destruction. And I think the correction very light, and not likely to be very effectual, if the strokes left no marks." All boys dream of running away to sea, Franklin reminded her, and many try. Even William had once tried run off to a privateer, Franklin reported, but this wasn't because Franklin had treated him cruelly: "Every one, that knows me, thinks I am too indulgent a parent, as well as master." And "as to clothes, I am frequently at New York, and I never saw him unprovided with what was good, decent, and sufficient" and, after all, "I never knew an apprentice contented with the clothes allowed him by his master, let them be what they would." Benny Mecom had told his mother he hadn't been able to go to Sunday meeting because his clothes were too ragged. It was a good story, Franklin allowed, but it was codswallop. Franklin, who had spent a Sunday at Parker's house, had seen the Parkers call Benny to church, again and again, only to discover him "delaying and shuffling till it was too late." This only amused Franklin, who had no small fondness for rebellious, impious, runaway boys:

I did not think it anything extraordinary, that he should be sometimes willing to evade going to meeting, for I believe it is the case with all boys, or almost all. I have brought up four or five myself, and have frequently observed, that if their shoes were bad, they would say nothing of a new pair till Sunday morning, just as the bell rung, when, if you asked them why they did not get ready, the answer was prepared, 'I have no shoes,' and so of other things, hats and the like; or if they knew of anything that wanted mending, it was a secret till Sunday morning.

Jane had sent her brother two letters to deliver: one for Benny and one for Parker. This Franklin refused to do: "I think your appearing to give ear to such groundless stories may give offence, and create a greater misunderstanding, and because I think what you write to Benny, about getting him discharged, may tend to unsettle his mind."

If Franklin already suspected the unsettled nature of Benny's mind, he waved those suspicions away. "I have a very good opinion of Benny in the main," he wrote Jane, "and have great hopes of his becoming a worthy man, his faults being only such as are commonly incident to boys of his years, and he has many good qualities, for which I love him."[4]

Benny Mecom had a knack for printing. Parker, Franklin said, "look'd on Benny as one of his best Hands."[5] But if the boy learned his trade, he never learned his place. In 1750, he tried, once again, to run away.[6] Two years later, when he was in the seventh year of his apprenticeship, Franklin called him to Philadelphia.

Earlier, Franklin had sent a young tradesman named Thomas Smith to Antigua to set up that island's first printing press. Smith was another of Franklin's former apprentices.[7] He had worked in Franklin's printing shop, and then he had worked in Parker's. In sending Smith to Antigua, Franklin made the same arrangement he had made with Parker: Franklin bought Smith type and a press, in exchange for a third of his profits.[8] Smith, however, drank himself to death, and Franklin needed to send another young tradesman in his place, lest he lose both his investment and his source of news: Smith had started a newspaper, the *Antigua Gazette*. Franklin wanted it to be continued. He also wanted a correspondent in Antigua, close to the equator, to make astronomical observations.

He proposed to send young Benny Mecom to Antigua, at once releasing him from an apprenticeship in which he was bridling and promoting him, in a stroke, from apprentice to master. He would be postmaster, too. The boy was only nineteen, but he was clever and an able tradesman: a franklin.

Franklin made haste. There was no time for the boy to go to Boston to say good-bye to his parents. On September 14, 1752, Franklin reported to his sister that Benny had sailed from Philadelphia and would soon land at Antigua. "The Island is reckoned one of the healthiest in the West Indies," he assured her (this was a lie). "My late Partner there enjoy'd perfect Health for four Years, till he grew careless and got to sitting up late in Taverns, which I have caution'd Benny to avoid, and have given him all other necessary Advice I could think of relating both to his Health and Conduct, and hope for the best." Benny, who was indentured for two more years, till the age of twenty-one, agreed to pay Parker for that part of his apprenticeship he had not completed. Franklin urged Jane to make amends with Parker, too: "You will not think it amiss to write Mr. and Mrs. Parker a Line or two of Thanks; for notwithstanding some little Misunderstandings, they have on the whole been very kind to Benny."[9]

Smith's print shop and post office was on Kerby's Wharf, in St. John's. Between St. John's and Boston lay a thousand miles of cobalt sea. Antigua was a sugar factory: three hundred sugar plantations owned by absentee landlords and worked by thirty thousand African slaves, mostly men, overseen by three thousand whites. It was brutal. In 1736, black men convicted of conspiring to murder their masters were burned at the stake, broken on the wheel, starved to death, and hanged from chains in public squares. It was a graveyard. Blacks died by the thousands. Whites either died or fled. An English agent for the Board of Trade filed a report on conditions in 1734 in which he concluded, "The Decrease of White Men I apprehend to be Owing to Several Causes. Epidemical Distempers have destroyed Numbers, Dry Weather, Want of Provisions, And inability to pay their Taxes have obliged Others to go off."[10]

Before he drank himself to death, Thomas Smith had run into debt, unable to keep a printing business afloat on an island where subscribers to his newspaper had a habit of not paying for it. Sending nineteen-year-old Benjamin Mecom there was not the path of wisdom.

Benny wrote to his mother, astonished at the place where he'd landed. He was unsettled. Maybe worse. Jane wrote to her brother, alarmed by what she'd read.

"In my opinion, if Benny can but be prevailed on to behave steadily, he may make his fortune there," Franklin wrote back. "And without some share of steadiness and perseverance, he can succeed no where." But he shared her concern. "That you may know the whole state of his mind and his affairs, and by that means be better able to advise him, I send you all the letters I have received from or concerning him. I fear I have been too forward in cracking the shell, and producing the chick to the air before its time." And then, in a postscript: "Please return to me the letters."[11]

Mad Benny Mecom was a stain on the Franklin family. The letters Franklin sent Jane must have chronicled the strange, erratic quality of Benny Mecom's mind. Franklin wanted those letters back. They do not survive.

Franklin had another reason for sending his nephew to Antigua. Under the terms of Josiah Franklin's will, the Blue Ball had to be sold following Abiah Franklin's death. Jane had lived in that house for almost the whole of her life. It was the only home that most of her children had ever known, a tumble of children, almost too many to count. (William signed off a letter to his aunt "with love to Mr. Mecom, Coz. Neddy, Sally, Jenny, Johnny, Polly, Josiah, Eben and Peter" adding, "I believe that's all of them.")[12]

Abiah Franklin died in May 1752. Benjamin Franklin sent Benny Mecom to Antigua that September. In October, two advertisements appeared in the *Boston Evening-Post*. One announced an auction of Josiah Franklin's movables:

> TO be sold by publick Vendue on Wednesday the 1st of *November* next, at the Sign of the BLUE BALL in Union-Street, sundry Sorts of Household Furniture, consisting of Beds, Bedding, Chairs, Tables, Looking-Glasses, a Desk, Pewter and Brass, a *Philadelphia* Fire Place, some wearing Apparel, and sundry other Articles, too many to be here enumerated.

The other, immediately below, advertised the real estate.

> TO be sold, a House and Land, known by the Name of the *Blue Ball,* very commodious for Trade, measuring on Union Street 38 Feet, on Hanover Street 93 Feet; any one inclining to purchase, may apply to *Wm. Homes,* Goldsmith in *Boston*.[13]

(William Homes, the goldsmith who handled the sale, was Jane's and Benjamin's nephew; he was the son of their sister Mary, who had died of breast cancer.)[14]

On November 1, 1752, Jane watched the house she had lived in for forty years being emptied of its beds and tables and chairs.[15] Edward Mecom, so far from being able to buy the house, remained in debt to the estate.[16] There were things in that house that Jane decided ought not to be sold. Privately, she made her own disquisitions. Her brother's daughter Sally had, at the age of five, made a pocketbook for her grandmother. "It was done in cross-stitch and was very beautiful," Jane wrote. She gave it to her Nantucket cousin Keziah Folger Coffin.[17] (Coffin, who often visited Jane in Boston, "was many years Like a Sister to me & a grat friend to my children," Jane said.)[18] These things belonged to women.

"I hear every thing is now sold," Franklin wrote their brother John at the beginning of 1753. "Who bought the House, and what did it sell for?" Franklin asked.[19]

But no one had bought the house yet; the Mecoms were still living there in the summer of 1753 when Franklin came to Boston to accept an honorary master of arts degree from Harvard.[20] *In prosperous fortunes be modest and wise,* Poor Richard says. *The greatest may fall, and the lowest may rise.*[21] The college he had been too poor to attend as a boy granted him its distinction for his "great Genius" and for "the high Advances he has made in Natural Philosophy, more especially in the Doctrine and Experiments of ELECTRICITY, whereby he has rendered himself justly famous in the Learned World." The honors would keep coming. Franklin received an honorary degree from Yale that same year. Not long after, he became "Doctor Franklin," when he received an honorary doctor of laws from the University of St. Andrews, in Scotland.[22]

During his visit to Boston in 1753, Franklin also attended to business ties in town. His seventy-five-year-old sister, Elizabeth, had married a ship's captain named Berry, and when he died, she had married another, named Richard Douse. She and her husband had been living in the North End, in a small brick house that she had inherited from her first husband. To support the widow Douse, Franklin had purchased the mortgage.[23] He charged Jonathan Williams Sr., the husband of his niece Grace Harris Williams, with handling the care of the Douse house.[24] Maybe he helped the Mecoms find a new house, too.

After Franklin left, Jane's family moved to a brick house on Hanover Street. In November 1753, an ad appeared in the *Boston Gazette*:

Edward Mecom, Hereby informs his Customers, that he has removed his Dwelling from the Blue Ball, to the uppermost Brick-House, except the Corner one, in the same Street, a little below the Orange Tree; where he provides Entertainment for Gentlemen as usual.[25]

The Orange Tree was an inn at the foot of Hanover Street, four blocks from the Blue Ball. The stagecoach stopped there. It was a good place to entertain gentlemen: a boardinghouse and a tavern. But Edward Mecom wasn't paying the rent.

When Franklin had sent Benny Mecom to Antigua, he had at first made the same arrangement with his nephew that he had made with Parker and

Smith: Franklin supplied the printing house and the type in exchange for one-third of the profits. But he soon arranged for different terms: Benny need send his uncle no more than a small amount of sugar and rum so long as he would pay his mother's rent.[26]

Meanwhile, in Antigua, Benny endured hurricanes. The wind blew cracks in his house; it broke canes of sugar as if they were reeds. And he suffered illness. Late summer was the worst. "Tis generally reckoned a sickly Time, for while People die much faster than usual," he wrote his aunt Deborah. "I can number about a Dozen, whom I was lately personally acquainted with, seemingly in good Health, that are now dead."[27]

Somehow, he steadied himself. But who, at such a distance, was to keep him steady? Franklin scarcely propped him up. "I take him to be a very honest industrious Lad," he wrote, recommending him to William Strahan, a bookseller in London who had supplied Smith with books and stationery, and had done the same with Mecom. But Benny faltered. He printed very little, and sold even less. He fell into debt. It wasn't long before Franklin began warning Strahan not to front Mecom too much inventory. "Pray keep him within Bounds," Franklin cautioned in April 1754, "and do not suffer him to be more than Fifty Pounds in your Debt." Franklin apologized: "He is a young Lad, quite unacquainted with the World."[28]

During Franklin's visit to Boston, his brother John, a soap boiler, was married to a widow named Elizabeth Hubbart, who had a son named Thomas, who was married to a woman named Judith Ray. Judith's sister Catharine had come to Boston, where she met both Benjamin Franklin and Jane Franklin Mecom.[29] Franklin and Caty Ray began a flirtatious correspondence; it lasted long after Caty Ray married William Greene, the son of Rhode Island's governor. But Jane and Caty exchanged visits, and letters, too. Caty would become one of Jane's closest friends.[30]

John Franklin died in 1756. "I condole with you on the loss of our dear brother," Franklin wrote Jane in February. "As our number grows less, let us love one another proportionably more." And then he added: "Benny, I understand, inclines to leave Antigua."[31]

"I shall be very glad to hear he does better in another Place, but I fear he will not for some Years be cur'd of his Fickleness," Franklin wrote a few months later.[32] Benny sailed to Philadelphia sometime after June; in December, Franklin gave him a horse, and Benny, determined to begin business again, rode to Boston.[33] "As he will keep a bookseller's shop, with his printing house," Franklin wrote his sister in February 1757, "I don't know but it might be worth his while to set up in Cambridge."[34]

Meanwhile, Franklin prepared to sail to London. On April 4, 1757, he left Philadelphia by carriage, with his son William and two slaves, Peter and King.[35] They reached New York four days later, ready to depart. Instead, Franklin found himself stuck in the city for more than two months.[36] Jane sent him three letters, and he wrote three letters back.

She wanted advice about Elizabeth Franklin Douse. Jane thought her sister ought to move out of her little brick house in the North End. Franklin disagreed. "As *having their own Way,* is one of the greatest Comforts of Life, to old People, I think their Friends should endeavour to accommodate them in that, as well as in any thing else," he advised. "When they have long liv'd in a House, it becomes natural to them, they are almost as closely connected with it as the Tortoise with his Shell, they die if you tear them out of it. Old Folks and old Trees, if you remove them, tis ten to one that you kill them. So let our good old Sister be no more importun'd on that head."[37] Douse stayed in her house.

Jane begged her brother's advice about her sons. She had known how to care for them when they were little. She had raised them and taught them their letters and breeched them. She had even found them apprenticeships. In choosing a trade, Jane's sons took the places their mother's brothers and cousins offered them, as charity; she had no money to pay their fees. Neddy was twenty-six and, having been trained by his father, had set up his own saddler's shop in Boston. But he was strangely sickly and found it hard to work. She was worried. Would he turn out as bad as his father? "As Neddy is yet a young man, I hope he may get over the disorder he complains of, and in time wear it out," Franklin answered.[38] Benny, twenty-four, was by this time in Boston. He had married Elizabeth Ross, a girl from New Jersey. "I don't doubt but Benny will do very well when he gets to work," Franklin offered, vaguely.[39] Eben, twenty-two and soon to be married, was living in Gloucester and hoping to open his own bakery; he had apprenticed with his uncle James Davenport, a baker on Fleet Street who had been married to Jane and Benjamin's sister Sarah.[40] "It gives me pleasure to hear, that Eben is likely to get into business at his trade," Franklin wrote. "If he will be industrious and frugal, 'tis ten to one but he gets rich, for he seems to have spirit and activity."[41] Peter, eighteen, had apprenticed with Jane and Benjamin's brother John, a soap boiler. "I am glad that Peter is acquainted with the crown soap business," Franklin wrote, although he would not take Jane's side in a dispute over whether Peter or John's widow, Elizabeth Hubbart Franklin, had more right to sell the family soap.[42] After John Franklin's death in January 1756, Peter Mecom had begun selling crown soap, until Elizabeth Hubbart Franklin took out an ad in the *Boston News-Letter* in October, informing the public, "That there are sundry Persons endeavouring to impose on People a Sort of Soap which *they call* Crown Soap, which a little resembles it in Appearance, but is vastly unlike it in Quality." She warned, "There never was in *New-England* any Person but the late Mr. *John Franklin,* that made the true Sort of CROWN-SOAP: It is now carried on by Mrs. Elizabeth Franklin."[43] It galled Jane, who thought that if anything was her rightful inheritance, and rightly belonged to her sons, it was the family recipe for soap.

Franklin wanted no part of this. He chided Jane, too, for having asked whether he might remove their brother's stepson, Tuthill Hubbart (a child of Elizabeth Hubbart Franklin's from her first marriage), from the position of postmaster to Boston and appoint Benny in his stead: "I have not shown any backwardness to assist Benny, where it could be done without injuring another. But if my friends require of me to gratify not only their inclinations, but their resentments, they expect too much of me."[44] He offered, instead, more advice: "I am glad to hear that Peter is at a place where he has full employ. A trade is a valuable thing; but, unless a habit of industry be acquired with it, it turns out of little use."[45] Johnny, sixteen, was apprenticed to Jane's nephew William Homes.[46] "I am glad to hear Johnny is so good and diligent a workman," Franklin wrote. "If he ever sets up at the goldsmith's business, he must remember, that there is one accomplishment without which he cannot possibly thrive in that trade, (i.e., *to be perfectly honest.*)"[47]

On the eve of sailing to England, Franklin filled his letters to his sister with advice for young tradesmen. One last thing Franklin did while waiting to leave for England, about which Jane never knew: he wrote a new will, forgiving Benny Mecom a debt of £50 and bequeathing to Jane the mortgage he held on Elizabeth Franklin Douse's house.[48]

And then, in his cabin, maybe even before the ship finally sailed, on June 20, he wrote the preface for that year's *Poor Richard's Almanack.* Instead of coming up with something new, he strung together ninety-odd proverbs from twenty-five years of *Poor Dicks.* They read like this:

Sloth, like Rust, consumes faster than Labour wears, while the used Key is always bright, as Poor Richard says. But *dost thou love Life, then do not squander Time, for that's the Stuff Life is made of*, as Poor Richard says. How much more than is necessary do we spend in Sleep! forgetting that *The sleeping Fox catches no Poultry*, and that *there will be sleeping enough in the Grave*, as Poor Richard says. If Time be of all Things the most precious, *wasting Time* must be, as Poor Richard says, *the greatest Prodigality*, since, as he elsewhere tells us, *Lost Time is never found again*, and what we call *Time-enough, always proves little enough:* Let us then be up and be doing, and doing to the Purpose; so by Diligence shall we do more with less Perplexity. *Sloth makes all Things difficult, but Industry all easy*, as Poor Richard says; and *He that riseth late, must trot all Day, and shall scarce overtake his Business at Night*. While *Laziness travels so slowly, that Poverty soon overtakes him*, as we read in Poor Richard, who adds, *Drive thy Business, let not that drive thee;* and *Early to Bed, and early to rise, makes a Man healthy, wealthy and wise.*[49]

Thinking about his sister's all but fatherless sons, Franklin collected all the advice to young tradesmen he had ever given: an argument against the kind of indolence that seemed to have plagued Edward Mecom and that had reduced his family to a state of misery and wretchedness.

He finished writing at sea, on July 7. Upon reaching England, he sent his essay back on the first westbound vessel. It was published as the preface to *Poor Richard Improved . . . 1758*, though it was reprinted—soon, often, and far and wide. It appeared in at least 145 editions and six languages even before the eighteenth century was over, usually with the title *The Way to Wealth*. He sent it to Benjamin Mecom. The very first time it was printed as a pamphlet, it contained this imprimatur:

BOSTON, NEW-England: Printed and Sold by Benjamin Mecom, at the NEW Printing-Office, Opposite to the Old-Brick Meeting, near the Court-House. NOTE, Very good Allowance to those who take them by the Hundred or Dozen, to sell again.[50]

The Way to Wealth has been read as an American creed: industry begets riches. Few pieces of writing have been more poorly understood.[51] "I often Recolect the Advice you wonce Gave won of my Sons," Jane wrote her brother: "do the right thing with Spirit."[52] This she never forgot. *Do the right thing with Spirit. The Way to Wealth* was an act of charity: a gift to Jane's son.

"Let me have a Line from you now and then while I am in London," Franklin wrote Jane before he sailed.[53] From Boston, from home, she wrote back.

PART THREE

Letters

1758–1775

CHAPTER XVI

Bad Writing

The first letter from Jane that survives is one she wrote not to her brother but to his wife.[1] It's dated January 29, 1758. She wrote it when she was forty-five years old. (Franklin first wrote to her when she was fourteen; more than three decades of her end of the correspondence are lost.) She crammed her words onto one side of a single sheet of paper, six inches by seven. This is her voice: gabby, frank, and vexed.

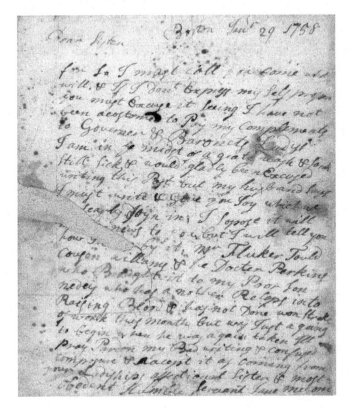

Dear Sister

For so I must call you come what will & If I don't Express my self
proper you must Excuse it seeing I have not been acostomed to Pay
my Complements to Governer & Baronets Ladys I am in the midst of
a grate wash & Sarah still sick, & would gladly been Excused writing
this Post but my husband says I must write & Give you Joy which we
searly Joyn in; I sopose it will not be news to you, but I will tell you
how I came by it, Mr Fluker Tould Cousen Williams & he Docter
Perkins who Brought it to my Poor Son nedey who has a nother
Relaps into Raising Blood & has not Done won stroke of work this
month but was Just a going to begin when he was again taken Ill pray
Pardon my Bad writing & confused composure & acept it as coming
from your Ladyships affectionat Sister & most obedient

> Humble Servant
> Jane Mecom

It needs translating. She was in the middle of a great wash and one of her
lodgers, Sarah, was ailing. Her poor son Neddy was sick again—weak and
listless and coughing blood. But she had heard from Neddy, who heard it
from Dr. Perkins, who heard it from Jonathan Williams Sr., the husband
of Jane's friend Grace, a daughter of her sister Anne, who heard it from
another Boston merchant, Thomas Flucker, that Benjamin Franklin had
been given a baronetcy. Jane's husband told her she must send her congratulations, "searly"—surely. She was miffed. If this ridiculous rumor was
true, why, for heaven's sake, was she the last to know about it?

"Your loving Sister" or "Your affectionate Sister" is how Jane usually
signed off—not "your Ladyships affectionat Sister & most obedient Humble Servant."[2] That was a jab. Must she curtsy? She was willing to follow the rules of civility, but only so far. She would not have forgotten the
satire Benjamin Franklin had written for the *New-England Courant* when
he was seventeen and she was ten, pointing out that there are no titles of
honor in the Old Testament: "Adam, was never called *Master* Adam," her
brother had written then, nor "Lot *Knight* and *Baronet*, nor the *Right Honourable* Abraham, *Viscount Mesopotamia, Baron of Carran;* no, no, they
were plain Men."[3]

With Deborah, Jane was frank: plain, honest, sincere, and uncurbed. They were close. Among other things, they shared a love, as Jane once put it, for "my Dear brother & yr Dear Husband."[4] Something else each valued in the other was a kind of epistolary equality: they both struggled with writing, tacking onto their letters the conventional apologies that were expected of unlettered women. "I have indevered to make as good a letter as I cold," Deborah wrote Jane, begging, "donte let aney bodey see my letter as I write so bad."[5]

They also shared an appetite for gossip. "Cousen willames Looks soon to Lyin," Jane wrote Deborah, "she is so big I tell Her she will have two." (This "Cousin Williams" was Jonathan Williams Sr.'s wife, Grace.)[6] "Greved to hear Poor Mrs. Smith has Got numb Palsey," Jane wrote— Mrs. Smith was a friend of Deborah's, and dying—"Pleas to Present my love & best wishes to her."[7] She could be sweet. And she could be cutting. Of Mrs. Elizabeth Hubbart Partridge, the daughter of Jane's brother John's widow, a woman Jane resented for having proved, Jane thought, insufficiently generous to Jane's son Peter in a dispute over the family soap recipe, she wrote, "I have not Heared whither she is Like to have another child. The Nabours say she Lay a bed afore with her Hare Poudered & a Grat Plum in it."[8] Powdered hair and a plume. Frippery. Of a younger woman whom Jane found stingy: "she is wise so far as that wisdom Reaches to keep her Dolars to her self."[9]

Jane called gossip "trumpery." "I have fill'd the Paper with such trumpery you will be vexed to give yr self the troble of Reading it," she wrote Deborah.[10] But she loved trumpery almost as much as she loved politics. She had great expectations for letters. Separated from people she loved by hundreds of miles of roads that no woman could travel alone, she cherished scenes and stories. By words on a page, she wanted to be carried away— out of her house, out of Boston, out into the world. The more details, the better. "The Sow has Piged," her friend Caty Greene reported from Rhode Island, reminding her, "You told me to write you all."[11]

Jane knew exactly what she wanted in a letter. She once scolded Deborah's daughter Sarah for writing letters that she found insufficiently chatty. "I want to know a Thousand litle Perticulars about your self yr Husband & the children such as your mother used to write me," Jane commanded, adding that "it would be Next to Seeing the little things to hear some of there Prattle (Speaches If you Pleas) & have you Describe there persons &

actions tell me who they Look like &c."[12] Stories, likenesses, characters: *Speeches, if you please.*

Jane's letters are different than her brother's—delightfully so. He wrote polite letters. She wrote impolite ones. She wrote the way she talked. If she weren't always so busy, she would have loved to write more; she told Deborah that she found "much Pleasure in conversing with you in this way."[13] In writing, she also found comfort, especially in times of trouble. "Pardon my writing you these aprehentions," she wrote her brother. "I do not take pleasure in gieving you an uneasy thought but it gives some Releif to unbousom wons self to a dear friend."[14]

Still, for all that pleasure and comfort, putting talk down on paper was hard, and harder when shaping the very letters was difficult. And she worried, too, that her letters—everything about them, including her penmanship—embarrassed her brother, pleading, "Dont let it mortifie you that such a Scraw came from your Sister."[15]

Women were expected to disavow their own writing. But, more, Jane had a particular concern: she worried that she had spelled so badly and failed to make herself clear—"my Blundering way of Expresing my self," she called it—that someone reading a letter she had written wouldn't be able to understand what she meant to say, wouldn't be able to *hear* her.[16] "I know I have wrote & speld this worse than I do sometimes," she wrote her brother, "but I hope you will find it out."[17]

To "find out" a letter was to decipher it, to turn writing back into speech. *If I don't Express my self proper you must Excuse it.* She knew—she understood very well—that letters weren't supposed to be speech written down; they were supposed to be more formal, more refined, more polite than speech. In her letters to Deborah, Jane was entirely at her ease. Neither of them knew how to write a polite letter, so they made no pretense of it. With her brother, everything was different. He had been her tutor, and she his student. He warned her that she was too free with him. "You Long ago convinced me that there is many things Proper to convers with a Friend about that is not Proper to write," she confessed.[18] But then he had also scolded her for not being free enough. "I was allways too Difident" she said he had told her.[19] Be more discreet. Be less diffident. What she couldn't be with him was free.

She studied. She had read more books than most women of her station had ever even seen. Two of her brothers were printers, and so were two of her sons. She may, then, have tried to learn the art of letter writing from one of the many books of instruction printed for boys and young men, such as *The American Instructor,* also known as *The Young Man's Best Companion,* and printed by Benjamin Franklin. She could have studied its templates, addressed to writers deficient in the art of letter writing, examples of *"Letters of proffered Assistance, Letters Consolatory, Letters of Thanks, Letters Congrat- ulatory, Ditto of Reproof, Ditto of Excuse, Ditto Accusatory, Ditto of Advice or Counsel, Ditto of Recommendation, Ditto Exhortatory, Ditto of Remonstrance, and Letters of Visit, properly called Familiar Letters, Letters of Business; and lastly, Mixed Letters, that is, on various Subjects, and different Affairs."*[20]

The manual Franklin printed was addressed to young men. But a hand- ful of writing manuals offered instruction to young women. The London printer Samuel Richardson issued a volume titled *Letters Written to and for Particular Friends, on the most Important Occasions. Directing not only the requisite style and forms to be observed in writing familiar letters; but how to think and act justly and prudently, in the common concerns of human life.* (It was more commonly known by a pithier title, *Familiar Letters on Important Occasions.*) Among the important occasions that demanded the writing of a letter, Richardson counted an attempted seduction. Here is the letter that etiquette required of *"A Father to a Daughter in Service, on hearing of her Master's attempting her Virtue"*:

My dear Daughter,

I Understand, with great Grief of Heart, that your Master has made some Attempts on your Virtue, and yet that you stay with him. God grant that you have not already yielded to his base Desires! For when once a Person has so far forgotten what belongs to himself, or his Character, as to make such an Attempt, the very Continuance with him, and in his Power, and under the same Roof, is an Encouragement to him to prosecute his Designs. And if he carries it better, and more civil, at present, it is only the more certainly to undo you when he attacks you next. Consider, my dear Child, your Reputation is all you have to trust to. And if you have not already, which God forbid! yielded to him, leave it not to the Hazard of another Temptation; but come away directly (as you ought to have done on your own Motion) at the Command of

Your grieved and indulgent Father.

And here is what, according to Richardson, etiquette required a daughter to reply:

Honoured Sir,

I received your Letter Yesterday, and am sorry I stay'd a Moment in my Master's House after his vile Attempt. But he was so full of his Promises of never offering the like again, that I hop'd I might believe him; nor have I yet seen any thing to the contrary: But am so much convinced, that I ought to have done as you say, that I have this Day left the House; and hope to be with you soon after you will have receiv'd this Letter. I am

Your dutiful Daughter.[21]

Jane could also have learned how to write letters by reading novels. While Richardson was preparing *Familiar Letters,* he had the idea to make a story out of them (that is, he thought to write a kind of book that was new: a novel). "Hence sprung *Pamela,*" as Richardson put it.[22] Richardson's first epistolary novel, *Pamela; or, Virtue Rewarded. In a Series of Familiar Letters from a Beautiful Young Damsel, To her Parents,* was published in London in 1740. It recounts the breathless story of a girl working as a servant to a wealthy family who finds herself in some peril of seduction from the gentleman of the house after the lady dies. Pamela is fifteen, and knows more than any servant girl should know.

"My Lady's Goodness had put me to write," Pamela boasts in a letter to her parents.

"Every body talks how you have come on, and what a genteel Girl you are, and some say, you are very pretty," her mother writes back. "But what avails all this, if you are to be ruin'd and undone!—Indeed, my dear Child, we begin to be in great Fear for you; for what signifies all the Riches in the World with a bad Conscience?"[23]

("I hear you are grown a celebrated beauty," Franklin had written Jane when she was fourteen and in some peril of seduction. "Remember that modesty, as it makes the most homely virgin amiable and charming, so the want of it infallibly renders the most perfect beauty disagreeable and odious."[24] His letter was as conventional as her danger.)

That Pamela writes so well is among her greatest problems—"I love Writing," she confesses—as it both raises her expectations for a life above her station and constitutes one of the attractions she holds to the gentleman of the house, who one day happens upon her in a dressing room, writing.

"Why, *Pamela*," he cries, "you write a very pretty Hand, and spell tolerably, too."[25]

But in the end, knowing how to write a fine letter is what saves this poor fifteen-year-old girl: the gentleman marries her—after having stolen and read her letters.

Franklin printed *Pamela*, beginning in 1742. In the eighteenth century, the cost of printing a book was generally borne by the author. Of all the

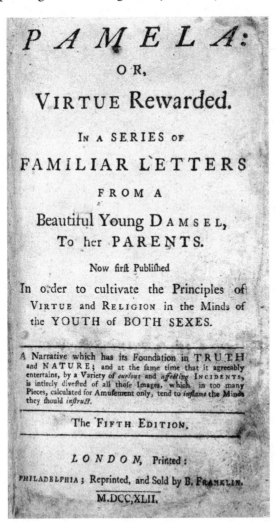

books Franklin printed, only sixteen—less than one a year—were at his own risk and expense. *Pamela* was the only novel among them. He very much admired it.[26] He once gave his daughter a copy of a French translation of *Pamela,* to help her with her French; she must have already read it in English.[27] He especially admired how Richardson had "mix'd Narration and Dialogue, a Method of Writing very engaging to the Reader, who in the most interesting Parts finds himself as it were brought into the Company."[28] *Speeches, if you please.*

Franklin printed *Pamela,* he admired it, and he liked to give it to women whose opinions he wished to mold. Likely, he gave a copy to Jane.[29] What must she have made of it?

Things ended differently for Jane, seduced at fifteen, than they did for Pamela. Jane didn't have "a very pretty Hand." Nor could she "spell tolerably." Nor write a polite letter. She could hardly expect to climb a ladder from tradesman's daughter to gentleman's wife on rungs of prose. She was Pamela, unimproved. She was Pamela, undone.

CHAPTER XVII

By the Post

"I am grown Impatient to hear from you," Jane once chided her brother.[1] (Her best letter was the Letter of Reproof.)

"It pains me that I have so long omitted writing to you," he admitted. (He excelled at the Letter of Excuse.) "And I do not complain that it is so long since I have been favour'd with a Line from you: for being so bad a Correspondent my self, I have no right to complain of others."[2]

She didn't always have much use for his excuses.

"I was almost Tempted to think you had forgot me," she wrote him during one of his stays in London, "but I check those thoughts with the consideration of the Difeculties you must Labour under in the station you are in in those difecult times."[3]

In the matter of letters, she kept, she said, "a Dr and Cr account"— a debtor and creditor account; as with books she lent out from her little library, she knew who owed her.[4] She was a stern creditor: "Cousin Bache knows she is a Leter in my Debt," she wrote to Deborah about Deborah's daughter Sally, who had married a man named Richard Bache, "& I will not Excuse her."[5]

A correspondence really is a kind of account, and not without its price. Posting letters "without Expence or troble" was a situation Jane both envied and lacked. The cost of postage was borne by the recipient. A one-page letter sent from Philadelphia to Jane in Boston cost her forty cents, a price she could hardly bear.[6]

For Franklin, letters were free. In 1753, Franklin had been appointed deputy postmaster general of America, a position he held jointly with William Hunter, a Virginia planter. Together, Franklin and Hunter made sending and getting letters faster, easier, and cheaper. They fixed postage rates, ordered post riders to carry all newspapers for free, discouraged the carrying of mail by anyone other than the official post riders and packet ships, required the keeping of strict accounts, and warned postmasters that they would lose their places if they were found franking letters for friends. Mail between Philadelphia and Boston, at one time fortnightly, was, by 1755, carried once a week.[7]

"Do not write; as no Letters can now go free in America but mine," her brother warned. She asked him whether she might have their letters franked. He refused. "The Privilege of Franking my own Letters," he explained, was an act of Parliament. "'Tis a Trust, which tis expected I will not violate by covering the Letters of others." Even his wife, he reminded her, had to pay postage.[8] He did, however, offer to reimburse Jane: "I expect your Bill, and shall pay it when it appears."[9]

Franklin kept very careful track of his correspondence, not only to remind himself of who owed him letters and what letters he owed but to keep track of the postal service. "I have just receiv'd your kind letter of the 2d instant," he wrote to his sister one April. "I wish you would also acknowledge, when you write the Recipt of those that have come to your hands since you wrote last. By that means I should have the satisfaction of knowing that they have not miscarried. You mention nothing of a letter from me dated Feb. 22, which went by the Post."[10]

Between Boston and Philadelphia, and across the Atlantic, their letters were often carried by ship, sometimes by Isaac Freeman, the ship's captain who, long ago, had told Franklin that his sister had grown a celebrated beauty.[11] "If you send it to my son He will find a vessel to send it by," Jane told Deborah when her son Benjamin was in Philadelphia.[12] She often wrote in haste, to get a letter into the mailbag on a departing packet. (A "packet" was a paper envelope, but the word had come to mean, too, a ship that sailed from port to port, carrying packets—that is, carrying mail.) "Beg you would forgive my sending you such very bad writing," Jane once wrote her brother, "but as the vesal is so near sailing this or nor none must go."[13] She sometimes sent her letters to her brother gratis, by way of travelers who offered to deliver a letter of hers in exchange for an introduction to him. (She explained to him that she thought these were usually her worst letters: "I have wrote by perticular persons who have desiered to be Introdused to yr Notice I have wrot in a hurry.")[14] Other strangers delivered letters, too. "Yr Leter was Brought me by a Negro who Did not know the man that gave it Him," Jane once wrote to Deborah.[15]

In Boston, people seldom used an address and, as Jane reported, few people even knew the names of the streets. "We have Accustomed our Selves so Litle to call the streets by there names that we who Live in them do not know it," she reported to her brother when he asked.[16] Letters went astray all the time. Many letters she sent—"I got it in to the bag"—she was disheartened to hear that he never received.[17] In some ways, the more important Franklin became, the easier it was to get letters to him. The lieutenant governor of Massachusetts was once to carry a letter from Jane to her brother in London. Another time, when Jane wanted to get a letter to Franklin in Paris, she sent it by way of the Marquis of Lafayette. But Franklin's public role placed constraints upon his correspondence, too. "My dear Sister, show this to no body," he warned in one letter. "I write it meerely for your Satisfaction."[18] The higher he climbed, the more careful Franklin had to be, even about his most mundane correspondence. "I am apprehensive that the Letters between us, tho' very innocent ones, are intercepted," he alerted her from London, warning her that the wax seal on her letters was often broken.[19] It didn't take espionage; there were plenty of ordinary ways for letters to go missing, too, especially in houses full of children. After Jane sent a letter to Deborah and didn't hear back, she concluded that her sister-in-law must have put the letter "under her cushing I sopose in order to Read at more Leasure & Prehaps never thought of it more & won of the children git it & tore it up."[20]

Letters were, very often, lost. This was truer for her letters than for his. By the time Franklin reached London in 1757, he was by far the most famous man ever to come from the North American continent. "You are the first Philosopher, and indeed the first Great Man of Letters for whom we are beholden to her," David Hume wrote Franklin.[21] Franklin's letters were prized. Even his private correspondence circulated; people passed around his letters, lending them out like books from a library. "I have just been reading a beautiful Letter of yours, written Feb. 22. 1756, on the Death of your Brother, which is handed about among us in Manuscript Copies," Mather Byles, a poet and a nephew of Cotton Mather's, told Franklin, remarking that he wasn't alone in cherishing Franklin's letters. "The Superstition with which we size and preserve little accidental Touches of your Pen, puts one in mind of the Care of the Virtuosi to collect the Jugs and Galipots with the Paintings of Raphael."[22]

Jane circulated her brother's letters, too. A letter he sent her in 1758 was read by a Philadelphia friend of the wife of one of Jane's sons who, in 1759, copied it, word for word, into her diary.[23] What had been his letter became part of her book.

What remains of anyone's life is what's kept. Jane kept the letters she got in the mail in a special place. "To go into the Litle Trunk," she wrote on the back of one of them.[24] But of the letters she herself wrote, she explained, "I keep no coppies."[25] Writing letters once took her long enough; she could never find time to write them twice. Very many people bothered to keep what Franklin wrote—as if the ink that came from his pen were paint from the brush of an Old Master. But for Jane's correspondence to have survived, both her brother and the people in charge of his papers after his death would have had to care enough about her letters to keep them. Generally, they did not. One year, Franklin in London sent to Jane in Boston at least four letters and she sent him at least six. In his letters to her, which survive because she kept them, he mentioned her letters to him, so that she would know which of her letters had reached him: "I received duly yours of Jan. 19., Apr. 20., May 5 and May 15"; "I received your kind Letter of June 28"; and, again, "I received your kind Letter of Dec. 11."[26]

He received her letters, but the letters themselves are lost. His four letters to her survive; her six to him are gone.

CHAPTER XVIII

You and I Only

D ear Sister," he wrote her on September 16, 1758. "I received your
Favour of June 17."

A letter was a favor. The word comes from Middle English, and it means kindness, an act of goodwill: to send a letter is an act of mercy.

In her favor of June 17, she had complained that she had not received a single line from him since he had left America. In his favor of September 16, he explained that he had written to her long since, and more than once:

> I wonder you have had no Letter from me since my being in England.
> I have wrote you at least two and I think a third before this; And, what
> was next to waiting on you in Person, sent you my Picture. In June last
> I sent Benny a Trunk of Books and wrote to him. I hope they are come
> to hand, and that he meets with Incouragement in his Business.

He had sent her two letters and a likeness: a miniature painted by Charles Dixon, which he had sent to Deborah with this instruction: "When you write to Boston, give my love to sister Jenney—as I have not often time to write to her. If you please you may send her the inclosed little picture."[1] He had sent Benny a trunk of books for the shop Benny was setting up in Boston.

Franklin told Jane she had no right to scold him. So he scolded her for scolding him, by telling her the story of how, over the summer of 1758, he had traveled to Ecton "and found some Relations in that part of the Country Still living." He had even found one of her namesakes.

Our Cousin Jane Franklin, daughter of our Unkle John, died but about a Year ago. We saw her Husband Robert Page, who gave us some old Letters to his Wife from unkle Benjamin. In one of them, dated Boston July 4. 1723 he writes "Your Unkle Josiah has a Daughter Jane about 12 years Old, a good humour'd Child."

"So Jenny keep up your Character," Franklin teased his sister, "and don't be angry when you have no Letters."[2]

Then he told her how their uncle Benjamin had sent this Jane Franklin, their cousin, "a little Book" of his poems, in which Franklin had found "an Acrostick on her Name, which for Namesakes' Sake, as well as the good Advice it contains, I transcribe and send you" (with *I*, again, doing service for *J*):

> I   lluminated from on High,
> A   nd shining brightly in your Sphere
> N   ere faint, but keep a steady Eye
> E   xpecting endless Pleasures there
>
> F   lee Vice, as you'd a Serpent flee,
> R   aise Faith and Hope three Stories higher
> A   nd let Christ's endless Love to thee
> N   -ere cease to make thy Love Aspire.
> K   indness of Heart by Words express
> L   et your Obedience be sincere,
> I   n Prayer and Praise your God Address
> N   ere cease' till he can cease to hear.

But Jane knew a great deal about their uncle's poetry; she even owned a volume of his poems. Maybe he had given it to her, before he died, on her fifteenth birthday. On its flyleaf, she had written,

> *Jane Mecom*
> *Her Book.*

This volume of their uncle's poetry is full of wordplay: mazes, anagrams, and abecedaries, as well as acrostics for Franklins named Benjamin, Hannah,

Samuel, Josiah, and Thomas but not one for Jane.[3] Maybe, when they were children, Benny and Jenny had read that book together. Maybe it had been a sore spot with Jane, that their uncle had never written an acrostic for her.

Her brother now copied this one down—JANE FRANKLIN—and sent it to her, as a gift and an apology. And then he did more. He amused himself. "After professing truly that I have a great Esteem and Veneration for the pious Author," he wrote her, "permit me a little to play the Commentator and Critic on these Lines." As much tutor as critic, he undertook a close reading of the line at the letter *R*—"Raise Faith and Hope three Stories higher"—with an eye to teasing his sister about their differences of opinion about religion. "The Meaning of *Three Stories* higher seems somewhat obscure," he began. This he then explained:

> *Faith, Hope* and *Charity* have been called the three Steps of Jacob's Ladder, reaching from Earth to Heaven. Our Author calls them *Stories*, likening Religion to a Building, and those the three Stories of the Christian Edifice; Thus Improvement in Religion, is called *Building Up*, and *Edification. Faith* is then the Ground-floor, *Hope* is up one Pair of Stairs.

He made sure she didn't miss his meaning: "My dearly beloved Jenny, don't delight so much to dwell in these lower Rooms, but get as fast as you can into the Garret; for in truth the best Room in the House is *Charity*." Don't dwell on your floor, Faith, but rise to mine, Charity.

> For my part, I wish the House was turn'd upside down; 'tis so difficult (when one is fat) to get up Stairs; and not only so, but I imagine *Hope* and *Faith* may be more firmly built on *Charity*, than *Charity* upon *Faith* and *Hope*.

("When one is fat"—this was a joke between them, about how they had both grown fat in middle age.) He went on:

> However that be, I think it a better reading to say Raise Faith and Hope *one Story* higher correct it boldly and I'll support the Alteration. For when you are up two Stories already, if you raise your Building three Stories higher, you will make five in all, which is two more than there should be, you expose your upper Rooms more to the Winds and

Storms, and besides I am afraid the Foundation will hardly bear them, unless indeed you build with such light Stuff as Straw and Stubble, and that you know won't stand Fire.

He had another edit to make, of the line at the letter *K:* "Kindness of Heart by Words express."

Stricke out *Words* and put in *Deeds.* The world is too full of Compliments already; they are the rank Growth of every Soil, and Choak the good Plants of Benevolence and Benificence, Nor do I pretend to be the first in this comparison of Words and Actions to Plants; you may remember an Ancient Poet whose Words we have all Studied and Copy'd at School, said long ago,

> *A Man of Words and not of Deeds,*
> *Is like a Garden full of Weeds.*

This poem is an English nursery rhyme—it turns up later in Mother Goose—that Jane and her brother might both have learned as children, though Jane was never at school. He gave, next, a sermon, about sermons:

'Tis pity that *Good Works* among some sorts of People are so little Valued, and *Good Words* admired in their Stead; I mean seemingly *pious Discourses* instead of *Humane Benevolent Actions.* These they almost put out of countenance, by calling Morality *rotten Morality,* Righteousness, *ragged Righteousness* and even *filthy Rags;* and when you mention *Virtue,* they pucker up their Noses as if they smelt a Stink; at the same time that they eagerly snuff up an empty canting Harangue, as if it was a Posie of the Choicest Flowers. So they have inverted the good old Verse, and say now

> *A Man of Deeds and not of Words*
> *Is like a Garden full of———*

I have forgot the Rhime, but remember 'tis something the very Reverse of a Perfume. So much by Way of Commentary.

He closed, that is, with a joke about shit.

· · ·

She didn't mind the coarseness. "You are very good in not resenting some Part of my Letter of September 16. which I confess was a little rude," he wrote her after receiving her reply (which is lost), "but you fatfolks can't bear Malice."[4] She did, though, worry that he was scolding her for her lack of charity.

He insisted that he was not. "If I were dispos'd to reprove you, it should be for your only Fault, that of supposing and spying Affronts, and catching at them where they are not. But as you seem sensible of this your self, I need not mention it; and as it is a Fault that carries with it its own sufficient Punishment, by the Uneasiness and Fretting it produces, I shall not add Weight to it. Besides, I am sure your own good Sense, join'd to your natural good Humour will in time get the better of it."[5]

He wrote to her, too, about having come across a gravestone with the words "Thomas Foulger" engraved on it. It wasn't just that trip to Ecton. There was something more going on in his mind—a casting back, a wondering about where he came from. He copied out the inscription and sent it to her with a request.

"I have never in my Life met with or heard of any Foulgers but those of our Family. Pray ask Cousin Abisha Foulger if he or any in Nantucket can tell what Part of England our Grandfather Peter Foulger came from. I think I have heard our Mother say he came out of Suffolk, but am not certain."[6]

Jane had kept up with the Folgers, especially her cousin Keziah Folger Coffin.[7] She knew, or found out for Franklin, that this Thomas Folger was not a relative; their grandfather Peter had come not from Suffolk but from Norfolk.

This wouldn't be the last time he would ask her about their family history. For the final quarter century of their lives, Benjamin and Jane were the last of Josiah Franklin's seventeen children still living.

"You & I only are now Left," she wrote him.[8]

The farther he, the closer she. She was, all his life, his anchor—and, in the end, his only anchor—to his past.

CHAPTER XIX

The Book of Nature

S he took out her Book of Ages:

my Eldest son Ed mecom Died Decr 7-1758

He was twenty-seven.

She turned the page:

January the 18 1762 this morning Died a worthy & Dutifull Son Ebenezer mecom

He was twenty-six.[1]

"I have had some children that seemed to be doing well," she wrote her brother, "till they were taken off by Death."[2]

Three of her children died in infancy. None died in childhood. Only in adulthood did the rest begin to fade, one by one. And then, so did their children.

Neddy left a wife and two children. His older daughter followed him to the grave; then his younger daughter, Jenny, began to fail. "Poor Litle Jeney Mecom," Jane wrote, "seems to be going the same way of her father & sister." She offered details: "She Pines a way Looses her Apetite but withal her Bowels swells Prodidgusly so that with a Litle slip out of a Chare she bust her self, She seems often to have something choaking in her throat & dont Incline to stir but mostly keeps in her cradle."[3] The baby died.

Jane understood affliction as a message from God. *Distrust not Providence.* Her doctor thought differently. John Perkins leaned toward Franklin's Newtonian view of the world: he was a natural philosopher; Franklin called him a fellow "Searcher into Nature."[4] Perkins made a particular study of meteors and tornadoes, corresponding with Franklin on these subjects at length. In recognition for his treatise *The True Nature and Cause of the Tails of Comets,* Perkins was elected to the American Philosophical Society.[5] In a philosophical essay, *Thoughts on Agency,* published by Benjamin Mecom—and, therefore, very likely read by Jane—Perkins examined "the origin, nature, and bounds of moral freedom." Shadowing Hume, he tried to reconcile self-determination with Providence; he did this by defining liberty as constrained by morality. "All Creatures do as they list," Perkins wrote, "but moral Freedom should be something very different from merely doing as one lists." To be free, Perkins argued, is to act in accordance with reason and discernment and in obligation to human and divine law, which no man can ignore because, no matter man's "Self-Direction," he is the object of God's "special Providence." In short, "Providence is not incompatible with Freedom."[6]

Perkins's attempt to straddle a providential and a liberal view of the world shaped his understanding of disease. He once wrote an essay called "A Few Thoughts on Epidemic Colds or Catarrh Fevers," containing his observations on bad cold and flu seasons in Boston in 1748, 1750, 1753, 1757, 1760, 1765, 1767, and 1768.[7] He sent it to Franklin. In another essay, "Of the Diseases & casualtys incident to Mankind," Perkins categorized diseases as natural, constitutional, or adventitious (further cleaving this last category into "some by our own faults, others by the people about us"). Perkins was trying to explain what made some years worse, and some people sicker, than others. He didn't blame an angry god; he made a study of circumstance. "Fevers are more frequent than any other illnesses of mankind, & more die of them," he wrote. "But it is hard to say whether the illness of itself or the imprudence of the person himself & those about him are the chief cause of fatality."[8]

Franklin, too, searched into nature. He took, for instance, a great deal of interest in Grace and Jonathan Williams Sr.'s oldest son, Josiah, a blind musical prodigy. "Let me know how the eldest does, who had the Misfortune of losing his Sight," Franklin wrote to Jonathan Williams Sr. in 1762. Franklin sent the boy a harpsichord. He began researching treatments.[9]

Jane accepted affliction as the workings of fate; Franklin and Perkins did not. But Perkins, for all his searching and speculating, could not possibly have understood what afflicted Jane's family because, in the eighteenth century, no one understood it. Nor is it possible, centuries later, for historians to diagnose diseases from the scant evidence recorded by people who understood sickness and health very differently.[10] All the same, it seems likely that Neddy, Eben, little Jenny, and Jenny's sister succumbed to what would later be called tuberculosis, which might be also what took the life of Jane's husband, her son Johnny, and her daughter Polly and affected her daughter Jenny, and possibly her sons Peter and Benjamin, too.

Tuberculosis—the term originated in the nineteenth century—is a bacterial disease. Infected with *Mycobacterium tuberculosis,* the body appears to be wasting away, exhausted, consuming itself, which accounts for the name by which such suffering was known in the eighteenth century: consumption.[11]

Edward, Neddy, Eben, Johnny, Polly, Jenny, and Neddy's two daughters all suffered periods of profound lassitude. What Jane's daughters endured she had "Grate Reason to fear Incureable," she wrote, describing one as suffering from "a Painfull Deseas" and "the other falling in to a Languishing."[12] Sometimes they could hardly get out of bed. During the French and Indian War, Edward and Neddy served only briefly, too weak to fight. Peter enlisted but deserted after five weeks; he came home from camp sick.[13]

The most common form of tuberculosis is pulmonary. Inhaled, the bacteria infect the lungs. When someone infected with tuberculosis coughs, the bacteria spread. Jane described Neddy as "Raising Blood": coughing blood, which is what happens when the infection is severe. Jane described how another of her sons suffered, in the last months of his life, from a list of symptoms that, a century later, would have readily been diagnosed as tubercular. "Johney has been sick," she wrote. He "has a Bad cough, & a chilly fitt & Fevour Every Day has not been Able to Do any work nor so much as write." There was nothing left of him but "Skin & Bons."[14] He died at twenty-nine.

Adults infected with tuberculosis often show no symptoms. Sometimes symptoms appear only when someone has become weakened for another reason—for instance, having endured the hardships of childbirth or war. In the eighteenth century, infected people often sickened and then lingered for years before finally wasting away. For infants, young children, and old people, the disease was usually more swiftly lethal.

Tuberculosis has existed for centuries. Jane and Benjamin's grandmother Jane White Francklin, who died in Banbury in 1662, in her mid-forties, when Josiah was five, seems to have been felled by it. (Their uncle Benjamin wrote about how his mother had languished "nere seven years undr. that flattering Lingering distemper, a consumtion.")[15] It had been in the colonies since their founding. But it became widespread only in the eighteenth century, when people began living closer together, in cities. By the beginning of the nineteenth century, tuberculosis is estimated to have accounted for between a quarter and a third of all deaths in New England.[16]

Some people got sick more easily, and more acutely, than others. Tuberculosis is a disease of crowding: the bacteria are typically inhaled in a closed space. It is most common in cities and among people whose lives are sedentary, and especially among people who live and work in confinement.[17] John Perkins was an astute observer of the relationship between circumstance and sickness. He knew that "Some businesses are unhealthful." Among these trades he counted "Glaziers, potters & painters."[18] Saddlers, soap boilers, dyers, and chandlers belong on this list, too: these trades involve working in a closed space and toiling over vats of fumes. Edward and Neddy were saddlers, and, with her daughters, Jane boiled soap and dyed cloth. Soaking leather, boiling lye, dipping candles, dyeing. People who did this kind of work indoors seemed to have trouble breathing.

Jane, like her parents and her brother Benjamin, enjoyed an extraordinarily stout constitution. But even she suffered from coughing spells, which she called asthma. "I have had a bad fit of Astme," she would report. "Coughing Shocks Every Part of the boddy," she complained.[19] She once wrote to her brother about gasping for air. He wrote back, "Your Shortness of Breath might perhaps be reliev'd by eating Honey with your Bread instead of Butter, at Breakfast."[20]

That might have helped the coughing; honey soothes the throat. But honey couldn't conquer lung disease. In treating signs of consumption, Perkins followed the best eighteenth-century medical practice: he recommended exercise and fresh air. "In general an active life is the most healthfull," he advised. "Few will bear a constant sedentary one."[21] A long journey by horseback and, especially, travel to the ocean were the most common treatments for lung trouble. (This prescription of sailing was occasionally challenged, as in an eighteenth-century tract called *An Account of the*

Effects of Swinging, employed as a Remedy in the Pulmonary Consumption and Hectic Fever, which recommended swinging—on a swing—instead; the idea was that swinging would pump air into the lungs.)[22]

Neddy's two daughters, Jane's grandchildren, died quickly, but Perkins would have urged the adults to get outdoors, especially to the ocean. This advice they appear to have complied with. "Sister wrote me word that Polley was gon to Nantuckit," Deborah reported to her husband, "and shee had heard that shee was better."[23] (Polly was not better; she was already dead by the time Deborah wrote this letter.) Eben moved to Gloucester, a seaport.

But glazers, potters, painters, saddlers, soap boilers, dyers, and chandlers were not often the sort of people who could afford to go for a long journey by horseback or move to the seaside. For patients too weak to get outdoors or too poor to follow his recommendations, Perkins suggested other remedies. None of his case notes for any of the Mecoms survive, but in 1750, Perkins treated another consumptive in Boston and recorded his treatment of this young man, named Gould, for an ailment Perkins wasn't quite sure about—it might have been an acute condition (pneumonia) or it might have been a chronic one (consumption). "Young Mr Gould being low constitution'd & dispos'd to Consumption I took small Quantities of Blood," Perkins wrote. He noticed that Gould's spit was "a little yellow at Times but mostly white & Frothy." Perkins recorded his treatment: "I vomited him at first & gave him the Pectoral opening Infusion but there appear symptoms of pleurisy."[24]

The tuberculosis bacteria often affect the lungs but can affect other parts of the body, too. Jane's granddaughter Jenny Mecom, the little girl Jane described as suffering from "choaking in her throat," may have had what would later be called laryngeal or pharyngeal tuberculosis. Extrapulmonary tuberculosis can also affect the central nervous system, and, like syphilis, it can lead to insanity.

The emotional unsteadiness of Jane's sons Peter and Benny seems likely to have been a hereditary condition. Or it could have had been caused by, or worsened by, a chronic bacterial infection like tuberculosis. Either way, it seems to have begun with Jane's husband, who may have contracted tuberculosis in debtors' prison, which is exactly the sort of place the bacteria thrive. In 1738, when Mecom was fending off creditors, Perkins was called in to treat one of Jane's children. By 1742, Mecom was unsteady enough, or unwell enough, that Jane was taking in boarders to support the family. Her husband seems never to have recovered.

Peter and Benny were, at first, only erratic. Peter, when he was twenty, was hauled into court after having attacked a tailor.[25] Two years later, he was unable to get anything done.[26] By the time he was twenty-four, he was violently insane.

Benny started out flighty. "I fear he will not for some Years be cur'd of his Fickleness," Franklin wrote about Benny at twenty-three.[27] But he was never cured of it. This looked to Franklin, who was forever urging industry, like laziness. It didn't look quite that way to Jane. It didn't look that way to William Franklin, either. "His Pride and Laziness are beyond any Thing I ever knew," William reported to his father, describing Benny in his thirties. And then he added something more: "I look upon him to have a Tincture of Madness."[28]

The Mecoms were a very sickly family, but no eighteenth-century doctor could have cured them. Jane was baffled. Whatever was wrong with the Mecoms, it's possible Jane unwittingly made it worse. "Physicians, after having for Ages contended that the Sick should not be indulg'd with fresh Air, have at length discover'd that it may do them good," Franklin once wrote, but Jane, like many poorer people, subscribed to the older view; she believed that fresh air could be dangerous. In winter, and even in summer, she kept the house shut up, preferring, as she explained to her brother, to be "Less Exposed to Doers opening on me which in cold wether Increeces my cough."[29]

"The *Aerophobia* that at present distresses weak Minds," Franklin observed, made people like his sister "choose to be stifled and poison'd, rather than leave open the Window of a Bedchamber, or put down the Glass of a Coach." Repeatedly he berated her, urging her "not to be afraid of her Friend Fresh Air."[30]

She tried to take this advice. "It is a very happy circumstance that you Injoy yr helth so perfectly," she wrote him, and "it is a Blesing vouchsaifed to me also Exept some trifeling Interuption & that but sildom which I a good deal atribute to my observation of yr former Admonitions respecting fresh Air & diet."[31]

But the problem wasn't only the air. New England winters are long, and dim. The windows in Jane's house were small, and shut. Fresh air would have helped, but what really seems to make people susceptible to tuberculosis, and what makes it worse for people who've got it, isn't lack of air. It's lack of sunlight.[32]

I have had some children that seemed to be doing well till they were taken off by Death. It may be that, at the height of the Enlightenment, the children and grandchildren of Benjamin Franklin's sister sickened, wasted, and died—and maybe even lost their minds—because they lived in darkness.

CHAPTER XX

Queer Notions

In 1758, settled in Boston, Benjamin Mecom had the idea to start a magazine.[1] He called it the *New-England Magazine of Knowledge and Pleasure.* It was, he explained, his stab at "undermining the Interests of Ignorance, Vice and Folly; and of attempting to substitute in their Stead,—Learning, Piety, and good Sense."[2]

Magazines were new. The *Gentleman's Magazine*—the first periodical called a "magazine"—appeared in London in 1731. It offered "a Monthly Collection, to treasure up, as in a Magazine, the most remarkable Pieces."[3] The metaphor is to weapons. A magazine is, literally, an arsenal; a piece is a firearm. A magazine is an arsenal of knowledge. It is also a library, dissected: bits of this book and bits of that. A magazine is a library—knowledge—cut into bits, so that more people can use it. Magazines, then, contained the great and soaring promise of the age: knowledge for all.

"No Man or Woman is obliged to learn and know every Thing," Benjamin Mecom wrote. "Yet all Persons are under some Obligation to *improve their own Understanding*, otherwise it will be like a barren Desart, or a Forest overgrown with Weeds and Brambles."[4] He meant his magazine for every reader. What he needed was writers: "ANY *Writers* who may incline to publish their Sentiments in this Magazine, are desired to send their Papers (Postage paid) under a Cover directed to *Benjamin Mecom*, Printer, at the *New* Printing-Office in Boston." He chose, for its motto, *E Pluribus Unum*.[5]

Unfortunately, writers were hard to come by. With no class of hacks—no equivalent of London's Grub Street—nearly everything printed in American magazines was a reprint. Mecom filled his magazine with Addisonian puffery, cribbing material from Swift, Hume, Bacon, and Pope and, above all, from his uncle, including "Advice to a Young Tradesman." In the magazine's inaugural issue, Mecom even printed, a little desperately, the epitaph Benjamin Franklin had written for Josiah and Abiah Franklin's gravestone.[6]

If writers were hard to come by, nearly as hard were readers. No magazine started in the colonies lasted for long. In 1741, Benjamin Franklin had launched what he'd expected would be the very first American magazine, the *General Magazine,* but his rival Andrew Bradford got out his own magazine three days before the first issue of Franklin's appeared, and with a better name, too. Bradford's was called the *American Magazine*. Neither publication finished out the year.[7] In 1757, James Parker had proposed a "New *American* Magazine," promising that its first issue would contain "A new and complete History of the *Northern Continent of America,* from the Time of its first Discovery to the present: Compiled with that Impartiality and Regard to Truth, which becomes a faithful Historian." Mecom sold Parker's magazine in Boston, but the *New American Magazine* didn't last three years.[8] "The expectation of failure is connected with the very name of Magazine," Noah Webster would one day write in his own *American Magazine*—which went the way of many another American magazine within the year.[9]

Mecom's *New-England Magazine* appeared while Parker's *New American Magazine* was still running. The colonies could barely support one magazine, let alone two. Still, Mecom aimed, by being various, to please many. "*Kind Reader,*—Pray, what would you have me do," he wrote, "If, out of Twenty, I should please but Two?"[10] He promised that his magazine would contain

> *Old Fashioned Writings and select Essays,*
> *Queer Notions, useful Hints, Extracts from Plays,*
> *Relations wonderful, and Psalm, and Song,*
> *Good-Sense, Wit, Humour, Morals, all ding-dong;*
> *Poems, and Speeches, Politics, and News,*
> *What Some will like, and other Some refuse.*[11]

Too many refused. The *New-England Magazine* folded after just three issues.

By 1761, Mecom's shop was growing. He advertised for a journeyman.[12] He sold a good number of imported books, advertising his stock as "very cheap indeed, Wholesale and Retail."[13] Still, he was forever missing his mark. On the strength of a loan from his aunt Deborah Franklin, he printed thirty thousand copies of *The New England Psalter,* then priced them too low to make a profit.[14]

Unable to repay the debt he owed his aunt, he named a daughter after her instead, writing to her, "If our Daughter proves as worthy a woman, we shall be contented." (He named all of his daughters after Franklin women: Sarah, Deborah, Abiah, and Jane.) "Debby is put out to a reputable Nurse at Charlestown," he reported to his aunt. "Betsy is weak yet, but has no Milk, & parted with her Child with great Regret."[15]

Mecom wrote polite and witty and kindhearted and affable letters. He was charming. He was also terribly odd. He wore a powdered wig and ruffles, even when operating his press. This was so very strange that the printers in Boston gave him a nickname: they called him, after one of his columns, Queer Notions.[16]

Queer Notions kept printing: sermons; psalters; almanacs; a parable titled *The Prodigal Daughter;* John Perkins's disquisition on storms at sea; James Otis Jr.'s essay on Latin prosody; a collection of Franklin's best writings, called *The Beauties of Poor Richard's Almanack;* and an edition of *Advice to a Young Tradesman.*[17] Much of what her son printed, Jane must have read, including his magazine (though she spelled the word "magizeen").[18] And he would surely have given her a copy of any of his uncle's books that he printed, books that would have been special to her: written by her brother, printed by her son. Jane's copy of his printing of *The Interest of Great Britain Considered* she inscribed, so that the half-title page bore all three of their names.[19] Written by Benjamin Franklin. Printed by Benjamin Mecom. Read by Jane Franklin Mecom.

While Benjamin Mecom lived near his mother in Boston, William Franklin lived with his father in London, where he acquired a fascination with royalty. He attended the coronation of George III. He acquired, too, a bastard son, William Temple Franklin (known as Temple), whom he abandoned. (It was Benjamin Franklin who paid for the boy's keep and his education.) Then he acquired a wife, Elizabeth Downes, not the mother of his child but the very wealthy daughter of a Barbadian plantation owner. And he acquired a sinecure: the king appointed him governor of New Jersey.

"I have no doubt but that he will make as good a Governor as Husband," Benjamin Franklin wrote his sister.[20]

Benjamin Franklin returned to America in November 1762. The following summer, he planned a visit to Boston, as part of a tour to inspect the post roads.[21]

"I purpose to lodge at your house if you can conveniently receive me," he wrote to his sister.[22] He brought his daughter with him. En route, they stopped to visit Caty Ray, now married and living in Warwick, Rhode Island.[23]

In Boston, Franklin learned that Peter Mecom had lost his mind. Franklin arranged for him to be sent to the country, to be cared for by a farmer's wife, where he may have been tied up in a barn, like an animal. There was very little else to do with a lunatic. There were no asylums; there was no hospital in Boston; and the almshouse refused to admit madmen. To pay for Peter's keep, Franklin used income from the Douse house, on Unity Street in Boston. Since Elizabeth Franklin Douse had died in 1759, the house had been rented. In 1763, Franklin told Jonathan Williams Sr. of his wish "that the Rent of the House be applied to assist my Sister Mecom in the Maintanance of her unhappy Son."[24]

By then, Benjamin Mecom had abandoned Boston, having failed once more. He went next to New York with his little brother Johnny as his apprentice—Johnny having abandoned his apprenticeship to the goldsmith William Homes—and opened yet another printing office, on Rotten Row, where he launched a newspaper called the *New York Pacquet*. It lasted only six weeks.[25] In April 1764, Mecom was ruined; he sold "The Remains of the Shop" at auction, not just his scant stock ("a Variety of valuable Pamphlets, a few bound Books, some Waste Paper") but the very shelves.[26] By July, John Mecom had given up his brief stint as a printer and returned to smithing. He opened up a shop in New Brunswick, where he sold everything from nails and chisels to sheep shears and scissors.[27]

Benjamin Franklin tried, once more, to save his nephew: he appointed Benjamin Mecom postmaster of New Haven and arranged for James Parker to set him up in business there.[28] (Years before, Mecom had been a wayward and ungrateful apparentice in Parker's shop in New York.) By the end of 1764, Mecom was printing Yale dissertations.[29] He had, as usual, grand plans. They fell through. Mecom's "lethargick Indolence" was his great fault, Parker reported to Franklin. "I can not get him to do any Thing hardly." He would not even answer letters. Up and down he went: bursts of extraordinary activity, followed by periods of profound indolence. "Benny Mecom continues—I fear on the going-back Road," Parker wrote. "My hopes of him wax fainter and fainter."[30] He grew queer, and even queerer.

In November 1764, Franklin sailed, once more, for London. Before he left, he sent copies of a likeness of himself to Boston, "it being the only way in which I am now likely ever to visit my Friends there." He shipped the miniatures to Jonathan Williams Sr. and suggested a few people who might like them: one for Jane's minister Samuel Cooper; one for John Withrop, a Harvard professor; one for Mather Byles. "And my Sister will possibly like to have one for herself, and one for her Doctor Perkins." A portrait—"I hope a long Visit in this Shape will not be disagreable to them"—a likeness, and no more.[31]

In New Jersey, Franklin's son moved into the governor's mansion. In New Haven, Jane's son struggled to keep out of debtors' prison.

~o CHAPTER XXI o~

Black Day

She was fifty-two years old. She took out her Book of Ages:

> *June the 12-1764 Died a beloved & Deservedly Lamented Daughter Sarah*
> *Flagg. She has Left four Children. Jane. Mary Josiah & Sarah.*

Jane's daughter Sarah had married a housewright named William Flagg.
And then, just before her twenty-seventh birthday—almost exactly the
same age at which Neddy and Eben had succumbed—she died, leaving
four children: Jenny, seven; Josiah, three; Mary (called Polly), two; and
Sally, one.

Sarah Mecom Flagg: beloved and deservedly lamented. "She always
appear'd to me of a sweet and amiable Temper," Franklin wrote Jane, consol-
ing her. "She is doubtless happy:—which none of us are while in this Life."[1]

The children came to live with their grandmother. The baby was sick.

> *Novr 9-1764 Died under my Care my Daughter flaggs youngest Child aged*
> *17 months.*

Under my Care. She thought it was her fault.[2] She wrote, at the beginning
of March 1765,

> *Died my Daughter Flagg Second Daughter Polly a sober Plesant Child*

"The sick child I mentioned to you in my Last Died the next Day," Jane
wrote to Deborah in April, "& the other childs Knee grows worce." Josiah
Flagg had fallen, badly, in Jane's house. He would be lame for life.[3]

Edward Mecom was in debt again. In 1764, he was sued twice. The sheriff came knocking on Jane's door. He left a summons. He took a chair. In January 1765, Mecom failed to show up in court.[4] He could scarcely rise from his bed.

Somehow, between March and May 1765, someone found the money to pay an artist named Joseph Badger to paint three-quarter-length oil portraits of the two surviving Flagg children, Jenny and Josiah.[5] Badger, who started out as a glazier and sign painter, and who never signed his work, painted, mainly, houses. (He had nothing of the talent of the much younger John Singleton Copley, whose *Boy with a Squirrel* was displayed in London that year.) He spent his sittings capturing faces, only later painting props and background and clothes, using a set of costumes he kept—a yellow dress for a girl, a blue cloak for a boy not yet breeched. Josiah, a fidgety four-year-old, would not have sat for long, and even his sober sister would have grown restless. In Jenny's hands Badger placed a flower; in Josiah's, an orange.[6]

Jane's grandchildren look very like each other, a great deal like Benjamin Franklin and probably a great deal like Jane: moon-faced, with dark hair, delicate brows, small features, and round blue eyes.

Badger painted charming portraits for very little money. For three-quarter-length portraits, he usually charged about two pounds, less for a pair.[7] This was a good deal of money for either Jane Franklin Mecom or William Flagg. Possibly it was Jane's brother who paid. Franklin had ties to Badger. Thomas Cushing, who became the Speaker of the Massachusetts General Assembly in 1766, had sat for Badger, and Franklin later acted in England as Cushing's agent and maintained a correspondence with him.[8] Jane knew Cushing, too. In a letter to her brother, she once referred to having read one of Franklin's letters to him.[9] Her cousins Jonathan and Grace Williams were Cushing's neighbors.[10] Then, too, the Mecoms, the Williamses, and the Cushings all belonged to the Brattle Street Church, and so did the Badgers. (Records of the baptisms of the Mecom and Badger children appear near to one another in the church's parish register.)[11] Franklin also sometimes asked Cushing and, later, Cushing's son to look after Jane. ("Mr Cushing has not been to see me as I understood by Mr Williams you Desiered Him," Jane once wrote to her brother.)[12] Maybe Franklin made arrangements for the portraits, through Cushing.[13] Or maybe Jonathan Williams Sr. gave them to Jane, as a gift.[14]

However they were gotten, the portraits must have been a consolation. Meanwhile, the times only grew harder. In Boston at midcentury, the rich grew richer, and the poor grew poorer. Never before in New England had such inequality of wealth been known. The French and Indian War had ended in 1763, leaving in its wake a crippling depression. Massachusetts had sent more men to that war than all of the other colonies put together. One in three men of age in Massachusetts went to fight.[15] Boston in the 1760s was a city of widows and orphans.

The poor roamed the streets and huddled in doorways. A wooden almshouse had been built before 1662, destroyed by fire in 1682, and replaced by a brick almshouse, built near the Common in 1686. A brick workhouse, also run by the Overseers of the Poor, was erected in 1739, next door to the prison that housed, mainly, debtors. The Society for Encouraging Industry and Employing the Poor built the Manufactory House in 1754. At midcentury, the numbers of admissions soared, from an average of 93 a year between 1759 and 1763 to 144 between 1763 and 1769. Only the size of the building stopped the number from rising higher. At capacity, some 300 people lived in the almshouse every year; 600 more received poor relief at home. Hundreds more, refugees, were warned out of town, their names recorded in the city's Warning Out Book, where the number of names grew from an average of 65 per year between 1745 and 1752, to 200 between 1753 and 1764, to 450 between 1765 and 1774.[16] The ranks of the poor swelled.

In these dire times, Parliament decided to levy new taxes on the colonies, passing, in 1764, the Sugar Act, a duty on imported sugars, and a Post Act, reforming the postal system. The next year brought the Stamp Act, requiring government-issued stamps on pages of printed paper—a tax on, that is, everything from indenture agreements and bills of credit to playing cards and newspapers. In London, Franklin, acting as an agent of the assemblies of Massachusetts, Pennsylvania, Georgia, and New Jersey, lobbied Parliament to repeal the Stamp Act. "It will affect Printers more than anybody," he warned.[17] He knew, too, that printers, more than anybody, could fight back.[18]

In Boston, printers filled their pages with protest. No newspaper, they insisted, could survive such a tax. With angry opinions about the Stamp Act, Jane reported to her brother, "You See the Newspapers full."[19] The hellfire tradition begun by James Franklin had been carried on by a man named Benjamin Edes, the son of a Charlestown hatter. In 1755, Edes, with his partner, John Gill, had taken over the *Boston Gazette.* Two years later, Boston's selectmen scolded him: "You have printed Such Pamphlets & such things in your News Papers as reflect grossly upon the received religious principles of this People which is very Offensive." Edes apologized, promising to "publish nothing that shall give any uneasiness to any Persons whatever." He didn't keep that promise. By the 1760s, Tories began calling Edes's paper the "Weekly Dung Barge."[20]

In the midst of all this, Benjamin Mecom had a very queer notion: he proposed to start a newspaper. The *Connecticut Gazette,* owned by James Parker, had stopped publishing in April 1764, a casualty of the postwar depression. ("Benny Mecom says he gets a good deal of small Work, but does not print a News-paper," Parker reported to Franklin in March 1765, adding, "He may make shift to rub along, but I believe will never do any great Matter.")[21] But just when the Stamp Act made printing a newspaper less profitable than ever before, Mecom decided to revive the *Gazette.* Mecom ardently supported the growing resistance to Parliament: in 1764, he printed a treatise titled *Reasons why the British colonies, in America, should not be charged with internal taxes, by authority of Parliament.*[22] He thought a newspaper in New Haven would help the cause. "Perhaps there never was a more unpromising Time for the Encouragement of another News-Paper," he admitted. "But, it is said there never was a Time when the Encouragement of such Papers was more necessary."[23] Mecom's *Gazette* began appearing in July 1765, just four months before the Stamp Act was to take effect. Mecom promised that his paper would be lively: "Bare Articles of News are not all we look for in the Weekly Gazettes."[24] He looked for hellfire.

In Boston, there was much hellfire to be found. On the floor of the Massachusetts General Assembly, gentlemen argued that Parliament had no right to levy taxes on the colonists, who were not represented in Parliament. On the streets, tradesmen and artisans and the suffering poor rioted. On August 26, 1765, a mob attacked Thomas Hutchinson's house on Hanover Street "with the rage of devils," as furious at Hutchinson's wealth as at his politics. Hutchinson barely escaped with his life, running through yards and gardens. "Nothing remaining but the bare walls and floors," Hutchinson wrote, inventorying his losses.[25] The rioters stripped the house of its contents and then began taking apart the house itself— tearing down walls and stripping slate from the roof. In the chaos, they set loose, fluttering to the winds, the entire manuscript of a book Hutchinson was writing, a history. Hutchinson's neighbor Andrew Eliot, the minister of Boston's New North Church, rescued the pages from gutters and puddles.[26] Hutchinson's losses ran to the thousands of pounds.

Jane's sympathies did not lie with the assembleymen nor with the mob. Violence terrified her. In the aftermath of one tumult, one of her grandnieces had died of fear: "Cousen Griffeth can asign no cause for the Death of her child Exept it was fright She Recved won Evening," Jane wrote, "when some men in Liquer next Dore got to fighting & there was screeming murther." (Cousin Griffith was Abiah Davenport Griffith, the daughter of Jane's sister Sarah Franklin Davenport.)[27] Jane had in her care young children, Jenny and Josiah Flagg. She wanted to keep them out of harm's way. She feared war. She feared, too, for her brother's family.

Before he left for London, Franklin had recommended his friend John Hughes for the post stamp distributor, an appointment Hughes was granted, leaving many in Pennsylvania to believe that Franklin supported the Stamp Act.[28] In September, a mob came to Franklin's house. Deborah, armed with a gun, fended them off. "I am amaizd beyond measure," Jane wrote. "I knew there was a Party that did not Aprove His Prosecuting the busness he is gone to England upon, & that some had used Him with scurrilous Language in some Printed Papers." But she could hardly believe it had come to this.[29]

The world she knew was coming to another end, too. In Boston, Edward Mecom worsened. Soon, he was gone. Jane opened her Book of Ages:

Sepr 11-1765 God sees meet to follow me with Repeeted correcti[ons] this morning 3 oclock Died my husband in a Stedy hope of a happy hear after

"It Pleased God to Call my Husband out of this Troblesom world where he had Injoyed Litle & suffered much by Sin & Sorrow," she wrote Deborah. Jane had been married for thirty-eight years and, at her husband's death, she wrote only of his suffering, his sin, and his sorrow.

She thought she was to blame. *God sees meet to follow me with Repeeted corrections.* "In fifteen months I have been bereved of four Near & Dear Relations," she reckoned.[30] She had very nearly lost her bearings. "Nothing but troble can you hear from me," she warned.[31] Still, she kept her sorrow close. *Weep not.* "I never Informed you of half I met with," she once reminded her daughter Jenny, but "I have Buried the best of Parents, all my Sisters, & Brethren Except one, how many of my children & in what circumstances you know, & some small Remembrance of my difficulties before your Fathers death & after you must have."[32] The difficulties she had before and after Edward Mecom's death: these were the darkest years of her life. She would not speak of them.

She dressed in black. About his sister's loss, Franklin said very little. "I condole with you on the Death of your Husband, who was I believe a truly affectionate one to you, and fully sensible of your Merit," he wrote.[33] No more than this. To be sensible was to be wise, but it had another meaning, too. To be sensible was to be sane. Mecom was sensible of Jane's merit. Was he sensible of anything more? Had he lost his mind?

Edward Mecom was either a bad man or a mad man. Every one of Jane's children who had children named a child after her. Not one of them named a child after their father.

She paid for a funeral and had her husband buried. Her minister, Samuel Cooper, preached a funeral sermon. Franklin, as a young man, writing as Silence Dogood, had mocked Puritan elegies, by writing a recipe for one: "Having chose the Person, take all his Virtues, Excellencies, &c., and if he have not enough, you may borrow some to make up a sufficient Quantity: To these add his last Words, dying Expressions, &c. if they are to be had; mix all these together, and be sure you *strain* them well. Then season all with a Handful or two of Melancholly Expressions, such as, *Dreadful, Deadly, cruel cold Death, unhappy Fate, weeping Eyes,* &c." Then, "having prepared a sufficient Quantity of double Rhimes, such as, *Power, Flower; Quiver, Shiver; Grieve us, Leave us; tell you, excel you; Expeditions, Physicians; Fatigue him, Intrigue him;* &c. you must spread all upon Paper, and if you can procure a Scrap of Latin to put at the End, it will garnish it mightily; then having affixed your Name at the Bottom, with a *Mœstus Composuit,* you will have an Excellent Elegy."[34]

Cooper offered no such encomium to the excellences of Edward Mecom. Jane, after hearing Cooper's sermon for her husband, copied down, in a letter to Deborah, the verse from which he had preached, 2 Corinthians 4:17: "for our Light Afflictions which is but for a moment worketh for us a far more Exceeding and Eternal weight of Glory." Her husband was afflicted. Her husband *was* an affliction. But no matter: this life was hard that the next might be soft. "To me," Jane wrote, "the Sermon was a master Peec."[35]

If 1765 was a dark year, for Jane, it was also an especially dreadful time to be widowed. From the moment of her husband's death, she was no longer a *feme covert*. A widow was a *feme sole;* she could own property; she could sign contracts; she could earn money; she had to pay debts; she was on her own. Jane was fifty-three years old when her husband died. For the first time in her life, she was, legally, alone. But she was also in trouble. Her husband had died without leaving a will. And he'd died in debt. She had still at home two daughters and two grandchildren. She ran a boardinghouse, but the house itself she did not own. Female heads of household did not fare well in Boston. More than a quarter of the city's households were headed by women, but less than 10 percent of the city's taxpayers were women.[36] Women in Jane's circumstances often ended up in the poorhouse.

In September 1765, the month Jane was widowed, "Sarah Burk & her Grand Child Sarah Cowley" were admitted to the almshouse. So was Ann Johns, "a poor Woman"; Edward Tavenue, "a little Boy"; George Glean; "Lydia Richardson big With Child"; Mary McGouin; and Anna Murrey, alias Taylor, "A Negrow Woman." Boston's population, in these years, held steady at about fifteen thousand. Over the course of the second half of the eighteenth century, more than ten thousand people were admitted to the almshouse. Some stayed for only a matter of days; over half stayed for more than three months. About a quarter of those admitted to the almshouse died there.[37]

On October 30, 1765, assessors came to Jane's house and made an inventory of everything in it. Downstairs: a desk, a table with nine chairs, a looking glass, and a tea chest. Upstairs: a case of drawers, five chairs, five beds, a great deal of bedding, and another looking glass. In the kitchen: pewter plates and dishes, tinware, a skillet, a kettle, a water pot, a coffee mill, pots and pans, andirons, bellows, gridirons, two old tables, two chairs, and Edward's clothing: "thickset coat 2 old coats, 1 Beaver hat 1 old hat 2 old wigs." In the shop: old saddlers' tools, girths, bridles, saddle trees, a bench, and a lamp. Edward Mecom's entire estate was valued at £41, placing him within the poorest tenth of the city's population. Then, too, this was an overestimate of his wealth: the claims on his estate were great. Very likely, he owed more than he owned.[38]

Two days after assessors came to Jane's house, the Stamp Act—the "fatal *Black-Act,*" James Parker called it in a letter to Franklin—was to go into effect.[39] November 1 would be a Black Day; to mark it, newspapers dressed in mourning. A Baltimore paper changed its title to *The Maryland Gazette, Expiring* and adopted a new motto: *In uncertain Hopes of a Resurrection to Life again.* The printer of the *Pennsylvania Journal* replaced his newspaper's masthead with a death's-head and framed his front page with a thick black border in the shape of a gravestone. "Adieu, Adieu!" whispered the *Journal* to its readers. The printer of the *New-Hampshire Gazette* edged his newspaper with black mourning borders and, in a column on page 1, the paper lamented its own demise, groaning, "I must *Die!*"[40]

In Boston, Benjamin Edes refused to buy stamps, draped his *Gazette* in black mourning ink, and changed the paper's motto to "A free press maintains the majesty of the people."[41] On November 1, Bostonians staged a Funeral for Liberty, burying a coffin six feet under the Liberty Tree. Edes's *Gazette* reported on similar funerals held all over the colonies. In Portsmouth, New Hampshire, a coffin was stamped with the word "LIBERTY." Everywhere the story ended the same way, with a resurrection. At Boston's Funeral for Liberty, the eulogy "was hardly ended before the Corps was taken up, it having been perceived that some Remains of Life were left."[42]

Jane's fate, too, turned on the imperial crisis. Her case—the matter of what was to be done with her husband's estate—went to court on December 19, 1765. Thomas Hutchinson served as a judge on the probate court. Out of Edward Mecom's estate of forty-one pounds, Jane requested four pounds, twelve shillings, to pay for his funeral, and five pounds "for what I am to pay the Dr for the last Sickness." These were her debts, not her husband's. Hutchinson, who that summer had lost the entirety of his own estate to rioters, and who knew very well that Edward Mecom's wife was Benjamin Franklin's sister, allowed her both of these expenses. Instead of impounding her husband's estate to pay his creditors—and remanding yet another widow to the poorhouse—he deeded to her the remainder of the estate, about thirty pounds, "for necessary Implements and her trouble as Administratrix."[43]

Hutchinson, as Jane wrote to her brother, "has shewn me the Gratest Clemency."[44] She was extraordinarily grateful. She also admired Hutchinson and regretted what he had suffered. She could not have known that, even while Hutchinson refused, publicly, to take the side of the mob in defying the Stamp Act, he had argued against it, privately, in letters to England.[45] But Franklin knew it.[46] "To my certain Knowledge," he told his sister, Hutchinson had written "warmly in favour of the Province and against that Act, both before it pass'd and since."[47]

Lest Franklin conclude that her opinion of Hutchinson was "Influenced by His Goodnes to me in perticular," Jane assured her brother, "my opinyon of the Gentileman was the same before I had any Busness with Him."[48] Something had changed: she had begun expressing her political opinions.

"I never atempt to give any acount of Publick affairs," she once wrote.[49] This was more than coy. Her education was slight, her intellect stunted, her vantage provincial, her views narrow. But she had opinions, and they were growing stronger.

"I do not Pretend to writ about Politics," she once wrote her brother, "tho I Love to hear them."[50] She did much more than listen.

CHAPTER XXII

To Be Sold

Her house was full. Her daughters Jenny and Polly, twenty and almost eighteen, long ill, seemed to be gaining. ("If I should now Repine or Distrust Provedenc I should be most ungratfull of all His Cretures," Jane wrote to Deborah, grateful that she had "two Daughters in Helth.")[1] Her grandchildren Jenny and Josiah Flagg, nine and five, were growing fast, the boy learning to walk with crutches. Then there were the boarders. In a December 1765 letter to her brother, she listed them: "I have son Flagg boards with me" (her daughter Sarah's bereaved and distracted husband, William Flagg), "cousen Ingersols two Daughters" (her grandnieces, the orphaned daughters of Elizabeth Davenport Ingersoll, a daughter of Jane and Benjamin's sister Sarah Franklin Davenport), and "Mrs. Bowls is also Returned after a twelve months absence" (Sarah Bowles, the widowed stepdaughter of Sarah Franklin Davenport). Her boarders, that is, were relatives who were worse off than she was: she charged them very little. "I have them all at a Low Rate," she explained, "because I can Do no beter." She was barely getting by: "my Income supys us with vitles fiering candles & Rent but more it cannot with all the Prudence I am mistres of." There wasn't much to be done about it, especially in the middle of the winter. "I must Rub along till Spring when I must strive after some other way."[2]

In 1766, she had a few better-paying boarders. When the Massachusetts General Assembly met, a half dozen of its members boarded at her house. Feeding them at her table, she listened avidly to their talk. "I have six good Honist old Souls who come groneing Home Day by Day at the Stupidety of there Bretheren," she wrote to her brother, adding, "I cant help Interesting my self in the case." Of one motion, she reported, they "cant yet git a Vote for it tho they sitt Late in the Evening."[3] The woman who read as much as she dared listened as much as she dared, too—day and night.

That spring, the assembly's first order of business was to elect a new speaker. Under the terms of the royal charter, the governor had to approve that election. When the assembly elected James Otis Jr., a fiery patriot, Governor Francis Bernard refused to accept him. Eventually, Thomas Cushing was elected and approved in Otis's place. But the divide between the governor and the assembly grew.[4]

Meanwhile, word of the Stamp Act protests had reached London. On February 13, 1766, Franklin was questioned by Parliament on the subject of colonial resistance. He made sure the transcript of his examination found its way across the ocean. It was printed all over the colonies: in Boston, by Benjamin Edes; in New York, by James Parker; and in Connecticut, by Benjamin Mecom.[5]

Why, Parliament wanted to know, did colonists object to paying for stamps on newspapers but not to paying for postage on letters?[6]

Franklin was asked, "Is not the post-office, which they have long received, a tax as well as a regulation?"

"No," Franklin insisted. "The money paid for the postage of a letter is not of the nature of a tax; it is merely a quantum merit for a service done." A colonist could avoid paying postage by delivering letters himself or having a servant or a friend do it.

"If the Stamp Act should be repealed," another minister inquired, "would it induce the assemblies of America to acknowledge the rights of Parliament to tax them, and would they erase their resolutions?"

"No, never."

"Is there no means of obliging them to erase those resolutions?"

"None that I know of; they will never do it unless compelled by force of arms."

"Is there no power on earth that can force them to erase them?"

"No power, how great soever, can force men to change their opinions."

Finally, Parliament and Franklin had this exchange:

"What used to be the pride of the Americans?"

"To indulge in the fashions and manufactures of G. Britain."

"What is now their pride?"

"To wear their old cloaths over again till they can make new ones."[7]

New clothes. The month Franklin was examined by Parliament, Jane received from her brother a trunk of new clothes. Franklin had shipped her three sets of fashionable English clothes—"credible cloathing," she called it. For "Each of us a Printed coten Gownd a quilted coat a bonit," she noted, and for "Each of the Garls," her daughters Jenny and Polly, "a cap & some Ribons." The bonnet, Jane wrote Deborah, "is very suteable for me to were now"—she was still in mourning—"being black & a Purple coten."[8]

Old clothes. In Philadelphia, Franklin's wife packed up Franklin's old clothes and sent them to be worn by Jane's deranged son Peter, who was being cared for in the country by a farmer's wife. Deborah wrote to her husband that she had sent "sume of yours for poor Petter who is still a live," explaining, "I shold not a disposed of aney thing of yours but the mothe is got in them."[9]

Since the death of her husband, Jane had wondered what she could do to bring in more income. She wanted to open a business. "I know my Dear Brother is allways Redey to asist the Indogent and I now Intreat your advice and Direction," she had written to him. At the almshouse in Boston, the Overseers of the Poor helped widows get business licenses. Jane had the same idea. "I feel now as if I could carey on some Biusnes if I was in it but at other times I fear my years are two far advancd to do any thing but jog on in the old track."[10]

Maybe it was the bonnets that she had lately unwrapped from their packing that gave her the courage to start a business. She gathered material and, with her daughters, began sewing. Jane, who wrote so ill, could stitch very well, and, she told her brother, "my Daughter Jeney with a litle of my asistance has taken to makeing Flowrs for the Ladyes Heads & Boosomes with Prity good acceptance."[11] She would turn her needle to profit.[12]

On March 17, 1766, Parliament, blindsided by the fervor of the colonial opposition, repealed the Stamp Act. "I congratulate you & my Countrymen on the Repeal," Franklin wrote Jane from London.[13] The times seemed hopeful. "I have a small Request to ask," she wrote her brother in November. Or, rather, she asked him to relay the request to his London landlady, Margaret Stevenson. "It is to Procure me some fine old Lining or cambrick (as a very old shirt or cambrick hankercheifs) Dyed into bright colors such as red & green a Litle blew but cheafly Red." She knew how to dye. She also kept, in her house, a little book she had brought with her from the Blue Ball: her uncle Benjamin's book of recipes, which he had carried with him from Banbury. But, she admitted, "with all my own art & good old unkle Benjamins memorandoms I cant make them good colors." She thought that with such vivid linen and cambric, "we shall git somthing by it worth our Pains if we live till Spring."[14] *No gains without pains.*

In March 1767, Franklin arranged for Mrs. Stevenson to send the fabrics, at his expense. "I send you per Capt. Freeman a little Box containing some few Articles of Millenery, which Mrs. Stevenson has bought for you," he wrote.

> Be so good as to accept them from me as the Beginning of a little Stock which if sold to Advantage after being made up by your good Girls, may by degrees become greater—for on your remitting the Produce to Mrs. Stevenson, she will always readily buy more for you, till by the repeated and accumulated Profits, the Girls grow rich. They may think it a very small beginning. But let them know 'tis more than I had to begin the World with; and that Industry and Frugality early practis'd and long persisted in, will do Wonders.[15]

She and her daughters were to stitch their way from rags to riches. The fabrics—fine English linens and lace and ribbons—were lovely. "They apear to me to be Extroydnary good of the kind," Jane wrote to Mrs. Stevenson in May, sending her "complyments & thanks" and adding, "& tho the fashons are new to most of us I make now Doubt they will Obtain by Degrees when our Top Ladys sett the Example." She begged for more material, requesting, further, that "if opertunity Presents & any new Fashon comes out of Caps, or Hankerchifs, Ruffels, Aprons, Cloaks, hatts, shaids or Bonets, & you will be kind anouf to send me Paterns cut in Paper with Directions how to make them, & how they are worn, it will Add still Grater obligations & shall be Gratfully Acknolidged."[16]

Jane and her daughters, sometimes sick, sometimes well, stitched and stitched. But the month after the fabric arrived, Parliament passed the Townshend Acts, instituting taxes on all tea, paper, glass, paint, and lead imported from England and mandating the establishment of a customs board to enforce the new taxes and regulate trade; the board was to be located in Boston. It would take weeks for word of the new taxes to reach

Boston. But when it did, Jane was faced with the grim and certain knowledge that she could not possibly have decided to venture into the business of making and selling new clothes at a worse time. Bostonians resolved to boycott not just tea, paper, glass, paint, and lead but everything imported from England—including fine fabrics, especially luxury items like ribbons, lace, and cloth. The boycott began in October 1767.

She had gone too far, had invested too much to abandon her stock of goods. That November, she took out an advertisement in the *Boston Evening-Post*. It was the first time her name appeared in print.[17]

TO BE SOLD *by*
Jane Mecom,
At her House a little below Concert-Hall,
A few Articles of Millenary,
of the newest Fashion, from *London*, by Captain *Freeman*. Among which are a few ready-made Caps, Handkerchiefs, Ruffs, Aprons, Terefas, Bonnets and Hats, Cloaks and Capuchins; and all the above Articles made at said House, with Care and Expedition.

But in Boston, where the boycott had inspired even the women Jane called the city's "Top Ladys" to spin flax and wear homespun—ostentatiously performing their civic virtue—there wasn't much money to be made in selling fancy hats of the latest English fashion and finest English fabrics.

Franklin offered his sympathy. "We suppose you did not then know, that your People would resolve to wear no more Millinery," he wrote her in December. And then he wanted to know, "Pray are those Resolutions like to be steadily stuck to?"[18]

She was vexed, sorely vexed.

"It Proves a Litle unlucky for me," she grumbled, "that our People have taken it in there Heads to be so Exsesive Frugal."[19]

What price, liberty? In 1766, Benjamin Mecom had begun using for his newspaper's motto something Franklin had once printed: "Those who would give up ESSENTIAL LIBERTY, TO PURCHASE A LITTLE TEMPORARY SAFETY, deserve neither LIBERTY nor SAFETY."[20] But no aphorism of Franklin's was better remembered, in these years, than his answer to Parliament when asked what was Americans' pride: *To wear their old cloaths over again till they can make new ones.*

Jane's trials during these years were, in her accounting, the price she paid for a boycott led by blusterers. She thought bluster usually came at the expense of the poor. She knew very well that her brother himself had fanned the boycotting fervor; she had read his examination before Parliament. She admired it. "Yr Ansurs to the Parlement are thought by the best Judges to Exeed all that has been wrot on the subject," she told him, "& being given in the maner they were are a Proof they Proceeded from Prinsiple."[21]

It was a pickle. "Our Blusterers must keep themselves Imployed & If they Do no wors than Perswade us to *were our old cloaths over again* I cant Disaprove of that in my Hart," she wrote her brother. Still, she added, "I should Like to have those that do bye & can afford it should bye what Litle I have to sell & Imploy us to make it."[22] She understood the principle behind the boycott. But did it have to ruin her?

CHAPTER XXIII

Spectacles

She picked up her Book of Ages:

> *September 19-1767 at my Nantuckett at the House and under the most Affectionat care of my Dear Friend Kezia Coffin Died my Dear & Beloved Daughter Polly Mecom.*
>
> *The Lord Giveth & the Lord taketh away oh may I never be so Rebelious as to Refuse Acquiesing & & saying from my hart Blessed be the Name of the Lord.*

These are the last lines she ever wrote in her Book of Ages: lines from the Book of Job.

From childhood, Jane had been close to her relatives on Nantucket. ("My Nantuckett," she called it.) Her cousin Keziah Folger Coffin was one of the island's richest merchants, a shrewd and well-known tradeswoman. J. Hector St. John de Crèvecoeur, who, in *Letters from an American Farmer*, asked, "What then is the American, this new man?" asked another question, too: "Who is he in this country, and who is a citizen of Nantucket or Boston who does not know Aunt Kesiah?"[1]

Jane and Keziah had traded daughters. Polly went to live on Nantucket, to get well; Keziah Folger Coffin's daughter Keziah came to live with Jane in Boston, to go to school.[2] Keziah thrived; Polly died. "Poor Aunt Mecom has meet with a Verry Severe affliction in the Death of her Daughter Polly Who Died in Nantucket at her Cousin Coffins," Jonathan Williams Sr. wrote to Franklin.[3] "Realy my Spirits are so much Broken with this Last Hevey Stroak of Provedenc that I am not capeble of Expresing my self as

I ought," Jane wrote to her brother. She had loved this daughter best. "Oh my Brother she was Every thing to me, Every word & Every Action was full of Duty & Respect, & I never Lookd on Her but with Pleasur Exept when she was sick or in troble." Polly was exactly the kind of daughter Jane had tried to be. "How to make me Easey & Happy was what she had most at Heart," Jane wrote. For her death, Jane blamed herself: "Rather than Give me Pain she concealed her own Infirmities & Did so much more than she was Able that it Increased Her Disorder & Hastened Her End."[4] Maybe stitching bonnets had made her worse. Jane could scarcely bear it. "Sorrows roll upon me like the waves of the sea." What had she done to so offend God? She read the Book of Job, again and again. "I am hardly allowed time to fetch my breath," she wrote. "I am broken with breach upon breach, and I have now, in the first flow of my grief, been almost ready to say, 'What have I more?' "[5]

She began to wonder whether the fate of her family might not have been her fault. Maybe her daughter had died because, as sick as she was, she stitched bonnets for rich women unwilling to buy them. Maybe her sons had failed not for lack of merit but because they were unable to overcome the disadvantage of an unsteadiness they had inherited from their father. Maybe her children had died because they were poor and lived lives of meanness and filth and crowding and squalor. Maybe. Maybe not only Providence but also men in power—politics—determined the course of human events. She wondered and wondered.

In her grief, she grew bold. It was at this moment, in the depth of her despair, that she asked her brother to send her "all the Pamphlets & Papers that have been Printed of yr writing." She wanted to read "all the political Pieces" he had ever written: "Do Gratifie me."[6]

"I could as easily make a Collection for you of all the past Parings of my Nails," he wrote back.[7]

Still, he sent what he could.

She loved best books about ideas. "I keep your books of Philosophy, and Politics, by me (tho I have Read them throw several times) and when I am dull I take won up & Read, and it seems as tho I were conversing with you, or hearing you," she once wrote. "I find a Pleasure in that."[8] She asked him, too, for books written by other authors—books she'd heard about and was keen to read.

"I will endeavour to get the Books you desire," he promised, warning her that "it will be difficult." Still, he usually managed it: "I send you by this Opportunity the two you wrote for." He sent her, too, London newspapers, with this caution: "If you think you see any thing of mine there, don't let it be publish'd as such."[9]

She read and read. She read till her eyes grew tired.

"I thought you had mentioned in one of your Letters a Desire to have Spectacles of some sort sent you," he wrote her from London, "but I cannot now find such a Letter."[10]

She had asked, in a letter he lost, for eyeglasses. Spectacles were, to Franklin, a kind of signature.[11] A student of Isaac Newton's *Opticks,* he had long been fascinated with lenses.[12] He had sat for many portraits, but one of the best known, and his favorite, was painted by the artist David Martin in 1767. The portrait had been exhibited in London, and Franklin had commissioned a miniature, which he sent home to Philadelphia. He may have given Jane, too, a miniature of the Martin portrait. He sent her many likenesses of himself, the next best thing, he said, "to waiting on you in Person."[13] Martin painted Franklin in lavish attire, seated in his study, with a bust of Isaac Newton on his desk. Franklin strokes his chin while reading a letter. He wears wire-rimmed temple spectacles. Man of learning, man of science, man of letters: reading.

He sent her the spectacles. "I send you a Pair of every Size of Glasses from 1 to 13," he wrote her. There followed careful instructions on how she ought to conduct her own eye exam. "To suit yourself, take out a pair at a time, and hold one of the Glasses first against one Eye, and then against the other, looking on some small Print.—If the first Pair suits neither Eye, put them up again before you open a second. Thus you will keep them from mixing. By trying and comparing at your Leisure, you may find those that are best for you." Two eyes, two lenses. "Few Peoples Eyes are Fellows," Benjamin Franklin told his sister, "and almost every body in reading or working uses one Eye principally, the other being dimmer or perhaps fitter for distant Objects."[14]

Look, Dear Reader, Dear Jenny, Dear Sister, and *see.*

In London, Franklin was beginning to believe that the imperial crisis might end in American independence. In January 1768, he published an essay in the *London Chronicle*—which he might well have sent to Jane—describing the colonists' vantage on the Townshend Acts from what he insisted was the disinterested position of a mere chronicler, "an impartial historian of American facts and opinions." Americans, Franklin explained, consider their royally appointed governors corrupt and their properly elected assemblies powerless. They are willing to contribute funds to the empire, but they dispute, entirely, the right of Parliament, a body "in which there is not a single member of our chusing," to levy direct taxes. However much affection and loyalty Americans felt toward the mother country, Franklin concluded, "this unhappy new system of politics tends to dissolve those bands of union, and to sever us forever."[15]

Franklin's plea for calm went unheard. In September 1768, British soldiers landed in Boston to suppress the growing rebellion. Two regiments of infantrymen disembarked from ships in the harbor, marched through the streets of the city, flying flags, drumming drums, and wheeling artillery. They set up camp in the Common. From New Jersey, William Franklin expressed at once relief and concern, believing that the army "will have to good Effect to prevent such scandalous Riots, and Attacks on the Officers of Government, as had before prevail'd," but warning that "no Force on Earth is sufficient to make the Assemblies acknowledge, by any Act of theirs, that the Parliament has a Right to impose Taxes on America."[16]

From Boston, Jane reported, "The whol conversation of this Place turns upon Politices."[17] The rest of the colonies might still be at peace, but Bostonians were living under an occupying army.[18] Benjamin Edes began producing a daily *Journal of the Times,* a chronicle of atrocities committed by redcoats on the people of Boston. "Working the political Engine" is what John Adams called writings for Edes, after a night spent "Cooking up Paragraphs" for "the Next Days newspaper."[19]

Jane didn't trust a word of it. She reported to her brother that, in Boston, politics was "managed with two much Biterness as you will see by the News Papers If you give yr self the Troble to Read them." The newspapers, she warned him, "will not Infalably Informe you of the Truth." By what Edes printed, she was disconcerted. "Every thing that any Designing Person has a mind to Propagate Is stufed into them, & it is Dificult to know whither Either Party are in the Right."[20] She was a remarkably discerning reader.

"Your Political Disputes I have no Objection to if they are carried on with tolerable Decency, & do not become outrageously abusive," Franklin wrote back. "They make People acquainted with their Rights & the Value of them."[21]

She had her doubts. The governor ordered the rebellious Massachusetts General Assembly to dissolve. Jane was miffed. She had lost her best boarders.

"I suppose the Dissolution of your Assembly will affect you a little in the Article of Boarders," Franklin wrote her, "but do not be discouraged."[22]

She reported to him about the spinning of Boston's women, which left her no choice but to close her millinery shop.

"The Acct. you write of the growing Industry, Frugality and good Sense of my Country-women gives me more Pleasure than you can imagine," he wrote back delicately. "I should be sorry that you are engag'd in a Business which happens not to coincide with the general Interest, if you did not acquaint me that you are now near the End of it."[23]

"For my Part I wish we had Let alone strife before it was medled with," she wrote him, "& followed things that make for Peace."[24]

CHAPTER XXIV

The Philosophy of Soap

In the fall of 1769, Jane left New England for the first time in her life. She was fifty-seven years old. Not since she was a girl had she had no children to care for. Her youngest child, Jane Mecom, was twenty-four. Her grandchildren, little Jenny and Josiah Flagg, twelve and eight, had gone to live with their father, who had married again.[1] She decided to venture into the world.

She proposed to go to Philadelphia, and when she didn't hear back from anyone she meant to visit, she determined to go anyway. "I have no leter from you nor my son since I wrot you I was Going to Philadelphia," Jane wrote Deborah from Boston on September 14, "but Still Persist in my Intent & Porpose to sit out in about a fortnight."[2]

She set out at the end of the month, by carriage. She went first to New Brunswick, New Jersey, to visit her son John. Earlier that year, as William Franklin had reported to his father, John Mecom had "gone and quarter'd himself and Wife on his Mother at Boston" (he "has turn'd out as bad as Ben," William warned).[3] But by the end of the summer, John and his wife had gone and quartered themselves on someone else: John's wife's family in New Brunswick. Jane stopped to see them. She rode next to Perth Amboy, to visit William. (New Jersey had at the time two capitals, Burlington in the west, and Perth Amboy in the east. The assembly met in Burlington; the governor lived in Perth Amboy.) From there she rode to Philadelphia, to see her son Benjamin and his family; they had settled in Philadelphia the year before.[4]

"Benney Macume and his Lovely Wife and five Dafters is Come hear to live and woork Jurney worke," Deborah had written to her husband.[5]

"I cannot comprehend how so very sluggish a Creature as Ben Mecom is grown, can maintain in Philadelphia so large a Family," Franklin had written back. "I hope they do not hang upon you."[6]

From William, Franklin had received a more candid account: "Coz. Ben. Mecom is starving at Philadelphia, and would have been, I suppose in Gaol by this Time, if it had not been for the Assistance my Mother and I have afforded him and his Family."[7]

Benjamin Mecom had hired himself out as a journeyman to just about every printer in the city of Philadelphia, William reported to his father, but "cannot agree with any Body, and is I believe now without any Employ."[8] To keep out of debtors' prison, he had borrowed money from everyone in the family, clutching at the hope that his uncle would set him up in business yet again. (This hope was groundless; Franklin had lost all patience with Mecom.)[9] That August, Mecom went back to Connecticut to make a desperate effort to collect what debts were owed him there.[10] Not long after, James Parker sold what was left of Mecom's inventory, in an attempt to regain his own losses.[11]

Visiting her unstable son would have been painful. But Jane was especially keen to visit her brother's wife. Deborah had earlier visited Jane in Boston, and the two women longed to see each other again.[12] Jane wrote Deborah that she was eager to "Have the Pleasure to convers with you by yr own Fier side."[13]

She reached Philadelphia by the middle of December. She had a great many people to visit, including her niece Sally, Franklin's daughter, whose husband, Richard Bache, a merchant, Jane had met the year before.[14] ("I am glad you approve the Choice they have made," Franklin wrote Jane.)[15] She grew especially fond of her grandnephew, Sally's son, Benjamin Franklin Bache, then four months old. "King Bird," Deborah called him. Jane thought he looked just like her brother.[16]

"Sister is verey a greabel to me and makes everey thing verey plesant to me," Deborah wrote to her husband, "and we air as hapey as we Cold expeckte."[17] Jane was so happy in Philadelphia that Franklin wondered whether she might consider settling there. "Since your family is so much reduced, I do not see why you might not as well continue there, if you like the place equally with Boston," he wrote to her. "It would be a pleasure to me to have you near me."[18] But in January 1770, she decided to go home.

"You had not, I hope, any Offence in Philadelphia, that induc'd you to leave it so soon," he inquired.[19]

There had been none.[20] Instead, she had other reasons to leave. She may have wanted to see her son John once more. "Johney has been sick Ever since His wife wrot me to Philadelphia," Jane explained to Deborah.[21] (John Mecom died in New Brunswick on September 30, 1770.)[22] And her son Josiah, who had become a sailor on a whaling vessel, was about to get married, to a girl who worked as a servant. It was a bad match, but "I have no Objection," Jane wrote Deborah, "for I am convinced Poverty is Intailed on my Famely."[23]

She was probably somewhere between Philadelphia and Boston on March 5, 1770, when, in Boston, British soldiers fired on a crowd in front of the Town House, killing five men. Two days after the shooting, in a city of some fifteen thousand people, twelve thousand turned out for the funeral of the first four victims (one injured man still lingered), marching past the Liberty Tree to the Granary Burying Ground, where the caskets were lowered into the ground beneath a single tombstone. Samuel Adams arranged for Edes to print a report about what happened on King Street under the title *A Short Narrative of the horrid Massacre in Boston;* Adams sent copies of it to London.[24] Revere engraved a picture of the scene that night (a copy, really, of a drawing made by the accomplished artist and witness to the massacre Henry Pelham, a half brother of John Singleton Copley's). He titled it *The Bloody Massacre perpetrated in King Street.*

Even if Jane had reached Boston by March 5, she wouldn't have been out on the streets that night. In Philadelphia, she had fallen down the stone steps at brother's house; she found it difficult to walk. "My Lamenes continus yet that it is with Grat Pain I walk as far as Dr Coopers meeting," she wrote Deborah.[25] ("I hope the Hurt you receiv'd will be attended with no bad Consequences," her brother wrote her.)[26]

She seems to have moved into her old house on Hanover Street, near the Orange Tree Inn. "Aunt Mecom is well Settled in the Old place tho almost a N House," Jonathan Williams Sr. wrote Franklin in August 1770, telling him, too, that he was soon to send his blind son, Josiah, to London, to live with Franklin at Mrs. Stevenson's house in order to to study music, accompanied by another of his sons, Jonathan Williams Jr., who would work as Franklin's clerk. Jane was glad that her favorite nephews, Jonathan and Josiah Williams, would be going with Franklin to London, but she wrote to her brother to take special care of blind Josiah. ("Josiah says He fears nothing He shall ha[ve] to Incounter so much as your Disaprobatio of His Sceme." She hoped Franklin wouldn't send the young man back. "I tell Him you have seen s[o] much of the Follies of Human Nature & so L[ittle] Els in the comon Run of man kind, that you will know Beter how to Pitty & Advice Him.")[27] But she was weary, and in pain. Her children gave her more trouble than consolation. ("She has indeed been very unfortunate in her Children," as Franklin gently put it.)[28]

She wrote to Deborah, to tell her how much she missed her. "I should Admire to come & see & hear all about every thing there wonc a year & stay a fortnight," she explained.[29] She had no company but her daughter Jane. She missed the friends she had made in Philadelphia. She missed the news. "I see so few Intilegent People that I know the Least News of any won in the world," she complained. "I am a Grat Deal a Lone Exept some young persons coming back on Erands, for as I cant go a broad People Dont come to see me & Jeney is a good Deal out."

She sent Deborah a flurry of questions:

When do you Expect cousen Bache Home? is His wife Like to have a nother child? How Does Mrs Smiths Daughter & Famely do if you will beleve me I cannot now think of her Name How is Dr Bond & Famely Do you Ever see my obliging Mr York. Did Mrs Leegay go to the West Indieas, is that Dr Shipin that is Dead whose child mad the Speech at yr House, How goes on Goard & his sister & Townly Did they Ever Pay my son the mony they owed Him, or Did you Ever git yr Rent. How Does yr Good Nibour Hadock, Duke of Wharton, Marquis of Rockingham has he got His Government. how do you Like Mr Foxcrofts Lady is Tomey married. Is Cousen All Turned Marchant & stay at home constantly.

She asked after everyone from family (Richard Bache) to members of the American Philosophical Society and the Pennsylvania Provincial Assembly and their wives to her son Benjamin's employers (the Philadelphia printer William Goddard and his sister), to Deborah's cousin Captain Isaac All. She knew she had run on too long: "I beleve by this time you are hartyly tiered with this trumpery," she sighed, adding, "In compashon to you I conclud."

She wished her granddaughter Jenny Flagg could come to live with her, but the girl's father refused; he wanted Jenny's help minding his children by his second wife. Jane's boarders came and went. "I wish I had such a constant Border to Pay me 3 Dolars a week the year Round," she thought. "I could then do Prity well."[30] She especially missed the children she had grown fond of in Philadelphia. "Your King Bird I Long to see," she wrote Deborah. "I have watched Every child to find some Resemblanc but have seen but won & that was only in Good Natuer & Sweet Smell."[31] No child smelled so sweet.

In London, Franklin's thoughts, too, turned to his family, if differently. Jane thought about her descendants; her brother thought about his ancestors. In 1771, thirteen days before he began writing his autobiography, he sent his sister a genealogical chart. It begins with "Thomas Franklin of Ecton in N. hamptonshire born 1598," and it ends with the children of Grace Harris Williams, Benjamin Mecom, and Sally Franklin Bache. (He left his illegitimate son, William, and William's illegitimate son, Temple, out of the chart.) Then Franklin asked his sister for a favor: "Having mentioned so many Dyers in our Family"—he had written to her about how their father learned dyeing from his older brothers—"I will now it's in my Mind request of you a full & particular Receipt for Dying Worsted of that beautiful Red, which you learnt of our Mother. And also a Receipt for making Crown Soap. Let it be very exact in the smallest Particulars."[32]

She wrote down the recipes. How to dye wool red. How to make soap. She sent them across the ocean. Her recipe for soap runs on for pages.[33] It's even more detailed than her brother's genealogical chart. She could hardly have been more particular. "There is a good deal of Phylosephy in the working of crown soap," she explained.[34]

"I thank you for the Receipts; they are as full and particular as one could wish," he wrote back, adding that he was glad "that those useful Arts that have so long been in our Family, are now put down in Writing."[35]

He was thinking of putting another useful art down in writing: the art of his life. "I should have no Objection to a Repetition of the same Life from its Beginning, only asking the Advantage Authors have in a second Edition to correct some Faults of the first," he remarked, using his favorite metaphor: his life was a book, and he was its author. But what if it could be more than a metaphor? What if he could make his life into a book? He could hardly live his life over again but, "since such a Repetition is not to be expected, the Thing most like living one's Life over again, seems to be a *Recollection* of that Life." A memory could be made "durable," so long as he busied himself "putting it down in Writing."[36] A book could be life, everlasting.

Two weeks after Franklin sent Jane their family's genealogy and asked her to send him the family recipes, he began writing the story of his life. It began with his origins. He meant for the story of his life to be copied.

> Having emerg'd from the Poverty and Obscurity in which I was born and bred, to a State of Affluence and some Degree of Reputation in the World, and having gone so far thro' Life with a considerable Share of Felicity, the conducing Means I made use of, which, with the Blessing of God, so well succeeded, my Posterity may like to know, as they may find some of them suitable to their own Situations, and therefore fit to be imitated.

It was another recipe: rags to riches.

CHAPTER XXV

On Smuggling

Patience Wright, an artist who worked wax beneath her skirts, warming it between her thighs, met Jane in Boston in 1771. Wright, a widow and a mother of three, was an artist on her way to London. She wished for an introduction to Franklin.

For years, Wright had amused her children by molding people out of bread dough. When her husband died, she, like Jane, went into business. She started making people out of wax, pulling life-size molded wax figures out from between her legs. It was astonishing, unrivaled, and scandalous. Abigail Adams called Wright "the queen of sluts."[1]

In New York in June 1771, as the newspapers reported it, "a Fire was discovered in the House of Mrs. Wright, the ingenious Artist in Wax-Work, and Proprietor of the Figures so nearly resembling the Life." Nearly everything was destroyed.[2] Wright then headed to Boston, with her children and what was left of her gallery of figures. By September, she was exhibiting her work.[3]

Maybe it was the idea of a female artist that fascinated Jane. Or the way Wright gave birth to her art. Or maybe it was the wax itself, so much like soap. Jane gave the artist a letter of introduction to her brother (something people often asked her to do, but which she rarely did).[4] When Wright arrived in London, she carried in her bag a letter from Jane to Franklin. "I have this Day receiv'd your kind Letter by Mrs. Wright," Franklin wrote Jane in March. "She has shown me some of her Work which appears extraordinary. I shall recommend her among my Friends if she chuses to work here."[5] Franklin became Wright's most important patron.

In London, Wright became an ardent advocate of the patriot cause. Franklin had promised Jane he would "do her all the Service in my Power," and he did.[6] By November, Jane could read in the Boston papers that "the ingenious Mrs. Wright" was taking likenesses of the king and queen and had already completed "the most striking likeness of the celebrated Dr. Franklin."[7] (It does not survive. Only a single piece of Patience Wright's work remains; the rest is lost. Most of it caught fire and melted.)

Jane and her brother shared other friends, too. "There seems now to be a Pause in Politics," Jane's minister, Samuel Cooper, wrote to Franklin in London in 1771.[8] (Cooper used the political pause to plan his church's move.)[9] Cooper and Franklin had been corresponding at least since the middle of the 1760s, when Cooper became a leader of the resistance movement; Franklin sent Cooper transcripts of speeches made in Parliament, and Cooper sent Franklin news of the doings of the Massachusetts General Assembly. "Your candid, clear, and well-written Letters, be assured, are of great Use," Franklin wrote to him.[10] "My Thanks are due to you for writing me with so much Freedom," Cooper returned, "and I endeavor to make the best Use of what you communicate to me."[11]

That May, Franklin sent to Jonathan Williams Jr., who had returned to Boston, a set of books written by Joseph Priestley; Williams sold them and gave the money to Jane.[12] Blind Josiah Williams returned from London unwell.[13] He died in August 1772. He was twenty-four. His father paid for a lavish funeral, giving away gold mourning rings. Jane consoled with Grace. And Grace consoled with Jane, whose daughter Jenny was threatening to marry a ship's captain named Peter Collas, a man whose merit Jane doubted.[14]

Jane expected her brother to visit Boston in 1773. He had run away from home in 1723. He had visited in 1733, in 1743, in 1753, and in 1763. "Aunt Mecom and all Friends are well," Jonathan Williams Jr. wrote to Franklin at the end of 1773, but "the Year 73 is now so near at hand without the prospect of seeing You, that we begin to fear you will break through your Intention of visiting every ten Years."[15]

Franklin could not come. Instead, he was busy trying to smuggle out of London letters written by Thomas Hutchinson. Francis Bernard, the royally appointed, feckless, and much despised governor of Massachusetts, had left the colonies in 1769. There had been some small speculation that Franklin might replace Bernard. Jonathan Williams Sr. wrote his uncle, "We Want a Governor and all most every Body Wishes Doctor Franklin

might Come."[16] But with Bernard gone, it was Hutchinson who was left
to handle the deepening crisis. The Massachusetts General Assembly, pro-
testing the military occupation, had refused to meet at the Town House
in Boston and instead met in Cambridge, at Harvard. In November 1772,
Hutchinson prorogued the assembly. In defiance, the Boston Town Meeting appointed an entirely extralegal twenty-one-member Committee of
Correspondence—replacing legislators with letter writers.

Sometime that fall, in London, a member of Parliament, probably
Thomas Pownall, a former governor of Massachusetts, showed Franklin—in confidence—a series of letters written to and from Thomas
Hutchinson and other officials between 1768 and 1771. Read very selec-
tively and, frankly, unfairly, Hutchinson's letters find him suggesting that
the colonists enjoyed too much liberty. Pownall showed Franklin the correspondence in order to prove to him that the colonists ought not to blame
Parliament for having sent an army to Boston but should instead blame
Hutchinson. Franklin would not let those letters alone.

On December 2, 1772, Franklin made a fateful decision. He sent the
letters to Thomas Cushing, writing to him:

> I think it fit to acquaint you that there has lately fallen into my Hands
> Part of a Correspondence, that I have reason to believe laid the Foun-
> dation of most if not all our present Grievances. I am not at liberty to
> tell thro' what Channel I receiv'd it; and I have engag'd that it shall not
> be printed, nor any Copies taken of the whole or any part of it; but I
> am allow'd and desired to let it be seen by some Men of Worth in the
> Province for their Satisfaction only. In confidence of your preserving
> inviolably my Engagement, I send you enclos'd the original Letters,
> to obviate every Pretence of Unfairness in Copying, Interpolation or
> Omission.

Franklin offered more caveats about how the letters were to be handled:

> I therefore wish I was at Liberty to make the Letters publick; but as
> I am not, I can only allow them to be seen by yourself, by the other
> Gentlemen of the Committee of Correspondence, by Messrs. Bowdoin,
> and Pitts, of the Council, and Drs. Chauncey, Cooper and Winthrop,

with a few such other Gentlemen as you may think it fit to show them to. After being some Months in your Possession, you are requested to return them to me.[17]

The letters reached Boston at the end of March 1773.[18]

They arrived along with rumors of a new tax. In 1770, Parliament had repealed the Townshend Acts—all but the tax on tea. That year, three hundred wealthy Boston women had signed a pledge to stop drinking tea.[19] But in the spring of 1773, Parliament passed the Tea Act to bail out the East India Company, which, with a surplus of tea and stiff competition from smugglers, was facing bankruptcy. By eliminating duties on tea in England and lowering the import tax to just three pence, the Tea Act actually reduced the price of tea in the colonies, but it offended by its assertion of Parliament's right to tax the colonies, and by its protection of a politically connected corporate monopoly. It wasn't the price; it was the principle.

Franklin counseled patience, writing, in a letter to Cushing on March 9, "I must hope that great Care will be taken to keep our People quiet, since nothing is more wish'd for by our Enemies, than that by Insurrections we should give a good Pretence for increasing the Military among us, and putting us under more severe Restraints."[20] But he knew that the letters he was sending would only fan flames.

Hunched over his desk, Franklin wrote, that same day, a letter to his sister. A printer named Samuel Hall who had married a daughter of James Franklin's owed Benjamin Franklin more than £100. Franklin, who rarely pursued debtors, had engaged John Adams to recover the debt. Adams had been successful, and Franklin, having received the payment in February, had ordered that it be given to Jane.[21] It was the most money she had ever had at once. She used it to make another go at running a millinery shop out of her house. Her brother sent her another trunk full of materials.[22] And he gave her advice: "If you possibly can, try to increase your Capital, by adding the Profits."[23]

Once word of the Tea Act reached Boston, Cushing abandoned Franklin's stipulations about keeping the Hutchinson letters private. On June 2, Samuel Adams read the letters aloud in the General Assembly. And then, on June 15, Benjamin Edes printed them in the *Boston Gazette*.[24] Calls came for Hutchinson's impeachment.

Jane sent her brother six letters in 1773; not one survives.[25] Franklin

ON SMUGGLING · 163

may well have destroyed them. His correspondence that year was especially dangerous. If his sister was more candid than she ought to have been, in describing events in Boston—and especially if she mentioned the Hutchinson affair, about which she might have known more than he wished—those letters, in the wrong hands, would have been damaging. In the letters Franklin exchanged with Jonathan Williams Sr. during those months, they spoke of the Boston poet Phillis Wheatley, a slave, who had traveled to London. Williams recommended that Franklin meet her. ("Upon your Recommendation I went to see the black Poetess and offer'd her any Services I could do her," Franklin wrote Williams.)[26] Whether Jane ever met Phillis Wheatley, or ever wrote to her brother about her, is unknown, since her letters from this year are all lost. What she wrote can only be deduced from his replies.

She urged him to make peace.

"I thank you for your good Wishes that I may be a means of restoring Harmony between the two Countries," he returned. "It would make me very happy to see it, whoever was the Instrument." He sent her his satire, "Rules for Reducing a Great Empire to a Small One," in which, echoing their grandfather Folger, he said, "I have held up a Looking-Glass in which some Ministers may see their ugly Faces, & the Nation its Injustice." Parliament was bullying the colonies, and the only way to deal with bullying was to hold your ground. "I grew tir'd of Meekness when I saw it without Effect," he wrote.[27] He gave her this piece of advice: *If you make yourself a Sheep, the Wolves will eat you.*[28]

In October, a ship carrying Jane's millinery supplies arrived from London. Jonathan Williams Sr., writing to Franklin to acknowledge the arrival of the goods, informed him that, under the circumstances, Jane, wisely, had decided to buy nothing else from London.[29] In November and December, three more ships, the *Beaver,* the *Eleanor,* and the *Dartmouth,* arrived from England, carrying tea (a fourth ship ran aground off Cape Cod). By law, they had twenty days to unload their cargo. The *Dartmouth*'s twenty days were set to expire at midnight on December 16. At ten o'clock that morning, seven thousand people showed up at the Old South Meeting House to decide what to do. A courier was sent to Hutchinson, asking him to let the ships return to England without unloading the tea. Hutchinson refused. Three groups of men, about fifty altogether, then headed to three meeting places, the Green Dragon, Edes's print shop, and a carpenter's house, where they disguised themselves as Mohawks, smearing their faces with soot. Then they marched to Griffin's Wharf, boarded the three ships, and dumped into the sea more than three hundred chests of tea.[30]

For the trouble in which he found himself, Hutchinson blamed Franklin. Hutchinson had surreptitiously obtained a copy of a letter Franklin had written to Cushing in July. In it, Franklin had urged the colonial assemblies "to engage firmly with each other that they will never grant aids to the Crown in any General War till those Rights are recogniz'd by the King and both Houses of Parliament; communicating at the same time to the Crown this their Resolution. Such a Step I imagine will bring the Dispute to a Crisis; and whether our Demands are immediately comply'd with, or compulsory Means are thought of to make us Rescind them, our Ends will finally be obtain'd."[31] This letter was more damning than any piece of Hutchinson correspondence that Franklin had sent to Cushing.

Hutchinson sent Franklin's letter to Lord Dartmouth, the colonial secretary, who judged it an act of treason. Dartmouth ordered Thomas Gage, commander of the British Army in America, who was stationed in Boston, to obtain the original, which Gage was unable to do (Cushing had likely burned it). On December 25, only after speculation about who had sent Hutchinson's letters to Boston had led to a duel, Franklin finally admitted that it was he. In January 1774, word of the dumping of the tea reached England. Franklin was denounced before the Privy Council as a thief, a villain, and a traitor. He was dismissed from his royally appointed position as deputy postmaster general of North America. He was upbraided, and disgraced.

"You will hear before this comes to hand, that I am depriv'd of my Office," he wrote his sister. "Don't let this give you any Uneasiness. You and I have almost finished the Journey of Life; we are now but a little way from home, and have enough in our Pockets to pay the Post Chaises."[32]

Remaining in London in his capacity as agent of four colonial assemblies, Franklin lobbied against a series of measures proposed in response to the dumping of the tea—to no avail. By March, Parliament had passed the first of what the colonists called the Intolerable Acts. The Boston Port Act closed the port of the city of Boston. The Massachusetts Government Act greatly constrained the activities of town meetings.

Hutchinson sailed for England in May, never to return.[33] He had become a liability to the Crown. Gage was appointed in his place. The port of Boston was closed on June 1; the only ships to arrive in Boston were those carrying still more British soldiers.

Jane wrote to her brother, frantic about rumors that he had abandoned the colonial cause, to which she had herself become more and more persuaded and devoted. He sent reassurance. "The Report you mention that I offer'd to desert my Constituents, and banish myself if I might continue in Place, is an infamous Falshood, as you supposed." He had not traded his integrity for a post. "For God knows my Heart, I would not accept the best Office the King has to bestow, while such Tyrannic Measures are taking against my Country." And then he closed: "All this to yourself. To the World such Declarations might seem incredible, and a meer puffing of ones own Character: therefore, my dear Sister, show this to no body: I write it meerly for your Satisfaction; and that you may not be disturb'd by such Idle Reports."[34]

Franklin was very often disingenuous. But he does seem to have been genuinely concerned that his sister thought ill of him. He had been lashed by the Privy Council. He had been assaulted in the press, called a traitor on two continents. When he didn't hear from her, he wrote her again: "I wish to know how you fare in the present Distress of our dear Country. I am apprehensive that the Letters between us, tho' very innocent ones, are intercepted. They might restore me yours at least, after reading them; especially as I never complain of broken patch'd-up Seals, (of late very common) because I know not whom to fix the Fact on." He wanted to be sure she knew that what was being reported in newspapers about his having accepted a political appointment was false. "I am anxious to preserve your good Opinion, and as I know your Sentiments, and that you must be much afflicted your self, and even despise me, if you thought me capable of accepting any Office from this Government while it is acting with so much Hostility towards my native Country, I cannot miss this first Opportunity of assuring you that there is not the least Foundation for such Report."[35]

She had not lost her faith in him. But life in Boston was dreadful, she wrote him, "the towns being so full of Proflegate soulders and many such officers there is hardly four and twenty hours Pases without some fray amongst them." Her daughter Jenny had married Peter Collas, without her mother's consent; luckily, they had moved to the countryside.[36] "She has not curidge to stay in town," Jane wrote. The Quartering Act meant that soldiers could occupy any house or shop they liked. Drunken soldiers went on rampages. People began stockpiling weapons in the countryside. In September, after Gage seized ammunition stored in Charlestown and Cambridge, the legislature established the Committee of Safety; in October, it created special units of "minutemen," who could be ready to fight at a moment's notice.

In November, Jane put on her spectacles and wrote a letter to her brother about the British soldiers in the city.

> Won can walk but a litle way in the street without hearing there Profane language, we were much surprised the other day upon hearing a Tumult in the street & looking out saw a soulder al Bloody damning His Eyes but He would kill Every Inhabatant He mett & Pressing into a shop oposite us with His Bayonet drawn bursting throw the Glas Dore & the man of the house pushing Him out & he to do what mischeif He could Dashing the chiney & Earthen were which stood on the window threw the sashes with the most terrable Imprecations, the case it seems was He Percved they sould liquer & went into the House Demanding some but being refused He went into the closet and took out a gon & said His comanding officer tould Him he might take any thing out of any house He had a mind to upon which the batle Ensued & the man & His servant were boath very much wounded there were to of them soulders but I saw but won, a Gaurd with an officer came & careyed Him away & I have heard nothing of Him since but this has made me more Timerous about what may be before winter is out.

"Damn your eyes!" a bloody soldier cried, with bayonet drawn, as he attacked a shopkeeper just across the street from Jane's house. "I will kill every inhabitant I meet!" Jane wrote Franklin that she sought consolation where she had always sought it: "My only comfort is God Reigns."[37]

The pace of the crisis quickened. In August 1774, John and Samuel Adams set off, by carriage, for Philadelphia, for the first meeting of the Continental Congress. "The distinction between Virginians, Pennsylvanians, New Yorkers, and New Englanders, are no more," Patrick Henry declared in Philadelphia. "I am not a Virginian, but an American."[38] Jane had her own ideas about what was going on. "The Uniteing of the Colonies" she considered nothing less than "a token of Gods Design to deliver us out of all our trobles."[39]

In London, Patience Wright, acting as an American spy, began writing reports to the Continental Congress. She heard a great deal of loose talk at her waxworks, while taking the likenesses of the king's ministers. She often went to Parliament and sat in the gallery, watching the debates. She had much to report. She smuggled her letters out of England, tucked inside heads made of wax.[40] Everything augured war.

CHAPTER XXVI

Exodus

Rumors chased rumors. In November 1774, Jane heard that her nephew William Franklin, the royally appointed governor of New Jersey, continued to support Parliament, even after its ministers had accused his father of treason. She probably heard this news from her son Benjamin, who, in August 1774, had abandoned printing and was making and selling the family soap in Burlington.[1]

She could not, would not, believe it. She wrote to her brother. "I think it is Presumeing on yr Patience but I must Just mention the Hored lie tould & Publishd hear about yr son." At first she thought "it might be trew," until "a litle consideration convinced me it was Imposable."[2]

But it was true. "You who are a thorough Courtier, see every thing with Government Eyes," Benjamin Franklin raged at his son.[3] There were more sources of estrangement between them than politics. Deborah Franklin suffered a stroke, her second, on December 14, 1774. Five days later, she was dead. Richard Bache sent an express to New Jersey, so that William might ride to Philadelphia in time to attend the funeral. Writing to his father to tell him the news, William made no attempt to hide his bitterness about his father's conduct. Deborah's death had long been expected, as her husband had known very well, and she had hoped to see him once more before she died. "I think her Disappointment in that respect preyed a good deal on her Spirits," he told his father.[4] Not to mention, if Franklin hadn't stayed so long in England, William argued, he might have attended the Continental Congress, where he might have done some good in healing the breach between England and America: "Had you been there you would have framed some Plan for an Accommodation of our Differences."[5]

William took a side, against his father, and stuck with it. In January 1775, he convened the New Jersey General Assembly and delivered a speech in which he urged legislators to break with the Continental Congress and instead seek reconciliation by submitting a petition to the king. "You have now pointed out to you, Gentlemen, two Roads," he said. "One evidently leading to Peace, Happiness, and a Restoration of the publick Tranquility—the other inevitably conducting you to Anarchy, Misery, and all the Horrors of Civil War."[6]

Benjamin Franklin left England on March 21, 1775, bringing with him his young grandson, Temple Franklin.[7] On April 6, Patience Wright smuggled a letter out of London. "Meny thousand fire arms sent out of the tower and shipt on bord the transports," she warned. "Meny hundrd Cags of flints marked BOSTON on Each Cagg with all Implements of WARR."[8] On April 14, General Gage, in Boston, received orders from London to arrest the leaders of the rebellion, the men who met at the Green Dragon Tavern.[9] On April 18, Joseph Warren, hearing that Gage planned to march to Lexington and Concord to seize the colonists' stores of arms, gave Paul Revere and William Dawes orders to set off to sound the alarm.[10] At daybreak, some seven hundred redcoats reached Lexington, where they found about seventy armed minutemen waiting for them. The British fired.[11]

Word of the battle reached Boston within hours. Gage had "sent out a party to creep out in the night & Slauter our Dear Brethern for Endevering to defend our own Property," Jane reported to her brother. "The distress it has ocationed is Past my discription," she wrote. "The Horror the Town was in when the Batle Aprochd within Hearing Expecting they would Proceed quite in to town, the comotion the Town was in after the batle ceasd by the Parties coming in bringing in there wounded men causd such an Agetation of minde I believe none had much sleep, since which we could have no quiet." She expected that the colonial militia would march into town and continue the battle in Boston: "We under stood our Bretheren without were determined to Disposes the Town of the Regelors." Instead, the militia surrounded the city. Occupied by the British Army, Boston became a city under siege. Jane wrote, "The Generol shuting up the town not Leting any Pass out but throw such Grate Dificulties as were allmost insoportable."[12]

Nevertheless, thousands fled. "The unhappy situation of this town, which, by the late cruel and oppressive measures gone into by the British Parliament, is now almost depopulated," the Reverend Andrew Eliot wrote. His wife and eight of his children fled; he stayed to preach to those left behind.[13] Of a population of fifteen thousand there were, in a matter of days, only three thousand people left in the city. Most of those who remained behind were loyalists, seeking the protection of the British Army. Others were simply unable to escape. They had to watch while the soldiers ransacked the city. Jonathan Williams Sr. wrote to Franklin that Boston "is now become a den of theaves and robers."[14] When wood grew scarce, British regulars gutted the Old South Meeting House, burned the pews and pulpit, and used the floor to exercise their horses. A party of soldiers broke into Edes's print shop, on Queen Street; failing to find him, they seized his son instead. Eighteen-year-old Peter Edes spent months as a prisoner of war. He watched from the window of his cell while a fellow captive, a Boston painter, was dragged to the yard and beaten until, broken, he finally called out, "God bless the King."[15]

Jane was among those who managed to escape. "I had got Pact up what I Expected to have liberty to carey out intending to seek my fourtune with hundred others not knowing whither," she wrote to her brother. She had all of her shop goods, her millinery supplies. She couldn't afford to lose them. Then there were her books and papers. She couldn't leave them behind. She knew, too, that the soldiers were imposing limits on what could be brought out of the city. With the harbor blockaded, the British soldiers occupying the besieged city would have to live off what they could raid from abandoned homes; they didn't want people leaving with much of use. Jane turned smuggler. "I Brought out what I could Pack up in trunks & chists & I so contrived to Pack em in our wereing Aparil Lining & Beding that they Pasd Examination, without discovery." (Franklin had once sent her a pamphlet he had written, condemning smuggling. So she joked, telling him about her escape, "This was not an unlawfull smuggling which you would have reproved for they were not owed for, nor any won cheated of Duties.") "The whol of my Houshold furniture," she told him, "Except a few small maters I put into my trunk I left behind." She secured the house "with locks & bars but those who value not to Deprive us of our lives will find a way to brake throw."[16]

She fled, first, to Cambridge. "My Poor litle little Delicat nabour Mrs Royall & Famely came out with me not knowing where she should find a Place," she related. Abigail Royall, an elderly widow, wasn't sturdy enough to travel far. "I left them at Cambridg in a most shocking Disagreable

Place," Jane reported, "but since hear she is gone to wooster." Jane's daughter, Jane Mecom Collas, living in Roxbury, was "obliged to fly in to the woods."[17] Jonathan Williams Sr. had been out of town, to Grace's distress. "His Poor wife slaved her self almost to Death to Pack up & Secure what She could & sent away her two Daughters Intending to go to Him & behold in comes he in to town the day before I came out Imagining (as I was told for I did not see him) that was the saifest Place." She feared he was dead. "I can hear nothing of Him since." (He was not. He was in Worcester.) Jane's "Daughter foot"—Neddy's widow, Ruth, who had married a cabinetmaker named Thomas Foot—had managed to escape but was "in a bad stat of helth," and had left all her belongings in Boston. Her son John's widow, Catherine Oakey Mecom, had married a British officer named Thomas Turner. Jane "left them in Boston" and "how it has faired with them can not hear tho I wish them saif for He realy appeared a Good sort of man." The civil war had divided even her own family: "O how horrable is our situation that Relations seek the Destruction of Each other."[18]

Worst of all, she thought, was the fate of her grandson Josiah Flagg, fourteen. Jane had never wanted Josiah and his sister Jenny to leave her house in the first place. It was their father, William Flagg, who had taken them from her when he remarried and who would not allow them to return to live with her. William Flagg's "storey is two long & two full of shocking sircumstances to troble you with," Jane wrote her brother, and I "shall only tell you that in the winter He was taken in a fitt which terminated in Distraction & confined Him some time." He then "sent out His wife & children Intending to follow them but was soon After taken in the same maner as in winter & Died in a few days." He had sent out of the city his second wife and her children, keeping Jane's grandchildren Josiah and Jenny behind. Jane was frantic. "Por Flagg tho He has used me very Ill I Deplore His Fate the more as there is two of my Daughters Children left I know not how they will be Provided for." Eventually Jenny Flagg—"an Grand Daughter who I could not leve if I had it would have been her Death"—made her way to her grandmother, somehow, but Jane could not find Josiah, hard as she tried.[19] She was forced to leave without him.

From Cambridge, Jane and her granddaughter made their way, on roads filled with fugitives, to Providence. William Franklin had sent his aunt an invitation to come stay with him in New Jersey, but she never received his letter. "Cousen Coffen has Invited me to nantuckett," she wrote her brother. "I don't know if it would be [prudent] for me to go now."[20] She went, instead, to Warwick, Rhode Island.

She fled from her home at the age of sixty-three, riding a cart through a city in turmoil, stowing her goods between sheets. Her house she left locked. She was the last of the Franklins of Boston. In a trunk, she carried her brother's letters, and her Book of Ages.

PART FOUR

History

———————

1775–1793

CHAPTER XXVII

Saif Back

Sailing across the ocean with his grandson Temple, Benjamin Franklin wrote, in the form of a letter to William, a twenty-thousand-word history of "the Misunderstandings between Great Britain and America."[1] He reached Philadelphia on May 5, 1775. The next day, he was elected by a unanimous vote of the Pennsylvania Provincial Assembly to the Second Continental Congress.

"God be Praised for bring you saif back to America," Jane wrote to her brother on May 14. Then she added a postscript: "Dear Brother I am tould you will be joynd to the Congress & that they will Remove to conetecut will you Premit me to come & see you there Mrs Green says she will go with me." Jane had found refuge in Warwick, in the home of her friend Catharine Ray Greene. They were as close as family. ("My Dear Mama," Caty called Jane. "The Epethet of Daughter which you Seem to like to use cannot be Disagreable to me," Jane answered.)[2] Caty was forty-four years old and running a house filled with five children, the oldest fifteen, the youngest not yet one. She opened her doors to sixteen refugees.[3] At the bottom of Jane's letter to Franklin, Caty added a note of her own. "When Shall We See you here?" she asked. "Do let it be as Soon as the Congress is adjournd or dont know but your good Sister and Self Shall mount our old Naggs and Come and See you."[4]

The rumor that Congress would remove to Connecticut turned out to be false. And Franklin didn't receive Jane's letter for weeks. Instead, he learned that she had escaped the siege of Boston from John Adams, who'd arrived in Philadelphia from Massachusetts. "I have just now heard by Mr. Adams that you are come out of Boston, and are at Warwick in Rhode-illand," he wrote her on May 26, in a letter that went first to Cambridge, where, Harvard students having been sent home, some seven hundred soldiers were quartered in the college. From Cambridge, the letter was sent to Newport, where it sat for three weeks before it was forwarded to Warwick. Jane didn't receive it until July 14.[5]

"I found my Family well," he told her, "but have not found the Repose I wish'd for."[6] Neither had she.

"Send me what News you can that is true," he urged her.[7]

"I am so much at a lose to know whether the News I hear be trew or no that prehaps I had beter leve it to other hands," she wrote back.[8]

He was worried. "I wish to hear from you," he pressed, "and to know how you have left your Affairs [in] Boston; and whether it will be inconvenient for you to come hither, or you wish rather that I should come to see you, if the Business I am engag'd in will permit."[9]

He was engaged in a great deal of business. Congress having no power to tax, Franklin argued that waging the war demanded that Congress print paper money—"Continental dollars"—to be issued by the "United Colonies." He was charged with their design. These bills would have no kings or queens. Instead, Franklin chose proverbs, illustrated by pictures. For the two-dollar bill, he used a picture of a hand threshing grain, with the motto *Tribulatio Ditat:* "tribulation enriches."[10]

That money was meant to help Congress raise an army. On June 10, John Adams proposed that the soldiers arrayed outside Boston be considered the Continental Army. Among them was Jane's thirty-two-year-old son Josiah, who enlisted in Captain Charles Furbush's company of Colonel Ebenezer Bridge's regiment. On June 15, Adams nominated a Virginian named George Washington to serve as general of the new army. Washington accepted the next day and began preparing to ride to Cambridge.

On June 17, Franklin wrote his sister another letter. He had, at last, received her letter of May 14, in which she had described her flight from the city. "I sympathise most sincerely with you and the People of my native Town and Country," he wrote. "Your Account of the Distresses attending their Removal affects me greatly." He had left his parents behind. He had run away from an apprenticeship with his brother. He had left his sister behind. He had left his wife behind, even on her deathbed. He had grown estranged from his son. He was determined not to abandon his sister.

"I wish you to be other wise provided for as soon as possible," he told her, "and I wish for the Pleasure of your Company, but I know not how long we may be allowed to continue in Quiet here if I stay here, nor how soon I may be ordered from hence; nor how convenient or inconvenient it may be for you to come hither." And, after all, the field of battle might soon come to Philadelphia. He wondered whether, rather than come to him, she ought to accept William's offer to stay with him at the governor's mansion in New Jersey. "Perhaps that may be a Retreat less liable to Disturbance than this: God only knows, but you must judge."[11] It was very hard to say where anyone would be safe. And there was Jane's age to consider. To Catharine Ray Greene, Franklin wrote a letter warning her not to try riding with Jane to Philadelphia. "It is much too long a journey for her who is no good Horsewoman."[12]

The day Franklin wrote those letters, shots were fired in what came to be called the Battle of Bunker Hill. Charlestown was burned to the ground. Two hundred and twenty-six British soldiers died, including Thomas Turner, the husband of Catherine Oakey Mecom, the widow of Jane's son John. One hundred and forty colonists were killed, including Josiah Mecom's captain, Charles Furbush, and at least one other soldier from Mecom's company. Four more men from Mecom's company were wounded, possibly including Mecom himself.[13] He died not long afterward.[14] He may have died of wounds; he may have succumbed to disease.[15] Some sixty thousand Americans died during the war. Most of them were soldiers. Only about forty-five hundred died in battle. The rest died of cold or accident or, above all, disease, most falling prey to smallpox, dysentery, or typhus.[16] Jane likely never found out how Josiah met his end.[17] She reckoned her losses. "As to Sons I have nothing but misery in those that are left," she wrote, thinking about Peter and Benjamin. "Boath of them Distracted."[18]

On July 3, George Washington reached Cambridge and took command of the Continental Army on the Cambridge Common. All summer, anyone who saw Franklin's sister sent him word of her. In June, Jonathan Williams Sr. visited her in Rhode Island and wrote to Franklin that she was well, "and happy for every one is so that thinks themselves so."[19] Jane worried about the Greenes; she was, she felt, "an Incumbrance to this good Famely."[20] Franklin shared her worry. Caty reassured him, "You are fear full She will be trouble Some but be assrd that her Company Richly Pays as She goes along and we are Very happy together and Shall not Consent to Spare her to any body."[21]

In Philadelphia, the matter of the post needed attention. The Pennsylvania printer William Goddard (who had once employed Jane's son Benjamin) had proposed a "Constitutional post," arguing that the royal post amounted to taxation without representation. The question had been raised but then tabled. Committees of Correspondence had already established an alternative postal network. Franklin headed the effort to launch a new, American post. Its inauguration, on July 26, amounted to a declaration of American sovereignty.[22]

Congress adjourned on the morning of August 2. That afternoon, Franklin wrote to Jane: "I think you had best come hither as soon as the Heats are over, i.e. sometime in September, but more of this in my next."[23] Congress resumed on September 13. Franklin, appointed to a committee charged with conferring with Washington in Cambridge, left Philadelphia on October 4. On October 16, he wrote to Jane from Washington's headquarters in Cambridge.

My dear dear sister

I arrived here last Night with two other Delegates of the Congress. I suppose we may stay here about a Week. In order to take you home with me, I purpose quitting their Company, purchasing a Carriage and Horses, and calling for you at good Mrs. Greene's. But let me hear from you in the mean time, and acquaint me with any thing you would have me do or get towards the Convenience of our Journey. My Love to that hospitable Family, whom I hope soon to have the Pleasure of seeing. I am ever Your affectionate Brother

B Franklin[24]

The next week, he rode to Warwick.

Jane and her brother hadn't seen one another for eleven years. Reunited, they set out for Philadelphia.

"My seat was Exeding Easey & Jurney very Pleasant," Jane wrote Caty. "My Dear Brothers conversation was more than an Equivelent to all the fine wether Emaginable."

They stopped to see William Franklin in New Jersey. The governor's mansion, Jane wrote Caty, "was very magnificient."[25] She said no more.

After his father and aunt departed, William Franklin convened the assembly and instructed the legislature to form a committee to draft a petition to the king "to express the great Desire this House hath to a Restoration of Peace and Harmony with the parent State." And then he told the assemblymen that he feared for his life.[26]

By the end of October, Jane and her brother reached Philadelphia, where, in his house, they lived under the same roof for the first time since they were children.

CHAPTER XXVIII

A Survey of Ages

The cause of America is in a great measure the cause of all mankind" declared a pamphlet printed in Philadelphia in January 1776.[1] It was called *Common Sense,* and almost no one knew who wrote it. "Some make Dr. Franklin the Author," a friend wrote to John Adams. "I think I see strong marks of your pen in it," wrote another. "I could not have written any Thing in so manly and striking a style," Adams admitted. But he soon found out the author: "His Name is Paine."[2]

Thomas Paine, born in England, was the son of a tradesman who sewed the bones of whales into stays for ladies' corsets. At twelve, he left school to serve as his father's apprentice. He ran away to sea. He came back, opened a shop, taught school, collected taxes, married and lost a wife and, in 1771, married again. Three years later, when he was thirty-seven, he was fired from a post with the excise office and everything he owned was sold at auction to pay off his debts (exactly what had happened to Benjamin Mecom in 1770, at about the same age). Ruined, Paine fled to America. He landed in Philadelphia in 1774 so sick he had to be carried off the ship. What saved his life was a letter found in his pocket: "The bearer Mr Thomas Pain is very well recommended to me as an ingenious worthy young man." It was signed "B. Franklin."[3]

Paine had met Franklin in London. In Philadelphia, Franklin's name gained Paine a position as editor of the *Pennsylvania Magazine.* In the summer of 1775, Paine's essay "An Occasional Letter on the Female Sex" had appeared in the magazine. "If we take a survey of ages and of countries, we shall find that women, almost—without exception—at all times and in all places, adored and oppressed," Paine wrote. "Man with regard to them, in all climates, and in all ages, has been either an insensible husband or an oppressor."[4] More than one revolution had begun.

That fall, while Paine was writing *Common Sense,* Jane was living in Philadelphia, in Franklin's house. "I offer nothing more than simple facts, plain arguments, and common sense," Paine wrote.[5] There's a reason people thought Franklin might have written *Common Sense.* Like Franklin, Paine wrote for everyone—even for the tradesmen's daughters. "As it is my design to make those that can scarcely read understand," Paine explained, "I shall therefore avoid every literary ornament and put it in language as plain as the alphabet."[6] He wrote for readers as plain as Jane.

She likely read *Common Sense.* Everyone read it. Under its influence, the tide of public opinion began to change. So did the tide of the war. The British Army and the Continental Army had been in a stalemate for months but in November 1775, Washington sent Henry Knox, who before the war had been a bookseller in Boston, to bring to Massachusetts artillery captured from the British at Ticonderoga. In February 1776, Knox reached New England with sixty tons of artillery, and the Continentals fortified Dorchester Heights. On March 2, they began shelling the city. Two months after *Common Sense* was published, the Continental Army blasted the British out of Boston and ended the siege. Before the British left, they carried away what they could and destroyed what they couldn't. They broke into Jane's house and plundered its contents.[7] On March 17, the British evacuated. Eleven thousand people, more than nine thousand of them soldiers, sailed out of Boston Harbor. The city was in ruins. Jane wondered whether she might go home. She decided against it. "I am afraid Boston is not sufficiently fortified yet," she wrote Caty that spring.[8]

Between *Common Sense* and the liberation of Boston, the time seemed right, to a great many people, to declare independence from Britain. In March, Abigail Adams wrote a letter to her husband. "I long to hear that you have declared an independency," she began. She had another hope:

And, by the way, in the new code of laws which I suppose it will be necessary for you to make, I desire you would remember the ladies and be more generous and favorable to them than your ancestors. Do not put such unlimited power into the hands of the husbands. Remember, all men would be tyrants if they could. If particular care and attention is not paid to the ladies, we are determined to foment a rebellion, and will not hold ourselves bound by any laws in which we have no voice or representation.[9]

Adams wrote back in April. "As to your extraordinary code of laws, I cannot but laugh," he returned. "We have been told that our struggle has loosened the bonds of government everywhere; that children and apprentices were disobedient; that schools and colleges were grown turbulent; that Indians slighted their guardians, and negroes grew insolent to their masters. But your letter was the first intimation that another tribe, more numerous and powerful than all the rest, were grown discontented." He was hardly more than vaguely amused. "Depend upon it, we know better than to repeal our masculine systems."[10]

One of the obstacles to declaring independence was William Franklin, who had forbidden Congress's New Jersey delegation to support it. On June 7, Richard Henry Lee of Virginia introduced a resolution "that these United Colonies are, and of right ought to be, free and independent States, that they are absolved from all allegiance to the British Crown, and that all political connection between them and the State of Great Britain is, and ought to be, totally dissolved." On June 11, John Adams, Thomas Jefferson, Benjamin Franklin, Robert Livingston, and Roger Sherman were chosen to serve on a committee—the Committee of Five—charged with drafting a declaration of independence. On June 14, New Jersey's Provincial Congress—an extralegal body, formed as an alternative to the colonial assembly—urged members of the New Jersey General Assembly to boycott a meeting called by William Franklin. The next day, New Jersey's Provincial Congress declared William Franklin "an enemy to the liberties of this country" and called for his arrest. The Continental Congress voted to order his arrest, too: Benjamin Franklin was absent that day. He'd stayed home with his sister.

Samuel Adams rode from Philadelphia to Burlington to inform the Provincial Congress of the vote. William Franklin was arrested on June 17. With New Jersey's royally appointed and obdurate governor out of the way, the path to independence was cleared. The New Jersey Provincial Congress elected a new set of delegates to the Continental Congress and charged them with supporting independence.

Jefferson agreed to draft the declaration. On the morning of June 21, he sent Franklin a draft, with a note: "Will Doctr. Franklin be so good as to peruse it and suggest such alterations as his more enlarged view of the subject will dictate?"[11]

Jefferson's draft begins, "When in the course of human Events, it becomes necessary for one People to dissolve the Political Bands which have connected them with another, and to assume among the Powers of the Earth, the separate and equal Station to which the Laws of Nature and of Nature's God entitle them, a decent Respect to the Opinions of Mankind requires that they should declare the causes which impel them to the Separation." The Declaration of Independence, as Adams always insisted, contained no new ideas. But this was its strength, not its weakness. Jefferson stated political truths derived from centuries of philosophical speculation.

"We hold these truths to be sacred and undeniable, that all men are created equal, and endowed with certain inalienable rights, and that among these are life, liberty, and the pursuit of happiness," Jefferson wrote. A plowman was no less a man than a king.

Adams and Franklin undertook an initial set of revisions. Adams's revisions did not include those requested by his wife. Franklin's revisions were slight but crucial. He struck out "sacred and undeniable" and wrote, instead, "self-evident."[12]

Franklin signed the declaration on July 4. Two weeks later, he received a letter from Burlington, written on behalf of Benjamin Mecom's wife, who was by now so terrified of her husband that she sought relief from Franklin himself, two citizens of Burlington sending him this plea:

At the Request of Mrs. Mecum (who has been an Inhabitant of this City for some time past and behav'd with Prudence and Industry) We take the Liberty to Inform you that her husband's Conduct is such, as to render her Scituation Disagreeable, and at times very Dangerous he being often Depriv'd of his Reason, and likely to become very Troublesome to the Inhabitants. If a place in the Hospital of Philada. can be Procur'd or any other way of Confineing which may be thought more Eligeable she begs your Assistance And that you wo'd be pleas'd to favor us with an Answer on the Subject of this Letter. From Sir Your most Obedient Humble Servants (in haste).[13]

Betsy Mecom wanted her husband locked up. In the 1750s, Franklin had helped found Pennsylvania Hospital, America's first hospital "for the relief of the sick poor of this province and for the reception and cure of lunaticks." Before the war, the hospital's directors had placed a cap on the number of lunatics admitted; by the end of the war, the proportion of lunatics among the patient population had risen from 31 to 56 percent. Pennsylvania Hospital became a madhouse, but only for lunatics whose families could afford to pay; the insane poor were turned away.[14]

Benjamin Mecom did not end up in Pennsylvania Hospital. Instead, Franklin arranged for him to be confined to a house in Burlington. One month after William Franklin was arrested, Benjamin Mecom was locked up, too, Franklin's son a traitor, Jane's a madman.[15]

William Franklin spent much of the war in solitary confinement, beginning in Burlington.[16] He would not renounce the Crown and refused to give his word that he would not try to escape. "No Office or Honour in the Power of the Crown to bestow, will ever influence me to forget or neglect the Duty I owe my Country," he insisted, "nor the most furious Rage of the most intemperate Zealots induce me to swerve from the Duty I owe His Majesty." He was thought to be so dangerous that, for years, he was denied the use of pen, ink, and paper.[17]

CHAPTER XXIX

A Vagrant

On October 27, 1776, Benjamin Franklin left Philadelphia to sail to France, seeking an alliance.[1] He brought with him two grandsons: Temple Franklin and Benjamin Franklin Bache.

Franklin was seventy years old; Jane was sixty-four. He was tired, and suffering from gout. "The Publick having as it were eaten my Flesh," he wrote to her, it "seem'd now resolv'd to pick my Bones."[2]

The war consumed Jane differently. She spent years wandering. "I am Grown such a Vagrant," she wrote.[3]

In Philadelphia, she tried to find her scattered family.[4] At first, she remained in Franklin's house, with Sally Franklin Bache and her family. She adored Sally's children, including little three-and-a-half-year-old William Bache. "Will as Harty & as lovely as ever," Jane wrote her brother, and "Says He wants to go to france to grandpapa & He must send a Boat for Him." But in the fall of 1776, as the British Army approached the city, Jane and Sally and the children fled Philadelphia. "On hearing the Enemy were advanting to wards us," Jane wrote Franklin, "we thought it nesesary to Retire to this place where we hope we are saif & are very comfortable."[5]

At Christmastime, Benjamin Mecom escaped the house in Burlington where he had been confined, "in His deplorable state," as Jane described it.[6] It was hard to keep a madman locked up in the chaos of war. "Poor Benjamin strayed a way soon affter the batle at Trenton & has never been heard of since," Jane wrote to her brother, but this was scarcely more than a rumor; she had no idea what had happened to her son. She had also lost track of Betsy Mecom and the children: "I can hear nothing of His Famely tho I have wrot several times to Inquier."[7]

By August 1777, Jane was back in Philadelphia, writing to Franklin to tell him that William Franklin's wife had died: "I loved her gratly, Temple will mourn for her much."[8] She said nothing of William, who had been carried to Hartford, Connecticut, where he was a prisoner of war. Stopping en route, in Hackensack, he had been allowed to write a letter to his wife. That letter was intercepted and handed over to George Washington. It detailed the governor's plan to escape. In June 1777, when Elizabeth Franklin lay dying in New York, her husband pleaded for permission to go to her. That permission had been denied.[9]

During the war, which Jane believed to have taken the lives of two of her sons, she succumbed to despair. "Dear Lady what Continued Sceenes of Misfortunes She has waded throw," Caty wrote Franklin.[10] Meanwhile, her conviction grew that all that had befallen her family was due to something other than the workings of fortune, chance, or Providence. "I think there was hardly Ever so unfourtunate a Famely," she wrote her brother. But "I am not willing to think it is all oing to misconduct."[11]

While Jane was in Philadelphia, Caty, in Rhode Island, took care of Jane's granddaughter Jenny Flagg. She taught her the ways of the country. "We have had another Killing lately our Spring Piggs and Jenny saw the whole process of them," Caty wrote Jane. "She thinks She Shall not love Sasages any more nor has She eat Cheese Since She Saw what the Runnet is made of." ("Im a tell tale you Know," Caty added.)[12] She learned to spin wool. "Jenny is gone to spinning," Caty would write Jane.[13] (Caty spun, too, and knit stockings, which Jane did as well. Caty wrote her, "Will you nit Brother a Couple of Pr of Very Nice Cotton ones if I Send the yarn"?)[14] Jane worried about her granddaughter, but by June 1776, Caty had begun hinting that she ought not to, confiding, "I don't Know but Jenny will be Provided for after a While by Somebody else." That year, Jenny Flagg married Elihu Greene, a cousin of Caty's husband and a brother of Major General Nathanael Greene, one of Washington's most trusted officers and the man in command of the city of Boston after the British evacuation.[15] ("I am told the Young Lady is very handsome and cleaver," the general wrote to his brother. "God grant you much happiness.")[16]

Jane fled Philadelphia once again at the end of September 1777, just before the British attacked and occupied the city. By October, she had made her way to Rhode Island. "I pity my poor old Sister, to be so harass'd & driven about by the Enemy," Franklin wrote.[17] By the time Jane reached Warwick, at the end of 1777, Jenny Flagg Greene already had a baby. Jane found Elihu Greene a sober, sensible, and kindly man, "a very Good sort of man of plain Sense & sound Judgment whose conversation is a greable when he talks," as she wrote her brother. "My child makes Him a frugal Industrious & discreet wife & they are very happy."[18]

Instead of seeking out the Greenes in Rhode Island, Jane might have gone to live with her daughter Jane Mecom Collas in Massachusetts, but this she had no desire to do. Collas had no home of her own. She was married to an unpleasant man. She was sickly and needy; even worse, in her mother's mind, was her affectation. Jane wrote to her, "Your aspiring so much to gentility, without means to support it, must appear as ridiculous in every prudent person's eye as it does in mine, tho' it does not concern them to let you know it." Collas expected her mother to take care of her, and this Jane had no wish to do; she didn't enjoy her company one bit. "My natural temper is none of the patientest, and tho' by age and experience I am brought in some measure to check the appearance of resentment," Jane wrote to her daughter, "I don't know but I am as much inwardly galled as ever, therefore think it prudent to avoid such occasions as much as may be."[19]

Collas visited her mother in Rhode Island to press her to come and live with her, not least because she could not support herself. Her husband, a ship's captain, was unreliable and untrustworthy and, in war, unfortunate; he was taken prisoner three times. Jane began to relent. "If my Daughters husband shuld still meet with bad suckses I beleve I must try to go in to some busnes with her," Jane wrote her brother, wearily, in 1778. "She is a wery Inferm woman was sick all the first winter after you left us. She is very desirous of haveing me with her."[20] A bit desperately, Jane urged her daughter to keep herself constantly employed, urging, "I find I cannot live without it." She could do better than spin; she could stitch: "You can not only do plain work, but make bonnets, cloaks, caps and any thing."[21]

Jane was happy to knit a pair of socks for her brother, at Caty's request. And she was forever urging her daughter to make and sell bonnets. But she was not at all interested in a sewing scheme of Sally Franklin Bache's. During the war, Bache made clothes for soldiers through what became the Ladies Association of Philadelphia. But when she wrote to her aunt, requesting her help in raising money, Jane balked: "I have as you Sopose heard of yr Ladies Noble & generous Subscription for the Army and honour them for it & if a harty good will in me would Effect it we would follow your Example but I fear what my Infleuence would procure would be so Deminuitive we should be ashamed to offer it, I live in an obscure place have but Litle Acquaintance & those not very Rich."[22]

While Franklin was in France, he wrote his sister precious few letters, to her considerable consternation. For this, Jane blamed Peter Collas, who was supposed to have delivered some of her letters to her brother but who failed. "I do not wonder if you are discuridged from writing to me," Jane wrote Franklin, "for I Fear you have never recved any of my leters but the won you mention that was to have gone by my son Collas & I think I have sent seven, I all-ways sent them threw the hands of Mr Beach, or Mr Williams, but two of them happened to go by my son Collas & we sopose he is Taken again he has had nothing but misfourtun."[23]

Meanwhile, Jane worried about her mad son Peter. "My own Perticular Famely has been as was comon to me all my life mostly distressing," Jane reported to her brother, "but what now distresses me much now is that the woman that keeps my son peter in the Country Demands five Dolars a week for takeing care of him to commence Sepr 1777 or she would send him to boston." Peter Franklin Mecom had been locked up, in a house in the country, since 1763, with rent from the Douse house paying for his care. If he were to be sent to Boston, Jane would have no place to put him. As she told her brother, "I wrot to Mr Williams to git Him Put in to the Alms house there but he says there is no provision for such persons there I have sent a second Leter to Urge it but have had no Ansure." It must have been appalling to have to beg this favor of her brother, on the other side of the ocean, but she didn't know what else to do. "I write this with grat Reluctance but as you desiered me to Inform you of my circumstances as well as helth & situation it will not be confideing in you as Such a Friend as you have all ways been to me." Panicking, she promised him that she had taken what care she could of what money she had. "I bye as litle as posable I also wrot you that what mony I had a mounting to four hundrid Dolars I had put to Intrest only reserving for nesesary Use that I Live comfortable with my Grand children & have my Helth but no Income but what that litle mony Produces which however I should do very well with were it not for this dredfull affair of Peter which you see will take the most I have if I am forced to pay it & if Mr williams cant git Him in to the Alms House God only knows what I shall do with him." And then she added a postscript, having remembered about the house in Boston that her brother owned— the house where their sister Elizabeth Douse had lived for so many years. "Prehaps Mr williams may prevail with the overseers to take in poor Peter paying the Rent of the House you used to alow me which I know you will have no objection to I had forgot to mention that to Him but shall now."[24]

That arrangement may have been made, but if it was, it didn't last long. Peter Mecom died in the summer of 1778.[25] ("Now that aunts unhappy Son is no more that Truble is over," Jonathan Williams Sr. wrote to Franklin, with no small relief.[26] No one mourned Jane's lunatic son. To the contrary: "It was a great satisfaction to me to learn that my Dear Sister, was relieved from that continual Distress She had so long labour'd under," Franklin wrote Williams.[27]) Jane reported the death to her brother directly: "It has now pleasd God to take poor Peter & by that has Releved me from great distress for tho I still Retained for Him the Affection of a Parent, the grat Dificulties of the times, & the Extreem Demands of the woman where he boarded contineualy Incresing, & my Inability to satisfie them, & not being able to procure him any other Place of Residence by any means, keept me in Perpetual anxiety, & you know he has been no comfort to any won nor capable of Injoying any Himself for many years."[28]

In the same letter, she revealed to her brother the nature of her concern for the last of her children, Jane Mecom Collas, who had "given her self up to Dispare as she is apt to sink under troble." It wasn't only that her daughter was depressed; it was that depression seemed, to a mother who had watched her sons lose their minds, the beginning of something worse. She prayed, "May God preserve her from the faite of her Brothers."[29]

Jonathan Williams Sr. suggested to Franklin that Jane's poverty was a consequence not of her lack of industry but of family who depended on her, instead of working. "I belive aunt would have had Somthing before-hand" (that is, she would have had a profitable business, Williams told Franklin) "if all that was a burden to her were Out of the way" (that is, if these hangers-on had let her alone). "For as Long as Som people Can find assissdence they will not provid for themselves," Williams observed. As for Jane, "my Aunt Mecom is as Worty a Woman a Live."[30]

Franklin, writing to his sister from "a fine airy House upon a Hill, which has a large Garden with fine Walks in it, about ½ an hours Drive from the City of Paris," could say little, except to condole with her about the whole course of her life.[31] "I hope you will have no more Afflictions of that kind," he wrote, "and that after so long and stormy a Day your Evening may be serene & pleasant."[32]

CHAPTER XXX

Publick Affairs

Jane and her brother had the idea that when he came back, if he came back, they might live together again.[1] "O my Dear Brother," she wrote him, "if this could be Accomplished it would give me more Joy than any thing on this side Heaven." She missed his company. "I feel the want of suitable conversation I have but litle hear," she wrote to him from Rhode Island. She admitted that she had been shy of him for much of her life. "I Suffered my defidence & the Awe of yr Superiority to prevent the femiliarity I might have taken with you & ought, & yr kindness to me might have convenced me would be acceptable; but it is hard over comeing a natural propensity, & Difedence is mine." But something had changed: "I think I could Asume more freedom with you now."[2] She wrote, too, more freely.

In the fall of 1778, Congress elected Franklin minister plenipotentiary, America's chief diplomat. His sister liked to report to him on what was being published about him in America, much of which she found very funny. ("I have half a mind to send it to you as I think it would make you Laugh," she once wrote, about a poem about him.)[3] When an attack in the newspaper ridiculed his airs, portraying him as an American who, having "rubbed off the mechanic rust," had become a courtier, a seducer of French ladies, she wrote to poke fun:

> I now & then hear of yr helth & Glorious Achievments in the politi-
> cal way, as well as in the favour of the Ladys ("Since you have rubd off
> the Mechanic Rust and commenced compleat courtier") who Jonathan
> Williams writes me clame from you the Tribute of an Embrace & it
> seemes you do not complane of the Tax as a very grat penance.[4]

She was teasing him, but on this point he was, with her, sensitive. In the debauched French court, a world away from war-strapped, Puritan New England, Franklin really had become something of a courtier, and he winced at her joking about it: "The Story you allude to, which was in the News Papers, mentioning 'mechanic Rust,' &ca is totally without Foundation," he insisted.[5]

She wrote back, assuring him that she didn't take what she read about him in the newspapers seriously, adding that the story "of the mechanice Rust served only to make me Laugh."[6]

He boasted of his great fame.

"Perhaps few Strangers in France have had the good Fortune to be so universally popular," he wrote her. "This Popularity has occasioned so many Paintings, Busto's, Medals & Prints to be made of me, and distributed throughout the Kingdom, that my Face is now almost as well known as that of the Moon."

She wrote back that the likenesses she had seen of him were so many and so different that his face must be "as changeable as the moon."[7]

Franklin liked, in France, to present himself as a bumpkin, with his mechanic rust and his coon hat. This was a serviceable sham. It was in this same spirit that he began giving to his fashionable French friends crumbly whitish-greenish cakes of soap made by his sister, using what she made—and what he no longer knew how to make—as a marker of his humble and obscure origins. From Passy, outside Paris, he wrote to Jane, asking her to make some soap and send it to him. "You will do me a great deal of Pleasure in sending me as You propose, some Crown Soap, the very best that can be made," he wrote. "I shall have an Opportunity of obliging some Friends with it, who very much admire the little Specimens I have been able to give them."[8] Jane, living with her granddaughter Jenny Flagg Greene and her family, dutifully rode to Caty's house and, cobbling together what barrels and vats she could, made dozens of cakes of soap. Then she went on a visit to Boston, to see her friend Grace and to give Jonathan some soap, to ship to France—all this so that her extraordinary brother could complete his costume as an authentic, homespun American original.

"I take this opportunity to Send you a small Box of Crown Soap that I Recd from your Sister Who has been here On a Visit," Williams wrote to Franklin, reporting that Jane was "in good helth & Spirits, & I belive more happy now then I ever new her." She insisted that she lacked for nothing. "I repeated to her that I Stood ready to advance her any money she stood in need of agreeable to your Orders her greatfull hart was effected," Williams told Franklin. But "she told me that she hoped the Income of the house would be soficient."[9]

Because a single shipment of soap could easily get lost at sea, Jane sent another box by way of Peter Collas ("Mrs. Mecom Desired me to Acquint you the Soap was not as white as she could wish," Collas wrote Franklin).[10] But she never liked to rely on Collas. So when John Adams sailed to France in 1779, he carried with him yet another box of soap Jane had made for her brother. She apologized that it wasn't as good as it ought to be: "I thought I could have made a little more beter but I don't think I have suckceded."[11] About the quality of her soap, she was most particular.[12]

During these years, Jane spent a good deal of time not only making soap but thinking about peace. She wasn't sure she would live to see it. "The Dismal Sound of fiveteen year from the comencment of the war Dwells on my mind which I wonce heard you say it might Last," she wrote her brother in 1779. "If it does it is not Likely I shall Last that long."[13] It didn't drag on for fifteen years, but it did go on and on. "The Ravages of war are Horrible," she wrote.[14]

She told her brother she was far from the worst scenes of war. "I . . . know but litle how the world goes Except seeing a Newspaper some times which contains Enough to give Pain but litle Satisfaction while we are in Armes aganst Each other."[15] But she saw a great deal of war. She saw armies march through cities. She saw blood on the streets. She heard the rumble of artillery and the thunder of cannons. She was witnessing the end of an empire and the birth of a republic. Despite her vantage, she rarely described any of this—the grand course of events—because, as she told her brother, "I do not pretend to say any thing about publick Affairs."[16]

Still, from Rhode Island, she begged him to write to her more of politics: "The few friends I have hear flock about me when I recve a leter & are much disapointed that they contain no Politicks, I tell them you Dare not trust a woman Politicks, & prehaps that is the truth but if there is any thing we could not posable misconstru or do mischief by knowing from you, it will Gratifie us mightly if you add a litle to yr future kind leters."[17]

This he did not do. During the war, he wrote her infrequently and circumspectly. Her letters to him seem rarely to have made their way into his hands. There were delays; one letter Franklin sent to his sister from France took eight months to arrive.[18] Other letters were lost or intercepted. "I have heard of several of mine to you has fell in to the hands of the Enemie," she wrote to him when he was in Paris in 1779.[19] Some of their letters miscarried.[20] The more often her letters were lost, the more often she wrote. "You mention other Letters you have written, but they are not come to hand," he told her in the spring of 1779. "Dont however be discouraged from writing as often as you can; for I am uneasy when long without hearing from you; and the Chance is greater that one Letter out of many should arrive, than one out of a few. . . . If you do not hear from me as often as formerly, impute it to the too much Business upon my Hands and the Miscarriage of Letters, or any thing rather than a diminution of Affection."[21] The loss of their correspondence distressed her mightily. She prayed, again and again, for peace, not least because it would mean more letters: "when shall we be at peace," she asked, "that we may at least have the comfort of Each others leters?"[22]

She was old and she was tired, but she loved living with her granddaughter, and she loved living near enough to Caty to visit her. She was, however, also overwhelmed by the number of people who stayed at Caty's house, and when the Greenes had guests, she kept away. "When we have the Emtyest house We Send for her to Stay with us She Cant Bear Company as She used to do," Caty reported to Franklin. Jane grew sick. Caty reported to Franklin that "our Dear Mrs Mecom" had suffered much from "her old Cough."[23]

Her comfort, in these years, was her granddaughter and her great-grandchildren. Jenny Flagg Greene had four children in five years. Celia, born in 1777, died within a year. Sarah was born in 1779. Her next two children were born in 1780 and 1781. She named them, a boy and a girl: Franklin and Jane.

Jane loved them, her little rogues. She was more than a great-grandmother to them; she was another mother. "She is as much Enguagd in Raising the third Generation as She was the first," Caty wrote Franklin.[24] But Jane found it painful to watch her granddaughter struggle with pregnancy, childbirth, and nursing, even as she boasted about the children. "I have a grat-grand Daughter Eighteen months old that will Equill any won of yrs for understanding & prity Deverting actions at Least I think so,"

Jane boasted to Sally Bache, "& we have now a fine Lusty Fellow we have Named Franklin five weeks old who bids fair to Equill Will in bulk how-ever it may be with His Intellects, His mother Fattns Him two fast to be very Strong her self but has been much beter this time than usal."[25] (Jane told her brother, too, about his namesake: "I do not write often my Time seemes to be filld up as the Famely I am in Increaces fast, my Grandaugh-ter has had two children in Seventeen monthes the Eldest is a Daughter, Sally, the other a son Franklin, not because we could forgit your Name but that we love to hear it.")[26]

She loved them, but it was hard, after raising her own children and then so many of her grandchildren, to spend the twilight of her life helping to raise her great-grandchildren. "As I grow older I wish for more Quiet & our Famely is more Incumbred we have had three children Born since I came & tho they give grat Pleasure in comon yet the Noise of them is some times troblesome," she admitted.[27] Or again: "I write among so much noise & confusion that if I had any thing of consequence I could not Recolect it."[28]

She had more obligations, too. She began making trips to see Jane Mecom Collas, who had removed to Cambridge, where she was taken care of by Jane's fifteen-year-old granddaughter, Jenny Mecom, one of Benja-min Mecom's daughters. Jane found Jenny Mecom "grown a woman well & harty" and expected that she would soon be able to "writ well anouf to writ to me."[29] She was fifteen, and she could not yet write well enough to compose a letter. Benjamin Mecom's children had not thrived.

Meanwhile, Jane, who so cherished letters, hadn't heard from her brother in a very long time. Weeks had stretched into months, and months into years. There is some evidence that Franklin directed gifts to be sent to his sister but they were never delivered. "If the Doctor desired me to ship anything for Mrs. Mecom I have shamefully forgotten it, and deserve his displeasure," an abashed Jonathan Williams Jr. wrote to Temple Franklin in April 1781. "Pray let me know by the return of Post what the articles are & say nothing about the matter 'till I inform you of having shipped them."[30] This Jane could not have known. "Your Dear Sister is tolerable well but exceeding Desireous to have a letter from her only Brother her second Self," Caty Greene wrote to Franklin that June.[31]

That October, Jane went again to Cambridge, to visit her daughter and granddaughter.[32] She also went there in search of books. If she couldn't read her brother's letters, she hoped to read more of his essays. She crossed the river to shop at bookstores. "I am this Day going to Boston in Pursuit of a coletcion of all your works which I hear is lately come from Europe," she told her brother in a letter dated October 23, 1781. In London in 1779, Benjamin Vaughan had edited a collection, *Political, Miscellaneous, and Philosophical Pieces . . . written by Benj. Franklin.* Jane seems to have had a good idea of which essays were included in the collection—"some of which I have been in posesion of & have lost." She must have left them behind when fleeing from the British Army before the siege of Boston. "You will say then I dont Deserve to have them again, but may be not if you knew all the circumstances," she wrote Franklin. She hoped, too, that the Vaughan collection contained a few essays she had missed. "There is many things I never had and I can hardly help Envieng any won that Pleasure without my Pertakeing."[33]

She probably also saw her name in a Boston newspaper dated October 22, in a list of people for whom letters were waiting at the post office.[34] She must have hoped it was a letter from her brother; it was not. Still, she did get word from him, from Jonathan Williams Sr., who had received a parcel of goods Franklin had sent to her: "Silk for Cloaks &c. Gauze, Lace Ribbon, Linnen, & Cambrick."[35]

In Boston, she visited friends and family she hadn't seen since the war began.[36] She wrote her brother again on October 29, at once thanking and scolding him: "I See you do not forgit me tho I have so Long mourned the want of a line from your own hand to convince me of it." The day she wrote this letter, she probably also read, in the *Boston Gazette,* that Cornwallis had surrendered at Yorktown, because she added, "The Glorious News we have now recd from the Southard makes us Flater our selves you may Return to us soon."

She missed him, and she hadn't been able to find that book after all: "I mentioned my being coming to Boston in Serch of a Book containing all yr Publick writings but I cannot yet find it."[37] She went back to Cambridge, very happy to have learned that the war had ended but very disappointed not to have found that book.

CHAPTER XXXI

Sweat Peace

Jenny Flagg Greene died in April 1782, "of a Short Consumption." She was twenty-five. Jane had adored her. "I Injoyd Sweat Peace in her Pleasant conversation."[1]

Jane had raised Jenny's mother, Sarah, and when Sarah died, Jane had raised Jenny.[2] During her last illness, Jenny had begged her grandmother never to leave her own children: Sally was three; Franky was not yet two; the baby, Jane, was less than two months. Their great-grandmother was seventy.

"A care Devouled on me that I find my Self unequel to," Jane wrote to Franklin in anguish, "& tho I made her no promis I find the Request to be very Powerfull."[3]

Caty was worried, writing to Franklin that his sister "injoys great health for a Person of her age But She has met with a Shock." Jenny had declined very suddenly after giving birth, leaving Jane out of her depth in caring for her great-grandchildren. "She is So fond of the Children that I fear it will be a Disadvantage to both," Caty worried. "She thinks She Cant leave them to Visit us Scarcely."

Jane had not received a letter from her brother for two years. Caty begged Franklin to send his sister some words of comfort. "The Dear Lady tis So long Since She has had a line from you that She Can Scarcely Speak of you with out a tear."[4] Franklin wrote her a letter, some while after, and never again left off writing her for so long.

Jane was exhausted, and overwhelmed by grief. "Something constantly Passes that keeps alive my sorrow," she wrote, that "tho I have Plenty of all Nesesarys & the same Beautiful Prospect arownd me & all the season Blooming I so much mis her sosiety that it spreads a gloom over all." She resolved on a compromise.[5] She would spend most of the year with Sally, Franky, and baby Jenny in Rhode Island, but she would spend the winters in Cambridge, which would be quieter. She could bring Sally along with her, since she would have her granddaughter Jenny Mecom to help out.[6] When, that fall, Jane brought the little girl with her to Cambridge, there lived, beneath one roof, four generations: Jane Franklin Mecom, Jane Mecom Collas, Jenny Mecom, and Sally Greene.

But by the time Jane reached Cambridge, she was so exhausted that she nearly collapsed, and was confined to bed. Only slowly did she regain her strength. "I go some times to Boston where I am kindly Entertained by Cousen Williams & famely and see a few other Friends," she wrote to her brother, letting him know that she planned to return to Elihu Greene's house come spring, when she was sure that during "all the warm wether" she would be able to "do a number of things nesesary for Him & the Children."

She was still frustrated that she was, as yet, unable to find a copy of that collection of her brother's political and philosophical essays: "I have never been able to come at a sight of the Book yet," she wrote Franklin. "I would gladly bye won if it were to be Purchased but cant find that it is, I wish my Brother would do me the favour to send me won & I may be so Lucky as to Recive it, I would be a grat Amusement to me & that is the most I have to seek after at Present."[7]

That spring, six-month-old Jenny Greene died in Rhode Island.[8] Meanwhile, Jane received a package from her brother, "after a Total Silance of three years," as she took pains to point out, "in which Time Part of an old song would Some times Intrude it self into my mind,

> *Does He love & yet forsake me*
> *for*
> *can he forgit me*
> *will he niglegt me.*[9]

Possibly, his letters to her were simply lost, as he intimated. But even if he hadn't written, he had hardly neglected her. That year, he arranged an annuity for her, handled by Jonathan Williams in Boston, so that she would never have to worry about money again.[10]

"[I] cannot find Expreshon suitable to acknowlidg my Gratitude," she wrote back. "How am I by my Dear Brother Enabled to live at Ease in my old Age (after a Life of Care Labour & Anxiety) without which I must have been miserable."[11]

Franklin, in Paris, had been negotiating the peace. "A Grate work Indeed you have Done God be Praised," Jane wrote him. "I hope now you, your self, will think you have done anouf for the Publick, and will now Put in Execution what you have sometimes wished to be premited to do; sit down & spend the Evening with your Friends."[12]

Benjamin Franklin, John Adams, and John Jay signed the Treaty of Paris on September 3, 1783. Franklin made sure American loyalists got very little from that agreement.[13] In 1778, William Franklin had been exchanged for an American prisoner; he had spent the remainder of the war in occupied New York, where he founded the Board of Associated Loyalists and served as its first president. In many ways, and for many years, William Franklin was considered the greatest traitor in the United States, second only to Benedict Arnold. He had remained in New York until the end of the war and had then evacuated with the departing British Army. He had been in London since 1782, eager to see his son and his father, who were in Paris. Franklin had rebuffed him. Only after the treaty was signed did Franklin allow Temple to cross the Channel, in 1784, carrying a letter. "Nothing has ever hurt me so much and affected me with such keen Sensations," Franklin wrote to William, "as to find myself deserted in my old Age by my only Son; and not only deserted, but to find him taking up Arms against me, in a Cause wherein my good Fame, Fortune and Life were all at Stake."[14]

He would not forgive him. And he refused to see him. He planned to all but disinherit him. But from his son, to whom he had once addressed the story of his life, he did want something: his manuscripts.

The story of Franklin's life survives in four parts. In England in 1771, he had written Part I, eighty-seven pages, carrying the story of his life from his birth in 1706 up until 1730. That manuscript he'd brought back with him when he'd returned to Philadelphia in 1775. Before leaving for France in October 1776, he had given a chest of his papers, including the manuscript, to Joseph Galloway for safekeeping, outside the city. The chest included "Rough Drafts of all my Letters while I liv'd in London." Franklin explained this when writing to William in 1784, telling him that, at one point, he had intended these papers to go to him. "These are missing," Franklin told William. "I hope you have got them. If not, they are lost."[15] In November 1776, Galloway, a loyalist, fled to British lines, leaving Franklin's papers behind. Galloway's house was ransacked, and the trunk was looted, in 1778. Galloway left the country. But his wife stayed behind, and she apparently took care to remove Franklin's manuscript before leaving the house; it was found among her papers after her death in 1781; the executor of her estate eventually returned it to Franklin. In his will, Franklin bequeathed to William some worthless lands in Nova Scotia, and one thing more: "I also give to him all my books and papers, which he has in his possession, and all debts standing against him on my account books, willing that no payment for, nor restitution of, the same be required of him, by my executors. The part he acted against me in the late war, which is of public notoriety, will account for my leaving him no more of an estate he endeavoured to deprive me of." To leave William those of his papers in his possession was to leave him nothing: William had very few of his father's papers. The rest—the great bulk of his literary remains—Franklin left not to his son, but to his grandson Temple.[16]

His thoughts had turned to his remains. He began to consider what he might leave his sister.

CHAPTER XXXII

Dr. Franklin's Sister's House

In January 1784, Jane moved into the house she would live in till the end of her days, a two-story brick house on Unity Street, in the North End, down the hill from Copp's Hill Burying Ground, and just behind the Old North Church.[1]

Her brother had owned this house since 1748, when he'd acquired the mortgage from their sister Elizabeth Franklin Douse. It had long been rented out, and from 1763 through 1778, the rent, handled by Jonathan Williams Sr., had been used to pay for the care of Jane's mad son Peter. Between 1763 and 1774, Franklin had spent £150 on repairs. More repairs must have been needed after the British evacuated from Boston, in 1776, but by 1778, the house was evidently being rented again, because that year, Jane asked Williams if the rent could be paid over to the almshouse, to pay for Peter's keep. That never came to pass; Peter died within the year. After the war, with Boston finally safe, Jane moved in, and Franklin decided to give her the house, writing to her that she should consider it her own, "And I hope you will be happy in it."[2]

She had never before lived so far from the center of town, but, knowing her brother's opinions about exercise and fresh air, she thought this might be all to the good. "It is far from the few Relations & Acquaintance I have in Town but I Remember your sentaments are that walking is a most Healthfull Exercise and I practice it when I am able," she wrote, "but am so weak I make but a Poor figure in the Street."[3]

As for her new home, she loved everything about it. "The House is Pleasant for Light and Air," she reported, "haveing a large opening back & forward (as nobody has bulded near it since you saw it) and is very convenant for our Small Famely which consists of my son & Daughter [Peter Collas and Jane Mecom Collas] and Jenny Mecom."[4] Built about 1715, the house had a gambrel roof and center stairs of heavy oak. There were two rooms on the first floor, a parlor and a kitchen, and on the second floor, one chamber facing the street, which Jane shared with Jenny, and another chamber in back, for the Collases.[5]

Between the furniture left behind by Douse and used by previous tenants and some furniture brought by the Collases, there was plenty. Eight leather-bottomed chairs and a square mahogany dining table filled the front room, along with two stuffed-back easy chairs and a tea table. In Jane's room, upstairs, were a bedstead, a cane-backed chair, a broken looking glass, five pictures (portraits of Franklin, probably, and Badger's portraits of Jenny and Josiah Flagg as children), and a desk, sized for a child. Her room is where she kept her books.[6]

There had been some difficulty in moving in, because in Cambridge, Peter Collas hadn't paid his rent for two years, and his landlord had seized his furniture. Collas also asked his mother-in-law for money all the time. He was so much in and out of debt that finally Jane had asked him to turn the title to all of his goods over to her (suggesting just how much she had learned from dealing with Edward Mecom, decades before). "I thought it Absolutly nesesary to secure there nesesary furniture Least it should be Atached by some other creditor & got him to make it over to me," she reported to her brother. Then she began lecturing Collas on industry. "I at lenth tould him he had no Right to live without Labour any more than another man he was strong & Able & if he could not git to be master of a vesel he must go mate. He should not chose to do that Nither. I tould him the Expences of the Famely when he was at home were Doble to what they were when he was absent & that if I continued to spend as I now did I should have not for my own soport."[7]

She skimped and saved and soon had enough money to have the house decorated. By October she could write her brother, "I am now Pritily settled have had two Rooms New Papered an Painted, have Procurd some conveniances for my own Chamber (for you know I Lost allmost every thing when the Town was Ravged) that if I should be confined to it I might be comfortable for I cant say I ever feel Perfectly well."[8] If she was going to die in that room, she wanted to like the wallpaper.

She loved to walk. She could walk to her church, the Second Church, just a few blocks away, on Hanover Street. She loved to walk up Copp's Hill. "I frequent go on the Hill for the sake of the Prospect & the walk," she wrote. She loved to look at the river, where a bridge was being built, connecting Boston to Cambridge. "It is Realy a charming Place," she wrote her brother, "they have Leveld the Riseing Ground that Led to it & Nicely Paved it, that at some Distance as you Aproach to it it is a Beautifull sight with a Litle Vilidg at the other End the Buildings all New the Prospect on Each side is Delightfull." Once, she even walked all the way across the bridge and into Cambridge. The Charles is wide. Crossing by foot from Boston to Cambridge is a very long walk for a woman of seventy-four. "I sopose you wont allow it as grat a feeat as yr walking ten miles befor Break-fast," she wrote her brother, "but I am strongly Inclined to Alow it my self, all circumstances considered."[9]

As she grew older, she worried, having witnessed so much insanity, that she might be losing her mind. Every time she forgot something, she fretted about dementia. She had always loved to read Swift, and she knew the story of how, in the years before he died, he went mad. "I am often Afflected with grat Dizenes & Expect or fear if I live much Longer to be in such Circumstances as Dean Swift was," she wrote her brother on the Fourth of July 1784. "If it Pleases God to hear my Prayer Death will be much Prefer-able, but who am I to Prescribe to the Allmighty." Franklin, who suffered from not only gout but also stones, was in considerable pain. She had heard of his illnesses, and wrote these words of comfort: "your Retaining your Intlectual Faculties & such Fortitude to bare up under it must be Prefer-able to a Senslis Stupidetie."[10]

Losing her wits worried her above all else. "The similarity of my Disor-der with Dean Swifts makes me often very Apprehensive," she wrote her brother. "I however Recreate my self in the best maner I can, I walk abroad often, viset my friends oftener than they do me hopeing they will Pay the debt in time of need."[11]

Free and independent in a way she had never been before, she wrote, brazenly, that she wished she had more intelligent people to talk to. "I Injoy all the Agreable conversation I can come at Properly, but I find Litle, very Litle, Equal to that I have a Right to by Nature but am deprived of by Providence."[12] It was a shocking thing to say, and to believe: that she had a right to intelligent conversation—a natural right—but had been deprived of it, by Providence.

In Paris, Franklin returned to the story of his life, writing Part II, twelve pages. "Histories of Lives are seldom entertaining, unless they contain something either admirable or exemplar," he had written, decades before, as Silence Dogood.[13] He wasn't sure he ought to publish his story, or even finish it. Benjamin Vaughan, who had edited Franklin's *Political, Miscellaneous, and Philosophical Pieces* (the collection Jane hadn't been able to get her hands on), urged him to keep at it. "Your history is so remarkable, that if you do not give it, somebody else will," Vaughan wrote."[14]

Jane kept reading, studying lives, studying philosophy, studying politics. She would soon have a syllabus, a list of books to read, containing the greatest ideas of the age. In 1778, a town in Massachusetts had been named after her brother. There was some question of whether Benjamin Franklin would give to the town, as a gift, a bell for the church tower. "They are poore, and in my Opinion, dont nead a *bell* any more then a toad Neads a Tail," Jonathan Williams Sr. wrote Franklin. Franklin decided to give not a bell for a church but books for a library.[15]

"I observe in won of your Leters to cousen Williams your Intention to Present to Franklin Town a number of Books as a Foundation for a Parish Library hopeing the Franklins will Prefer Sense to Sound," Jane wrote her brother, much amused. She didn't quite like the idea—she never had—that her brother had more use for a library than for a church. So she pestered him: "I cant doubt but such a Library will consist of some Authers on Divine Subjects I therefor hope you will not think it too Presuming in me to Propose won, Viz Discourses on Personal Religion in two Volumes by Samuel Stnnett D D Printed in London by R Hett in 1769 I borrowed them and Read them with a grat deal of Pleasure and I think you yourself would if you could find time tho there may be many things in them not altogether Agreable to your Sentiments, which I sopose may be the case with Every Volume you Read on any Subject"—and which was the case with nearly every volume she read on any subject, too.[16]

Here was she, full of opinions, telling *him* what to read. He took her advice. He wrote a letter to his friend the Welsh clergyman Richard Price asking for his help in drawing up a list of books for the Franklin library. "Besides your own Works," Franklin wrote Price, "I would only mention, on the Recommendation of my Sister, Stennet's Discourses on personal Religion, which may be one Book of the Number, if you know it and approve of it."[17]

Price had been a friend of Franklin's since the two men first met, in 1757. He maintained a considerable correspondence in Boston.[18] He was an ardent supporter of American independence, having published several influential tracts in favor of the American cause during the 1770s, along with a pamphlet called *Observations on the Importance of the American Revolution,* in 1784. He approved of Stennett, an English Baptist and hymn writer who was just the sort of theologian Jane admired. In 1785, Price prepared a list of books for the town of Franklin; early the next year, Jonathan Williams Jr. shipped them to Massachusetts.[19]

Jane asked Franklin for a copy of the list.[20] "My Reason for this Request is I have a grat deal of time on my hands," she explained. "I Love Reading, it is a Present Amusement tho my memory is so bad that I cannot Retain it as many others do; now I am sure that will be a collection worth Reading & I dont doubt I can Borrow of won & a nother of my Acquaintance from time to time such as I have a mind to Read."[21]

She got the catalog.[22] If she read from that list of 116 volumes, she would have read Locke, Sydney, Montesquieu, Blackstone, Newton, Priestley, and Price.[23] She would have pored over everything she could get her hands on. She found company, and pleasure, in pages, more pleasure than she had ever known. She not only had more time to read, and a mind for it, but more time to write, and a mind for that, too. Between 1785, when she was well settled in her own house, and 1790, when her brother died, she wrote more letters than survive for all of the years of all the rest of her life put together.[24]

She had never been happier. "As to my self I Live very much to my Likeing, I never had a Tast for High Life, for Large companys, & Entertainments," she wrote her brother, adding, philosophically, "I am of Popes mind that Health, Peace, and Competance, come as near to Happynes as is Atainable in this Life, and I am in a good measure In possession of all three at Present, if they are at Times a Litle Infringd ocationaly or by Accedent, I Vew it as the common Lot of all and am not much Disturbed."[25] Health, peace, and competence. Quiet, at last.

"It is trew I have some Trobles," she admitted, but "when I Look Round me on all my Acquaintance I do not see won I have Reason to think Happier than I am."[26] She was happy, and she was proud. "I have this Spring been new planking the yard made New gate, & new Cedar Dores," she one day boasted, "& am Painting the Front of the House to make it look Decent that I may not be Ashamed when any Boddy Inquiers for Dr Franklins Sister in the Neibourhood."[27]

CHAPTER XXXIII

Thirteen Stars

In July 1785, Benjamin Franklin sailed for home. He arrived in Philadelphia in September. He was seventy-nine years old. His sister was seventy-three.

"I Perceive by the News papers you are not to be suffered to Rest as long as you are Alive," she wrote him, having heard that he had accepted the post of president of Pennsylvania (the equivalent, under the state's new constitution, of a governorship). She was furious. "I was in hopes you would have Resolutely Rersisted all Solicitations to Burdern yr Self any more with the concerns of the Publick, & Flattered my self if I were with you I should Injoy a litle familiar Domestic Chit Chat like comon folks, but now I Imagine all Such Attempts would be Intrusion."[1]

They would never have that domestic chitchat, like common folks, except in letters, which now traveled between them in a matter of days, and were chatty in a way they had never been before, Jane less diffident, Franklin less busy.

"I can not find in my Hart to be Pleasd at your Accepting the Goverment of the State and Therefore have not congratulated you on it," Jane wrote, miffed. "I fear it will Fatigue you two much."[2]

"I do not wonder at your blaming me for accepting the Government," he wrote back. And then he teased her. "We have all of us Wisdom enough to judge what others ought to do, or not to do in the Management of their Affairs; and 'tis possible I might blame you as much if you were to accept the Offer of a young Husband. My Example may teach you not to be too confident in your own Prudence; as it teaches me not to be surpris'd at such an Event should it really happen."[3]

She let that pass.

She told him all about her house. He told her all about his. He was renovating and expanding, adding a new library, with shelves for four thousand books.

"The Library is to be even with the Floor of my old Chamber," he wrote her. "I hardly know how to justify building a Library at an Age that will so soon oblige me to quit it."[4]

"If we may Judge of the fittnes of things," she allowed, "we may Surely Expect won who has Imployd His whol Life to Defuse Happines to all the world has a Right to live in a comodious House."[5]

He kept casting his mind back to home. "When you have a little Leisure write me an Account of all the Relations we have left in New England," he asked her.[6]

"I have begun the Acount of our Relations and shall send it in my Next," she promised.[7]

After she sent it, he received an inquiry. "I have lately receiv'd a Letter from a Person who subscribes himself Stickney, says he is a Grandson of my Sister Davenport, and has a son named Benj Franklin," he told her. "You have not mentioned this Family in the List you sent me. Do you know any thing of them?"[8]

Jane loved this sort of question, reporting, in her gabby way, in the middle of a snowy winter:

> Our Sister Davenport had a Daughter Dorcas who married to a Mr Stickney & lived at Newbury he was a chare maker by traid but never loved work, but that is not the thing, thay had been so long Dead & I had no Remembrance of there Leaveing any Children & had never seen any of them that I sopose I did not think of the Famely when I wrot the List, when I recd your Leter our Streets were unpasable by any means for old folks but a few Days after I Sent to Mrs Williams to Inquier what She knew about them, & had for Ansure all she knew of the man who wrot to you, was that he was a good for nothing Impudent Lazey Felow Just like his Father, I thought however as he had an Aunt in the Town I would know somthing farther before I ansured your Leter.

That is to say: their niece Dorcas Davenport had married a layabout named Stickney. Jane couldn't recall whether they had any children, but she had decided to find out. She asked Grace Harris Williams, who told her that Dorcas had had a son. This was the man—Anthony Somersby Stickney—who had written to Franklin. Grace thought him "a good for nothing Impudent Lazey Felow Just like his Father." This only made Jane more curious, so she went to visit the young man's aunt. ("I therefore Got a Carrage & went to her & Inquierd about the Famely.") Reporting all this to her brother, she included, too, a rather breathless history of the Stickney family, more elaborate than usual, since she had been gently chided by her brother for having left this branch of the Franklin family off the list of all their relatives that she had just sent him. So she went on, about the aunt:

> She Tould me that when her Sister was married her Husbands mother & Grandfather were Liveing on a Litle Estate they had in Newbury where he also carried his Wife after trying to live by Shopkeeping in this Town, but haveing so litle means of soport they became exdding Poor, in which time she says you went to see them & made them a hansom Present (I sopose at the time you Put out yr Shoulder at Portesmouth) His Grandfather Lived to be above 90 year old but He and his Daughter Dieing Left the house to our cousen but they could not feed long upon that, he Therefore took a Prudent Step sould it & bought a good Farm at Derry, & went to Live on it where his wife helpd. to work on it & thay got to Live Extradinery well, but She Mrs Rodgers thinks shortned her Days by too hard Labour, & her husband Died soon After her & left the Farm to this man & a sister who are all the children they left & who live to gather on it & do very well, She says he has a Good charecter as a Sober Honest man but does not Increce his Estate as won tould her he Entertaind too many Strangers in hopes of Entertaing Angels unawares.

That is to say, Anthony Stickney wasn't a bad man, but he was dreamy, awaiting riches rather than working for them. Finally, Jane reached the end of her history:

> She says she saw Him about a year & half a go & he tould her he had such a Son that he Named for you, that he gave him all the Education he was able, but she thinks him very Bold in writing to you She is shure she shuld not have don it, as to the Boy I omited to Inquire Perticularly about him as the carriage waited for me Put it out of my mind.[9]

Anthony Stickney wanted Franklin to help educate his son, Benjamin Franklin Stickney. To this end, he not only wrote to Franklin but also, no doubt after hearing that Jane had visited his aunt, traveled from New Hampshire to Boston to plead his case to her in person.

He was not well received. Jane took a dim view of the idea that just because Stickney had named the boy "Benjamin Franklin" her brother owed him an education.

"I tould him if you were to take such Notice of all who had been named In Respect to you," she dryly reported, "you must build an Academy for there Reception." And not only that, she told him, but, "that I had a Grate-Grandson Prehaps would clame Admitance when it was well Established."[10]

They wrote and wrote. Her brother asked her to make him some more crown soap. "I wish it to be of the greenish Sort that is close and solid and hard like the Specimen I send; and not that which is white & curdled and crumbly."[11]

She rode to Rhode Island, to Caty's house, and boiled up sixty pounds of soap. Jonathan Williams Jr., who had served as an agent for the American commissioners in France, came to watch her work. (Williams had replaced his father as a kind of guardian of Jane's affairs. "How has my poor old Sister gone thro' the Winter?" Franklin asked him. "Tell me frankly whether she lives comfortably or is pinched? For I am afraid she is too cautious of acquainting me with all her Difficulties tho' I am always ready and willing to relieve her when I am acquainted with them.")[12] To the soap boiling, Williams brought a pen and paper. He wanted to learn the family recipe. "I have gone through the Operation of making the soap and by taking Notes throughout the whole, I have a tolerable Idea of both Theory and Practice," he reported to Franklin, who had once again lost the recipe. "Aunt Mecom will soon send you the Recipe, and the soap is ready to be sent to you by the first Vessel."[13]

Jane had stopped calling it crown soap. The people who, she thought, had stolen the name had ruined it ("dirty Stinking Stuff," she called it). "The Crown Soap now vended among us," she said, "is as contemptible as the British Head that now wears won." She didn't have a crown stamp anymore, anyway, but she wouldn't use it if she did. If she were to stamp her soap, she had a better idea than to stamp it with a British crown. "It would be cleaver," she thought, to stamp it with a stamp of "thirteen Stars."[14] American soap.

CHAPTER XXXIV

The Petition of the Letter *J*

He wrote her on the first day of January 1786: "Our good God has brought us old Folks, the last Survivors of 17 Brothers & Sisters, to the Beginning of a new Year."[1]

She wrote back on January 6, his eightieth birthday. She wanted more to read. "I have two favours to Ask of you," she begged. "Your New Alphabet of the English Language, and the Petition of the Letter Z."[2]

Franklin had written "The Petition of the Letter Z," a satire, in 1778; it had been published in the *Tatler* in 1779. In it, the letter *Z*, distressed at being the last letter in the alphabet, complains, "That he is not only plac'd at the Tail of the Alphabet, when he had as much Right as any other to be at the Head; but is, by the Injustice of his Enemies totally excluded from the Word WISE, and his Place injuriously filled by a little, hissing, crooked, serpentine, venomous Letter called S." The letter *Z*'s petition is denied, however, the judges urging "that Z be admonished to be content with his Station, forbear Reflections upon his Brother Letters, & remember his own small Usefulness, and the little Occasion there is for him in the Republick of Letters, since S, whom he so despises, can so well serve instead of him."[3]

"The Petition of Z is enclos'd," Franklin replied. "My new Alphabet is in a printed Book of my Pieces, which I will send you the first Opportunity I have."[4]

In April, he sent her the Vaughan edition of his collected writings, *Political, Miscellaneous, and Philosophical Pieces,* a book she had wanted for a very long time. It contains the essay she was after, which is called "A Scheme for a New Alphabet and Reformed Mode of Spelling."[5]

Franklin had written it in 1768. He had been making a study of phonetics. The English language, as he argued, is a poor fit with a Greek-derived alphabet; some letters, like *c,* have more than one sound, and some sounds, like *sh,* require more than one letter. "If we go on as we have done a few Centuries longer," Franklin warned, "our words will gradually cease to express sounds." Franklin, like many another tinkerer both before and after him, offered a solution whereby there might be a one-to-one correspondence between sounds and letters. He proposed deleting the letters *c, w, y,* and *j* and adding six new letters. He explained:

> Az to oz hu du nt spel uel, if i tu difikltiz er kmpêrd, at v titi em tru speli in i prezent mod, and at v titi em i nu alfabet and i nu speli akrdi to it; i am knfident at i latr uuld bi bi far i liist. ê natrali fl into i nu med alredi, az mt az i imperfekn v er alfabet uil admit v; êr prezent bad speli iz onli bad, bikz kntreri to i prezent bad ruls: ndr i nu ruls it uuld bi gud. i difiklti v lrni to spel uel in i old uê iz so grêt, at fiu atên it; uzands and uzands riti n to old ed, uiut ever bii ebil to akuir it.

That is to say:

> As to those who do not spell well, if the two difficulties are compared, that of teaching them true spelling in the present mode, and that of teaching them the new alphabet and the new spelling according to it; I am confident that the latter would be by far the least. They naturally fall into the new method already, as much as the imperfection of their alphabet will admit of; Their present bad spelling is only bad, because contrary to the present bad rules; under the new rules it would be good. The difficulty of learning to spell well in the old way is so great, that few attain it; thousands and thousands writing on to old age, without ever being able to acquire it.[6]

Nothing had come of Franklin's new scheme for spelling.[7] But when, in the spring of 1786, Jane read about it, she attempted to learn it. "My Daughter & I sat down to Study the Alphabet," she wrote her brother, "Imagining we should soon Larn it so as to write you in that way." She gave it a great deal of thought. "I sopose you meen to have the writing and Printing as near alike as Posable." She found it hard to write but easy to read: "It must be a more Acute Pen than mine that can Imitate it, I however could Read it Perfectly."[8] *The difficulty of learning to spell well in the old way is so great, that few attain it; thousands and thousands writing on to old age, without ever being able to acquire it.* Jane found this a relief, "Since I am but won of the Thousands, & thousands, that write on to old Age and cant Learn." She would not accept, though, that this meant that she was worthless. "I know the most Insignificant creature on Earth may be made some Use of in the Scale of Beings, may Touch some Spring, or Verge to some wheel unpercived by us."[9]

"You need not be concern'd in writing to me about your bad Spelling," Franklin wrote back, "for in my Opinion as our Alphabet now Stands, the bad Spelling, or what is call'd so, is generally the best, as conforming to the Sound of the Letters and of the Words." And then he told her a story:

A Gentleman receiving a Letter in which were these Words, Not finding Brown at hom, I delivered your Meseg to his yf. The Gentleman finding it bad Spelling, and therefore not very intelligible, call'd his Lady to help him read it. Between them they pick'd out the meaning of all but the yf, which they could not understand. The Lady propos'd calling her Chambermaid; for Betty, says she, has the best Knack at reading bad Spelling of any one I know. Betty came, and was surpriz'd that neither Sir nor Madam could tell what y, f was; why, says she, y,f spells Wife, what else can it spell? And indeed it is a much better as well as shorter method of Spelling Wife, than by Doubleyou, I ef, e, which in reality Spells, Doubleyifey.[10]

Jane loved that. "I think Sir & madam were deficient in Sagasity that they could not find out y f as well as Bety," she wrote back. "Some times," she ventured, "the Betys has the Brightst understanding."[11]

In January 1786, Jane's twenty-five-year-old grandson, Josiah Flagg, wrote to Benjamin Franklin—whom he had never met—seeking assistance. "My mother was Sally Mecom Daughter of Mrs Jane Mecom of Boston, and Niece to your Excellency," he began, by way of introduction. His mother having died when he was three, Josiah had then lived in Jane's house. Reduced to a state of "unhappy Lameness" by a fall before the age of five, he had been taken from his grandmother's house when his father remarried. When Jane fled Boston in 1775, she had been unable to find the boy. The ailing William Flagg had not survived the occupation; not long after the Battle of Bunker Hill, he was poisoned by a British Army surgeon. Josiah Flagg once wrote about what happened next: "I was left a helpless orphan at the age of fourteen, and during the whole of the Revolution suffered very much."[12] He probably ended up in the almshouse; from there, he was bound into service as an apprentice to a shoemaker, the lowliest of the trades. Since the end of the war, he had been working as a cobbler in Boston. But he had pretensions to gentility; he wanted to climb his way up the trades, and then out. He went to Lancaster, a farming town north of Worcester, where his father's family came from.[13] In November 1785 he had left Massachusetts to seek his fortune in Virginia.

"Dear Coz," he wrote to his cousin Jenny Mecom from Virginia. "This is the most dirty place I ever saw." He found the place melancholy and slavery grotesque: "The Virginians as a people are given to Luxury and Dissipation of every kind, and are supported in their Extravagance by Afric's sable sons, who they consign to the most Abject Slavery."[14]

Josiah Flagg was bright and ambitious and, for a self-taught man, a fine writer. ("I endeavour to behave as well as my slender Education and Knowledge of the World will admit," he wrote his "Dear Grandma.") From Virginia, Flagg wrote to Benjamin Franklin, expressing a hope that his granduncle might help find him a position as a clerk.[15]

"Loving Kinsman," Franklin wrote back. "If you should call here in your Way, I will give you some Writing to do for me."[16]

When Jane found out, from Jonathan Williams Jr. (to whom she was still trying to teach the art of making soap), that her grandson had gone knocking on her brother's door, she was mortified.[17] Flagg was as bad as Stickney. "Cousen Jonathan has Just now Informed me that my Grandson Josiah Flagg has Aplied to you to Put him in to Busness," Jane wrote to her brother. "Tho he is my Grandson & I wish him well settled to somthing he can git his Liveing by I am Angry with him for his Audacity in writing to you on such an Acount." She had sympathy for him: "He is a Poor unfortunate youth." But she didn't like the way he put on airs, accusing him of having "too Proud a Spirit to conform to the occupation he was Taught" and refusing to recommend him: "What his capasety is for Any other I am not qualified to Inform you." She was, uncharacteristically, uncharitable:

"Tho I am his Grandmother, he has been at so Grat a Distance from me Ever since the war commencd, but in ansure to all my Inquiries I have allways heard he behaved Honestly & uprightly & he has Apeared so when he has been to see me but has had so few advantages that it must be the highest Impropriety in him to Adres you on such an ocation."[18]

Flagg wheedled himself into his grandmother's good graces when he wrote to her using Franklin's new mode of spelling. "Anyrd Grandma," he began, thanking her for her "tu letrys."[19] But Jane was vexed that he hadn't written to her before imposing himself on Franklin ("I think it was Disrespectfull in him to me not to ask my advice," she wrote her brother).[20] And Flagg made matters worse when, in a letter asking Jane to use her "Influence with him in a Recommendation of me," he begged her not to tell Franklin that he had been a shoemaker. She found this "Ridiculous Vanety." Instead of complying, she forwarded Flagg's letter to Franklin, "wherein you will see the man as he is, & I can Add nothing to it as it contains all I believe about him."[21]

"I am sorry you are as it were forced to bare the Burden of soporting my whol Famely," Jane wrote her brother. "He is the son of a Dear worthy Child; his sister was Remarkably Dutyfull & affectionat to me, & I wish him well but should never consented to his throwing himself upon you." Still, she regretted having been so hard on him, in her first, and miffiest, letter.[22] "I believe I have wrote too sevre to Poor Josiah & as he is among all strangers & so much His Superours it may Depres his Spirits & I Realy think him a good young man in the main I know no fault he has but his Vanety." She asked Franklin to guide the boy. "I beg my Dear Brother you will as far as you can without Interfering with your other Affairs Inspect his conduct, his Disposion, and his capasety, & Reprove, Advise, an Direct him, in what you see to be most Proper for him; which if he does not observe he need not Expect Prosperity any way." (Nor was she stinting with her own advice: "I have allways made it my Pratice in my conduct towards my first children [to] Reprove & advise where it apeared to me to be Nesesary," she wrote her grandson, "and I Still Presist in the beleif of its being Proper & usefull." Be humble, she advised him, and do not despair: "By no meenes suffer your self to Dispond & Perticularly on account of the Lose of yr Leg.")[23]

"Your Grandson behaves very well, and is constantly employ'd in writing for me," Franklin reassured her. "As to my Reproving and Advising him, which you desire, he has not hitherto appeared to need it, which is lucky, as I am not fond of giving Advice, having seldom seen it taken."

This stung. "I percive you have some Exeptions to the Lose of your Advice," Jane wrote back, "& I flater my self I am won."[24]

Maybe it had something to do with the Fourth of July. But in the summer of 1786, some combination of events stirred in her a new spirit of equality. It was the nation's tenth birthday. "There is much Rejoicing in Town to day," Franklin wrote to his sister, "it being the Anniversary of the Declaration of Independence, which we sign'd that day Ten years, and thereby hazarded Lives and Fortunes."[25]

Or maybe it had something to do with Franklin's simplified spelling scheme. *Some times the Betys has the Brightst understanding,* Jane thought.

Or maybe it was thinking about her crippled grandson, struggling to make his way in the world. Doubtless it had something to do with the growing unrest in Massachusetts. Josiah Flagg had fled to Virginia in 1785 because he could no longer earn a living in Massachusetts. The state's economy was failing. Revolutionary War veterans were broke and, by the hundreds, were being hauled into court for unpaid debts.

But maybe, most of all, what led Jane to think differently about equality that summer stemmed from the reading she had been doing, using that list of books Franklin had intended for the library of the town of Franklin. She had been studying Richard Price's *Four Dissertations.* Franklin might have sent it to her. Or Price might have, after Franklin mentioned his sister in a letter to him. Or her minister, John Lathrop, might have loaned her his copy; Lathrop had been corresponding with Price.[26] Either she owned a copy or she had borrowed one from someone in Boston, because, after Josiah Flagg wrote to her lamenting his condition, she recommended that, especially to avoid feeling sorry for himself, he read "The first Sec. of Dr Price's Dessertations on Provedence," suggesting, "My Brothers Liberary will firnish you with it I dont doubt if not try to borrow it." She found it beautiful. She advised her grandson, "It will be a usefull Subject for your Reflection in your Laesure Hours, He thinks Every Persen Injoys more happynes than Adversity therefore take your share and be content."[27]

In the passage Jane recommended to her grandson—Section I of the first dissertation—Price attempted to prove that nothing happens in the world but that God directs it, and for good ends. "I am, suppose, in affliction," Price began. "The author of my existence, who is almighty and righteous, knows my condition, and sees what I feel. Would he, if he saw that my affliction is improper, or that I labour under any real grievance, suffer it for one moment? 'Tis utterly impossible. A God without a Providence is undoubtedly a contradiction."[28] It was in this argument that Jane had taken comfort, all her life.

But the passage that really caught her eye came in a section titled "On the Objections against Providence." One objection to Providence, Price remarked, is the great waste in the natural world, in "the untimely deaths that happen among our own species": "Many perish in the womb; and the greater part of those that see the light, and are put in the way to the enjoyments and happiness of grown men in the present life, fall short of them, and are nipped in their bloom."

Jane must have marked these pages. She read them carefully. She even read Price's footnote to this passage, in which he describes the findings of a member of the Royal Academy of Sciences, who "computes that an elm every year, at a medium, produces 330,000 seeds, and, therefore, supposing it to live a hundred years, 33 millions during its whole age." And yet so few, so few of those seeds ever grow into trees. "A spider lays, as naturalists tell us, five or six hundred eggs." And yet so few, so few ever grow into spiders. "What an infinity then of these eggs must be lost for want of falling into favourable situations?" The same could be said of humanity, which exhibits every "*capacity of improvement*" and yet "the greatest part of men have, from the beginning of the world, been in a state of darkness and barbarism"—unenlightened "by the invention of arts and sciences, and the establishment of the best schemes of civil policy."

What is true for elms and spiders and the human species is true, even, Price went on, for "the individuals of mankind": "Thousands of Boyles, Clarks and Newtons have probably been lost to the world, and lived and died in ignorance and meanness, merely for want of being placed in favourable situations, and enjoying proper advantages." But these, even these, "are capable of an *endless* future progress in knowledge and happiness." There *was* no wasted humanity. There was only a "seeming waste": "The *seeming waste* may, for ought we know, answer important ends."[29] No one dies for naught.

Richard Price was the eighteenth-century philosopher who spoke to Jane more clearly, more concisely, more forcefully, even, than her brother did.[30] He supported civil liberty; he denounced slavery; he advocated American independence.[31] But he believed in a providential god, and he explained to her, better than any other preacher or writer ever had, why she had given birth to twelve children and lost eleven.

She wrote to her brother. At her desk, in her own room at last, she had her paper, her pot of ink, a blotter, and Richard Price's *Four Dissertations*, pressed open to a page she had marked. And then she copied out, letter by letter, word by word, the passage in Price on Providence that spoke so powerfully to her, except that, instead of following Price's spelling, she spelled the way she liked to spell. She wrote: "Dr Price thinks Thousand of Boyles Clarks and Newtons have Probably been lost to the world, and lived and died in Ignorans and meanness, merely for want of being Placed in favourable situations, and Injoying Proper Advantages."

This was the most revolutionary thought Jane Franklin Mecom had ever put down in writing. But there was more. To this, she added an opinion of her own—in her own words.

"Very few we know," she wrote, "is Able to beat thro all Impediments and Arive to any Grat Degre of superiority in Understanding."[32]

Franklin knew, and Jane knew, very well, that very few people in their world ever beat through. Three hundred thousand seeds to make one elm. Six hundred eggs to make one spider. Of seventeen children of Josiah Franklin, how many had beat through? Very few. Nearly none. Only one. Or, possibly: two.

CHAPTER XXXV

Swords Beat into Plow-shares

Josiah Flagg left Philadelphia on September 4, 1786, carrying in his pocket a recommendation praising his "great Ability, Diligence and Fidelity." It was signed by B. Franklin.[1] Jane had a different piece of paper to give her grandson. She had made for him a copy of her recipe for soap.

"I porpose to Learn him the Art of makeing the Crown Soap if I can git an opertunity," she wrote her brother.[2]

"I think you will do well to instruct your Grandson in the Art of making that Soap," he returned. "It may be of use to him, and 'tis pity it should be lost."[3]

That year, Josiah Flagg turned twenty-six; his cousin Jenny Mecom turned twenty-one. "I expect when I come to Boston to have the pleasure of seeing you connected in the Hymeneal Band with some Gentleman of merit," he wrote to her. "O, how does Mr. What dy'e call him do, that pretty little Lord who pleasured us with his company one Sunday Ev'ning at Grandma's"? he wanted to know. "I began to think from his Ogles and manovres, he intended to make a Conquest."[4] If Jenny Mecom had suitors, she denied them. She was to be the granddaughter of her grandmother's old age.

Flagg reached Boston on September 9, probably having passed through Annapolis, where delegates from five states were about to begin meeting to discuss how to strengthen the Articles of Confederation, which, drafted in 1776 and adopted in 1781, had governed the states during the war. In Boston, he gathered intelligence about the crisis in Massachusetts. Three days later, he sent a report to Franklin.

"Our affairs wear a very gloomy aspect, and Business is entirely at a stand, owing to the late illegal Conventions," Flagg began. Led by poor, indebted, and disaffected veterans, gatherings had been held all over the state. It was a debtors' rebellion. Resolutions had been passed, stating objections to the economic policies of the Massachusetts government. Armed protesters had forced courts—where debtors were arraigned and sentenced—to close their doors. "There has been a Mob at Worcester, which prevented the supreme Court from proceeding in their Business," Flagg reported. "This day, at Concord the Court sets for the County of Middlesex, provided they meet with no interruption, but the country People are determin'd they shall not, what the Consequences will be time will discover." The governor, James Bowdoin, was intent on suppressing the rebellion, whose strength lay in the western part of the state.[5]

On September 19, the Massachusetts Supreme Judicial Court indicted eleven leaders of the rebellion for sedition; if captured, they were to be hanged. Revolutionary war veteran Captain Daniel Shays began leading eleven hundred men to an arsenal in Springfield. Jane's sympathies lay with the debtors, many of whom had been conscripted into military service and had never received the pensions they had been promised. More, she was weary of strife.

"I wish our Poor Distracted State would atend to the many good Lesons which have been frequently Publishd for there Instruction," she wrote her brother, "but we seem to want Wisdom to Giued, & honesty to comply with our Duty, & so keep allways in a Flame."

She never got the chance to give Josiah Flagg the recipe for soap. "My Grandson was hear he went to Lancaster & I have not heard from him since," she wrote to her brother.[6] But Mecoms were still making soap. In Elizabeth-town, New Jersey, Elizabeth Ross Mecom, Jenny's mother, advertised that she was making and selling "Fine Crown Soap, For the washing of fine Linens, Muslins, Laces, Silks, Chintzes, Calicoes, And for the use of Barbers."[7] (In some ads, she offered a genealogy explaining how the Franklin family soap had become the Mecom family soap.)[8] In Boston, Jenny Mecom stitched her mother a pocketbook.[9]

The winter of 1786–87 was, Jane said, a "most Intolarable hard Winter," especially wearing for an old woman.[10] Between October and March, she was hardly able to get out the door. "I do walk, some times in the House but I don't think of it offten anouf," she admitted to Franklin.[11] It snowed and snowed. "The Snow has been so Deep & we no man in the House that we might have been Buried Alive were it not for the care of some good Neibours who began to Dig us out before we were up in the morning," Jane wrote her brother, "& cousen Williams came Puffing, & Sweating, as soon as it was Posable to see how we were & if we wanted any thing, but thank God we had no want of any thing Nesesary if we had been Shutt up a fortnight. Except milk." Ever since Jane had moved to the house in the North End, Franklin had arranged for firewood to be delivered to her every winter. "It is impossible for me always to guess what you may want," he told her, "and I hope therefore that you will never be shy in letting me know where I can help to make your Life more comfortable."[12]

In January and February 1787, after Bowdoin sent an army of more than four thousand volunteer militia to suppress the rebellion, the Springfield arsenal was defended. On March 10, Franklin signed a proclamation on behalf of the state of Pennsylvania, pledging support for the capture of Shays and other leaders of the rebellion by offering rewards.[13] That spring, Franklin was elected as a Pennsylvania delegate to a convention, to be convened in Philadelphia, to address the inadequacies of the Articles of Confederation. At eighty-one, he was the oldest delegate in the convention, which was scheduled to begin on May 14, 1787.

"I wanted to tell you how much Pleasure I Injoy in the constant and lively mention made of you in the New papers, which makes you Apear to me Like a young man of Twenty-five," Jane wrote him on May 22. But Franklin had been ailing. "I don't see how this world can do without Him," Jane wrote to Sally the next day. "If we had a few more Such men I should hope for beter Times but I fear they Die of faster than they come forward in the world."[14]

Years before, Abigail Adams had asked her husband, John, to "remember the ladies."[15] Jane had, for her brother, on the eve of the Constitutional Convention, a different request. *Remember war*, she urged him:

I hope with the Asistance of Such a Nmber of wise men as you are connected with in the Convention you will Gloriously Accomplish, and put a Stop to the nesesity of Dragooning, & Haltering, they are odious means; I had Rather hear of the Swords being beat into Plow-shares, & the Halters used for Cart Roops, if by that means we may be brought to live Peaceably with won a nother.[16]

222 · BOOK OF AGES

It was a nice twist on what must have been two of her favorite books of
the Old Testament, Micah 4:3 ("they shall beate their swords into plow-
shares . . . neither shall they learne warre any more") and Isaiah 5:18 ("Woe
unto them that draw iniquitie with cords of vanitie, and sinne, as it were
with a cart rope"). *I had Rather hear of the Swords being beat into Plow-
Shares, & the Halters used for Cart Roops, if by that means we may be brought
to live Peaceably with won a nother.*

"I agree with you perfectly," he wrote back.[17]

The Constitution of the United States is four sheets of parchment, each
about the size of any eighteenth-century newspaper. It is a book of law.

"We the People," the first three words of the Preamble, are written in
a flourishing hand, like the title of Jane's "Book of Age's." On Monday,
September 17, 1787, the Constitution was read out loud in a chamber on
the first floor of Pennsylvania's State House. Franklin had written a speech
for the occasion. "I confess that there are several parts of this constitution
which I do not at present approve, but I am not sure I shall never approve
them," Franklin wrote. "For having lived long, I have experienced many
instances of being obliged by better information, or fuller consideration, to
change opinions even on important subjects, which I once thought right,
but found to be otherwise." He and his sister both knew this: that people
so often believe themselves to be right is no proof that they are. "Most men
indeed as well as most sects in Religion, think themselves in possession of
all truth, and that wherever others differ from them it is so far error." The
only difference between the Church of Rome and the Church of England,
Franklin joked, is that the former is infallible while the latter is never in the
wrong. Urging, therefore, humility, he closed, "Thus I consent, Sir, to this
Constitution because I expect no better, and because I am not sure, that it
is not the best."[18]

He signed his name: "B. Franklin."[19] And then he went home. During
the convention, the delegates had been sequestered. The first letter Franklin wrote after the convention adjourned, he wrote to Jane.

"You will see the Constitution we have propos'd in the Papers," he told
her. "The Forming of it so as to accomodate all the different Interests and
Views was a difficult task and perhaps after all it may not be receiv'd with
the same Unanimity in the different States, that the Convention have

given the Example of, in delivering it out for their Consideration. We have, however, done our best, and it must take its Chance."[20]

It wasn't over yet. The United States Constitution is one of the oldest written constitutions in the world and the first, anywhere, submitted to the people for their approval.[21] As James Madison explained, the Constitution is "of no more consequence than the paper on which it is written, unless it be stamped with the approbation of those to whom it is addressed . . . THE PEOPLE THEMSELVES."[22] But critics charged that it was so difficult to read that it amounted to a conspiracy against the understanding of a plain man. "A constitution ought to be, like a beacon, held up to the public eye, so as to be understood by every man," Patrick Henry argued. He believed that what was drafted in Philadelphia was "of such an intricate and complicated nature, that no man on this earth can know its real operation."[23] No one wondered whether any woman could read it.

Rhode Island, the only state to hold a popular referendum on the Constitution, rejected it. Elsewhere, in state ratifying conventions, the Constitution passed by only the narrowest of margins: 89 to 79 in Virginia; 30 to 27 in New York. The Massachusetts convention ratified the Constitution by one of the narrowest votes of all: 187 to 168. "You Percive we have some quarilsome spirits against the constetution," Jane wrote to her brother, "but it does not apear to be those of Superior Judgment."[24]

He was worried about the coming winter. It had been so hot. It could get cold so quickly. Did she have enough firewood?

"I blame myself for not sooner desiring you to lay in your Winter's Wood, and drawing upon me for it, as last year," he apologized in that first letter he wrote after the Constitutional Convention. "But I have been so busy."[25]

CHAPTER XXXVI

Crooked Lines

This Day my Dear Brother compleats his 84th year," Jane wrote to Franklin on January 17, 1790. (They had lived through such a momentous century that the very calendar had changed, from the Julian to the Gregorian. In 1752, eleven days were added to the calendar, shifting Franklin's date of birth from the sixth of January to the seventeenth.) She knew his birthday, but he didn't know hers.

"I am as you sopose six years younger than you Are being Born on the 27th march 1712," she informed him, adding, "but to Apearance in Every wons sight as much older."[1]

Franklin had been ill, and in a great deal of pain, for some time. "May God mitigate your Pain & continue yr Patience yet many years," Jane wrote him, "for who that Know & Love you can Bare the thoughts of Serviving you in this Gloomy world."

He was no less worried about her than she was about him.

"You always tell me that you live comfortably," he wrote to her, "but I sometimes suspect that you may be too unwilling to acquaint me with any of your Difficulties, from an Apprehension of giving me Pain. I wish you would let me know precisely your Situation that I may better proportion my Assistance to your Wants. Have you any Money at Interest, and what does it produce? Or do you do some kind of Business for a Living?"[2]

"I never mean to Decive you by Any thing I write but your Penetrating Eye Discovers the Smallest simton & the Remotest consequences," she wrote back. "I do indeed Live comfortable, (but can not Indulge such a childish disposition as to be Runing to you with every complaint when I know it will give you Pain.)" She offered, then, by way of assurance, a full account of her daily life.

I have a good clean house to Live in my Grandaughter constantly to atend me to do whatever I desier in my own way & in my own time, I go to bed Early lye warm & comfortable Rise Early to a good Fire have my Brakfast directly and Eate it with a good Apetite and then Read or work or what Els I Pleas, we live frugaly Bake all our own Bread, brew small bear, lay in a litle cyder; Pork, Buter, &c. & suply our selves with Plenty of other nesesary Provision Dayly at the Dore we make no Entertainments, but some Times an Intimate Acquaintance will come in and Pertake with us the Diner we have Provided for our selves & a Dish of Tea in the After noon, & if a Friend sitts and chats a litle in the Evening we Eate our Hasty Puding (our comon super) after they are gone.[3]

He also received word of her from Catharine Ray Greene. "Im now on a Viset to your good Sister who I find Very Comfortable, and as much Health as Can expeckt for a Person So far advanst," Caty wrote Franklin from Boston. "We have had a real feast on you you may rejoice you was not between us as we might Posibly each took a Peice."[4] And yet, knowing how often, in the early and middle years of her life, his sister had not acquainted him with her troubles, he wrote to her pastor, John Lathrop, to inquire. "I am glad my poor dear Sister has so good and kind a Nieghbour," he began. But "I sometimes suspect she may be backward in acquainting me with Circumstances in which I might be more helpful to her. If any such should occur to your Observation, your mentioning them to me will be a Favour I shall be thankful for."[5]

"Yours must be Esteemed a Glorious Life," Jane wrote her brother. He had tried to take the measure of that life, by writing his history, but had left the work unfinished. Having written Part I in London and Part II while in France, he had brought what pages he had back with him upon his return in 1785. In Philadelphia in 1788, he had revised Parts I and II and written Part III—more than one hundred pages, taking the story of his life up till about 1756.[6] He never once mentioned it to his sister, at least in any letter that survives.

He did, however, tell other people about it. "I am recovering from a long-continued gout, and am diligently employed in writing the History of my Life," he wrote to Benjamin Vaughan in October 1788. In 1783, Vaughan had urged Franklin, in the strongest terms, to finish what he had begun: "Sir, I *solicit* the history of your life." It would contain, Vaughan believed, a history of the United States itself, as if in miniature. Moreover, he argued, "all that has happened to you is also connected with the detail of the manners and situation of *a rising* people; and in this respect I do not think that the writings of Caesar and Tacitus can be more interesting to a true judge of human nature and society." And there was more: "These, Sir, are small reasons in my opinion, compared with the chance which your life will give for the forming of future great men; and in conjunction with your *Art of Virtue,* (which you design to publish) of improving the features of private character, and consequently of aiding all happiness both public and domestic." Then, too: "Your Biography will not merely teach self-education, but the education of *a wise man;* and the wisest man will receive lights and improve his progress, by seeing detailed the conduct of another wise man. And why are weaker men to be deprived of such helps, when we see our race has been blundering on in the dark, almost without a guide in this particular, from the farthest trace of time. Shew then, Sir, how much is to be done, *both to sons and fathers;* and invite all wise men to become like yourself; and other men to become wise." And for Vaughan, himself a radical, there was, finally, this: it "will shew that you are ashamed of no origin."[7]

Franklin had begun, in 1771, by addressing the story of his life to his son. That no longer made sense. Vaughan urged him to write what would be read, instead, by *every* son. Franklin explained to Vaughan how he understood his task. He made no pretense of telling the whole of his story: "To shorten the work, as well as for other reasons, I omit all facts and transactions that may not have a tendency to benefit the young reader, by showing him from my example, and my success in emerging from poverty, and acquiring some degree of wealth, power, and reputation, the advantages of certain modes of conduct which I observed, and of avoiding the errors which were prejudicial to me. If a writer can judge properly of his own work, I fancy on reading over what is already done, that the book may be found entertaining, interesting, and useful, more so than I expected when I began it."[8]

In the spring of 1788, Franklin fell down the stone steps to his house—the same steps Jane had fallen down—and hurt his arm, his writing arm. At the time, in addition to working on Part III of his autobiography, he was drafting a new will, in which he left his sister the house in which she lived, as well as £50 a year for the rest of her life.[9]

"Death, however is sure to come to us all, and mine cannot now be far off," he wrote her, "but that may be to me no misfortune, and I shall take care to make it as small a one to you, as possible."[10]

This she heard as a rebuke. "I see you are Angry with me and I cannot bare my Brothers Displeasure," she returned. "I am Anxous for your Life it is true, but also for your Sufferings hear as I had Reason from my own Expearance of a fall from the Same Place, the Efects of which I felt for some years, but is it posable my Dear Brother can think my concern for Him is mearly for my own Soport." After she wrote that, though, Reverend Lathrop stopped by and showed her the letter he had received from Franklin, asking him to be sure to let him know if Jane needed anything. This led her to reread Franklin's letter: "On Reading it several times since I bigin to Doubt whither you were Angry or no, if you were not Pray dont let this make you so, but Impute all to a weakness of mind depraved by *my* Old Age which was never very strong."[11]

"There are in life real evils enough," he returned calmly, "and it is a folly to afflict ourselves with imaginary ones."[12]

She had real worries, too. In the summer of 1788, Jenny Mecom, Jane's "Constant Atendant and comfort," now twenty-three years old, nearly died. "For Eight & forty hours we dispared of her Life," Jane wrote her brother. "Her Phisicion said Afterwards tho he had long Practice he had never a Patient with all the Simptomes of Death on them as she had that Recovered, but thank God she is again about House & we have hopes of a Perfect Recovery."[13]

More often, her family was a comfort, especially when her great-grandchildren visited. Jenny Flagg Greene's daughter Sally Greene came in the spring of 1789.[14] Jane missed having young children around. "I long to have Every won to Kiss & Play with," she wrote.[15] She found, in visits, relief from the aches of old age. "I have Even in my self in times Past Lost the snse of Paine for some time by the Injoyment of good Company." She was happy that her brother had the pleasure of his own mind, writing to him that she was glad his "Intellets . . . thank God Apear as sound as Ever, which must suply you with a Source of Entertainment beyond what comon mortals can Expearance."[16] But she took pleasure, too, in her own intellect: in the company of her own mind.

Franklin wrote to her about his favorite grandson, Benjamin Franklin Bache, who had begun work as a printer in Philadelphia. Franklin sent Jane a box of books Bache had printed: *Lessons for Children,* by Anna Letitia Barbauld.[17] (Barbauld was one of eighteenth-century England's most celebrated and accomplished poets and critics. She was also an astute political commentator.) "They are really valuable for the purpose of teaching Children to read," Franklin told his sister. "The largeness and plainness of the Character, and the little Sentences of common occurrence which they can understand when they read, makes them delight in reading them, so as to forward their Progress exceedingly." But booksellers in Boston were either unable or unwilling to sell them. Jane reported to her brother, "They are Jealous of a young Printer who so far surpases them in the Art & accuracy of his Profeshion & are not willing to Incuridge him by Disposeing of his work."[18]

Franklin told his sister that Sally Franklin Bache had given birth again, to her eighth child.

"Mrs. Bache may make up my Number Twelve," Jane admitted, even "tho she did not begin so young."[19]

Franklin inquired after the Folgers: "By the way, is our Relationship in Nantucket quite worn out?"[20]

"I beleve there are a few of our Nantucket Relations who have still an Affection for us," Jane answered. "But the war time which made such Havock every where Devided & scatered them about." She got gabby:

> Those I was most Intimate with were Abisha Fougre; His Brother, & Sons, Timothy won, the Jenkinss & Kezia Coffin, who was many years Like a Sister to me & a grat friend to my children. She sent me two very Affectionat Leters when the Town was shut up Inviting me to come to Her & She would Sustain me that was her word, & had I Recd them before I left the Town I should certainly have gone.

It was just as well for Jane that she had turned down Coffin's invitation to come spend the war on Nantucket. "A Wise & Good Providence ordered it otherways," Jane wrote. As to Coffin: "She Took to the wrong side & Exerted Her Self by Every method she could devise Right or rong to Accomplish her Designs, & Favour the Britons, went in to Large Traid with them, & for them, & by mis-management & not suckceding in her Indevours has sunk Every Farthing they were Ever Posesed of & have been in Jail both Her Husband at nantuket & her self at Halifax."[21] During the war, Coffin, a loyalist, turned smuggler. In 1779, she was accused of treason; in 1780, she was tried and acquitted in Watertown.[22] In 1782 she was again arrested, charged with attempting to steal a vessel owned by the Continental Army; by the end of the war, she was ruined. She fled to Halifax, where by 1787 she was in debtors' prison.[23] By then, Jane and Keziah had stopped writing to each other.[24]

"She was allway thought to be an Artfull Wooman, but there are such Extraordinary stories tould of her as is hard to be leved," Jane wrote Franklin. (Keziah Folger Coffin died in 1798, after falling down a flight of stairs. The stories that were told about her were so hard to believe that, in the early nineteenth century, she became the subject of a swashbuckling novel which, in turn, inspired Herman Melville to write *Moby-Dick*.)[25] The war had divided the Franklins from the Folgers, and Jane was a Franklin. As for the rest of the Folgers, Jane wrote her brother, "I dont know if they come to Boston if they do they do not know where to find me."[26] She didn't mind. She had no wish to be found.

In December 1789, Benjamin Franklin wrote to his sister with a request: "As I imagine it might be some Pleasure to you, if you knew of anything agreable to me, that you could send me, I now acquaint you, that I have lately wished to regale on Cod's Tongues and Sounds"—that is, a New England delicacy, cods' tongues and bladders—"and if you could now and then send me a small Keg of them, containing about two Quarts, they would be very acceptable and pleasing to your affectionate Brother."[27]

Franklin had been, all his life, a "great Lover of Fish," especially cod.[28]

She sent him "a Keg of souns & Toungs."

"I have Tasted them and think them very Good," she wrote to him on his eighty-fourth birthday. "I hope now you have been able to Regale on them more than wonce as I beleve they are so throwly Preserved they will

Reman sweet all the cool wether." It was cold enough in Boston that winter that she was shut in: "I do not Atempt to go abroad my Breath but Just Serves me to go about the House."[29]

Shut in her house, and mostly confined, as her brother was, to bed, Jane read. In March and April 1790, the *Massachusetts Magazine* published a two-part essay called "On the Equality of the Sexes." Its author was a writer from Gloucester named Judith Sargent Murray. Murray inquired, as Mary Astell had a century earlier, about the cause of men's intellectual superiority, asking, "May we not trace its source in the difference of education, and continued advantages?" To make this case, Murray asked her reader to imagine the lives of a brother and sister, born very much alike:

> Will it be said that the judgment of a male of two years old, is more sage than that of a female's of the same age? I believe the reverse is generally observed to be true. But from that period what partiality! how is the one exalted, and the other depressed, by the contrary modes of education which are adopted! the one is taught to aspire, and the other is early confined and limitted. As their years increase, the sister must be wholly domesticated, while the brother is led by the hand through all the flowery paths of science. Grant that their minds are by nature equal, yet who shall wonder at the *apparent* superiority, if indeed custom becomes *second nature;* nay if it taketh place of nature, and that it doth the experience of each day will evince. At length arrived at womanhood, the uncultivated fair one feels a void, which the employments allotted her are by no means capable of filling. What can she do? to books she may not apply; or if she doth, *to those only of the novel kind,* lest she merit the appellation of a *learned lady.*

The sister has the misfortune, in watching her brother's education, to see the lack of her own. "She feels the want of a cultivated mind." Her misery is profound, her solitude inevitable. If she marries a man of discernment, she is pained by her inferiority. "Doth the person to whom her adverse fate hath consigned her, possess a mind incapable of improvement, she is equally wretched, in being so closely connected with an individual whom she cannot but despise." Either way, she is alone.[30]

On March 24, 1790, Benjamin Franklin wrote the last letter he would ever write to his sister. His hand was poor, weak and quavering. The fish, he told her, "give me pleasure." He had been thinking about their child-hood and about what had become of everyone. Their sister Lydia Franklin, born in 1708, had married a ship's captain named Robert Scott, borne a daughter, and died in 1758.

"Do you know anything of our sister Scott's daughter," Franklin asked Jane, and "whether she is still living, and where?"

He was sure Jane would be able to find out.[31] But he was tired. He added a postscript:

"P.S. It is early in the morning, and I write in bed. The awkward position has occasioned the crooked lines."[32]

He wrote only two more letters.[33] He died on April 17.

Richard Bache sent Jane the news: "My duty calls upon me to make you acquainted with an event which I know will be a sore affliction to your affectionate Breast."[34]

Her brother had been the fellow of her mind's eye. "To make society agreeable there must be a similarity of circumstances and sentiments, as well as age," she wrote, when she learned of his death. "I have no such near me." She had felt such want. "My dear brother supplied all. Every line from him was a pleasure." No one else came as close. "He while living was to me every enjoyment."[35]

CHAPTER XXXVII

Private Life

In May 1790, a month after Benjamin Franklin died, the "History of the Life and Character of Benjamin Franklin" began appearing in Philadelphia in the *Universal Asylum and Columbian Magazine*.[1] Starting in July, much the same account ran in another Philadelphia magazine, the *American Museum, or Universal Magazine*. Both consisted of extracts taken from Franklin's account of his own life. The editors didn't call what they were printing an "autobiography"; that word wasn't coined until 1797.[2] Nor did they print what Franklin had written. Instead, they read what Franklin wrote, summarized the facts, modernized the style, and changed the first person to the third. "At Ten Years old, I was taken home to assist my Father in his Business, which was that of a Tallow Chandler and Sope-Boiler," Franklin had written. "I dislik'd the Trade." This became: "Benjamin had a most decided aversion to the business of soap-boiling."[3] Franklin's editors replaced a memoir with a history.

Meanwhile, the memoir itself—the manuscript and as many as four copies—had begun to travel. In November 1789, Franklin, knowing that he was dying, had sent one copy to Louis-Guillaume Le Veillard, soon thereafter the mayor of Passy, requesting that it be read by him and by the French politician Louis-Alexandre de La Rochefoucauld.[4] He wanted to know, from these men, what to do with what he had written.

"I am not without my Doubts concerning the Memoirs, whether it would be proper to publish them, or not, at least during my Lifetime," he wrote La Rochefoucauld. "I am persuaded there are many Things that would, in Case of Publication, be best omitted. I therefore request it most earnestly of you, my dear Friend, that you would examine them carefully and critically, with Mr. Le Veillard, and give me your candid and friendly Advice."[5]

Two days after writing to La Rochefoucauld, Franklin sent a copy of the manuscript to Benjamin Vaughan in London, requesting that he arrange for Richard Price to read it.[6] He knew Vaughan wanted him to publish it; he wanted to hear Price's views. Price, unaware that Franklin was already dead, replied in May 1790, sending his letter by way of Jonathan Williams Jr.

"Your life has been so distinguished that your account of it must, if made public, excite much curiosity and be read with *eagerness*," Price wrote Franklin. Then he equivocated: "I cannot however help wishing that the qualities and talents which produced this eminence had been aided by a faith in Christianity and the animating hopes of a resurrection to an endless life."[7]

The story of Franklin's life contains within it a story about skepticism. Price found that dangerous. Franklin's readers in France didn't share that

THE

PRIVATE LIFE

OF THE LATE

BENJAMIN FRANKLIN, LL.D.

LATE MINISTER PLENIPOTENTIARY FROM THE UNITED
STATES OF AMERICA TO FRANCE, &c. &c. &c.

Originally written by Himself,
AND NOW TRANSLATED FROM THE FRENCH.

TO WHICH ARE ADDED,

SOME ACCOUNT OF HIS PUBLIC LIFE, A VARIETY OF
ANECDOTES CONCERNING HIM, BY M. M. BRISSOT,
CONDORCET, ROCHEFOUCAULT, LE ROY, &c. &c.

AND THE EULOGIUM OF M. FAUCHET,
CONSTITUTIONAL BISHOP OF THE DEPARTMENT OF CALVADOS,
AND A MEMBER OF THE NATIONAL CONVENTION.

Eripuit cœlo fulmen, mox fceptra tyrannis.   TURGOT.
A Paris, ce grand homme, dans notre ancien régime, feroit refté dans l'obfcurité; comment employer le fils d'un chandelier?   LE ROY.

LONDON:

PRINTED FOR J. PARSONS, NO. 21, PATER-NOSTER ROW.

1793.

fear. In 1791, a French translation of Franklin's memoirs was published in Paris as *Mémoires de la Vie Privée de Benjamin Franklin, Écrits par Lui-même, et Adressés a Son Fils.*[8] Within months of the Paris publication of *La Vie Privée de Benjamin Franklin*, retranslations back into English began appearing in London, often with the title *The Private Life of the Late Benjamin Franklin . . . , Written by Himself.*

In 1793, there appeared in London a two-volume anthology titled *Works of the late Doctor Benjamin Franklin: Consisting of His Life, Written By Himself, Together with Essays Humorous, Moral, and Literary.* These editions, poor translations of a poor translation, did preserve Franklin's first person, if not his prose. But their publication alarmed Temple Franklin, Franklin's literary executor, who, in a letter sent to London newspapers, condemned the *Works* as spurious and unauthorized.

"I am arranging and methodizing the original manuscripts for the press," he promised, "and before the conclusion of this year, I propose publishing the genuine Life of Dr. FRANKLIN as really written by himself."

This he did not do. Temple Franklin, raised in England and having spent much of his life with his grandfather in Paris, was never happy in America. In 1792, he sailed from Philadelphia to London, where he was reunited with his father, who had married his landlady, an Irish widow named Mary D'Evelyn; they lived with Mary's sister-in-law, with whom Temple soon began an affair. Temple Franklin was something of a scoundrel. And, as for preparing his grandfather's Life for publication, he procrastinated.[9] Meanwhile, American publishers began proposing an American edition of the 1793 London version of the *Works*. In September 1793, Benjamin Franklin Bache printed his cousin's caution against unauthorized editions in his newspaper, the Philadelphia *General Advertiser.*[10] None of this halted the unauthorized publication of Franklin's memoirs, either in England or in America. Editions cribbed from the French publication continued to make their way into print.[11]

Did Jane read her brother's memoirs? She must have known about them. She could have learned about them in the *General Advertiser*, which she read whenever she could.[12] Or she might have heard about them from Jonathan Williams Sr. His wife, Grace, had died two weeks before Franklin did. ("Aunt Mecom is poorly a good deal overCome by the Loss of her Niece," Jonathan Williams Sr. had written to Franklin then, "for She was her bosom friend She Could unbosom to her more freely then to anyone except yourSelf.")[13] After Grace's death, Jane remained close to the rest of the Williamses. In 1789, the older Williams had assured the dying Franklin that he would never fail Jane: "She is Intitled to every ade and Assistence in Our power and shall Niver want it."[14] The next year, Williams left Boston for Philadelphia. "Considering His Age & circumstances I think it unlikely I Shuld Ever see him more," Jane wrote Sally. "It is Like cutting off Another Limb." She missed him. "I feal the Diminution of my few friends very Sensibly tho I am grown almost Stupid to Every other Sensation, Except the Joy I recive on Seeing the Just Encomiums continually Expressed & Repeated of the Vertues & Honours Due to my Venerable Brother." News of him she followed above all else.[15] She was lonely. She found joy in reading about her brother in the newspaper. She could scarcely have failed to learn about the publication of his memoirs.

One other person from whom Jane might have heard about Franklin's memoirs was Jonathan Williams Jr. Jane had taught him how to make soap. She adored him. (She took pleasure, she once wrote Franklin, in "the sight of Him whom I Love like a child.")[16] The last letter written in Jane's hand, dated August 11, 1792, is addressed to him. "Be Assured there is Love at the Heart & a wish to be Affectionatly Reme'd," she closed.[17] These are the last words of hers to survive.

As old and frail and far away as she was, Jane had remained close to each of her nephews. Temple Franklin, Benjamin Franklin Bache, and Jonathan Williams Jr. all played a role in the story of Benjamin Franklin's memoirs. Temple owned the rights, Bache had tried to help protect those rights, and Williams had carried Price's letter to Franklin. They also seem to have conspired to keep from her a secret. In 1793 an advertisement appeared in Bache's newspaper for crown soap, to be sold by Benjamin Mecom, in Burlington, New Jersey. Apparently, Benny Mecom hadn't died during the Battle of Trenton after all.[18]

In March 1793, Jane turned eighty-one. She was housebound. She had few visitors; she didn't much like visitors. What she did or did not read that year is impossible to know. Did she read Mary Wollstonecraft's *A Vindication of the Rights of Woman*, excerpted in the *Massachusetts Magazine*?[19] The tragedy of women's ignorance, Wollstonecraft argued, is that women could think about nothing but private life; they could not comprehend public affairs or understand politics; they could not possibly have any interest in the past.[20] Abigail Adams read *A Vindication of the Rights of Woman*, leading her husband to accuse her of being a "Disciple of Wolstoncraft."[21] Whether Jane read it is harder to say. It's not clear whether, that year, she could any longer read at all, even with her spectacles.

Nor is it possible to know whether she read her brother's memoirs. But she had tried for decades to read everything her brother ever wrote. If it was within her power, she would have tried very hard to get her hands on the story of his life.

Supposing she did. Supposing she was able to get a copy. And supposing she was still able to read, squinting and rubbing her eyes. What then?

She would have opened the first volume to find a preface, which included an excerpt from a letter written by Richard Price, in which he observed that the story of Franklin's life, written by himself, showed, plainly, strikingly, "how a man, by talents, industry, and integrity, may rise from obscurity to the first eminence and consequence in the world."[22] Finishing the preface, she would have turned the page to read a story about a rise from rags to riches. *It wil teache you to live, and learne you to die.* It wasn't a Bible or a psalter or an almanac or a conduct manual or a constitution. It was something new.

If she did read the story of her brother's life, written by himself, she would have pored over every letter, every word. And she would have discovered: he never mentioned her.

CHAPTER XXXVIII

Partial, Prejudiced, and Ignorant

In the autumn of 1791, in an English town not more than ninety miles south of Ecton, a fifteen-year-old girl named Jane picked up her pen. On the first page of a tiny notebook made of stitched vellum, she wrote a title: "The History of England from the Reign of Henry the 4th to the Death of Charles the 1st, by a Partial, Prejudiced, & Ignorant Historian." And then she added, at the bottom of the page, "N.B. There will be very few Dates in this History."

Jane Austen was clever and she was sharp and she was wry. She was the littlest of the eight Austen children. She was, it was said, "very like her brother Henry."[1] Her father was a rector and a schoolmaster. He sent her to a dame school and then, when she was ten, to a boarding school, in Reading. There was a lending library in Reading, and Jane read everything she could get her hands on—Addison, Fielding, Richardson, and the *Lady's Magazine*. In 1787, when she was twelve, she started writing stories. She thought it would be very funny to write a fake history.

Jane Austen's "History of England" is a parody of Oliver Goldsmith's march-of-the-monarchs four-volume chronicle of kings: *The History of England, from The Earliest Times to the Death of George II.* Once in a great while, Austen happened to bump into a fact or two, for which she apologized, "Truth being I think very excusable in an Historian."[2]

Austen's "History" consisted of thirteen perfectly dunderheaded character sketches of the crowned heads of England. Of Henry V: "During his reign, Lord Cobham was burnt alive, but I forget what for." Of the Duke of Somerset: "He was beheaded, of which he might with reason have been proud, had he known that such was the death of Mary Queen of Scotland; but as it was impossible that he should be conscious of what had never happened, it does not appear that he felt particularly delighted with the manner of it." As for Lady Jane, the Nine Days' Queen, "an amiable young woman, & famous for reading Greek while other people were hunting": "Whether she really understood that language or whether such a study proceeded only from an excess of vanity for which I believe she was always rather remarkable, is uncertain."[3]

Austen had a thing or two to say about women as readers of histories written by men, not just in her fake history, but in her fiction. In *Northanger Abbey*, Austen's heroine confesses that she finds history both boring and impossible to credit: "It tells me nothing that does not either vex or weary me. The quarrels of popes and kings, with wars or pestilences, in every page; the men all so good for nothing, and hardly any women at all—it is very tiresome: and yet I often think it odd that it should be so dull, for a great deal of it must be invention."[4] In Austen, history written by men is, to women readers, fiction.

"All histories are against you," Captain Harville insists, in *Perusasion*, when Anne Elliot claims that women are more constant than men. "But perhaps you will say, these were all written by men."

"Men have had every advantage to us in telling their own story," Anne answers, insisting. "I will not allow books to prove anything."[5]

Fiction was Austen's answer to history, to biography, to the memoirs of great men. But it wasn't only Austen's answer; it was the eighteenth century's answer: fiction, not history, could tell the stories of ordinary lives, something that's necessary because there's more to the past than the march of monarchs. "There have been as great Souls unknown to fame as any of the most famous," Benjamin Franklin once wrote. No one, Jane Franklin Mecom knew, was worthless, not even "the most Insignificant creature on Earth."[6] Fiction is the history of the obscure.

Novels like Austen's didn't only critique history; they *were* history. In the eighteenth century, when the novel was born, novelists called their books "histories," smack on their title pages.[7] In the preface to *Robinson Crusoe,* Daniel Defoe wrote, "The Editor believes the thing to be a just History of Fact; neither is there any Appearance of Fiction in it." But of course Defoe was not the editor of a journal kept by a man named Crusoe; there was no journal. Defoe made it up. Of what Defoe meant by this imposture, one critic wrote, "I know not; unless you would have us think, that the Manner of your telling a Lie will make it a Truth."[8] Samuel Richardson, too, insisted that he was merely the editor of Pamela's letters; the letters themselves, he claimed, were real: genuine historical documents. That this was a lie doesn't mean it was a hoax; Richardson wanted his novels to be read with "Historical Faith," since, he believed, they contained a kind of truth, the kind of truth you can find in poetry: the truth of the possible, the truth of what it means to be human.[9] The truth of fiction was its intimacy. A novel, as Defoe put it, was a "private History," a history of private life. In *The Life and Opinions of Tristram Shandy, Gentleman* (1759–67), Laurence Sterne implied that his book was a history "of what passes in a man's own mind." No one was more brash about this than Henry Fielding. It is "our Business to relate Facts as they are," Fielding told his readers, classing himself among "historical writers who do not draw their materials from records" but, rather, from "the vast authentic Doomsday-Book of Nature." In his 1749 *History of Tom Jones, a Foundling,* he included a chapter called "Of Those Who Lawfully May, and of Those Who May Not, Write Such Histories as This." Fielding insisted that what flowed from his pen was "true history"; fiction was what historians wrote.[10]

Fielding was not without his critics. "A new Sect of Biographers (founded by Mr. *Fielding*)" was much lamented by one, who in 1751 attempted "to put a Stop to the unbounded Liberties the Historians of this comic Stamp might otherwise indulge themselves."[11] Novelists really had founded a new kind of biography, a new kind of history: there was history based in fact (whose truth is founded in documentary evidence) and history based in fiction (whose truth is founded in human nature). Novelists believed the second was truer than the first. "Dismiss me from the falsehood and impossibility of history, and deliver me over to the reality of romance," William Godwin pleaded in "Of History and Romance." (In 1794, Godwin titled his first novel *Things as They Are*.) There is and never can be any such thing as "genuine history," Godwin insisted: "Nothing is more uncertain, more contradictory, more unsatisfying, than the evidence of facts." Every history is incomplete; every historian has a point of view; every historian relies on what is unreliable: documents written by people who were not under oath and cannot be cross-examined. (That is to say, every historian is, like Jane Austen's historian, "Partial, Prejudiced, & Ignorant.") Before his imperfect sources, the historian is powerless: "He must take what they choose to tell; the broken fragments, and the scattered ruins of evidence." He could decide merely to reproduce his sources, to offer a list of facts, "but this is in reality no history. He that knows only on what day the Bastille was taken, and on what spot Louis XVI perished, knows nothing."

Like Fielding, Godwin believed that the novel was not only another kind of history but "the noblest and most excellent species of history." History made claims to absolute truth, Godwin observed, but "the reader will be miserably deluded if, while he reads history, he suffers himself to imagine that he is reading facts." Instead, he is reading the historian's always partial, prejudiced, and ignorant interpretation of facts. The novelist is the better historian because he *admits* these deficiencies. The novelist, not the historian, Godwin argued, is "the writer of real history."[12]

American writers like Charles Brockden Brown made this argument, too, Brown exploring it both in his novels, especially *Wieland* (1798), and in essays like "The Difference Between History and Romance" (1800).[13] History concerns facts, Brown argued, but facts have to be arranged and explained. The historian, then, "is a dealer, not in certainties, but probabilities, and is therefore a romancer."[14] Brown went further, arguing that history's grossest distortion of reality stems not from its false claims to truth but, instead, from its exclusive interest in the great.[15]

In the eighteenth century, history and fiction split. Benjamin Franklin's life entered the annals of history; lives like his sister's became the subject of fiction. Histories of great men, novels of little women.

Franklin's story doesn't fit neatly on one side of that divide, nor Jane's on the other. Their lives were messier than that. John Adams found Benjamin Franklin impossible to account for. "His name was familiar to government and people," Adams wrote Jefferson, "to kings, courtiers, nobility, clergy, and philosophers, as well as to plebeians, to such a degree that there was scarcely a peasant or a citizen, a *valet de chamber,* coachman or footman, a lady's chambermaid or a scullion in a kitchen, who was not familiar with it, and who did not consider him a friend to human kind. When they spoke of him, they seemed to think he was to restore the golden age." Adams knew, though, that a large part of Franklin's fame, high and low, was a consequence of the eighteenth century's revolution in reading and writing: "Throughout his whole life he courted and was courted by the printers, editors, and correspondents of reviews, magazines, journals, and pamphleteers, and those little busy meddling scribblers that are always buzzing about the press," Adams fumed. "If a collection could be made of all the Gazettes of Europe for the latter half of the eighteenth century, a greater number of panegyrical paragraphs upon '*le grand Franklin*' would appear, it is believed, than upon any other man that ever lived." But there was more behind Franklin's fame, too: something to do with history itself. Writing his biography, Adams believed, would require telling the story of an entire century; explaining Franklin would require writing a book of ages. "To develop that complication of causes, which conspired to produce so singular a phenomenon, is far beyond my means or forces," Adams wrote. "Perhaps it can never be done without a complete history of the philosophy and politics of the eighteenth century. Such a work would be one of the most important that ever was written; much more interesting to this and future ages than the 'Decline and Fall of the Roman Empire.' "[16]

John Adams was puzzled by the insufficiency of history. As history, the story of a life like Franklin's is, finally, a mystery, unless it's told alongside the story of a life like Jane's. In 1806, Charles Brockden Brown hinted at this in an essay called "Historical Characters Are False Representations of Nature." Brown, who believed fiction to be truer than history, blamed historians for blinding readers to the pathos of small lives. "The human character appears diminutive, when compared to those we met with in history," Brown wrote, "yet am I persuaded that domestic sorrows are not less poignant, and many of our associates are characters not inferior to the elaborate delineations which so much interest in the deceptive page of history." This, for Brown, was the historian's darkest deception, the idea that only the great are good: "Popular prejudice assists the illusion, and because we are accustomed to behold public characters occupy a situation in life that few can experience, we are induced to believe that their capacities are more enlarged, their passions more refined, and, in a word, that nature has bestowed on them faculties denied to obscurer men." This is history's deceit: "The fascination which thus takes possession of us is, therefore, the artifice of the historian, assisted by those early prejudices of that superiority which we attach to great characters." But great characters are *not* superior to obscure men, who are, alas, condemned to obscurity by history itself. The solution was to write fiction, Brown decided, but one day, he hoped, it might be possible to write a new kind of history. "If it were possible to read the histories of those who are doomed to have no historian, and to glance into domestic journals as well as into national archives," Brown wrote, "we should then perceive the unjust prodigality of our sympathy to those few names, which eloquence has adorned with all the seduction of her graces."[17]

If it were possible to read the histories of those who are doomed to have no historian, we should then perceive the unjust prodigality of our sympathy. What would it mean to write the history of an age not only from what has been saved but also from what has been lost? What would it mean to write a history concerned not only with the lives of the famous but also with the lives of the obscure? What would it mean to turn the pages of Jane Franklin's Book of Ages?

PART FIVE

remains

––––––

1794–

CHAPTER XXXIX

A New and More Beautiful Edition

On February 17, 1794, Benjamin Franklin's sister, eighty-one years old, "weak in Body yet of sound mind and memory," signed her will. The will itself is written in another hand. She could no longer write.[1]

She had lived through a century of revolution. In 1771, Massachusetts's poor laws had, for the first time, required that girls be taught to write. This hadn't changed matters as much as it might have. "We don't pretend to teach the female part of the town anything more than dancing," one Boston teacher reported in 1782.[2]

Jane reckoned her estate. She had some small items of value: things made of silver and gold. To her grandson Josiah Flagg, she gave a silver porringer that had belonged to her brother Peter Franklin.[3] To her great-grandson Franklin Greene: "my Gold sleeve Buttons." To her great-granddaughter Sally Greene: "a mourning Ring, which was given to me at the funeral of my kinsman Josiah Williams."[4] To her friend Elizabeth Lathrop, the wife of her minister: "a White Medallion of Dr. Franklin."[5]

To her granddaughter Jenny Mecom, nearly thirty and unmarried, she gave things made of wool and flax, things made of wood, things made of copper and iron and brass:

> In consideration of the extraordinary attention paid me by my Grand Daughter Jane Mecom exclusive of her common and necessary concerns in domestic affairs & the ordinary business of the Family, I think proper to give and bequeath unto her several articles of household furniture, particularly as follows The Bed, Bedstead, and Curtains which I commonly use, the three pair of homespun sheets lately

made and the Bedding of every kind used with this Bed both in Summer and Winter, consisting of two Blankets, a White Counterpane and two Calico Bedquilts, one of which is new; The Chest of Drawers and Table which usually stand in my Chamber, and six Black Walnut Chairs with green bottoms also two black Chairs, my looking Glass which I bought of Samuel Taylor and which commonly hangs in my Chamber, a large Brass Kettle, a small Bell mettle skillet, a small Iron Pot, a large Trammel, a pair of large Iron hand irons, a shovel and pair of Tongs, a Black Walnut stand and tea board, two brass Candle sticks, a small Copper Tea Kettle and one half of my Wearing Apparel of every kind.

Believing her son Benjamin to be dead, Jane left the remainder of her estate, including the house itself, in the hands of her executors, her minister, John Lathrop, and Benjamin Summers, a merchant, stipulating that the only one of her twelve children still alive, her daughter Jane Mecom Collas, would be allowed to occupy the house for as long as she lived.

She considered what to do with her papers. A letter she loved best she decided to show to Benjamin Edes. Edes printed it on the front page of the March 3 issue of the *Boston Gazette,* under this head:

THE FOLLY OF MAKING WAR.

Extract from a letter written by that great Philosopher, and wise politician, the late DR. FRANKLIN, to a friend in Boston, not long before his death.

There followed a paragraph from a letter Franklin had sent Jane on September 20, 1787, three days after he signed the Constitution. It begins, "I agree with you perfectly in your disapprobation of war."[6] Franklin's letter was an answer to a letter of his sister. "I had Rather hear of the Swords being beat into Plow-shares, & the Halters used for Cart Roops, if by that means we may be brought to live Peaceably with won a nother," she had written him.[7] Edes didn't print Jane's letter or mention it. *To a friend in Boston* is all he said.

·   ·   ·

Six weeks later, on April 17, America's first best-selling novel, *Charlotte: A Tale of Truth,* was published in Philadelphia.[8] Its author, Susanna Rowson, grew up in Boston; later, she founded Boston's Young Ladies' Academy, where she taught not only writing but also history.[9]

Charlotte is the tale of a fifteen-year-old girl who is seduced, gives birth, and dies.[10] In eighteenth-century novels, women do not generally survive seduction at the age of fifteen. At fifteen, Jane Franklin hadn't married a gentleman, like Pamela. She hadn't died miserably, like Charlotte. Instead, she'd married a poor man, raised her children. She'd raised her grandchildren. She'd raised her great-grandchildren. And only then did she meet her end.

She died at home on Wednesday, May 7, 1794.[11] Of "old age, & a Cold," John Lathrop wrote in his church record book.[12] Edes reported the event in the "Deaths" column of the *Boston Gazette.* The notice was picked up in New York, Philadelphia, and Newport.

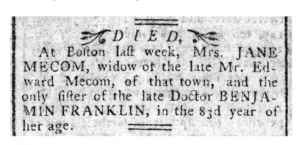

Her funeral was held in her house at five o'clock on May 10. "Her friends, and the friends of the late Dr. Franklin are requested to attend," read one notice.[13] Mourners must have been few. She had outlived almost everyone she'd ever loved.

No account of the funeral survives. Jane Mecom Collas and Jenny Mecom would have been there. Josiah Flagg would likely have come from Lancaster. Franklin and Sally Greene, thirteen and sixteen, might have ridden from Rhode Island, but maybe not.

John Lathrop would have delivered the sermon. It does not survive. At the funeral of his first wife, Lathrop had preached on resurrection: "The unwieldy carcass which is now with difficulty moved from place to place, shall be changed for a body such as God shall please to give."[14] Maybe he said much the same for Jane.

No one knows where she is buried. The records of the administration of her estate include "funeral Charges" of more than seven pounds but no mention of any payment to the engraver of a stone.[15]

She had kept with her, all her life, a scrap of paper on which her brother had written an epitaph for himself:

> The Body of
> B. Franklin Printer;
> Like the Cover of an old Book
> Its Contents torn out
> And stript of its Lettering and
> Gilding,
> Lies here, Food for Worms.
> But the Work shall not be wholly lost:
> For it will, as he believ'd, appear once more
> In a new & more perfect Edition,
> Corrected and amended,
> By the Author.[16]

She thought she was a book, too. In the twilight of her life, she wrote to her brother that she looked forward to both of them attaining "the Injoyment of that New & more Beautifull Edition."[17]

She believed that every life mattered, even her own. "I am willing to Depart out of it when ever my Grat Benifactor has no farther Use for me," she wrote her brother, for "I know the most Insignificant creature on Earth may be made some Use of in the Scale of Beings, may Touch some Spring."[18] She loved, too, a poem about death written by her uncle Benjamin: "Thy Journeys End." She had once copied it out:

> Let Joy sit on thy Brow
> Down Hill art going now
>   Next stage may give the flight
> From all those Earthly things
> Up to the King of Kings
>   In uncreated Light

("Tho the Poitry is not so good," she wrote, discerningly, "I have taken Grat satisfaction in Reading it.")

My soul still thither bend
Thy steps all this way tend
 Thy all to this Aply
When thow art wonce got there
Past want & woe & care
 Thou'rt Blest Eternaly.[19]

She might have liked that, for an epitaph: *Past want & woe & care. Blest Eternaly.*

 She may have been buried near her parents, in the old Granary Burying Ground.[20] By the time she died, the inscription on the stone her brother had placed there had begun to wear and fade. A few decades more and it was "nearly obliterated."[21] In 1825, Boston marked the fiftieth anniversary of the revolution. "Those who established our liberty and our government are daily dropping from among us," Daniel Webster said at the dedication of the Bunker Hill Monument on the battle's fiftieth anniversary, June 17, 1825.[22] The city from which a very young Benjamin Franklin had fled, and to which he had rarely returned, wanted to count him among its founders. People began raising money to replace the stone Franklin had placed in the Granary Burying Ground with something grander. (A campaign was launched, too, to rename the burial ground "Franklin Cemetery"; this proved unsuccessful.)[23] In 1827, Franklin's marker was removed and replaced with a massive, five-tiered, twenty-foot-high obelisk made of granite taken from the same quarry as the Bunker Hill Monument. It dwarfs every other stone in the burying ground. On its face, brass letters read, simply, FRANKLIN.[24] Jane's bones might lie there somewhere, underfoot, beneath her brother's name. If she ever had a gravestone, it's long since sunk underground.

 Silver and gold. Copper, iron, brass. Wool and flax. Wood and stone. Flesh and bone. What had become of her books and papers?

CHAPTER XL

The Librarian

She gave her papers to an archivist and her books to a librarian.

She had kept hold of her papers, scraps saved against time, in trouble and strife, in war and peace. A letter her brother had written to their mother, in 1749, she had tucked away. "From my Brother to His Father & Mother," she wrote on the back of it.[1] "To go into the Litle Trunk," she wrote on the back of another.[2]

In 1794, knowing she was dying, she gave the bulk of her papers to her granddaughter and namesake, Jenny Mecom, with the provision that her minister, John Lathrop, could go through them and take what he wanted.[3] Lathrop was a member of the American Academy of Arts and Sciences. In 1791, he was elected Librarian and Keeper of the Cabinet.[4] He was an archivist. He died in 1816. At his death, his five surviving children, including a daughter named Jane, inherited his estate. In 1821, Jane Lathrop married a Boston merchant named Caleb Loring; Jane Franklin Mecom's papers remained in Lathrop and Loring family hands for more than a century.[5]

Sometime before Jane died, she gave her Book of Ages to her grandson Josiah Flagg. Not long after traveling from Philadelphia to Boston in 1786, Flagg had settled in Lancaster, Massachusetts. He married in 1789. In 1790, he was among the original proprietors of the town's first library, founded to promote "a general diffusion of knowledge."[6]

He made his grandmother's Book of Ages his own. On its blank pages, he recorded the story of his own life. "According to the best information I can obtain, there were two Brothers, Flagg, came over from England, one settled in Boston," he began. "My father William Flagg married Sarah Mecom a Niece of the illustrious Dr Benjamin Franklin." His own life story was brief: "I was born Nov 12 1760 and married June 7 1789 to Dolly Thurston." Then he recorded the births and deaths of his own children. He had, eventually, six. His first daughter, born in 1791, he named Sarah, after his mother.[7]

In 1800, he began serving on both the school committee and the board of selectmen. He was also appointed the town's librarian.[8] In 1801, he was elected Lancaster's town clerk, a position he held for thirty-four years. In the town books—books of ages—he recorded births, marriages, and deaths. He was curious about history and found, in an attic, and copied out, an "ancient Record Book"—a list of births and deaths beginning in 1635. In 1803, he bought a beautiful edition of the King James Bible. In it, the printer had left, following Revelation, four blank pages headed "Family Record."[9] On those blank pages, Flagg recorded his family history, repeating there, and carrying much further, the record he had begun in his grandmother's Book of Ages. "Blessed are the dead," he wrote there, when his wife died.[10]

He kept careful records of his books. He purchased for the town library a collection of John Lathrop's sermons. He signed the books he owned. When the American Antiquarian Society opened in Worcester in 1812, to "encourage the collection and preservation of the Antiquities of our country," he donated to its library his copies of Benjamin Franklin's books.[11] In 1816, he was nominated to serve as Worcester County's register of deeds.[12]

In 1836, at the age of seventy-five, Josiah Flagg decided against seeking reelection to the office of Lancaster town clerk, whereupon the town gave public thanks for his service, noting that, among his many other talents, "his penmanship is almost as legibile as good print." He died in 1840.[13] His daughter Sally recorded his death in the family Bible. "Departed this life Feby 11th 1840 Josiah Flagg Esq in the 80th year of his age. The kind tender & affectionate Husband and the beloved Father. 'The Dust shall return to the earth as it was and the Spirit to God who gave it.'"[14]

In 1845, a group of Boston men founded the New England Historic Genealogical Society, the nation's first genealogical organization, dedicated to preserving the records of New Englanders' ancestors. In 1853, William Flagg Bliss, a genealogist researching the Flagg family, went to Lancaster. He met two of Josiah Flagg's children, Sally Flagg and Samuel Ward Flagg, and was said to have "obtained much valuable genealogical history from them."[15] Sally Flagg had other kinds of treasures, too. A member of the

New England Historic Genealogical Society met her in 1858, when she was sixty-six. He wrote himself a note: "Miss Sarah Flagg, of South Lancaster, has in her possession many letters written by Dr. Franklin to his sister."[16]

Sally Flagg was known in town as a quirky, old-fashioned spinster. In 1862, when Lancaster opened a public library, she made a gift of twenty books that had once belonged to her father. They included books that Josiah Flagg had inherited from his grandmother. Jane's books ended up in a library.[17]

Samuel Ward Flagg died in 1871. In 1872, the Cambridge estate lawyer and New England Historic Genealogical Society member Benjamin A. G. Fuller reported that "certain descendants of Josiah Flagg, late of Lancaster, Mass., with a view to their better preservation in the archives of some fitting institution," wished to give six letters to the society. Fuller, presenting the gift, said, "These papers, I do not doubt, will be regarded as valuable, and worthy of a place in the archives of the society, by the side of the many rare and choice documents, already in the possession of this useful and honored institution."[18] Included in this bequest was Jane's Book of Ages.

It was not the last of her remains.

CHAPTER XLI

The Editor

The letters Jane left behind were eventually collected and edited by the nineteenth century's most important American historian, not because he was interested in her life but because he was interested in her brother's. Jared Sparks, a former chaplain of Congress and editor and owner of the United States' first literary magazine, the *North American Review,* wanted to write the history of America from original documents: unpublished manuscripts, like the papers of Benjamin Franklin. But first, he had to collect them.[1]

In 1826, in an essay called "Materials for American History," Sparks explained his philosophy of history:

> Sometimes the historian fails, on account of his subject; at other times, for the want of materials. It is not in the power of the greatest mind to make that dignified and interesting, which in its nature is low and unattractive. The first step to be taken by a historian, therefore, is to exercise his judgment in selecting a subject, which will not cause him to run the hazard of wasting his powers in developing and recording events, that have nothing in them to command the admiration, or awaken the sympathy of mankind. Next come the materials of history, and in no part of his task are the resolution, the patience, the ardor of the historian, more seriously tried than in collecting these.

He measured the merits of Herodotus and Hume, of Gibbon and Lucian. Some of these historians had chosen unworthy subjects. Some had been good researchers, others good writers, but a great historian must be both. American historians, Sparks believed, suffered a disadvantage: the problem wasn't that they lacked talent or worthy subjects; the problem was that American historians lacked sources.

"Nothing is more obvious, than the scattered and loose condition of all materials for history in the United States," he warned. "Many have been lost, and those which remain will gradually suffer the same fate, unless some special means shall be used to collect and preserve them." He was especially concerned about documents chronicling the origin and progress of the revolution. "Two or three years ago," he reported, "a large bundle of letters was brought to light in a baker's shop in New York, which proved to be the private correspondence of Paul Jones."[2] Sheaves of Benjamin Franklin's papers had wound up in a tailor's shop on St. James's Street in London; some of them had been cut into sleeve patterns.[3] Sparks made a plea: "Individuals, who possess manuscripts of public interest as affording materials for history, should deposit them in the archives of public institutions, where the chance of their being preserved will be much greater than in private hands."[4] And he made a promise: he would dedicate his life to gathering the lost, scattered, and junked papers of the revolutionary generation.

In 1827, Sparks helped plan the erection of the Franklin monument. Then he left Boston for Mount Vernon, where he read George Washington's papers.[5] After that, he embarked on a two-year tour of Europe.[6] In London, Sparks found a great many papers written by Benjamin Franklin. In Paris, he sought out Temple Franklin's widow. Temple Franklin had died in poverty in 1823. After having advertised in 1793 that he was in the midst of preparing a complete edition of his grandfather's papers, Temple had proved a malingerer.[7] William Franklin, despairing, died in exile in 1813.[8] Temple Franklin's six-volume *Memoirs of the Life and Writings of Benjamin Franklin* was published, between 1808 and 1818, by William Duane (the husband of the widow of Benjamin Franklin's grandson Benjamin Franklin Bache).[9] But Sparks was disappointed to discover that Temple Franklin's widow no longer had any of Benjamin Franklin's papers.

Sparks sailed home. In Boston he heard rumors that there were Franklin papers in his very backyard: "50 to 60 original letters of Dr Franklin to his sister," now in the hands of Mrs. Caleb Loring.[10] Sparks went to see her. He wanted the letters. She refused to give them to him.[11]

In 1831, Sparks left Boston for Philadelphia, where he met with Baches and Duanes and with the descendants of Jonathan Williams.[12] He also finally found out what had happened to the papers Benjamin Franklin had left to his grandson. "Before Wm. T. Franklin went to Europe, after Dr. Franklin's death," Sparks wrote in his diary, "he put into the hands of Mr. Fox of Philadelphia a large collection of papers and articles which had belonged to Dr Franklin."[13] When Temple Franklin had left America for England, he had brought with him only a small number of his grandfather's papers, leaving the great bulk of them behind in the hands of a friend, George Fox. Fox died in 1828; the papers descended to his son Charles. In 1831, Sparks went with Charles Fox to his estate in Champlost, outside of Philadelphia, where he discovered that Fox had stored the papers—some thirteen thousand manuscripts—in a stable.[14]

Sparks returned to Philadelphia the next year.[15] On this visit, he learned that Fox had given many of the papers from his stable to the physician Franklin Bache, Benjamin Franklin's great-grandson (the son of Benjamin Franklin Bache).[16] Sparks went to see Bache and wrote in his diary, "I visited Dr. Franklin Bache, who has a volume of Mss., containing copies of many letters from Franklin to his mother & sister, which have never been printed."[17] Sparks was delighted. He found Franklin's family letters charming. He thought they ought to be published. When he got back to Boston, he began a correspondence with Franklin Bache and arranged to borrow the manuscript volume.[18]

"In my researches I have collected somewhat more than one hundred original letters of Dr. Franklin, which have not been printed, and these chiefly on private and domestic subjects," Sparks wrote Bache in December 1832. "They exhibit the author in so amiable and engaging a light, that I have thoughts of publishing them separately in a small volume. . . . Kind feelings and an indulgent temper are everywhere manifested, and rendered doubly attractive by the peculiar charm & simplicity of his style." He wondered whether Bache had any more unpublished letters; except "such as were written to his relations in Boston," Sparks explained, "I probably have the originals."[19]

In all, Sparks collected more than a hundred letters from Franklin to friends and family in Boston. But one set he had not been able to collect: Mrs. Loring's letters. In January 1833, Sparks begged Mrs. Loring's brother-in-law to intervene on his behalf. Sparks was able to *see* some of the letters, and to copy them, but not to have them.[20] He wrote to Bache on February 27, 1833: "There are in this town in the hands of one lady 20 or 30 original letters from Dr. F. to Mrs Mecom. I should suppose they more properly belonged to her granddaughters, & if applied for, I presume they would be given up to them."[21]

Meanwhile, Sparks was busy working on Washington's letters; he had eight boxes of manuscripts shipped from Mount Vernon to Boston. On April 2, 1833, Sparks moved, with his boxes, into the house in Cambridge— now a boardinghouse—that had served as Washington's headquarters in 1775, so that he could edit the papers where the great man himself had once written them.[22] Henry Wadsworth Longfellow, a Harvard professor of belles lettres, boarded there, too. In that house, Sparks finished editing Washington's papers and began editing Franklin's, embarking on what would become a ten-volume edition of *The Works of Benjamin Franklin*. (It would be in the *Works* that Sparks established the custom of calling the story of Franklin's life an "autobiography.")[23] But first he wanted to publish that set of more than a hundred delightfully charming family letters. Ten days after he moved into the house, Sparks wrote to Bache, returning a volume of manuscript letters Bache had sent to him and promising to send Bache a copy of his volume of Franklin's family letters as soon as it appeared, declaring, "It affords the best and most favorable exhibition of his private feelings and character, which has ever appeared."[24]

Sparks's *Collection of Familiar Letters and Miscellaneous Papers of Benjamin Franklin* was published in June.[25] Readers would have recognized *Familiar Letters* as an allusion to Samuel Richardson. The collection consists of 128 letters; 21 are to Jane, including the letter Franklin wrote to her on January 6, 1727, the day he turned twenty-one.[26] In 1833, Sparks had seen that letter; he'd copied it, edited it, and redacted it. What he printed is curiously preachy. And then: the original letter disappeared. It has never been seen by a scholar since.[27]

The first volume of Sparks's twelve-volume *Writings of George Washington* appeared in 1833, just after Franklin's *Familiar Letters*. Sparks adored Washington, and even his handwriting, which he found "close and handsome."[28] But he had not been pleased to discover that Washington was not often a forceful writer. In editing Washington's papers, Sparks corrected Washington's spelling and punctuation. What he found badly expressed, he rewrote. When Washington called too little money a "flea-bite," Sparks changed this to "a sum totally inadequate to our demands."[29] Passages in which Washington criticized New England men, as when he remarked on the "unaccountable kind of stupidity in the lower class of these people," Sparks simply struck out. All this he did silently.[30]

Sparks's problem with Franklin was different from his problem with Washington. Franklin was a delightful writer, the best writer in eighteenth-century America. Sparks much admired "the peculiar charm and simplicity of his style."[31] He did, nevertheless, make changes. Capitalizing nouns had gone out of style. So had the use of italics, except for emphasis. These changes had begun even before Franklin's death and, as a printer, he greatly regretted them; he thought they made type much harder to read. "Lately another Fancy has induced some Printers to use the short round *s* instead of the long one," Franklin complained to Noah Webster. "Certainly the omitting this prominent Letter makes the Line appear more even; but renders it less immediately legible; as the paring all Men's Noses might smoothe and level their Faces, but would render their Physiognomies less distinguishable."[32] Sparks shrank Franklin's capitals, romanized his italics, and changed his long *s*'s to short ones. He cut off Franklin's nose.

Sparks wished his collection of Franklin's *Works* to be entire. In August 1833, he wrote to Franklin Bache to tell him about Mrs. Loring, who, he said, had in her possession "about 25 original letters to Mrs Mecom." (The number had diminished since he'd first learned of them.) In the *Familiar Letters*, Sparks explained, he hadn't been able to print any of Mrs. Loring's letters in full; she had allowed him to copy only small portions. (Mrs. Loring, Sparks told Bache, "has scruples about letting them be printed, though she permitted extracts to be taken.") Sparks asked for Bache's assistance: "I think she would give up these letters to Mrs. Mecom's granddaughters, if they were to make a proper application."

"Will you be the medium of this application?" Sparks asked. "It is desirable that the letters should be printed entire, & if the granddaughters obtain them, they would no doubt give copies for this purpose. You can write to *Caleb Loring, Esq* on the subject, who is Mrs Loring's husband. They are highly respectable people. I wish you would keep my name entirely out of the matter, as I have made unavailing efforts to get the letters. The only objection is Mrs Loring's conscientious scruples, as to her right to part with them unless it be to the descendants of Mrs Mecom."[33]

At the time, "Mrs Mecom's granddaughters" were the surviving daughters of Benjamin Mecom, who were, by 1833, three: Sarah, Abiah, and

Jenny.[34] Sarah Mecom had married Benjamin Smith, of Burlington, New Jersey; she was a widow, living in Philadelphia.[35] Abiah Mecom, never married, was also living in Philadelphia. She kept a shop.[36] In Boston, Jenny Mecom had moved out of the house in the North End not long after her grandmother's death.[37] In 1800, at the age of thirty-five, Jenny Mecom had married a shipwright named Simon Kinsman. They had no children. Simon Kinsman had died in 1818.[38]

Sometime between 1836 and 1840, when Jane Mecom Kinsman, now in her seventies, was living in either Boston or Philadelphia, Sparks went to see her. He asked her about her grandmother, who, she said, had had thirteen children, not twelve. In his notebook, he took down their names. Whatever else Sparks asked Kinsman, he didn't record her answers. Instead, he wrote down names, and nothing more.[39] He had no use for old wives' tales. He cared not one whit about the lives of the obscure. He had no curiosity about the short and simple annals of the poor.

The first volume of Sparks's *Works of Benjamin Franklin* appeared in 1836. Then he returned to Europe. "I have brought home rich treasures,— two large trunks full of his papers, which belonged to Franklin, which have slumbered in a garret 40 years," Sparks wrote in 1837.[40] The next year, he joined the faculty at Harvard as McLean Professor of Ancient and Modern History. He was the first professor of history at Harvard, and the first professor of American history anywhere.[41]

The year Sparks published Franklin's *Familiar Letters,* he launched a book series called *The Library of American Biography.* His plan was to publish "the lives of all persons, who have been distinguished in America, from the date of its first discovery to the present time." He had the idea that a collection of biographies would add up to "a perfect history of the country."[42] Between 1833 and 1849, he oversaw the publication of twenty-five volumes. People called him the American Plutarch. In 1849, he became the president of Harvard.[43]

Lives have been written for centuries, but the word *biography* was coined only late in the seventeenth century, and the modern genre didn't really begin to take shape until 1791, with the publication of Boswell's *Life of Johnson.* The United States was new; the presidency was new; biography was new. How the lives of the founders would be written would set a precedent for the writing of biography in a republic. Sparks believed that the proper role of the historian was to burnish the reputation of great men, even in the United States, a nation founded on the idea that all men are created equal. He held that the aim of biography was "to bring together a series of facts which should do justice to the fame and character of a man, who possessed qualities, and performed deeds, that rendered him remarkable and are worthy of being remembered."[44] Stories about nobodies he hated. "The present unfortunate propensity of filling tomes of quartos and octavos with marvellous accounts of the lives of men and women, who, during their existence, produced no impression on the publick mind, and who were not known beyond the circle of their immediate friends, or the mountains, which bounded the horizon of their native villages, is preposterous and absurd," Sparks wrote. "Why should the world be called off from its busy occupations to listen to an ill told story of their little concerns?"[45]

He kept hunting for Franklin's letters.[46] The final volume of Sparks's *Works of Benjamin Franklin* appeared in 1840. (That year, Charles Fox gave his collection of Franklin papers to the American Philosophical Society.) Trawling through archives in the United States, England, and France, Sparks had found 650 pieces of Franklin's writing that had never been collected—450 of which had never before been printed.[47]

In the *Works,* Sparks published letters from Franklin to Jane that he had found in Philadelphia. And he included, too, some very short excerpts from letters from Jane to Franklin. In editing Jane's prose, Sparks took far greater liberties than he had taken with either George Washington's or Benjamin Franklin's. In 1789, Jane wrote her brother a long letter, in the middle of which she wondered whether she should address him as "Exellency," now that he was no longer governor of Pennsylvania:

I was a Litle suspicious wither Exellency was acording to Ruel in Adress to my Brother at this time but I never write any my self & of Late Because He Lives nearer than cousen Willims have sent them to Dr Lathorps who is very obliging to me, & I thought must know what was Right & gave no Directions about it, but shall another time.[48]

Sparks's extract reads:

I was a little suspicious whether *Excellency* was according to rule in addressing my brother at this time; but I did not write the address; and of late, because he lives nearer than cousin Williams, I have sent my letters to Dr. Lathrop, who is very obliging to me, and I thought he must know what is right, and I gave no directions about it. But I shall do it another time.[49]

Sparks had his reasons for correcting Jane's writing, which is difficult to decipher. But in meddling, he erased her lack of learning, and put her remarks about titles and rank in a quite different light. Jane could be very funny. Not in Sparks.[50]

No one noticed Sparks's editorial methods until 1851, when several of his emendations to Washington's letters were observed by a British historian and by a contributor to the *New York Evening Post*. Sparks was accused of painting the president with "patriotic rouge" and "setting Washington on stilts."[51] Some critics remarked that the controversy might be an occasion to codify editorial standards: "The question, then, is—What are the rules?"[52] But, others countered, the rules were already fairly well established. The *Democratic Review* concluded, "Mr. Jared Sparks has made biography what it never was before—the lie to history."[53]

Another critic dubbed Sparks's editorial work as "one of the most flagrant injuries" ever done by an editor to a writer or by a biographer to his subject.[54] But it was of a piece with all of his work. Sparks believed that "the machinery of society and government is kept in motion by the agency of a few powerful minds." He kept only what he valued: the worthy political writings of great men. Letters he didn't find interesting he cut up, handing the scraps out as mementos.[55] In the margin of a seventy-three-page draft of Washington's first inaugural address, he wrote, "Washington's handwriting but not his composition"; then he cut it up and gave the cuttings to friends.[56]

Sparks saw, but did not save, a letter Jane wrote to her brother in October 1767, just after her daughter Mary died, at the very moment when, in her grief, she had stopped writing in her Book of Ages. Sparks printed an extract from that letter in *The Works of Benjamin Franklin*, editing it as he saw fit:

> Sorrows roll upon me like the waves of the sea. I am broken with breach upon breach, and I have now, in the first flow of my grief, been almost ready to say, 'What have I more?' But God forbid, that I should indulge

that thought, though I have lost another child. God is sovereign, and I submit.[57]

This is what Jane felt, in the depth of her mourning. It is not, however, what she wrote, which is lost.

No one ever noticed what Sparks had done to Jane's papers. Or maybe Jenny Mecom Kinsman noticed, and kept quiet about it. Elizabeth Duane Gillespie, a great-granddaughter of Benjamin Franklin's, found Kinsman uncommonly canny.[58] "Her cleverness is frequently spoken of by those who knew and respected her," Gillespie remembered. And she was coy. "Once when asked by some impertinent friend what her income was, she answered, 'If I were to tell you, you would know as well as I do myself, but I always like to keep a few secrets.'"[59]

Kinsman was still alive in 1856 when a notice about her appeared in the newspaper: "A great niece of Franklin, Mrs. Jane Kinsman," it was reported, "resides in Philadelphia, born in Boston, and now in her ninetieth year; she is one of the few of those yet surviving who remember the famous 'Tea Party.'"[60] Kinsman made that year's news because 1856 marked the 150th anniversary of Benjamin Franklin's birth. To commemorate the occasion, an eight-foot-tall bronze statue of Franklin was erected in Boston by a committee whose members included Jared Sparks. It was at Sparks's urging that the statue had first been discussed, over dinner on Franklin's birthday, January 17, in 1854.[61] Two years later, on the day of the unveiling, Robert Winthrop, a U.S. senator and former Speaker of the House of Representatives, delivered an oration celebrating Franklin as "the greatest of our native-born sons, and peculiarly the man of the People." He described the Ecton tithe book sent by Thomas Carlyle to Edward Everett, to prove that Franklin was "descended of from a sturdy stock of blacksmiths, which this curious and precious relic enables us to trace distinctly back to their anvils and their forge-hammers." The statue was draped with an American flag. "Let the Stars and Stripes no longer conceal the form of one who was always faithful to his country's Flag, and who did so much to promote the glorious cause in which it was first unfurled!" cried Winthrop as the veil was drawn. "Behold him!"[62]

The Franklin statue was paid for by the Massachusetts Charitable Mechanic Association, whose members wanted to claim Franklin as one of their own: a mechanic, an artisan. But the association's real hero was Paul Revere. When Revere died, in 1818, the notice of his passing in the "Deaths" column of the *Boston Gazette* was even shorter than Jane Franklin Mecom's: "In this town, yesterday morning, Paul Revere, Esq., aged 83." No mention was made of his ride.[63] But he would soon have his rise.

Sparks retired from Harvard in 1853. He spent the rest of his life attempting to write a history of the American Revolution. He never finished it.[64] He died in 1866. No scholar was more important to American history, Robert Winthrop said at a memorial service at the Massachusetts Historical Society, "nor can any one write that history, now or hereafter, without acknowledging a deep indebtedness, at every step, to his unwearied researches."[65]

In December 1860, the month Henry Wadsworth Longfellow's poem "Paul Revere's Ride" appeared on newsstands in Boston, making Revere a legend, Jenny Mecom Kinsman died in Philadelphia.[66] She was ninety-five. She was clever and witty and had never been wealthy and she liked to keep her secrets. She was the last of the Jane Mecoms. She was the last of the Franklin Janes.

CHAPTER XLII

The Biographer

In 1928, fifty-nine letters written by Franklin to Jane, the property of one Robert Harcourt, Esq., were auctioned by Sotheby's of London.[1] Robert Vernon Harcourt, born in 1878, was the son of Sir William George Granville Venables Vernon Harcourt, a liberal member of Parliament, and an American woman, Elizabeth Cabot Motley. Elizabeth Cabot Motley was John Lathrop's granddaughter; her mother was Ann Lathrop Motley. Jane Lathrop Loring was her aunt. The papers Jane had left to Jenny Mecom Kinsman, and that Kinsman had given to John Lathrop, had stayed in family hands since Jane's death in 1794.[2]

The year Franklin's letters to Jane were auctioned in London, Virginia Woolf turned her attention to the question of women's writing. She had just finished writing *Orlando,* a parody of biography that took up themes Woolf had long wrestled with, especially in "The Lives of the Obscure," a meditation on books shelved in a "faded, out-of-date, obsolete library": biographies of nobodies.[3] (Woolf's father was a founding editor of the *Dictionary of National Biography,* a dictionary of somebodies.) "The obscure sleep on the walls, slouching against each other as if they were too drowsy to stand upright," Woolf wrote. "Why disturb their sleep?"[4]

In October 1928, Woolf delivered a series of lectures to women undergraduates at Cambridge University, soon after published as *A Room of One's Own.* It was Woolf's odd work to turn Thomas Gray's elegy to the short and simple annals of the poor into rage about the unwritten literary work of women.[5] What, she wanted to know, "would have happened had Shakespeare had a wonderfully gifted sister, called Judith"?

Maybe that fall, Virginia Woolf, casting about for ideas for a lecture series, rummaging about in a bookstore, came across a catalog from Sotheby's of London, slumbering upon a shelf, and, inside, an entry that read:

A MOST REMARKABLE AND EXTENSIVE SERIES OF LETTERS
WRITTEN BY BENJAMIN FRANKLIN
TO HIS SISTER JANE MECOM

Someone who did learn about those letters was Carl Van Doren. Born in Illinois in 1885, Van Doren had earned a PhD from Columbia in 1911. His greatest passion was biography. He was a signal contributor to the *Dictionary of American Biography*. Van Doren was just embarking on a biography of Benjamin Franklin. He wanted to rescue Franklin from the likes of Jared Sparks. To Van Doren, Franklin was a cosmopolitan, a revolutionary, and a wit. "The dry, prim people seem to regard him as a treasure shut up in a savings bank, to which they have the lawful key," Van Doren fumed. "I herewith give him back, in grand dimensions, to his nation and the world."[6]

In 1939, Van Doren's *Benjamin Franklin* won a Pulitzer Prize. That same year, Virginia Woolf published an essay called "The Art of Biography":

The question now inevitably asks itself, whether the lives of great men only should be recorded. Is not anyone who has lived a life, and left a record of that life, worthy of biography—the failures as well as the successes, the humble as well as the illustrious? And what is greatness? And what is smallness?[7]

Also in 1939: Jane's house was demolished. In 1856, the 150th anniversary of Benjamin Franklin's birth, the house had even been decorated for the celebration. But so little was known about Jane that the claim that Franklin's sister had ever lived there was eventually deemed dubious.[8] In 1939, Jane's brick house was torn down to make room for a memorial to Paul Revere. The house wasn't in the way of the Revere memorial; it simply blocked a line of sight.[9] Jane's house, that is, was demolished to improve the public view of a statue to Paul Revere, inspired by a poem written by Henry Wadsworth Longfellow, Jared Sparks's roommate.[10]

Van Doren found this crushing. While writing about Franklin, he had become fascinated by Jane. His affection for her grew into something of an obsession.[11]

He determined to collect her papers and write her biography.[12] Some of her letters were, at the time, in the possession of Franklin Bache. In 1936, Bache's descendants had given his eleven hundred Franklin papers—including thirty-seven letters written by Jane—to the American Philosophical Society.[13] Van Doren also knew that the cache of letters auctioned in London in 1928 had been purchased by the Rosenbach Company, based in Philadelphia. In 1943, Rosenbach listed the letters in an auction catalog, touting the collection as "The Longest Franklin Correspondence in Existence," "AN ACCOUNT OF HIS LIFE FROM ABOUT 1729 UNTIL THE YEAR PRIOR TO HIS DEATH, IN A SERIES OF LETTERS TO HIS FAVORITE SISTER," amounting to "FRANKLIN'S UNOFFICIAL AUTOBIOGRAPHY."[14]

In July 1950, Van Doren had a heart attack while digging up a root in his yard. His *Letters of Benjamin Franklin and Jane Mecom* appeared after his death. He wrote, in the book's preface, "Jane Mecom at last takes her true place in history."[15] His biography *Jane Mecom, the Favorite Sister of Benjamin Franklin: Her Life Here First Fully Narrated from Their Entire Surviving Correspondence* was published that October.[16] "A belated act of justice," he called it.[17] Not many people read it. But he had made his point. A reviewer remarked, "Mr. Van Doren was too civilized a man to be interested only in the great."[18]

CHAPTER XLIII

The End

Igrew up in a house a dozen miles from the library where Jane's books ended up, on a street that got its name in 1906, on the two hundredth anniversary of Benjamin Franklin's birth. I grew up on Franklin Street.

A winter not long past, I headed out that way to visit the Lancaster library. I walked down the stairs to the basement and knocked on the door of a locked room I'd never been in before. I'd spent years hunting for everything Jane had left behind. I'd found letters and books and recipes. I'd held them and read them.[1] I'd found the ring she'd left, in her will, to her great-granddaughter Sally Greene. Curators at the Museum of Fine Arts in Boston had taken a box out of storage and handed it to me. I'd reached in and picked up a gold ring. I'd slipped it on. It barely fit on my pinkie. She must have been so small.

I'd gone to the library following the trail of another one of Jane's great-granddaughters, Sally Flagg. She'd died unmarried on July 24, 1881, at the age of eighty-nine. The "many letters written by Dr. Franklin to his sister" that she had had in her house in 1858 had disappeared. But she had left the bulk of her estate, including the Flagg family Bible, to the Lancaster library.[2]

Inside that underground room, I found that Bible. Then I saw, hanging on a wall, something unexpected: a pair of three-quarter-length portraits, a boy and a girl, very young and very alike. I stared at their faces. They looked, uncannily, exactly how I had always pictured Franklin and Jane. I pulled the paintings down from the wall and read the tag on the back: "A gift of Sally Flagg, 1881."

These were the portraits of Josiah Flagg and Jane Flagg, painted in 1765 by Joseph Badger, when Josiah was four and Jenny was eight.[3] Sally Flagg had saved, for posterity, the only likenesses of Jane's little rogues.

And then I found, on another wall of that room, something else Sally Flagg had left to the library: a needlepoint sampler she had embroidered and signed in 1802, when she was ten years old.[4]

On linen, with silk, she had stitched these words:

The book the needle and the pen divide.

And that's when I knew I had come to the last page of my own book of ages.

Sorrows rolled upon Jane Franklin like waves of the sea. She left in their wake these gifts, her remains: needles and pens, letters and books, politics and opinions, this history, this archive, a quiet story of a quiet life of quiet sorrow and quieter beauty.

Methods and Sources

Do the right thing with Spirit.
—JANE FRANKLIN MECOM, JULY 4, 1784

Methods

In writing this book I have had to stare down a truism: the lives of the obscure make good fiction but bad history. For an eighteenth-century woman of her rank and station, Jane Franklin Mecom's life is exceptionally well documented, but, by any other measure, her paper trail is miserably scant. She was born in 1712. No letter written by her before 1758 survives; the earliest piece of her prose that survives is not a letter but an addendum to a letter, a sentence, a scrap—a postscript she wrote, when she was thirty-nine, on a letter written by her mother.

This is dispiriting. For a long time, I was so discouraged that I abandoned the project altogether. I thought about writing a novel instead. But I decided, in the end, to write a biography, a book meant not only as a life of Jane Franklin Mecom but, more, as a meditation on silence in the archives. I wanted to write a history from the Reformation through the American Revolution by telling the story of a single life, using this most ordinary of lives to offer a history of history and to explain how history is written: from what remains of the lives of the great, the bad, and, not as often, the good.

This book is a history, a biography, but, in the spirit of the age in which Jane lived, it borrows from the conventions of fiction. (The eighteenth century's most influential historians, Hume and Gibbon, greatly admired the novels of Henry Fielding, and Fielding, in turn, considered reading history essential preparation for writing novels. "History, like tragedy, requires an exposition, a central action, and a denouement," Voltaire wrote in 1757. "My secret is to force the reader to wonder: Will Philip V ascend the throne?")[1] My difficulty was evidence. I searched for what there was to find. Then I pondered its insufficiency.

270 · METHODS AND SOURCES

For different problems, I tried different solutions. Instead of skipping over Jane's girlhood, I dwelled on it, making her silence the object of my investigation rather than an obstacle to it. In writing about the early years of her marriage and motherhood, I tried to bring her Book of Ages to life. I relied on public records, too, like the records of Edward Mecom's debts, and on newspapers, and especially on the writings of Benjamin Franklin, to describe his sister's world.

Throughout, I leaned heavily on what letters do survive. I rendered some epistolary exchanges in the form of dialogue, because that's how Jane understood exchanging letters—as a conversation—and because that's what Franklin thought was most remarkable about the novels of his day, like *Pamela,* which "mix'd Narration and Dialogue, a Method of Writing very engaging to the Reader, who in the most interesting Parts finds himself as it were brought into the Company."[2]

Occasionally, in describing Jane's early years, I quoted from letters she wrote much later in life. For example, there exists not a single description, in Jane's own words, of what it was like to take care of all those children in the 1730s and 1740s. (She *wrote* letters in those decades; the problem is that they are gone.) But she happens to have described the tumult of life with young children in letters that she wrote many decades later, when she was raising her great-grandchildren: "My litle wons are Interupting me Every miniut," she wrote to her brother in 1782, "& I can add no more but that I wish for the comfort of a leter from you."[3] In the text, I quote this passage in a chapter about Jane's life as a young mother. An endnote identifies the date of the letter and the circumstances under which it was written. I mean no sleight of hand; I mean only to allow the reader to enjoy Jane's company.

This book aims to be at once a history and a work of literary criticism. It includes new readings of the principal writings of Benjamin Franklin, including his Silence Dogood essays, *Poor Richard's Almanack, The Way to Wealth,* and his autobiography. I have attempted, too, to bring a new vantage to his contributions to the Declaration of Independence, the Treaty of Paris, and the Constitution. But I have worked hard not to lose sight of Jane. Given Franklin's staggering literary remains, a biography of his sister might easily become a book only about Franklin himself. The risk is of her voice being, at best, a murmur. That I have strived to avoid.

Finally, I have tried, throughout, to call attention to the conventions of different kinds of writing about lives—history, biography, autobiography, and fiction—in order to argue that Jane's life doesn't fit neatly into any one of those genres. Nor do most lives.

A NOTE ABOUT NAMES

There are a great many Janes and Benjamins and Franklins and Mecoms in this book, as well as three different people named "Jane Mecom": Jane, Jane's daughter Jane, and Jane's son Benjamin's daughter Jane. I elected to refer to Jane Franklin Mecom, as "Jane" and to her brother Benjamin Franklin as "Franklin." This seemed the best way to distinguish my two main characters from everyone else.

When referring to women before and after their marriages, I have used maiden names as middle names to make it easier for the reader to keep track of women over the course of their lives, making it possible to distinguish, for instance, among Jane Franklin Mecom (1712–1794), Jane Mecom Collas (1745–1802), and Jane Mecom Kinsman (1765–1860). Similarly, when writing about Jane Colman, who later married Ebenezer Turell, I refer to her, after her marriage, as Jane Colman Turell, just as I refer to Keziah Folger, after her marriage to John Coffin, as Keziah Folger Coffin, which, in this instance, also helps to distinguish her from her daughter, Keziah Coffin.

Sources

Searching for Jane's papers, I traced her descendants, reported in appendix C. (The better-known genealogy of Benjamin Franklin's ancestors is reproduced as appendix B.) I also spent a great deal of time trying to reconstruct Jane's library, an inventory of all the books I believe she read or owned. That inventory is reproduced as appendix F. A calendar of letters written to and from Jane is provided as appendix D. (That appendix also notes the early collections of Franklin's writings in which correspondence between Jane and her brother appeared.)[4] Because fuller information about Jane's letters, and also about Franklin's letters to Jane, can be found in that appendix, I have, in the notes, listed for those letters only the writer, recipient, and date. Letters written to and from Benjamin Franklin through 1785 can be found in the printed volumes of the *Papers of Benjamin Franklin;* the online edition, at franklinpapers.org, includes letters through 1790. For Franklin's letters to and from correspondents other than Jane, I have, in the notes, listed only the writer, recipient, place, and date. For all other correspondence, I have supplied standard citations.

In part 5 of this book, I relate much of the story of Jane's lost letters. Here I chronicle the fate of those letters more minutely, in the hope that, one day, more of her papers might be found.

JANE MECOM KINSMAN

After Jane Franklin Mecom's death in May 1794, her minister, John Lathrop, went through her papers and took what he wanted. Lathrop was given permission to do this by Jane's granddaughter Jenny Mecom, later Jane Mecom Kinsman ("I find it was Mrs. Kinsman, that allowed Dr. Lathrop . . . to select what letters he chose from the Dr's correspondence, from among Mrs. Mecom's papers," Benjamin Franklin Bache's son Franklin Bache told Jared Sparks in 1833). Before she allowed Lathrop to go through them, Kinsman would likely have looked through the papers herself. People tend to take back from a dead relative whose papers they have a chance to rummage through letters they themselves have written or letters that concern them. If, before allowing Lathrop to choose what he wanted, Kinsman kept a number of the papers for herself, she would most likely have selected letters written by members of her own family: her father (Benjamin Mecom), her mother (Elizabeth Ross Mecom), and her sisters (Sarah Mecom Smith, Abiah Mecom, and Elizabeth Mecom Britt).

Noticeably missing from the letters that survive is almost any mention of the madness of Benjamin Mecom. Jane and Franklin had been, themselves, discreet on the subject. "That you may know the whole state of his mind and his affairs, and by that means be better able to advise him, I send you all the letters I have received from or concerning him," Franklin had written to Jane on November 30, 1752, from Philadelphia, adding in a postscript, "Please return to me the letters." None of these letters—not a single letter written by Benjamin Mecom to either his mother or his uncle—survive.[5] Not even this letter survives. But it was still in Boston in 1833, because Sparks saw it and made a transcription—doubtless a redaction—which he printed.[6] That Kinsman was in charge of the papers may explain why so few documents chronicling the madness of her father survive: she might have destroyed them. Or, if Benjamin Mecom was really still alive in 1794, she might have given those papers back to him. This remains a mystery.

John Lathrop

The pick of the correspondence would have been any letter written by Benjamin Franklin. As early as the 1750s, letters in Franklin's hand were prized, as Mather Byles put it, as much as "the Paintings of Raphael."[7] Fifteen letters that are known to have been written by Franklin to Jane—Franklin and Jane refer to them, by date—were unseen, even by Sparks. These fifteen letters might have ended up in the hands of members of Jane's family and then vanished. The rest seem to have ended up with Lathrop. At John Lathrop's death, his papers may have been scattered among all five of his children. Jane Franklin Mecom's papers went to at least two of them.

Jane Lathrop Loring

Both Jared Sparks and Carl Van Doren were confused and finally defeated by John Lathrop's daughter Mrs. Caleb Loring. In 1830, Sparks heard that some of Franklin's letters to his sister were still in Boston. "Mr. Gray tells me that Mrs. Caleb Loring of Boston has in her possession 50 to 60 original letters of Dr Franklin to his sister Mrs. Williams, which have never been printed," Sparks wrote in his diary in December 1830. (Hilliard, Gray was Sparks's publisher.) "Mr G has seen them, and he says they are in Franklin's peculiar manner, & highly interesting." Who was this Mrs. Caleb Loring? Sparks asked Gray, who told him, "Mrs Loring is the daughter of the late Dr. Stillman, who was the executor of Mrs. Williams, and thus the papers came into her hands."[8] This was a red herring. "Mrs. Williams" was not Franklin's sister but his niece, Jane's very dear friend Grace Harris Williams. "Aunt Mecm was hear yesterday and Sends her love to you," Grace Harris Williams had written to her uncle Benjamin Franklin in 1771, in the only letter of hers to him that survives. One of his to her survives, too, but that is all: two letters.[9] Gray was mistaken in more ways, too. Not only was "Mrs.

Williams" not Franklin's sister, but Mrs. Caleb Loring was not "the daughter of the late Dr. Stillman, who was the executor of Mrs. Williams," either. Mrs. Caleb Loring was Jane Lathrop, the daughter of Jane's minister and the executor of her estate. The Franklin letters still in Boston in 1830 weren't letters to Grace; they were letters to Jane.

The source of Van Doren's confusion was different. Van Doren was unable to figure out, first, how Jane's papers had come into the hands of Mrs. Caleb Loring sometime before 1833 and, second, how they had ended up at an auction in London in 1928. "The course of the letters is obscure from the date of Sparks's appeal to Dr. Bache," he concluded, "down to December 18, 1928, when they were sold at Sotheby's in London as the property of Robert Harcourt, Esq."[10] He also assumed—wrongly, I believe—that the letters Mrs. Loring had in 1833 were the same as the letters sold in London in 1928.

Van Doren made a series of errors. But his first, from which all the rest derive, is that he believed that Mrs. Caleb Loring was a woman named Love Hawk.[11] That sent him down the wrong path. He never found out that Mrs. Caleb Loring was really Jane Lathrop, because, although he read Sparks's appeal to Bache, a letter housed in the American Philosophical Society, he did not read Bache's reply, which is among Sparks's papers at Harvard.

Van Doren knew that on August 6, 1833, Sparks wrote to Bache, asking him to make an appeal to Mrs. Loring. "I wish you would keep my name entirely out of the matter, as I have made unavailing efforts to get the letters," Sparks pleaded. "The only objection is Mrs. Loring's conscientious scruples, as to her right to part with them unless it be to the descendants of Mrs. Mecom."[12] Van Doren did not know that, one week later, Bache wrote back, with specific instructions:

> I advise you to apply to Mr. & Mrs. Loring by letter for permission to take copies from the letters in question, provided the Granddaughters of Mrs. Mecom have no objection. If the answer is yes, provided they are willing, then apply by letter to Miss Mecom, Mrs. Kinsman, & Mrs. Smith for permission, addressing it to Mrs. Smith as the eldest, to my care, asking the permission. They would grant your request at once, or otherwise, ask Mrs. Loring to send them copies of the letters.

Bache had also gotten more information, probably by calling on one or more of Jane's granddaughters—his cousins—whom he plainly knew well. He then explained to Sparks how it was that Mrs. Loring had come to have the letters in her possession: "I find it was Mrs. Kinsman, that allowed Dr. Lathrop, whom I presume was Mrs. Loring's father, and was the Executor to Mrs. Mecom's will, to select what letters he chose from the Dr's correspondence, from among Mrs. Mecom's papers. Mrs. Kinsman, after giving them, would not like to require their return."[13]

Sparks saw at least some of the papers in Mrs. Loring's hands, in 1833. He did not acquire them, and I believe he made, chiefly, redacted copies or extracts. The originals of all of Jane's papers once in the possession of Mrs. Loring have either been lost or remain in private hands.

ANN LATHROP MOTLEY

Another of John Lathrop's daughters, Ann, married a Boston merchant named Thomas Motley. This may explain why Sparks at first thought Jane Lathrop Loring had fifty or sixty letters and later told Bache she had twenty-five. Suppose that, in 1794, Lathrop had taken from Jane Franklin Mecom's papers dozens of letters written to her by her brother and that, at Lathrop's death in 1816, these letters went not to his sons but to his two daughters: twenty-five letters to Jane Lathrop Loring and fifty-nine to Ann Lathrop Motley. In the 1830s, Sparks saw twenty-five letters—the letters in the possession of Jane Lathrop Loring. Then they were lost.

The letters belonging to Ann Lathrop Motley were saved. Her first son, born in 1814, was John Lothrop Motley. (Somewhere along the way, the spelling of the family name changed from Lathrop to Lothrop.)[14] In 1832, when John Lothrop Motley was eighteen, he went to Göttingen to study history. While he was there, he wrote a letter home, thanking his parents for having sent him a letter of his grandfather's: a letter from George Washington to John Lathrop. "I am very much obliged to you for Washington's letter," young Motley wrote home, "and you may be quite sure I shall keep it very religiously, and should like very much to have Franklin's letters, which mother speaks of, and can certainly very easily send."[15]

Sparks was on good terms with the Motleys. In January 1833, he had written to Thomas Motley, asking him to intervene with Mrs. Loring. ("I hope in a day or two to have the pleasure of seeing Mrs. Loring and will not fail in making known your wishes," Motley wrote back, but he seems to have been unable to convince his wife's sister to allow Sparks to have her set of the letters.)[16] In 1837, by which time John Lothrop Motley had returned from Europe, Sparks, who had finished the *Familiar Letters* but was still collecting material for his *Works of Benjamin Franklin,* and who was also bankrupt (having lost a fortune in the Panic of 1837), wrote to him. He wanted Motley's help in finding some letters from Franklin to John Lathrop. Motley consulted with his mother and father. Then he wrote to Sparks, "My father begs me to inform you that the only letter which my mother or any of her family have preserved, from Dr Franklin to Dr Lathrop, is the one of September 1788 already published in your collection." Motley went on: "They looked carefully through the collection of letters to Mrs. Mecom & others but have not been able to find the one to which you allude."[17]

Motley, meanwhile, tried writing historical fiction. But after receiving poor reviews for novels published in 1838 and 1839 and set in colonial Massachusetts, he began writing history. In this field, he achieved considerable renown. His most important work, *The Rise of the Dutch Republic,* was enthusiastically reviewed by Sparks's *North American Review* in 1856, as the product of "the matured powers of a vigorous and brilliant mind, and the abundant fruits of a patient and judicious study and deep reflection"; it was judged "one of the most important contributions to historical literature that have been made in this country."[18]

John Lothrop Motley spent much of his life abroad, serving as a U.S. diplomat in Russia and, later, Austria. From 1869 to 1870, he was the American minister to Great Britain; in 1871 he moved to The Hague. He visited America in 1875, but after returning to Europe, he lived in England from 1875 until his death.

His children were raised in England. The year before Motley died, his daughter Elizabeth Cabot Motley was married in Westminster Abbey to Sir William George Granville Harcourt, a liberal member of Parliament and later the home secretary. They had one son, Robert Vernon Harcourt, born in 1878.[19]

Lady Harcourt died in 1928; everything in her estate went to her son. That year, Sotheby's of London printed a catalog listing, as the property of Robert Harcourt, fifty-nine letters from Benjamin Franklin to his sister. Jane's papers had been in the hands of her minister and his descendants since 1794.[20]

Van Doren made sure this collection was purchased by the American Philosophical Society.[21] That made a significant enough set of letters that Van Doren proposed publishing a properly edited collection of the complete correspondence. The American Philosophical Society gave him a grant, a secretary, and a research assistant.[22]

In the 1940s, Van Doren gathered together a collection of all the letters then available: ninety-eight letters from Franklin to Jane and sixty-eight from Jane to Franklin or other relatives, from originals held in more than a dozen archives. Edited by Van Doren and under the auspices of the American Philosophical Society, *The Letters of Benjamin Franklin and Jane Mecom* was published in 1950, three months after Van Doren's death.

Three letters from Jane to Franklin were purchased by the Historical Society of Pennsylvania. (The society already owned four other letters written by Jane: one to Franklin, one to Sarah Bache, and two to the executors of Franklin's estate.) Remarked a collector, "What would Jane, who always needed money so badly, have thought if she had known that one of her poor letters would bring even ten dollars at auction!"[23] Letters written by Jane to recipients other than Franklin are few, but letters written by Jane to her friend Catharine Ray Greene were carefully kept by Greene and remained in the Greene homestead, in Warwick, Rhode Island, until 1946, along with letters Jane received from Franklin while staying with Greene; these letters were acquired by the American Philosophical Society in 1946.[24]

FRANKLIN GREENE

The people most likely to have gone through Jane's papers, with Jane Mecom Kinsman's permission, are the other members of the family named in Jane's will: Jane Mecom Collas, Franklin Greene, Sally Greene, and Josiah Flagg. Nearly all of these people corresponded with Jane, but only one original letter from Jane to Jane Mecom Collas survives (in private hands), while another, a copy, descended through the family of Josiah Flagg, and no letters written by Jane to either Franklin or Sally Greene survive. Of all of what Jane's children and grandchildren and great-grandchildren took out of her house in the days after her death in 1794, only what Josiah Flagg selected has been found. He took from that house letters he himself had written, as well as a letter Franklin wrote to Jane in May 1786— presumably, because that letter is about him—along with the letter Richard Bache wrote to Jane in 1790, informing her of Franklin's death.

Some things Jane left to her Greene grandchildren can be traced. In 1758, Franklin had his portrait painted, in London, in miniature. He sent the miniature to his wife, asking her to send it to his sister. Jane either gave it to Franklin Greene or else he took it from her estate. The miniature was handed down, in Franklin Greene's family, for generations, along with the name: by Franklin Greene to his son Franklin Greene Jr., who gave it to his daughter Agnes, who married a man named Balch, with whom she had a son named Franklin Greene Balch, born in Roxbury in 1864, and he, in 1899, loaned the miniature to the Museum of Fine Arts, in Boston. Franklin Greene Balch had a son, also named Franklin Greene Balch, born in Jamaica Plain in 1896, and who, in 1943, gave the miniature to the museum as a permanent gift, writing to the museum's director, "I think it will be in a much more appropriate spot than it would be in my safe deposit box."[25]

Balch told a curator at the Museum of Fine Arts that he had something else he might be interested in giving to the museum: "a mourning ring of Benjamin Franklin's." Balch had no idea the ring had belonged to Jane Franklin Mecom. In her 1794 will, Jane had left to Sally Greene "a mourning Ring, which was given me at the funeral of my kinsman Josiah Williams." (Jane's blind nephew, Josiah Williams, a son of Grace and Jonathan Williams Sr., died in 1772, at the age of twenty-four; Jane had been given the ring at his funeral.)[26] Sally Greene died of a fall from her horse in 1795, at the age of seventeen. Her brother ended up with the ring. Like the miniature of Benjamin Franklin, Jane Franklin Mecom's ring remained in the Greene family, descending through the Franklin Greene Balches. Over time, they forgot that it had ever belonged to Jane Franklin Mecom; they decided it must have belonged to Benjamin Franklin.

Balch expected that the museum wouldn't be interested in it; the connection to Franklin, after all, was not very well established. "Do you suppose the Massachusetts Historical Society would care to have the ring?" he asked. And then he added, as an afterthought, in the very last line of his letter: "I have two letters of Jane Mecum's."[27] He didn't think anyone would want those, either. He was right. The museum declined the ring, informing Balch, "The same applies to the letters of Jane Mecum."[28] The Massachusetts Historical Society, too, declined.[29]

In 1946, Katherine T. Balch, Franklin G. Balch's sister-in-law, left half of her estate—hundreds of thousands of dollars—to the museum. This led the curators to reverse their decision to decline the ring.[30] In 1949 the ring entered the museum's collections. In the museum's catalog, it is described as "traditionally owned by Benjamin Franklin."[31]

After Van Doren's biography of Jane, *Jane Mecom*, appeared, Benjamin Franklin's sister was suddenly—briefly—somebody. In 1955, the art historian Charles Coleman Sellers, who had been hired to prepare an exhibit of portraits of Franklin for the American Philosophical Society's marking of the 250th anniversary of Franklin's birth the next year, discovered the miniature in the Museum of Fine Arts in Boston. Digging through the accession files, he discovered, too, that the portrait had once belonged to Franklin's sister. In 1955, he published a two-page account of the miniature in the society's proceedings. It was probably Sellers who pointed out to museum staff that Balch had once mentioned that he had some of Jane Franklin Mecom's letters.[32] A member of the staff wrote to Balch, asking about the letters. Ailing and in his nineties, Balch replied with bad news. He had once had "two letters signed Jane Mecum and they were in my safe deposit box for years," he began. But "then I took them out to show them to someone and now they are not in my box."[33]

These two letters, alone among the dozens and dozens of letters Jane Franklin Mecom must have written to Jane Flagg Greene, Franklin Greene, and Sally Greene, had survived for two centuries, only to be misplaced. Balch's sister went back to the bank and double-checked the safe deposit box: no letters. Balch's son rifled through the drawers of his father's desk: no letters. Balch was stumped.[34] The originals of the letters disappeared, but in 1956, a daughter of Balch's sent photostats of them to the editor of the Benjamin Franklin Papers, at Yale.[35]

No one at the museum ever tied the mourning ring to Jane Franklin Mecom. The ring is a band of gold inlaid with black enamel. An inscription reads, "JOSIAH WILLIAMS 1772." Atop the band is set a beveled piece of glass in the shape of a coffin, under which rests a tiny slip of paper, onto which is sketched a skeleton, smaller than a fly.[36]

JOSIAH, SAMUEL, AND SALLY FLAGG

Jane's grandson Josiah Flagg inherited her collection of books, including her Book of Ages, as well as a number of papers, her portraits of Josiah Flagg and Jane Flagg Greene as children, and, apparently, a miniature of Benjamin Franklin. Some of these materials were inherited by Josiah Flagg's son Samuel, some by his daughter Sally, and others (all now lost) by his other surviving children. Some of what Samuel and Sally Flagg inherited they gave to the New England Historic Genealogical Society in Boston, and some to the Thayer Memorial Library in Lancaster.

AFTER VAN DOREN

A few more letters have turned up since Carl Van Doren published his collection of the correspondence in 1950. A letter from Franklin to Jane dated March 2, 1767, was purchased by the University of Virginia, at auction, in 1951.[37] In 1976, a letter from Jane to Jonathan Williams Jr., dated August 12, 1792, entered the collections of Philadelphia's Rosenbach Museum with the Jonathan Williams Papers. Resources not available to Van Doren in the 1940s yielded information about letters unknown to him. The Cripe and Campbell index to American manuscripts in auction records and dealers' catalogs, published in 1977, lists two letters sent by Jane and five letters received by her. Two letters written by Jane, one auctioned in 1892, the other in 1895, either have been lost or remain in private hands.[38] Three letters from Franklin to Jane were auctioned by Sotheby's in 1985. They remain in private hands.[39] Copies of two letters from Franklin to Jane, previously unknown to scholars, turned up as recently as 2006. (These two were among twelve letters— some are only fragments of letters—between Franklins and Mecoms that were sent in 1825 by William Duane Jr., in Philadelphia, to the London Magazine for publication but were not published.)[40]

Meanwhile, Franklin's papers were being collected and edited, for a modern edition. In 1954, Yale University and the American Philosophical Society launched *The Papers of Benjamin Franklin*. So far, thirty-nine volumes of a projected forty-seven volumes have been published.

In 2008, the Jane Franklin Mecom letters in Van Doren's 1950 edition were also made available through a digital collection known as *North American Women's Letters and Diaries,* published by Alexander Street Press. That same year, a digital edition of the *Papers of Benjamin Franklin,* sponsored by the Packard Humanities Institute, was made available online. Readers interested in taking a look at Jane's letters can do so easily at franklinpapers.org but should be advised that early editors working at Yale's Franklin Papers project made significant changes to Jane's prose, correcting some of her spelling and punctuation. The most faithful transcription of Jane's correspondence is still to be found in Van Doren, *Letters.*

A PLEA

Jared Sparks once destroyed a draft of George Washington's first inaugural address. "Washington's handwriting but not his composition," Sparks wrote in the margin. He sliced up the manuscript and gave the cuttings to friends. This left John C. Fitzpatrick, a twentieth-century editor of Washington's papers, in the awkward position of begging people who might have a scrap of Washington's first inaugural address to mail it to the Library of Congress. "The curious activities of Jared Sparks seem to have deprived us at this point of what might have proved the most valuable political document of Washington's entire career," Fitzpatrick wrote. "Unfortunately, it seems certain that only a small percentage of the entire document will ever be recovered, but it is to be hoped that any possessor of a sheet of paper about seven by eight inches, covered on both sides with Washington's handwriting, which has neither beginning nor end but is numbered in the upper corners, in ink, by Washington, will communicate with the Manuscript Division of the Library of Congress."[41]

In that same spirit, it is hoped that anyone who knows about any of Jane Franklin Mecom's papers would be so kind as to write to me at the History Department, Harvard University, Cambridge, Massachusetts 02138.

A Franklin Genealogy

Thomas Francklyne
wife unknown

Jane Franklyne   B. 1565   D. 1565
Henry Franklyne   B. MAY 26, 1573   D. OCT. 23, 1631
   M. OCT. 30, 1595   Agnes Joanes or James   D. JAN. 29, 1646
Thomas Francklin   B. OCT. 8, 1598   D. MARCH 21, 1682
   M. *date unknown*   Jane White   B. CA. 1617   D. OCT. 30, 1662

Thomas Franklin   1637–1702
Samuel Franklin   1641–1664
John Franklin   1643–1691
Joseph Franklin   1646–1683
A twin son
A twin son
Benjamin Franklin   1650–1727
Hannah Franklin   1654–1712
Josiah Franklin   B. DEC. 23, 1657   D. JAN. 16, 1745
   M. *date unknown*   Ann Child

Elizabeth Franklin (Douse)   1678–1759
Samuel Franklin   1681–1720
Hannah Franklin   1683–1723
Josiah Franklin   1685–CA. 1715
Anne Franklin (Harris)   1687–1729
Joseph Franklin   1688–1688
Joseph Franklin   1689–1689

M. NOV. 25, 1689   Abiah Folger

John Franklin   1690–1756
Peter Franklin   1692–1766
Mary Franklin (Homes)   1694–1731
James Franklin   1697–1735
Sarah Franklin (Davenport)   1699–1731
Ebenezer Franklin   1701–1703
Thomas Franklin   1703–1706
Benjamin Franklin   1706–1790
Lydia Franklin (Scott)   1708–1758
JANE FRANKLIN (Mecom)   1712–1794

APPENDIX C

A Jane Genealogy

The attempt to trace Jane's descendants began with the executors of Franklin's last will, in which Franklin made the following bequest: "To the children, grandchildren, and great-grandchildren of my sister Jane Mecom that may be living at the time of my decease, I give fifty pounds sterling, to be equally divided among them."

After Franklin's death in 1790, the executors of his estate wrote to Jane, inquiring about her descendants. Jane sent them a document titled "Descendants of Jane Mecom":

> Jane Collas only daughter of Jane Mecom at Boston Josiah Flagg grandson at Lancaster now in Boston, Sally Green and Franklin Green great grand children, at Rhode Island, Children of Elishu Greene by Jane Flagg, her son Benjamin Mecom has living five children his daughter Jane with her in Boston, a daughter Abiah at Amboy in the Jerseys, a single woman, a daughter Mary Carra at Elizabeth Town in the Jerseys with one child Mary Carra, a daughter Elizabeth a single woman in Philadelphia and Sarah Smith with six children at Philadelphia. We the Subscribers being present in Boston do give full power to Jane Mecom Widow to receive of the Gentlemen Executors our proportionate parts of the Legacy as set forth in the will of the late Doctor Franklin, and to discharge the said Executors therefrom; also the said Jane Mecom becomes surety for what she may be entrusted with for her great grand children Sally Greene and Franklin Greene.[1]

The next year, Jane wrote requesting a slightly different arrangement for the New England branch of her family.[2] The records of the administration of Franklin's estate contain considerable additional information about Jane Franklin Mecom's descendants.[3] Those records also demonstrate that although Jane did not list her son Benjamin Mecom as among her living descendants, he was still alive. Franklin's executors at first presumed, too, that Benjamin Mecom was dead: "Mrs Jane Mecom's Son Benja. Said to be deceased." But on June 29, 1791, the account books record that seventeen pounds, five shillings were disbursed as "Cash pd Elizabeth Mecom for Maintenance of B. Mecom."[4] This sum appears to have been an annuity.[5] I have been unable to trace his fate.

JANE FRANKLIN   B. MAR. 27, 1712   M. JULY 27, 1727   D. MAY 7, 1794
M. *Edward Mecom*   B. DEC. 15, 1704   D. SEPT. 11, 1765

Josiah Mecom I   B. JUNE 4, 1729   D. MAY 18, 1730

Edward "Neddy" Mecom   B. MAR. 29, 1731   M. JULY 22, 1755   D. DEC. 7, 1758
M. *Ruth Whittemore*   B. ?   D. ?

[girl] Mecom   B. AFTER 1755   D. CA. 1758
Jane Mecom   B. BEFORE 1758   D. 1760

Benjamin "Benny" Mecom   B. DEC. 29, 1732   M. CA. 1757   D ?
M. *Elizabeth "Betsy" Ross*   B. CA. 1729?   D. NOV. 29, 1807

Sarah Mecom   B. CA. OCT. 1, 1758   M. ?,   D. ?
M. *Benjamin Smith*   B. ?   D. SEPT. 6, 1800

Deborah Mecom   B. DEC. 1760?   D. ?
Elizabeth Mecom   B. ?   M 1798   D. BEFORE 1833
M. *Daniel Britt*   B. ?   D. ?

Abiah Mecom   B. 1761?   D. AUG. 6, 1841
Jane Mecom   B. CA. 1765   M. FEB. 13, 1800   D. DEC. 16, 1860
M. *Simon Kinsman*   B. NOV. 21, 1752   D. JAN. 1818

Mary Mecom   D. BEFORE 1833
M. *? Carr*

John Ross Mecom   B. OCT. 24, 1771   D. ?

Ebenezer Mecom   B. MAY 2, 1735   M. JULY 21, 1757?   D. JAN. 18, 1762
M. *Susannah Hiller*   B. ?   D. ?

Sarah "Sally" Mecom   B. JUNE 28, 1737   M. MAR. 18, 1756   D. JUNE 12, 1764
M. *Wiliam Flagg*   B. JULY 10, 1732   M. APR. 22, 1756   D. JUNE 1775

Jane "Jenny" Flagg   B. JAN. 22, 1757   M. DEC. 5, 1775   D. APR. 6, 1782

M. *Elihu Greene*   B. DEC. 10, 1746   D. AUG. 1, 1827

Celia Greene   B. JAN. 27, 1777   D. MAR. 26, 1778

Sarah Greene   B. MAR. 16, 1778   D. OCT. 10, 1795

Franklin Greene   B. SEPT. 3, 1780   M. JUNE 29, 1806   D. OCT. 2, 1841

Jane Greene   B. 1781   D. 1782

Mary "Polly" Flagg   B. ?   D. MARCH 1765

Josiah Flagg   B. NOV. 12, 1760   M. JUNE 7, 1789   D. FEB. 11, 1840
M. *Dolly Thurston*   B. NOV. 6, 1766   D. JUNE 1, 1835

> William Flagg   B. JULY 29, 1790   D. FEB. 7, 1806
>
> Sarah "Sally" Flagg   B. NOV. 19, 1791   D. JULY 24, 1881
>
> Dolly Flagg   B. JULY 25, 1793   M. NOV. 20, 1820   D. MAY 17, 1878
>
> Rebecca Flagg   B. MAY 8, 1795   M. MAR. 30, 1818   D. ?
>
> George Washington Flagg   B. JAN. 31, 1797   D. OCT. 17, 1819
>
> Samuel Ward Flagg   B. APR. 22, 1803   M. ?   D. 1871

Sarah Flagg   B. JUNE 1763   D. NOV. 9, 1764

Peter Franklin Mecom   B. MAY 13, 1739   UNMARRIED   D. BEFORE FEB. 14, 1779

John Mecom   B. MAR. 31, 1741   M. SEPT. 11, 1765   D. SEPT. 30, 1770
M. *Catherine Oakey*

Josiah Mecom   B. MAR. 26, 1743   D. 1775

Jane Mecom   B. APR. 12, 1745   M. MAR. 23, 1773   D. 1802
M. *Peter Collas*

James Mecom   B. JULY 31, 1746   D. NOV. 30, 1746

Mary "Polly" Mecom   B. FEB. 29, 1748   D. SEPT. 19, 1767

Abiah Mecom   B. AUG. 1, 1751   D. APR. 23, 1752

A Calendar of the Letters

DATE	FROM	TO	PLACE
1/6/1727	Benjamin Franklin	Jane Franklin	Philadelphia
June 1730	Benjamin Franklin	Sarah Franklin Davenport	Philadelphia
5/26/1731	Jane Franklin Mecom	Benjamin Franklin	Boston
6/19/1731	Benjamin Franklin	Jane Franklin Mecom	Philadelphia
7/28/1743	Benjamin Franklin	Jane Franklin Mecom	Philadelphia
1744–45	Benjamin Franklin	Jane and Edward Mecom	Philadelphia
10/16/1747	Benjamin Franklin	Abiah Folger Franklin	Philadelphia
1748	Jane Franklin Mecom	Benjamin Franklin	Boston
1748	Jane Franklin Mecom	Benjamin Mecom	Boston
1748	Jane Franklin Mecom	James Parker	Boston
1748	Benjamin Franklin	Jane Franklin Mecom	Philadelphia
9/7/1749	Benjamin Franklin	Abiah Folger Franklin	Philadelphia
4/12/1750	Benjamin Franklin	Abiah Folger Franklin	Philadelphia
9/11/1750	Jane Franklin Mecom	Benjamin Franklin	Boston
9/20/1750	Benjamin Franklin	Jane Franklin Mecom	Philadelphia
10/14/1751	Abiah Folger Franklin and Jane Franklin Mecom	Benjamin and Deborah Read Franklin	Boston
10/24/1751	Benjamin Franklin	Jane Franklin Mecom	Philadelphia
May 1752	Benjamin Franklin	Abiah Folger Franklin	Philadelphia
5/21/1752	Benjamin Franklin	Jane Franklin Mecom and Edward Mecom	Philadelphia
9/14/1752	Benjamin Franklin	Jane Franklin Mecom and Edward Mecom	Philadelphia
11/30/1752	Benjamin Franklin	Jane Franklin Mecom and Edward Mecom	Philadelphia
9/21/1754	Benjamin Mecom	Deborah Read Franklin	Antigua
2/12/1756	Benjamin Franklin	Jane Franklin Mecom	Philadelphia
5/30/1754	William Franklin	Jane Franklin Mecom	Philadelphia
6/10/1756	Benjamin Franklin	Jane Franklin Mecom	Philadelphia
June 1756	Jane Franklin Mecom	Benjamin Franklin	Boston

Please note that in this table a letter referred to as "missing" was once seen and copied but has since disappe *while a letter referred to as "lost" has never been recorded and its contents are unknown.*

ORIGINAL	NOTES ON PROVENANCE AND PRINTINGS
Missing	A) Duane, *Works*, 6:3; Sparks, *Familiar Letters*, 3–4; C) Sparks, *Works*, 7:2.
APS	A) Sparks, *Familiar Letters*, 4–5; B) Sparks, *Works*, 7:3.
Lost	Referred to by BF in 6/19/1731.
Missing	A) Duane, *Works*, 6:3–5; B) Sparks, *Familiar Letters*, 5–7; C) Sparks, *Works*, 7:4–6.
APS	A) Duane, *Works*, 6:5–6; B) Sparks, *Familiar Letters*, 8–9; C) Sparks, *Works*, 7:8–9.
Missing	A) Sparks, *Familiar Letters*, 10; B) Sparks, *Works*, 7:10.
Missing	A) Duane, *Works*, 6:8; B) Sparks, *Familiar Letters*, 16–17; C) Sparks, *Works*, 7:41–42.
Lost	Referred to by BF in letter to JFM June 1748.
Lost	Referred to by BF in letter to JFM June 1748.
Lost	Referred to by BF in letter to JFM June 1748.
Missing	Sparks, *Familiar Letters*.
Missing	A) *London Magazine* xii (1825): 606; B) Sparks, *Familiar Letters*, 15–16; C) Sparks, *Works*, 7:39–41.
Boston Athenaeum	A) Sparks, *Familiar Letters*, 17–19; B) Sparks, *Works*, 7:42–43.
Lost	Referred to by BF in letter to JFM 9/20/1750.
Missing	Sparks, *Familiar Letters*, 19–20.
APS	Duane, *Letters*, 9–10.
Missing	A) Sparks, *Familiar Letters*, 21; B) Sparks, *Works*, 7:54.
Missing	Sparks, *Familiar Letters*, 20–21 (misdated as 1751).
Missing	A) Sparks, *Familiar Letters*, 22–23; B) Sparks, *Works*, 7:58–59.
APS	A) Sparks, *Familiar Letters*, 24–26; B) Sparks, *Works*, 7:59–61.
Missing	Sparks, *Familiar Letters*, 27.
APS	
Private hands	A) Sparks, *Familiar Letters*, 38; B) Sparks, *Works*, 7:112–13.
copy at LCP	A copy of a letter sent to the *London Magazine*.
APS	
Lost	Referred to by BF in letter of 6/28/1756.

DATE	FROM	TO	PLACE
6/28/1756	Benjamin Franklin	Jane Franklin Mecom	New York
7/5/1756	Jane Franklin Mecom	Benjamin Franklin	Boston
7/12/1756	Benjamin Franklin	Jane Franklin Mecom	New York
12/27/1756	Benjamin Mecom	Benjamin Franklin	Antigua
12/30/1756	Benjamin Franklin	Jane Franklin Mecom and Edward Mecom	Philadelphia
Feb. 1757	Jane Franklin Mecom	Benjamin Franklin	Boston
2/21/1757	Benjamin Franklin	Jane Franklin Mecom	Philadelphia
Apr. 1757	Jane Franklin Mecom	Benjamin Franklin	Boston
4/19/1757	Benjamin Franklin	Jane Franklin Mecom	New York
5/9/1757	Jane Franklin Mecom	William Franklin	Boston
5/9/1757	Jane Franklin Mecom	Benjamin Franklin	Boston
5/9/1757	Jane Franklin Mecom	William Franklin	Boston
5/16/1757	Jane Franklin Mecom	Benjamin Franklin	Boston
5/21/1757	Benjamin Franklin	Jane Franklin Mecom	Woodbridge, NJ
5/26/1757	William Franklin	Jane Franklin Mecom	New York
5/30/1757	Benjamin Franklin	Jane Franklin Mecom	New York
1/29/1758	Jane Franklin Mecom	Deborah Read Franklin	Boston
1/30/1758	Benjamin Mecom	Deborah Read Franklin	Boston
4/10/1758	Benjamin Mecom	Deborah Read Franklin	Boston
6/17/1758	Jane Franklin Mecom	Benjamin Franklin	Boston
8/15/1758	Jane Franklin Mecom	Benjamin Franklin	Boston
9/16/1758	Benjamin Franklin	Jane Franklin Mecom	London
9/26/1758	Benjamin Franklin	Jane Franklin Mecom	London
10/2/1758	Benjamin Franklin	Jane Franklin Mecom	London
11/11/1758	Benjamin Franklin	Jane Franklin Mecom	London
1/31/1759	Jane Franklin Mecom	Benjamin Franklin	Boston
7/14/1759	Benjamin Franklin	Jane Franklin Mecom	London
9/10/1759	Benjamin Mecom	Benjamin Franklin	Boston
Fall of 1759	Jane Franklin Mecom	Benjamin Franklin	Boston
1/9/1760	Benjamin Franklin	Jane Franklin Mecom	London
3/17/1760	Jane Franklin Mecom	Deborah Read Franklin	Boston

ORIGINAL	NOTES ON PROVENANCE AND PRINTINGS
APS	A) Duane, *Works*, 6:11–13; B) Sparks, *Familiar Letters*, 40–43; C) Sparks, *Works*, 7:117–19.
Lost	Referred to by BF in letter of 7/12/1756.
Missing	Sparks, *Familiar Letters*, 43–44.
APS	
APS	A) Sparks, *Familiar Letters*, 47; B) Sparks, *Works*, 7:126–27.
Lost	Referred to by BF in letter of 2/21/1757.
Missing	A) Sparks, *Familiar Letters*, 48; B) Sparks, *Works*, 7:129.
Lost	Referred to by BF in letter of 4/19/1757.
APS	A) Duane, *Works*, 6:14–15; B) Sparks, *Familiar Letters*, 50–51; C) Sparks, *Works*, 7:132–33.
Lost	Referred to by WF in letter of 5/26/1757.
Lost	Referred to by BF in letter of 5/21/1757 and 5/30/1757.
Lost	Referred to by William Franklin in letter of 5/26/1757.
Lost	Referred to by BF in letter of 5/30/1757.
Missing	A) Duane, *Works*, 6:16–17; B) Sparks, *Familiar Letters*, 52–53; C) Sparks, *Works*, 7:133–35.
Missing	A) Extracted by Josiah Flagg ca. 1794; B) Duane, *Works*, 6:17.
Private hands	A) Duane, *Works*, 6:18–20; B) Sparks, *Familiar Letters*, 54–57; C) Sparks, *Works*, 7:142–44.
APS	Duane, *Letters*, 183.
APS	
APS	
Lost	Referred to by BF in letter of 9/16/1758.
Lost	Referred to by BF in letter of 11/11/1758.
SC Historical Society	A) Duane, *Works*, 6:39–42; B) Sparks, *Works*, 7:182–85.
Lost	Referred to by BF in letter of 11/11/1758.
Lost	Referred to by BF in letter of 11/11/1758.
APS	
Lost	Referred to by BF in letter of 7/14/1759.
APS	
Lost	Referred to by BF in letter of 1/9/1760.
Lost	Referred to by BF in letter of 1/9/1760.
APS	Sparks, *Familiar Letters*, 9n, 63n (excerpts).
APS	

DATE	FROM	TO	PLACE
2/9/1761	Benjamin Mecom	Deborah Read Franklin	Boston
8/19/1762	Benjamin Franklin	Jane Franklin Mecom	Portsmouth, England
11/1/1762	Jane Franklin Mecom	Benjamin Franklin	Boston
11/11/1762	Benjamin Franklin	Jane Franklin Mecom	Philadelphia
11/12/1762	Jane Franklin Mecom	Benjamin Franklin	Boston
11/25/1762	Benjamin Franklin	Jane Franklin Mecom	Philadelphia
12/30/1762	Benjamin Franklin	Jane Franklin Mecom	Philadelphia
2/21/1763	Benjamin Franklin	Jane Franklin Mecom	Philadelphia
4/11/1763	Jane Franklin Mecom	Benjamin Franklin	Boston
5/20/1763	Benjamin Franklin	Jane Franklin Mecom	Philadelphia
6/19/1763	Benjamin Franklin	Jane Franklin Mecom	New York
11/7/1763	Benjamin Franklin	Jane Franklin Mecom	Philadelphia
12/15/1763	Benjamin Franklin	Jane Franklin Mecom	Philadelphia
7/10/1764	Benjamin Franklin	Jane Franklin Mecom	Philadelphia
7/24/1764	Benjamin Franklin	Jane Franklin Mecom	Philadelphia
Nov. 1764	Jane Franklin Mecom	Deborah Read Franklin	Boston
3/5/1765	Deborah Read Franklin	Jane Franklin Mecom	Philadelphia
4/6/1765	Jane Franklin Mecom	Deborah Read Franklin	Boston
Aug. 1765	Jane Franklin Mecom	Benjamin Franklin	Boston
8/29/1765	Benjamin Franklin	Jane Franklin Mecom	London
9/28/1765	Jane Franklin Mecom	Deborah Read Franklin	Boston
Nov. 1765	Jane Franklin Mecom	Benjamin Franklin	Boston
11/12/1765	Jane Franklin Mecom	Benjamin Franklin	Boston
12/20/1765	Jane Franklin Mecom	Benjamin Franklin	Boston
12/30/1765	Jane Franklin Mecom	Benjamin Franklin	Boston
Jan. 1766	Deborah Read Franklin	Jane Franklin Mecom	Philadelphia
2/27/1766	Jane Franklin Mecom	Deborah Read Franklin	Boston
3/1/1766	Benjamin Franklin	Jane Franklin Mecom	London
Nov. 1766	Deborah Read Franklin	Jane Franklin Mecom	Philadelphia
11/8/1766	Jane Franklin Mecom	Benjamin Franklin	Boston
11/24/1766	Jane Franklin Mecom	Deborah Read Franklin	Boston
3/2/1767	Benjamin Franklin	Jane Franklin Mecom	London
5/9/1767	Jane Franklin Mecom	Margaret Stevenson	Boston
5/9/1767	Jane Franklin Mecom	Benjamin Franklin	Boston
10/23/1767	Jane Franklin Mecom	Benjamin Franklin	Boston

ORIGINAL	NOTES ON PROVENANCE AND PRINTINGS
APS	Duane, *Letters,* 184–85.
LCP	A copy of a letter sent to the *London Magazine.*
Lost	Referred to by BF in letter of 11/11/1762.
APS	
Lost	Referred to by BF in letter of 11/25/1762.
APS	
APS	
APS	
Lost	Referred to by BF in letter of 5/20/1763.
APS	
APS	
APS	
APS	Sparks, *Familiar Letters,* 88n (excerpt).
Yale	
APS	
Lost	Referred to by DRF in a letter to BF, 1/8/1765.
Lost	Referred to by JFM in letter of 4/6/1765.
APS	
Lost	Referred to by JFM in letter of 12/30/1765.
APS	
APS	
Lost	Referred to by JFM in letter of 12/30/1765.
Lost	Referred to by BF in letter of 3/1/1766.
Lost	Referred to by BF in letter of 3/1/1766.
APS	
Lost	Referred to by JFM in letter of 2/27/1766.
APS	Duane, *Letters,* 186–88.
APS	Sparks, *Familiar Letters,* 98–99n (excerpt).
Lost	Referred to by JFM in letter of 11/24/1766.
APS	Duane, *Letters,* 29–31.
APS	
UVA	
APS	
Lost	Referred to by JFM in letter of 5/9/1767 to Margaret Stevenson.
Missing	Referred to by JFM in letter of 12/1/1767, by BF in letter of 12/24/1767, and partially printed by Sparks, *Works,* 7:515n.

DATE	FROM	TO	PLACE
12/1/1767	Jane Franklin Mecom	Benjamin Franklin	Boston
12/24/1767	Benjamin Franklin	Jane Franklin Mecom	London
1768	Jane Franklin Mecom	Keziah Coffin	Boston
2/21/1768	Benjamin Franklin	Jane Franklin Mecom	London
5/11/1768	Jane Franklin Mecom	Benjamin Franklin	Boston
8/6/1768	Keziah Folger Coffin	Jane Franklin Mecom	Nantucket
9/20/1768	Benjamin Franklin	Jane Franklin Mecom	London
9/26/1768	Jane Franklin Mecom	Deborah Read Franklin	Boston
10/7/1768	Jane Franklin Mecom	Benjamin Franklin	Boston
11/7/1768	Jane Franklin Mecom	Benjamin Franklin	Boston
11/20/1768	Benjamin Franklin	Jane Franklin Mecom	London
1/30/1769	Jane Franklin Mecom	Benjamin Franklin	Boston
2/23/1769	Benjamin Franklin	Jane Franklin Mecom	London
4/27/1769	Benjamin Franklin	Jane Franklin Mecom	London
6/13/1769	Jane Franklin Mecom	Benjamin Franklin	Boston
9/14/1769	Jane Franklin Mecom	Deborah Read Franklin	Boston
9/29/1769	Benjamin Franklin	Jane Franklin Mecom	London
1/3/1770	Jane Franklin Mecom	Benjamin Franklin	Philadelphia
3/15/1770	Benjamin Franklin	Jane Franklin Mecom	London
6/25/1770	Deborah Read Franklin	Jane Franklin Mecom	Philadelphia
7/6/1770	Jane Franklin Mecom	Benjamin Franklin	Boston
7/15/1770	Deborah Read Franklin	Jane Franklin Mecom	Philadelphia
Before Aug. 1770?	Jane Franklin Mecom	Deborah Read Franklin	Boston
August 1770	Jane Franklin Mecom	Deborah Read Franklin	Boston
9/25/1770	Jane Franklin Mecom	Benjamin Franklin	Boston
9/29/1770	Jane Franklin Mecom	Benjamin Franklin	Boston
9/29/1770	Deborah Read Franklin	Jane Franklin Mecom	Philadelphia
11/7/1770	Benjamin Franklin	Jane Franklin Mecom	London
11/9/1770	Benjamin Franklin	Jane Franklin Mecom	London
12/30/1770	Benjamin Franklin	Jane Franklin Mecom	London
1771	Jane Franklin Mecom	Benjamin Franklin	Boston
5/10/1771	Jane Franklin Mecom	Benjamin Franklin	Boston
7/17/1771	Benjamin Franklin	Jane Franklin Mecom	London

ORIGINAL	NOTES ON PROVENANCE AND PRINTINGS
APS	
APS	Sparks, *Familiar Letters*, 22n (excerpt).
Lost	"Receiv'd all your Letters," Coffin wrote to JFM on 8/6/1768.
APS	
Lost	Referred to by BF in letter of 9/20/1768.
APS	
APS	
Lost	Referred to by BF in letter of 2/23/1769.
Lost	Referred to by BF in letter of 2/23/1769.
APS	
APS	
Lost	Referred to by BF in letter of 4/27/1769.
APS	A) Sparks, *Familiar Letters*, 119–20n (excerpt); B) Sparks, *Works*, 7:437–38n (excerpt).
APS	A) Sparks, *Familiar Letters*, 117n; B) Sparks, *Works*, 7:442–44.
Lost	Referred to by BF in letter of 9/29/1769.
APS	
APS	
Lost	Referred to by BF in letter of 3/5/1770.
Missing	Sparks, *Familiar Letters*, 123–24. Copy sent to *London Magazine* in Aug. 1825.
Lost	Referred to by JFM in letter of Aug. 1770.
Lost	Referred to by BF in letter of 11/7/1770.
Lost	Referred to by JFM in letter probably dated before Aug. 1770.
APS	Duane, *Letters*, 192–95.
APS	
APS	
Lost	Referred to by BF in letter of 11/9/1770 (included with 11/7/1770).
Lost	Referred to by JFM in letter begun in Aug. 1770.
APS	
APS	
Private hands	Transcript at APS. A) Sparks, *Works*, 7:495–98; B) Smyth, *Writings*, 5:288–92; auctioned by Sotheby's in 1985.
Lost	Referred to by BF in letter of 1/13/1772.
Lost	Referred to by BF in letter of 7/17/1771.
APS	A) Sparks, *Familiar Letters*, 22–23n, 133n (excerpts); B) Sparks, *Works*,, 7:380n.

DATE	FROM	TO	PLACE
9/2/1771	Jane Franklin Mecom	Deborah Read Franklin	Boston
9/12/1771	Jane Franklin Mecom	Benjamin Franklin	Boston
11/9/1771	Jane Franklin Mecom	Benjamin Franklin	Boston
1/13/1772	Benjamin Franklin	Jane Franklin Mecom	London
1772	Jane Franklin Mecom	Benjamin Franklin	Boston
3/30/1772	Benjamin Franklin	Jane Franklin Mecom	London
4/13/1772	Benjamin Franklin	Jane Franklin Mecom	London
1772	Jane Franklin Mecom	Deborah Read Franklin	Boston
May 1772?	Deborah Read Franklin	Jane Franklin Mecom	Philadelphia
12/30/1772	Jane Franklin Mecom	Benjamin Franklin	Boston
1/19/1773	Jane Franklin Mecom	Benjamin Franklin	Boston
3/9/1773	Benjamin Franklin	Jane Franklin Mecom	London
4/20/1773	Jane Franklin Mecom	Benjamin Franklin	Boston
5/5/1773	Jane Franklin Mecom	Benjamin Franklin	Boston
5/15/1773	Jane Franklin Mecom	Benjamin Franklin	Boston
6/28/1773	Jane Franklin Mecom	Benjamin Franklin	Boston
7/7/1773	Benjamin Franklin	Jane Franklin Mecom	London
7/9/1773	Jane Mecom Collas	Benjamin Franklin	Boston
10/9/1773	Benjamin Franklin	Jane Franklin Mecom	London
11/1/1773	Benjamin Franklin	Jane Franklin Mecom	London
12/11/1773	Jane Franklin Mecom	Benjamin Franklin	Boston
2/17/1774	Benjamin Franklin	Jane Franklin Mecom	London
3/23/1774	Benjamin Franklin	Jane Franklin Mecom	London
5/1/1774	Jane Franklin Mecom	Benjamin Franklin	Boston
5/18/1774	Jane Franklin Mecom	Benjamin Franklin	Boston
7/28/1774	Benjamin Franklin	Jane Franklin Mecom	London
8/18/1774	Benjamin Franklin	Jane Franklin Mecom	London
9/3/1774	Benjamin Franklin	Jane Franklin Mecom	London
9/26/1774	Benjamin Franklin	Jane Franklin Mecom	London
9/28/1774	Benjamin Franklin	Jane Franklin Mecom	London
Oct. 1774	Jane Franklin Mecom	Benjamin Franklin	Boston
Oct. 1774	Jane Franklin Mecom	Jonathan Williams Jr.	Boston
11/3/1774	Jane Franklin Mecom	Benjamin Franklin	Boston

ORIGINAL	NOTES ON PROVENANCE AND PRINTINGS
APS	
Lost	Referred to by BF in letter of 1/13/1772.
Lost	Referred to by BF in letter of 1/13/1772.
Private hands	Incomplete draft at APS. A) *London Magazine* (Aug. 1825): 607–8; B) *Worcester Magazine* (Oct. 1825): 75–76; C) Sparks, *Familiar Letters,* 145–47; D) Sparks, *Works,* 7:541–43.
Lost	Referred to by BF in letters of 3/30/1772 and 4/13/1772.
APS	
APS	
Lost	Referred to by DRF in letter of May 1772.
APS	
Lost	Referred to by BF in letter of 3/9/1773.
Lost	Referred to by BF in letter of 7/7/1773.
LC	Smyth, *Writings,* 6:21.
Lost	Referred to by BF in letter of 7/7/1773.
Lost	Referred to by BF in letter of 7/7/1773.
Lost	Letter of 5/15/1773 referred to by BF in letter of 7/7/1773.
Lost	Referred to by BF in letter of 11/1/1773.
LC	Smyth, *Writings,* 6:93–94.
APS	
APS	
APS	Sparks, *Familiar Letters,* 120n (excerpt).
Lost	Referred to by BF in letter of 2/17/1774.
HSP	
APS	
Lost	Referred to by BF in letter of 7/28/1774.
Lost	Referred to by BF in letter of 7/28/1774.
APS	
Lost	Referred to by JFM in letter of 11/3/1774.
APS	
APS	A) Sparks, *Familiar Letters,* 150–51; B) Sparks, *Works,* 8:136–37.
Lost	Referred to by JFM in letter of 12/5/1774.
Lost	Referred to by JFM in letter of 11/3/1774.
Lost	Referred to by JFM in letter of 12/15/1774.
APS	

DATE	FROM	TO	PLACE
12/5/1774	Jane Franklin Mecom	Benjamin Franklin	Boston
12/15/1774	Jane Franklin Mecom	Benjamin Franklin	Boston
2/26/1775	Benjamin Franklin	Jane Franklin Mecom	London
5/14/1775	Jane Franklin Mecom	Benjamin Franklin	Warwick, RI
5/26/1775	Benjamin Franklin	Jane Franklin Mecom	Philadelphia
6/17/1775	Benjamin Franklin	Jane Franklin Mecom	Philadelphia
7/14/1775	Jane Franklin Mecom	Benjamin Franklin	Warwick, RI
8/2/1775	Benjamin Franklin	Jane Franklin Mecom	Philadelphia
10/16/1775	Benjamin Franklin	Jane Franklin Mecom	Cambridge
11/24/1775	Jane Franklin Mecom	Catharine Ray Greene	Philadelphia
1/5/1776	Jane Franklin Mecom	Catharine Ray Greene	Philadelphia
2/7/1776	Catharine Ray Greene	Jane Franklin Mecom	Warwick, RI
2/20/1776	Catharine Ray Greene	Jane Franklin Mecom	Warwick, RI
3/12/1776	Catharine Ray Greene	Jane Franklin Mecom	Warwick, RI
5/8/1776	Jane Franklin Mecom	Catharine Ray Greene	Philadelphia
June 1776	M. Walker	Jane Franklin Mecom	Philadelphia
6/1/1776	Jane Franklin Mecom	Catharine Ray Greene	Philadelphia
6/21/1776	Catharine Ray Greene	Jane Franklin Mecom	Warwick, RI
8/4/1776	Ray Greene	Benjamin Franklin and Jane Franklin Mecom	Warwick, RI
12/8/1776	Benjamin Franklin	Jane Franklin Mecom	Nantes, France
12/16/1776	Jane Franklin Mecom	Benjamin Franklin	Goshen, PA
8/18/1777	Jane Franklin Mecom	Benjamin Franklin	Philadelphia
10/5/1777	Benjamin Franklin	Jane Franklin Mecom	Passy, France
12/22/1777	Benjamin Franklin	Jane Franklin Mecom	Passy, France
1/9/1778	Jane Mecom Collas	Benjamin Franklin	Boston
2/28/1778	Benjamin Franklin	Jane Franklin Mecom	Passy, France
Apr. 1778	Jane Franklin Mecom	Jane Mecom Collas	Coventry, RI
5/5/1778	Jane Franklin Mecom	Benjamin Franklin	Warwick, RI
5/7/1778	Jane Franklin Mecom	Jonathan Williams Sr.	Warwick, RI
5/16/1778	Jane Franklin Mecom	Jane Mecom Collas	Warwick, RI
8/15/1778	Jane Franklin Mecom	Benjamin Franklin	Warwick, RI
11/26/1778	Benjamin Franklin	Jane Franklin Mecom	Passy, France
12/7/1778	Jane Franklin Mecom	Benjamin Franklin	Warwick, RI

ORIGINAL	NOTES ON PROVENANCE AND PRINTINGS
Missing	Transcript at Harvard. Copied by Sparks between 1836 and 1840. Printed in *Southern Literary Messenger*, May 1839, p. 304.
Missing	This is a continuation of JFM to BF, 12/5/1774.
APS	Printed in facsimile in *Library Bulletin* 1944 of the APS.
Yale	
Marietta College	Sparks, *Works*, 8:154–55.
APS	
APS	Duane, *Letters*, 62–66 (postscript from Greenes, 66–67).
APS	Roelker, *BR and CRG*, 56–57.
APS	
Missing	A copy is in the APS. Roelker, *BF and CRG*, 61–63.
Missing	Referred to by CRG in letter of 2/20/1776.
APS	Roelker, *BF and CRG*, 65–66.
APS	Roelker, *BF and CRG*, 67–69.
APS	Roelker, *BF and CRG*, 69–70.
APS	
Missing	Extract in APS.
	Roelker, *BF and CRG*, 73–75.
APS	
APS	In facsimile in *Library Bulletin* 1944 of the APS.
APS	
HSP	*Pennsylvania Magazine of History and Biography* LXXII (1948): 265–66.
APS	
Lost	Referred to by JFM in letter of 5/5/1778.
APS	
Lost	Referred to by JFM in letter of 5/5/1778.
Missing	A copy is at the NEHGS.
HSP	*Pennsylvania Magazine of History and Biography*, LXXII (1948): 267–70.
Lost	Referred to by Jonathan Williams Sr. in a letter to BF, 5/7/1778.
Private hands	Sold by Sotheby's in 1984. Corrected copy at NEHGS.
APS	Duane, *Letters*, 81–84.
Lost	Referred to by JFM in letter of 7/27/1779.
Lost	Mentioned by BF in letter to William Greene, 6/4/1779.

DATE	FROM	TO	PLACE
1/4/1779	Jane Franklin Mecom	Benjamin Franklin	Warwick, RI
1/17/1779	Jane Franklin Mecom	Sarah Franklin Bache	Warwick, RI
2/14/1779	Jane Franklin Mecom	Benjamin Franklin	Warwick, RI
4/12/1779	Peter Collas	Jane Franklin Mecom	
4/22/1779	Benjamin Franklin	Jane Franklin Mecom	Passy, France
6/22/1779	Richard Bache	Jane Franklin Mecom	Philadelphia
6/23/1779	Jane Franklin Mecom	Benjamin Franklin	Warwick, RI
7/21/1779	Jane Franklin Mecom	Richard Bache	Warwick, RI
7/27/1779	Jane Franklin Mecom	Benjamin Franklin	Warwick, RI
8/18/1780	Sarah Franklin Bache	Jane Franklin Mecom	Philadelphia
9/12/1779	Jane Franklin Mecom	Benjamin Franklin	Warwick, RI
10/25/1779	Benjamin Franklin	Jane Franklin Mecom	Passy, France
3/5/1780	Benjamin Franklin	Jane Franklin Mecom	Passy, France
3/16/1780	Benjamin Franklin	Jane Franklin Mecom	Passy, France
3/27/1780	Jane Franklin Mecom	Benjamin Franklin	Warwick, RI
Oct. 1780	Jane Franklin Mecom	Sarah Franklin Bache	Warwick, RI
12/24/1780	Jane Franklin Mecom	Benjamin Franklin	Warwick, RI
3/3/1781	Jane Franklin Mecom	Benjamin Franklin	Warwick, RI
6/13/1781	Jane Franklin Mecom	Benjamin Franklin	Warwick, RI
10/23/1781	Jane Franklin Mecom	Benjamin Franklin	Cambridge
10/29/1781	Jane Franklin Mecom	Benjamin Franklin	Boston
6/17/1782	Jane Franklin Mecom	Benjamin Franklin	Warwick, RI
6/25/1782	Jane Franklin Mecom	Benjamin Franklin	Warwick, RI
10/6/1782	Jane Franklin Mecom	Benjamin Franklin	Warwick, RI
12/4/1782	Richard Bache	Jane Franklin Mecom	Philadelphia
12/26/1782	Jane Franklin Mecom	Benjamin Franklin	Cambridge
Late 1782?	Benjamin Franklin	Jane Franklin Mecom	Passy, France
4/11/1783	Jane Franklin Mecom	Richard Bache	Cambridge
4/29/1783	Jane Franklin Mecom	Benjamin Franklin	Boston
5/18/1783	Jane Franklin Mecom	Sarah Franklin Bache	Boston
8/23/1783	Josiah Flagg	Jane Franklin Mecom	Lancaster, MA
9/13/1783	Benjamin Franklin	Jane Franklin Mecom	Passy, France
12/26/1783	Benjamin Franklin	Jane Franklin Mecom	Passy, France
2/12/1784	Catharine Ray Greene	Jane Franklin Mecom	Warwick, RI
6/17/1784	Benjamin Franklin	Jane Franklin Mecom	Passy, France

ORIGINAL	NOTES ON PROVENANCE AND PRINTINGS
APS	
Missing	A corrected copy is at Yale.
APS	Duane, *Letters*, 94–96.
Lost	Referred to by JFM in a letter of 7/21/1779.
APS	
Lost	Referred to by JFM in a letter of 7/21/1779.
APS	Duane, *Letters*, 96–98.
APS	Auctioned by S. V. Henkels in 1892.
APS	Duane, *Letters*, 99–101.
Lost	Mentioned by JFM in letter of Oct. 1780.
APS	Duane, *Letters*, 102–4.
APS	A) Sparks, *Familiar Letters*, 171–72; B) Sparks, *Works*, 8:401–2.
Lost	Mentioned by JFM in letter of 12/29/1780.
Lost	Mentioned by JFM in letter of 6/13/1781.
APS	
Princeton	
APS	Van Doren dates this letter 12/29/1780, but the manuscript reads 24.
APS	
APS	
APS	Duane, *Letters*, 115–16.
APS	Duane, *Letters*, 116–17.
APS	
APS	
Princeton	
Lost	Mentioned by JFM in letter of 4/11/1783.
HSP	*Pennsylvania Magazine of History and Biography* LXXII (1948): 270–72.
Lost	Mentioned by JFM in letter of 4/29/1783.
NYPL	
APS	Duane, *Letters*, 123–26.
Missing	A copy is at Yale.
NEHGS	Donated by the Flagg family in 1872.
MHS	Printed in *Collections of the Massachusetts Historical Society*, Series 6, IV, 260–61.
LCP	A copy of a letter sent to the *London Magazine*.
APS	
APS	

DATE	FROM	TO	PLACE
7/4/1784	Jane Franklin Mecom	Benjamin Franklin	Boston
8/16/1784	Jane Franklin Mecom	Benjamin Franklin	Boston
10/16/1784	Benjamin Franklin	Jane Franklin Mecom	Passy, France
10/21/1784	Jane Franklin Mecom	Benjamin Franklin	Boston
4/12/1785	Benjamin Franklin	Jane Franklin Mecom	Passy, France
5/26/1785	Jane Franklin Mecom	Benjamin Franklin	Boston
7/13/1785	Benjamin Franklin	Jane Franklin Mecom	St. Germain, France
9/19/1785	Benjamin Franklin	Jane Franklin Mecom	Philadelphia
9/23/1785	Jane Franklin Mecom	Benjamin Franklin	Boston
10/1/1785	Benjamin Franklin	Jane Franklin Mecom	Philadelphia
10/1/1785	Jane Franklin Mecom	Benjamin Franklin	Boston
10/19/1785	Jane Franklin Mecom	Benjamin Franklin	Boston
10/27/1785	Benjamin Franklin	Jane Franklin Mecom	Philadelphia
11/7/1785	Jane Franklin Mecom	Benjamin Franklin	Boston
11/30/1785	Jane Franklin Mecom	Benjamin Franklin	Boston
12/29/1785	Jane Franklin Mecom	Benjamin Franklin	Boston
1/1/1786	Benjamin Franklin	Jane Franklin Mecom	Philadelphia
1/6/1786	Jane Franklin Mecom	Benjamin Franklin	Boston
1/24/1786	Benjamin Franklin	Jane Franklin Mecom	Philadelphia
2/21/1786	Jane Franklin Mecom	Benjamin Franklin	Philadelphia
4/8/1786	Benjamin Franklin	Jane Franklin Mecom	Boston
4/17/1786	Josiah Flagg	Jane Franklin Mecom	Philadelphia
4/22/1786	Jane Franklin Mecom	Benjamin Franklin	Boston
4/25/1786	Benjamin Franklin	Jane Franklin Mecom	Philadelphia
5/2/1786	Benjamin Franklin	Jane Franklin Mecom	Philadelphia
5/3/1786	Jane Franklin Mecom	Benjamin Franklin	Boston
5/29/1786	Jane Franklin Mecom	Benjamin Franklin	Boston
5/29/1786	Jane Franklin Mecom	Sarah Franklin Bache	Boston
May–July 1786?	Jane Franklin Mecom	Benjamin Franklin	Boston
6/3/1786	Benjamin Franklin	Jane Franklin Mecom	Philadelphia
7/4/1786	Benjamin Franklin	Jane Franklin Mecom	Philadelphia

ORIGINAL	NOTES ON PROVENANCE AND PRINTINGS
APS	Duane, *Letters,* 130–32.
APS	
Lost	Mentioned by JFM in letter of 5/26/1785.
APS	
Lost	Mentioned by JFM in letter of 9/23/1785.
HSP	*Pennsylvania Magazine of History and Biography* XXXVI (1912): 119–20.
APS	A) Sparks, *Works,* 10:213n (only first paragraph); B) Smyth, *Writings,* 9:363–64. Copy in another hand at APS.
SC Historical Society	
APS	Duane, *Letters,* 132–33.
APS	
APS	Duane, *Letters,* 133–34.
APS	A) Sparks, *Works,* 10:326n (excerpt); B)Duane, *Letters,* 135–36.
APS	
APS	Duane, *Letters,* 137–38.
APS	Duane, *Letters,* 138–40.
APS	
LC	
APS	Duane, *Letters,* 140–42 (without enclosures).
LC	Sparks, *Familiar Letters,* 203–4n (3rd and 5th paragraphs only). Petition of Z printed in Sparks, *Works,* 6:304–5.
APS	
LC	A copy is in the LC. Smyth, *Writings,* 9:506–8.
APS	
APS	
LC	
NEHGS	Donated by the Flagg family in 1872. Printed in *New England Historical and Genealogical Register* XXVII (1873): 249.
APS	
Private hands	
APS	
APS	Duane, *Letters,* 142–44.
LC	A) Sparks, *Familiar Letters,* 129n (excerpt); B) Smyth, *Writings,* 9:514–15.
LC	A) Sparks, *Familiar Letters,* 209–10; B) Sparks, *Works,* 10:264–65; C) Smyth, *Writings,* 9:522–23.

DATE	FROM	TO	PLACE
7/21/1786	Jane Franklin Mecom	Benjamin Franklin	Boston
7/21/1786	Jane Franklin Mecom	Josiah Flagg	Boston
7/30/1786	Benjamin Franklin	Jane Franklin Mecom	Philadelphia
8/5/1786	Jane Franklin Mecom	Benjamin Franklin	Boston
8/18/1786	Josiah Flagg	Jane Franklin Mecom	Philadelphia
9/4/1786	Benjamin Franklin	Jane Franklin Mecom	Philadelphia
9/13/1786	Jane Franklin Mecom	Benjamin Franklin	Boston
9/21/1786	Benjamin Franklin	Jane Franklin Mecom	Philadelphia
10/12/1786	Jane Franklin Mecom	Benjamin Franklin	Boston
10/12/1786?	Jane Franklin Mecom	Benjamin Franklin	Boston
11/5/1786	Jane Franklin Mecom	Benjamin Franklin	Boston
12/3/1786	Benjamin Franklin	Jane Franklin Mecom	Philadelphia
12/17/1786	Jane Franklin Mecom	Benjamin Franklin	Boston
1/6/1787	Jane Franklin Mecom	Benjamin Franklin	Boston
3/9/1787	Jane Franklin Mecom	Benjamin Franklin	Boston
5/22/1787	Jane Franklin Mecom	Benjamin Franklin	Boston
5/23/1787	Jane Franklin Mecom	Sarah Franklin Bache	Boston
5/30/1787	Benjamin Franklin	Jane Franklin Mecom	Philadelphia
8/16/1787	Jane Franklin Mecom	Benjamin Franklin	Boston
9/20/1787	Benjamin Franklin	Jane Franklin Mecom	Philadelphia
11/4/1787	Benjamin Franklin	Jane Franklin Mecom	Philadelphia
11/9/1787	Jane Franklin Mecom	Benjamin Franklin	Boston
11/11/1787	Jane Mecom Collas	Benjamin Franklin	Boston
12/11/1787	Benjamin Franklin	Jane Franklin Mecom	Philadelphia
1/8/1788	Jane Franklin Mecom	Benjamin Franklin	Boston
4/12/1788	Benjamin Franklin	Jane Franklin Mecom	Philadelphia
5/5/1788	Jane Franklin Mecom	Benjamin Franklin	Boston
5/31/1788	Benjamin Franklin	Jane Franklin Mecom	Philadelphia
6/25/1788	Jane Franklin Mecom	Benjamin Franklin	Boston
8/31/1788	Benjamin Franklin	Jane Franklin Mecom	Philadelphia
9/5/1788	Jane Franklin Mecom	Benjamin Franklin	Boston
9/16/1788	Benjamin Franklin	Jane Franklin Mecom	Philadelphia
9/26/1788	Jane Franklin Mecom	Benjamin Franklin	Boston

ORIGINAL	NOTES ON PROVENANCE AND PRINTINGS
APS	Duane, *Letters,* 145–46.
NEHGS	Donated by the Flagg family in 1872. Printed in *New England Historical and Genealogical Register* XXVII (1873): 250–51.
LC	
APS	Duane, *Letters,* 146–48.
Houghton	Purchased, 1941.
LC	
APS	Duane, *Letters,* 148–49.
LC	A printed copy is in the LC.
APS	Duane, *Letters,* 149–50.
APS	
APS	
LC	
APS	Duane, *Letters,* 151–52.
APS	Duane, *Letters,* 152–54.
APS	Duane, *Letters,* 155–56.
APS	Duane, *Letters,* 157–59.
Private hands	
Private hands	A copy is in the LC. Auctioned in 1995.
APS	Duane, *Letters,* 159–60.
LC	A) *New York Evening Signal,* Oct. 23, 1839; B) Sparks, *Works,* 10:444–46; C) Smyth, *Writings,* 9:612–14.
Private hands	Sparks, *Works,* 10:325–27. Auctioned in 1985.
APS	Duane, *Letters,* 161–62.
APS	
LC	A copy is in the LC. Smyth, *Writings,* 9:623–24.
APS	Duane, *Letters,* 162–66.
LC	A copy is in the LC.
Lost	Referred to by BF in letter of 5/31/1788.
Missing	Copied by Sparks in the 1830s; MS Sparks 44.
APS	
Lost	Referred to by JFM in letter of 11/21/1788.
APS	
Lost	Referred to by JFM in letter of 9/26/1788.
APS	Duane, *Letters,* 169–71.

DATE	FROM	TO	PLACE
11/11/1788	Jane Franklin Mecom	Benjamin Franklin	Boston
11/21/1788	Jane Franklin Mecom	Benjamin Franklin	Boston
11/26/1788	Benjamin Franklin	Jane Franklin Mecom	Philadelphia
1/10/1789	Jane Franklin Mecom	Benjamin Franklin	Boston
2/22/1789	Benjamin Franklin	Jane Franklin Mecom	Philadelphia
4/2/1789	Jane Franklin Mecom	Benjamin Franklin	Boston
4/27/1789	Benjamin Franklin	Jane Franklin Mecom	Philadelphia
May 1789	Benjamin Franklin	Jane Franklin Mecom	Philadelphia
6/8/1789	Jane Franklin Mecom	Benjamin Franklin	Boston
7/1/1789	Benjamin Franklin	Jane Franklin Mecom	Philadelphia
7/23/1789	Jane Franklin Mecom	Benjamin Franklin	Boston
8/3/1789	Benjamin Franklin	Jane Franklin Mecom	Philadelphia
8/29/1789	Jane Franklin Mecom	Benjamin Franklin	Boston
9/10/1789	Jane Franklin Mecom	Benjamin Franklin	Boston
10/19/1789	Benjamin Franklin	Jane Franklin Mecom	Philadelphia
11/24/1789	Jane Franklin Mecom	Benjamin Franklin	Boston
11/25/1789	Jane Franklin Mecom	Benjamin Franklin	Boston
11/30/1789	Benjamin Franklin	Jane Franklin Mecom	Philadelphia
12/17/1789	Benjamin Franklin	Jane Franklin Mecom	Philadelphia
1/17/1790	Jane Franklin Mecom	Benjamin Franklin	Boston
1/29/1790	Benjamin Franklin	Jane Franklin Mecom	Philadelphia
2/6/1790	Jane Franklin Mecom	Benjamin Franklin	Boston
3/24/1790	Benjamin Franklin	Jane Franklin Mecom	Philadelphia
4/19/1790	Richard Bache	Jane Franklin Mecom	Philadelphia
7/2/1790	Jane Franklin Mecom, Jane Mecom Collas, Josiah Flagg, and Jane Mecom	Henry Hill et al.	Boston
9/6/1790	Jane Franklin Mecom	Sarah Franklin Bache	Boston
10/20/1790	Jane Franklin Mecom	Sarah Franklin Bache	Boston
12/2/1790	Jane Franklin Mecom	Sarah Franklin Bache	Boston
6/28/1791	Jane Franklin Mecom		Boston
8/6/1791	Jane Franklin Mecom	Henry Hill	Boston
9/24/1791	Jane Franklin Mecom	Edward Duffield	Boston

ORIGINAL	NOTES ON PROVENANCE AND PRINTINGS
APS	Duane, *Letters,* 171–73.
APS	
Private hands	Sparks, *Works,* 10:366–67. Auctioned by Sotheby's in 1985.
Lost	Referred to by BF in letter of 2/22/1789.
APS	
APS	Duane, *Letters,* 174–75.
SCHS	
Lost	Mentioned by BF in letter of 1789.
Lost	Mentioned by BF in letter of 7/1/1789.
NEHGS	A) Extracted by Josiah Flagg ca. 1794; B) Printed in *New England Historical and Genealogical Register* XXVII (1873): 250.
APS	
LC	A) Sparks, *Familiar Letters,* 216–17; B) Sparks, *Works,* 10:394–95; C) Smyth, *Writings,* 10:33–34.
APS	A) Sparks, *Works,* 10:395n (excerpt); B) Duane, *Letters,* 175–78.
APS	
LCP	
APS	
APS	
LC	A copy in another hand is in the LC.
APS	Sparks, *Works,* 10:411–12.
APS	Duane, *Letters,* 179–80.
Lost	Referred to by JFM in letter of 2/6/1790.
APS	
Missing	Sparks, *Works,* 10:425–26.
NEHGS	Donated by the Flagg family in 1872. Printed in *New England Historical and Genealogical Register* XXVII (1873): 252–53.
APS	Copied into the records of BF's estate.
Private hands	Sold by Sotheby's in 1979. Corrected copy at Yale.
Private hands	
HSP	
HSP	
HSP	In another hand.
Yale	Auctioned by S. V. Henkels in 1895.

DATE	FROM	TO	PLACE
10/31/1791	Henry Hill	Jane Franklin Mecom	Philadelphia
8/11/1792	Jane Franklin Mecom	Jonathan Williams Jr.	Boston
8/14/1792	Henry Hill	Jane Franklin Mecom	Philadelphia
7/24/1793	Jane Franklin Mecom	Henry Hill	Boston

ORIGINAL	NOTES ON PROVENANCE AND PRINTINGS
ASP	Copied into the records of BF's estate.
Rosenbach	
APS	Copied into the records of BF's estate.
HSP	

The Editorial Hand of Jared Sparks

Jared Sparks's ideas about editing came from the world of magazines, where he had a very heavy hand.[1] One of his *North American Review* writers, the historian George Bancroft, was forever warning him, "You must not make any alterations or omissions without consulting me," and Sparks was forever ignoring him.[2] "Make no *omissions,* nor alterations, except grammar and good sense require it," Bancroft wrote his editor. "I have written with great care, will be personally responsible for every word of the article, and also for the selections."[3] Sending in a review of a book by the lexicographer Joseph Worcester, Bancroft made abundantly clear that he wanted to read the proofs before anything went to press. "Pray remember my desire to have the sheets sent me before they appear," Bancroft wrote. "I repeat: reject that on Worcester if you will, & write yourself a short general one of praise without vituperation. Or print what I have been compelled to say."[4] Sparks wrote back, without apology, that he had not only edited the review but already sent it to the printer: "Worcester I have cut off a good deal, and made a short review for the miscellaneous head. I have added a word or two of praise, just to take off the edge of your sharp criticism."[5]

Notably, while Sparks was preparing Franklin's and Washington's papers, more than one person urged him not to change their words, requesting that if he must make omissions, he mark them with an asterisk. In 1833, Supreme Court justice Joseph Story wrote Sparks, "To correct the grammatical errors (it seems to me) will be deemed by every person an appropriate duty of the editor. But the change of words merely to express the thought more appropriately, or the change of the form of the sentence merely to make it read more clearly, or, in a literary sense, more correctly, will perhaps be deemed a liberty not required, and very unfair, in the opinion of some, to the *veritable* character of the documents themselves." Story continued, "I am not sure that, on this account, it might not be well to mark with an asterisk every place where any alteration whatsoever occurs in printing the future volumes. This would obviate every possible objection."[6] Sparks did not take Story's advice.

At least one reader complained. "I wish you had printed Franklin's letter to me without altering an iota of it," Benjamin Waterhouse wrote to Sparks, after a letter Franklin had sent him appeared in *Familiar Letters*.[7] But what really troubled Sparks was that Franklin could be filthy. In editing Franklin's letters, Sparks redacted his prose, possibly even more severely than he bowdlerized Washington's; although, since so many of the originals have been lost, it's hard to tell. Sparks did not approve of earthiness, and he struck it out. In making extracts from Jane's letters, Sparks chose only what reflected well on Franklin.

Here I have supplied examples. In the following two letters, Sparks's additions are in boldface; his deletions are struck through.

1. Franklin wrote to Jane from London on September 16, 1758. The original of this letter is in the collections of the Historical Society of Pennsylvania. Sparks published it in *The Works of Benjamin Franklin*, volume 7, pp. 182–85.

London Sept 16 1758
Dear Sister

I received your ~~F~~**f**avour of June 17**th**. I wonder you have had no ~~L~~**l**etter from me since my being in England. I have wrote you at least two and I think a third before this~~; A~~ **,** **and**, what was next to waiting on you in ~~P~~**p**erson, sent you my ~~P~~**p**icture. In June last I sent Benny a ~~T~~**t**runk of ~~B~~**b**ooks and wrote to him. I hope they are come to hand, and that he meets with ~~I~~**e**ncouragement in his ~~B~~**b**usiness. I congratulate you on the ~~C~~**c**onquest of Cape Breton, and hope as your ~~P~~**p**eople took it by ~~P~~**p**raying the first ~~T~~**t**ime, you will now pray that it may never be given up again, which you then forgot. Billy is well, but in the Country. I left him at Tunbridge ~~Wells~~, where we spent a fortnight, and he is now gone with some ~~C~~**c**ompany to see Portsmouth.

We have been together over a great part of England this ~~S~~**s**ummer~~;~~, and among other places visited the ~~T~~**t**own our ~~F~~**f**ather was born in and found some ~~R~~**r**elations in that part of the ~~C~~**c**ountry ~~S~~**s**till living. Our ~~C~~**c**ousin Jane Franklin, daughter of our ~~U~~**u**nc~~k~~le John, died but about a ~~Y~~**y**ear ago. We saw her ~~H~~**h**usband, Robert Page, who gave us some old ~~L~~**l**etters to his ~~W~~**w**ife from unk~~c~~le Benjamin. In one of them, dated Boston July 4~~th~~**th,** 1723 he writes "~~Y~~ **that** your ~~U~~**u**nk~~c~~le Josiah has a ~~D~~**d**aughter Jane about ~~12~~ **twelve** years ~~O~~**o**ld, a good-humour'ed ~~C~~**c**hild" . So ~~Jenny~~ keep up **to** your ~~C~~**c**haracter, and don't be angry when you have no ~~L~~**l**etters.

In a little ~~B~~**b**ook he sent her, call'ed "*None but Christ,*" he wrote an ~~A~~**a**crostick on her ~~N~~**n**ame, which for ~~N~~**n**amesakes' ~~S~~**s**ake, as well as the good ~~A~~**a**dvice it contains, I transcribe and send you, **viz.**

"Illuminated from on ~~H~~**h**igh,
And shining brightly in your ~~S~~**s**phere,
Nere faint, but keep a steady ~~E~~**e**ye,
Expecting endless ~~P~~**p**leasures there.

"Flee ~~V~~vice, as you'd a ~~S~~serpent flee~~,~~;
Raise ~~Faith~~ *faith* **and** hope ~~Hope~~ three ~~S~~stories higher
And let Christ's endless ~~L~~love to thee
N-ere cease to make thy ~~L~~love ~~A~~aspire.
Kindness of ~~H~~heart by ~~W~~words express,
Let your ~~O~~obedience be sincere,
In ~~P~~prayer and ~~P~~praise your God ~~A~~address,
Nere cease' till he can cease to hear."

After professing truly that I have a great ~~E~~esteem and ~~V~~veneration for the pious ~~A~~author, permit me a little to play the ~~C~~commentator and ~~C~~critic on these ~~L~~lines. The ~~M~~meaning of ~~T~~*three ~~S~~stories higher* seems somewhat obscure. ~~, y~~You are to understand, then, that ~~F~~*faith, ~~H~~hope* and ~~C~~*charity* have been called the three ~~S~~steps of Jacob's ~~L~~ladder, reaching from ~~E~~earth to ~~H~~heaven~~. O~~; our ~~A~~author calls them ~~S~~*stories,* likening ~~R~~religion to a ~~B~~building, and those the three ~~S~~stories of the Christian ~~E~~edifice~~;~~ . Thus ~~I~~improvement in ~~R~~religion, is called ~~B~~*building ~~U~~up,* and ~~E~~edification. *Faith* is then the ~~G~~ground-floor, ~~H~~*hope* is up one ~~P~~pair of ~~S~~stairs. My dear~~ly~~ beloved Jenny, don't delight so much to dwell in these lower ~~R~~rooms, but get as fast as you can into the ~~G~~garret~~;~~, for in truth the best ~~R~~room in the ~~H~~house is ~~C~~*charity.* For my part, I wish the ~~H~~house was turn'd upside down; 'tis so difficult (when one is fat) to get up ~~S~~stairs; and not only so, but I imagine ~~H~~*hope* and ~~F~~*faith* may be more firmly built on ~~C~~*charity,* than ~~C~~*charity* upon ~~F~~*faith* and ~~H~~*hope.* However that be, I think it a better reading to say "Raise ~~F~~faith and ~~H~~hope *one ~~S~~story* higher." ~~C~~Correct it ~~boldly~~, and I'll support the ~~A~~alteration~~;~~. ~~F~~for when you are up two ~~S~~stories already, if you raise your ~~B~~building three ~~S~~stories higher, you will make five in all, which is two more than there should be, you expose your upper ~~R~~rooms more to the ~~W~~winds and ~~S~~storms~~;~~; and, besides, I am afraid the ~~F~~foundation will hardly bear them, unless indeed you build with such light ~~S~~stuff as ~~S~~straw and ~~S~~stubble, and that you know won't stand ~~F~~fire.

Again~~,~~ where the ~~A~~author ~~S~~says, "Kindness of ~~H~~heart by ~~W~~words express," ~~S~~strike out ~~W~~*words* and put in ~~D~~*deeds.* The world is too full of ~~C~~compliments already~~.~~; ~~T~~they are the rank ~~G~~growth of every ~~S~~soil, and ~~C~~choak the good ~~P~~plants of ~~B~~benevolence and ~~B~~benificence~~;~~; ~~N~~nor do I pretend to be the first in this comparison of ~~W~~words and ~~A~~actions to ~~P~~plants; you may remember an ~~A~~ancient ~~P~~poet, whose ~~W~~words we have all ~~S~~studied and ~~C~~copy~~'~~ied at ~~S~~school~~, said long ago,~~.

"A ~~M~~man of ~~W~~words and not of ~~D~~deeds,
Is like a ~~G~~garden full of ~~W~~weeds."

~~'T~~ **It** is pity that ~~G~~*good ~~W~~works,* among some sorts of ~~P~~people are so little ~~V~~valued, and ~~G~~*good ~~W~~words* admired in their ~~S~~stead; I mean seemingly *pious ~~D~~discourses* instead of ~~H~~*humane ~~B~~benevolent ~~A~~actions.* These they almost put out of countenance, by calling M~~m~~orality *rotten ~~M~~morality,* ~~R~~righteousness, *ragged ~~R~~righteousness* and even *filthy ~~R~~rags*; ~~and when you mention~~ *~~Virtue~~*~~, they pucker up their Noses as if they smelt a Stink; at the same time that they eagerly snuff up an empty canting Harangue, as if it was a Posie of the Choicest Flowers. So they have inverted the good old Verse, and say now~~

> ~~A Man of Deeds and not of Words~~
> ~~Is like a Garden full of ——~~

~~I have forgot the Rhime, but remember 'tis something the very Reverse of a Perfume. So much by Way of Commentary.~~

My ~~W~~wife will let you see my ~~L~~letter containing an ~~A~~account of our ~~T~~travels, which I would have you read to ~~S~~sister Dou~~w~~se, and give my ~~L~~love to her. I have no thoughts of returning 'till next year, and then may possibly have the ~~P~~pleasure of seeing you and yours~~;~~, take~~i~~ng Boston in my ~~W~~way home. My ~~L~~love to ~~B~~brother and all your ~~C~~children, concludes at this time from, ~~D~~dear Jenny, your affectionate ~~B~~brother,

B Franklin

2. Jane wrote to Franklin from Boston on August 29, 1789. The original of this letter is housed at the American Philosophical Society. Sparks published an extract from this letter in *The Works of Benjamin Franklin,* volume 10, p. 395n.

~~Boston August 29. 1789.~~
~~My Dear Brother~~

~~O that I could with Truth, begin with the old fashoned still I hope this will find you well, but that I dispar of Exept I could confine all to your Intellets which thank God Apear as sound as Ever, which must suply you with a Source of Entertainment beyond what comon mortals can Expearance. I have Even my self in times Past Lost the sense of Paine for some time by the Injoyment of good Company.~~

~~Yrs of Aug 3 by Cousen Jonathan was very Pleasing the knoing you had recd. mine so soon and was Pleasd with the contents gave me grat satisfaction and the sight of Him whom I Love like a child was a grat Addition. He is Truely a worthy man.~~

~~You Introduce your Reproof of my Miffy temper so Politely, won cant aVoid wishing to have conquered it as you have if you Ever had any, that disagreable Temper.~~

~~I have Drawn as you Premited Recd. the money and Paid of my Docr. Bill. I added the thirty Dolars for the wood which you give me orders constantly to Draw thinking it would be Less Troble to you and fearing Cousen Jonathan may not have the succes he wishes and Endevours about the Books and shall Take in the wood next week.~~

~~I have also Recved the Leter you sent by our Neibour Jemmy Leach.~~

I was a ~~L~~little suspicious wh~~e~~ither ***Excellency*** was according to ~~Ruel~~ **rule** in ~~A~~addressing ~~to~~ my ~~B~~brother at this time**; but I did not write the address**; ~~I never write any my self &~~ and of ~~L~~late, ~~B~~because ~~H~~he ~~L~~lives nearer than cousi~~e~~n Williams, I have sent ~~them~~**my letters** to Dr. Lath~~orrops,~~ who is very obliging to me, ~~&~~and I thought **he** must know what ~~wa~~is ~~R~~right, and I gave no ~~D~~directions about it~~;~~. ~~b~~But I shall **do it** another time. ~~He de[mands?] allways to be Respectfully Remembred to you when I write.~~

~~I beleve there are a few of our Nantucket Relations who have still an Affection for us, but the war time which made such Havock every where Devided and scatered them about, those I was most Intimate with were Abisha Fougre; His Brother, and sons, Timothy won, the Jenkinss and Kezia Coffin, who was many years Like a sister to me and a grat friend to my children. She sent me two very Afectionate Leters when the Town was shut up Inviting me to come to Her and she would sustain me that was her word and had I Recd. them before I left the Town I should certainly have gone, but a Wise and Good Providence ordered it other ways. She Took to the wrong side and Exerted Her self by Every method she could devise Right or rong to Accomplish her Designs, and Favour the Britons, went in to Large Traid with them, and for them, and by mismanagement and not suckceding in her Indevours has sunk Every Farthing they were Ever Posesed of and have been in Jail both Her Husband at nantuket and her self at Halifax. She was allway thought to be an Artfull Wooman, but there are such Extraordinary stories tould of her as is hard to be leved.~~

~~The two Jenkins' Seth and Thomas stood in the same Relation to us and always very Friendly and Afectionat to me. They were at Pheladelphia when I was there. You spok something for them at Congres). They were men of considerable Property and had a grat quantity of Oyl in there stores when a Vesel Belonging to the Tories went Down and Robd them of all, it was Proved that Kezia Pointed it out to Them, the owners Prosecuted her and she was Brought up to Boston to stand tryal, but I think there was no final condemnation at Court. She says they could not find Evedence. They say the Evedence was so strong that had they suffered them to come in to court it would have hangd her and so they supresd it not being willing it should Proceed so far. They settled at Provedence a few years whose Famelies I used to stop at when I went backwards and forwards and the were very kind to me sent there sons to carrie me from there to my [torn] and some thirteen miles [torn]er [?] and Every other obliging thing in there Power, but Afterwards they settled a Township on North River. I forgot the Name. There is a City and Thomas Jenkins is the Mayer. I have not seen Ither of them since. I dont know if they come to Boston. If they do they do not know where to find me, and tho the Foulgers some of them sail out of this Place I Beleve it is the same case with them for I have not seen a Nantuket Person since I Lived hear, I have a Next Dore Neibour who Lived there wonce and I now and then hear somthing of them by~~

Him. I know I have wrote and speld this worse than I do sometimes but I hope you will find it out. Remember my Love to your children and Grandchildren. Tell my Niece Betsey that I sent her Pocket Book to Mrs. Coffins Daughter and I dont doubt seh had it but she was at Halifax. I am yr Affectionat and Gratfull Sister

Jane Mecom

Addressed: To / Doctr Benjamin Franklin Esqr / In / Philadelphia
Endorsed: Sister

Jane's Library

As a child, Jane Franklin would have been able to read any book in her father's library, whose scantiness Benjamin Franklin mentioned in his autobiography, and whose contents are listed in an inventory of Josiah Franklin's estate taken in 1744. She would also have read her uncle Benjamin's writing, and she appears to have inherited his books. Reading whatever of her brother Benjamin's writing was published was, I suspect, a practice she began in their childhood.

After her marriage in 1727, she remained at the Blue Ball. Franklin sent *Poor Richard's Almanack* to his mother while Jane was living there, and he probably sent home more of his output as a writer and printer.[1] Because Jane also distributed books sent by Franklin to Boston to friends in the city, she would have had the opportunity to borrow books from a significant number of people, including John Perkins, Jonathan Williams Sr., and Thomas Cushing. It seems likely that she paid attention to what her son Benjamin printed, especially from 1758 to 1762, when he ran a print shop and bookstore in Boston.

Beginning in 1767, she made a dedicated effort to read all of her brother's published writing. "I think I desiered you to send me all the Pamphlets & Papers that have been Printed of yr writing," she wrote to him that year. "Do Gratifie me & I will contineu to be as Ever yr affectionat & most obliged Sister." In his reply, Franklin pledged, "I will send you what I write hereafter." This he does seem to have tried to do. "You desired I would send you what I published from time to time, and I am willing to oblige you," he wrote to her in 1773, "but often they are things out of your way so much that I omit sending them, and sometimes I forget it, and sometimes I cannot get a Copy to send."[2]

When Jane lived with her brother in Philadelphia in 1775 and 1776, she would have been able to read any book in his library. For the remainder of the war, and especially while living in Rhode Island, she found it difficult to get hold of books. Returning to Boston in 1784, she appears to have spent a great deal of her time reading. She might well have borrowed books from her minister, John Lathrop. In 1785, she requested a catalog of the library of books Franklin sent to the Massachusetts town named in his honor, with the idea of reading as many of them as she could get her hands on.[3] She did receive the catalog, and she certainly read some of these books, which number 116 volumes, including works by Locke, Sydney,

Montesquieu, Blackstone, Newton, and Priestley. I have not listed those books here. (A full catalog was printed in 1812.)[4]

In the inventory of her estate taken after her death in 1794, Jane is recorded as having had in her house "5 Volumes of Books," valued at six shillings. No titles were listed. I have been able to locate five volumes inscribed with her name: her own Book of Ages; volume 3 of *The Ladies Library;* Benjamin Franklin's *Experiments and Observations on Electricity;* a volume of her uncle Benjamin's poetry; and Granville Sharp's *Declaration of the People's Natural Right to Share in the Legislature.* I have no reason to suppose these five volumes are the same five volumes found in her house after her death. Her letters reveal her to have either owned or read a wealth of books, magazines, and newspapers; she was certainly familiar with many more books than she ever owned.

This reconstruction of her library is by no means meant as an exhaustive bibliography of what Jane read over the length of her lifetime; that list I am unable to compile—it would, of course, be much longer. This is, instead, a list of works I am almost certain she actually did read.

Barbauld, Anna Letitia. *Mrs. Barbauld's Lessons for Children, from Two to Four Years Old; Mrs. Barbauld's Lessons for Children of Four Years Old; Mrs. Barbauld's Lessons for Children, from Four to Five Years Old; Mrs. Barbauld's Lessons for Children of Five Years Old.* Philadelphia: B. Bache, 1788.

Franklin sent his sister this set of children's books, printed by his grandson, in 1788. She didn't like them one bit.[5]

Berkeley, George, comp. *The Ladies Library.* 3 vols. London, 1732.

Franklin gave Jane this book as a gift in 1733. Her copy of the third volume is in the American Antiquarian Society's collection. It is inscribed: "Jane Mecom her book given her by her Brother Benjamin Franklin 1733 anno Domini." The society acquired this book in 1978, a bequest of the estate of Arthur Tourtellot, a biographer of Franklin's. She at one time lent the second volume to Deborah, writing to her, on November 24, 1766, "Pray be so good as to Let me know by next opertunity, there is also a Book of mine among my Brothers the second volum of the Ladys Libriary, wrot in a blank Leaf borrowed of Sister Mecom, if you have a convenant opertunity I shuld be glad you would send it as it breaks the sett."

The Bible.

Jane's letters are full of references to the King James Bible. She especially loved the Book of Job. For instance, in her Book of Ages, she wrote, "The Lord Giveth & the Lord taketh away oh may I never be so Rebelious as to Refuse Acquiesing & & saying from my hart Blessed be the Name of the Lord." She also, of course, listened to sermons her whole life. In 1765, after the death of her husband, she wrote to Deborah that she considered the sermon delivered by her pastor, Samuel Cooper, to be "a master Peec." Cooper preached on 2 Corinthians 4:17, which Jane cited as: "for our Light Afflictions which is but for a moment worketh for us a far more Exceding and Eternal weight of Glory." Then she apologized: "I am not Good at Repeeting or Remembring tho I hope I Retain so much of the Sence as in some measure to Enable me with the asistance of Gods Spirit to Influenc my conduct Hear in this world and throw the merits of Christ Give me Hopes of a Gloryous Eternity."[6]

Boston Gazette. Printed by Benjamin Edes and John Gill, beginning in 1755. And other Boston newspapers.

Jane was an avid reader of news. She never mentioned the *Boston Gazette* by title, but she wrote about reading the newspaper often, and also about the political excesses of the Boston patriot papers, something for which the *Gazette* was infamous. On December 30, 1765, for instance, she wrote to Franklin, "The confusion & distres those Opresive Actts have thrown us Poor Americans into is un Discribable by me, but you see the Newspapers full of them." And on November 7, 1768, she told Franklin that the political and religious controversies of the time were "managed with two much Biterness as you will see by the News Papers If you give yr self the Troble to Read them, But they will not Infalably Informe you of the Truth; for Every thing that any Designing Person has a mind to Propagate Is stufed into them, & it is Dificult to know whither Either Party are in the Right." (This suggests that Jane read not only patriot papers, like the *Gazette,* but also loyalist papers.) Her ability to get newspapers was compromised during the war. For instance, she wrote to Franklin from Warwick on June 13, 1781, "I . . . know but litle how the world goes Except seeing a Newspaper some times which contains Enough to give Pain but litle Satisfaction."

Cooper, Samuel. Sermons.

Jane frequently referred to reading Cooper's sermons and made scattered references to reading other sermons as well. In a letter to Franklin dated June 13, 1781, for instance, she wrote, "I had no rembrance how I came by the Peece of the whig Sermon I inquiered of all I thot Like to have such a thing." (This letter, written when Jane was living in Rhode Island during the war, supplies further evidence for Jane's resourcefulness in getting books. She explained, "I then sent it to Cousen Williams to serch the Printers Shops but he says it was not to be found.") Van Doren identified this sermon as a piece of writing by three Boston ministers: Samuel Cooper, John Lathrop, and Samuel Stillman.[7]

Defoe, Daniel. *An Essay upon Projects.* 1697.

This work was in Jane's father's library. Franklin mentions it in his autobiography.

Edwards, Jonathan. *Some Thoughts Concerning the Present Revival of Religion in New-England.* Boston, 1742.

Franklin referred Jane to this book in a letter dated July 28, 1743: "Read the Pages of Mr Edward's late Book entitled Some Thoughts concerning the present Revival of Relgion in N.E. from 367 to 375."

"An Essay, Towards discovering the Authors and Promoters of the memorable Stamp Act," *Pennsylvania Journal,* September 18, 1766.

Jane alluded to this essay in a letter to her brother dated November 8, 1766: "The vile Pretended Leter which no Doubt you have seen gave me some uneaseyness when I heard of it before I could git a sight of it, as considering when a grat Deal of Durt is flung some is apt to stick but when I Read it I see it was filld with such bare faced falshoods as confuted them selves. theyre treetment of you among other things makes the World Apear a miserable world to me not withstanding yr good opinyon of it."

Franklin, Benjamin. *The Examination of Doctor Benjamin Franklin.* Boston, 1766.
Jane might have read this in the newspaper, or she might have read the pamphlet. She referred to it more than once. In a letter to her brother dated November 8, 1766, she wrote, "Yr Ansurs to the Parlement are thought by the best Judges to Exeed all that has been wrot on the subject & being given in the maner they were are a Proof they Proceeded from Prinsiple & suficent to stop the mouths of all gain-sayers." She alluded to its most famous line, about wearing old clothes, in a letter to her brother dated December 1, 1767; that letter contains further evidence of her reading of newspapers: "It Proves a Litle unlucky for me that our People have taken it in there Heads to be so Exsesive Frugal at this Time as you will see by the Newspapers our Blusterers must keep themselves Imployed & If they Do no wors than Perswade us to were our old cloaths over again I cant Disaprove of that in my Hart tho I should Like to have those that do bye & can afford it should bye what Litle I have to sell & Imploy us to make it up."

―――――. *Experiments and Observations on Electricity . . . To which are added, Letters and Papers on Philosophical Subjects.* London, 1769.
Franklin sent his sister a copy from London on February 23, 1769, writing, "There has lately been a new Edition of my philosophical Papers here. I send Six Copies to you, which I desire you would take care to have delivered as directed. There is one for your Trouble." Jane's copy of this edition is housed at Princeton Library. It is inscribed "Jane Mecom, Her Book." Van Doren probably acquired this book in the 1930s; it went to Princeton with Van Doren's papers following his death in 1950.[8]

―――――. *The Interest of Great Britain Considered.* Boston, 1760.
Jane's copy is at the Thayer Memorial Library in Lancaster.

―――――. *Maritime Observations. Philadelphia,* 1786.

―――――. *Miscellaneous.*
Franklin also sent Jane various miscellaneous and unidentified writings. "This is just to let you know I am well, and to cover a Newspaper containing one of my Scribblings, which please to give to my Sister with my Love: I have not now time to write to her," Franklin wrote Jonathan Williams Sr. in 1773.[9]

―――――. "On Smuggling," *London Chronicle,* November 24, 1767.
Franklin enclosed a copy of this essay in a letter to his sister dated December 24, 1767.[10]

———. "Petition of the Letter Z." 1778.
Franklin sent this essay to his sister on January 24, 1786.

———. *Philosophical and Miscellaneous Papers.* London, 1787.

———. *Plain Truth.* Philadelphia, 1747.
"I beg'd your Plain Truth of Mrs. *Mecom* a few Weeks since which I had never seen before," John Perkins, Jane's doctor, wrote to Franklin from Boston on February 17, 1752.

———. *Political, Miscellaneous, and Philosophical Pieces.* Ed. Benjamin Vaughan. London, 1779.
Jane's attempts to acquire this work began in 1781 when she wrote to her brother, "I am this Day going to Boston in Pursuit of a coletcion of all your works which I hear is lately come from Europe. some of which I have been in posesion of & have lost, you will say then I dont Deserve to have them again, but may be not if you knew all the circumstances, however there is many things I never had and I can hardly help Envieng any won that Pleasure without my Pertakeing."[11] She was unable to find it.[12] Complying with a request from his sister, Franklin sent her this edition of his works in 1786.[13] Of all of the books Jane owned, she treasured these two volumes the most, writing to her brother on August 25, 1786: "I keep your books of Philosophy, and Politics, by me (tho I have Read them throw several times) and when I am dull I take won up & Read, and it seems as tho I were conversing with you, or hearing you to some who can understand and I find a Pleasure in that."

———. *Poor Richard's Almanack.* Philadelphia, 1732–58.

———. "Rules for Reducing a Great Empire to a Small One," *Public Advertiser,* September 11, 1773.
Franklin enclosed a copy in a letter to Jane dated October 9, 1773.

Franklin, Benjamin, the Elder. Commonplace book.
Jane's copy of the second volume is in the American Antiquarian Society's collection. It is inscribed "Jane Mecom Her Book."

Lee, Arthur. *An Appeal to the Justice and Interest of the People of Great Britain.* London, 1774.
Franklin sent his sister a series of pamphlets along with a letter dated July 28, 1774, writing, "The Inclos'd Pamphlets were encourag'd by me, being written by Friends of mine, and printed at my Expense." Van Doren supposed Lee's *Appeal* to have been among them.[14]

———. *A True State of the Proceedings in the Parliament of Great Britain.* London, 1774.

Van Doren supposed Lee's *True State* to have been also among the pamphlets Franklin sent his sister in 1774.[15]

Lelyveld, Frans van. "Of the Stilling of Waves by means of Oil. Extracted from Sundry Letters between Benjamin Franklin, LL. D. F. R. S. William Brownrigg, M. D. F. R. S. and the Reverend Mr. Farish," *Philosophical Transactions* 64 (1774): 445–60.

On November 3, 1774, Jane wrote to her brother, "I thank you for the Pamphlits you then sent & another I have Just recved concerning the stilling the wavs with oyl."

Letter to the People of Pennsylvania: Occasioned by the Assembly's passing that important Act for constituting the Judges of the Supreme Court and Common Pleas, during Good Behaviour. Philadelphia: William Dunlap, 1760.

Jane asked Deborah for a copy of this tract in a letter dated March 17, 1760: "I have a favour to Ask which is that you would send me won of them Leters to the People of Pensylvania Advertised in yr Paper to be sould by Mr Dunlap." An advertisement had appeared in the *Pennsylvania Gazette* on March 6, 1760.

The Life of the Late Earl of Chesterfield; or, The Man of the World. Philadelphia: John Sparhawk, 1775.

In a letter to Franklin dated January 6, 1786, Jane wrote, "I want much to know how you are and have been since you have been at home but fear to be two often Inquisitive Least I should Provoke you to Return me such an Ansure as chesterfeild did to his sons widdow on such an Ocation." After this she wrote, then crossed out: "which would brake my hart I remember you wonce bad me not be fussy." The remark to which Jane alludes is in an October 27, 1771, letter from Chesterfield to his son's widow; Chesterfield wrote: "Upon my word, madam, you interest yourself in the state of my existence more than I do myself; for it is worth the care of neither of us." Franklin wrote back, on January 24, that he found this reference obtuse: "I don't know what the Answer was which Chesterfield gave to his Son's widow."[16]

Massachusetts Gazette.

Jane referred to reading this newspaper in a letter from 1765, writing to Deborah on April 6, "We have Grat Joy with you at the News of our Brothers arival in England tho we know it no other way than by that smal line in the News Paper." The only Massachusetts newspaper to report Franklin's arrival was the *Massachusetts Gazette,* which, on March 21, 1765, noted, under a London byline, "On Monday evening last the ingenious Dr. Benjamin Franklin arrived here from Philadelphia."

Miscellaneous.

There are references in the Franklin-Mecom correspondence to other works Jane read that I have not been able to identify.

1. A sermon Jane believed her brother wrote, ca. 1769: "The Sermon which you call mine, I know nothing of," he wrote to her on September 29, 1769, in reply to a letter of hers dated June 13, 1769, now lost. "I have only heard of it: I never saw it. It was wrong to give me as the Author of it. Whether it be good or bad, I have no Right to the Reputation or the Censures it may deserve."

2. An unspecified pamphlet, ca. 1770: "I am Desiered by a Lady of my Acquaintanc to send for the Pamphlit Discribed by this note," Jane wrote to her brother on September 25, 1770. The enclosed note does not survive. Jane added that this lady "says if I will send for two she will make me a Present of won, she is won I should be Glad to oblige & think it may be Agreable to have won." Franklin obliged in a letter dated December 30, 1770: "I send you by this opportunity the two books you wrote for."

3. An unidentified book by Franklin, ca. 1786: "the Book I recd and sent it to cousen Jonathan," Jane wrote Franklin on August 25, 1786, "who tells me he has a nother & will Return it to me for my Son Collas, to whom it may be of Grat Service, I Read it my self before I sent it and found a grat deal of Pleasure in it as I do in all you write as far as my capasety Enables me to under stand it, and farther too."

New-England Courant, 1721–25.
I believe Jane must have read the newspaper her brother James printed.

New-England Magazine, 1758–59.
I believe Jane must have read this magazine during its very brief run, when it was printed in Boston by her son Benjamin. She also read at least one Philadelphia magazine, in 1765, as she writes to Deborah on April 6 of that year, "Rec the magizeen for which I thank you."

Odell, Jonathan. "Inscription for a Curious Chamber-Stove, in the Form of an Urn, so contrived as to make the Flame descend, instead of rise, from the Fire: Invented by Doctor Franklin." 1776.
This poem appeared in various newspapers and magazines. Jane refers to it in a letter to Franklin dated June 13, 1781: "Parson Odell has been Exersiseing His Poetical Talant on yr Invention of the Chamber Fireplace it came to me throw the hands of Crasey Harry Badcock & I have half a mind to send it to you as I think it would make you Laugh." Crazy Harry Badcock—Jane's misspelling of his name may well have been intentional—was Henry Babcock, who was discharged from the Second Rhode Island Regiment for mental unfitness in May 1776.[17]

Paine, Thomas. *Common Sense.* Philadelphia, 1776.
Jane never mentioned reading *Common Sense,* but she was living in Franklin's house in Philadelphia in January 1776 when it was published. She could scarcely have avoided it.

Pennsylvania Gazette.

Jane referred to reading the *Pennsylvania Gazette* of March 6, 1760, in a letter to Deborah Franklin dated March 24, 1760 (see the *Letter to the People of Pennsylvania,* above), which suggests that she may have received the paper regularly, and within weeks of its publication.

Pennsylvania Packet.

In a letter to her brother dated June 23, 1779, Jane quoted from an article about him that had appeared in the *Pennsylvania Packet* on October 27, 1778. The *Packet* reported, "A gentleman just returned from Paris informs us, that Dr. Franklin has shaken off entirely the mechanical rust, and commenced the compleat courtier." Jane wrote to Franklin (and this is one of the only occasions, in all of her correspondence, where she uses quotation marks), "I now & then hear of yr helth & Glorious Achievments in the political way, as well as in the favour of the Ladys ('Since you have rubd off the Mechanic Rust and commenced compleat courtier') who Jonathan Williams writes me clame from you the Tribute of an Embrace & it seemes you do not complane of the Tax as a very grat penance." It is unclear where Jane read this remark, or from what source she copied it. She might have read the *Pennsylvania Packet.* She might have seen this phrase reported in another newspaper. It appeared originally in the *London Chronicle* in the summer of 1778 and was also picked up by several American papers, including the *New Hampshire Gazette* (December 22, 1788). Or, as is I think most likely, Williams might have quoted it in a letter to her. Franklin was abashed to learn that she had seen it ("The Story you allude to, which was in the News Papers, mentioning 'mechanic Rust,' &ca is totally without Foundation"), but she wrote back to him on her sixty-eighth birthday with this reassurance: "I seldom meet with any thing in the Newspapers but what is to yr honour, that of the mechanice Rust served only to make me Laugh."[18]

Perkins, John. *Thoughts on Agency.* New Haven: B. Mecom, 1765.

It seems likely that Jane would have taken an interest in this philosophical treatise, written by her doctor and printed by her son.

Plutarch's *Lives.*

This work was in Jane's father's library when she was growing up. Franklin mentions it in his autobiography.

Pope, Alexander. *An Essay on Man.* 1734.

"I do my Endeavour to adopt the Gra Popes Doctrin with Regard to the Providence of God whatever is is Right," Jane wrote to Deborah on September 28, 1765. This is a reference to Epistle I of Pope's *Esssay on Man:*

> All nature is but art, unknown to thee;
> All chance, direction, which thou canst not see;
> All discord, harmony not understood;

All partial evil, universal good;
And spite of pride, in erring reason's spite,
One truth is clear, Whatever is, is right.

And in a letter to her brother dated November 7, 1785, she referred to Epistle IV of Pope's *Essay on Man:* "I am of Popes mind that Health, Peace, and Competance, come as near to Happynes as in Atainable in this Life." Jane might have known Pope well without ever having read the *Essay;* it was much spoken about, and preached about, and referred to.[19]

Price, Richard. *Four Dissertations on Providence.* London, 1777.
Jane referred to this book in a letter to her grandson Josiah Flagg dated July 21, 1786 ("I would advise you to Read The first Sec. of Dr. Price's Dessertations on Providence, my Brothers Liberary will firnish you with it"), and she quoted from it, at length, in a letter to her brother with the same date. She had probably come across it in the catalog of the Franklin town library.

Priestley, Joseph. *An Address to the Protestant Dissenters of all Denominations.* London, 1774.
Van Doren supposed Priestley's *Address* to have been among the pamphlets Franklin sent Jane in 1774.[20]

Romilly, Samuel. *Observations on "Thoughts on Executive Justice."* London, 1786.
Van Doren believes that this is the "Pamphlit" to which Jane refers in a letter to Franklin dated May 22, 1787.[21]

Sharp, Granville. *A Declaration of the People's Natural Right to Share in the Legislature.* London: B. White, 1774.
Jane's copy is in the Thayer Memorial Library. It is inscribed "Jane Mecoms."

Shipley, Jonathan. *A Speech intended to have been spoken on the Bill.* London, 1774.
Van Doren supposed Shipley's *Speech* to have been among the pamphlets Franklin sent Jane in 1774.[22]

Stennett, Samuel. *Discourses on Personal Religion.* 2 vols. London, 1769.
Jane recommended this book to her brother, for inclusion in the library for the town of Franklin, in a letter dated October 21, 1784: "I cant doubt but such a Library will consist of some Authers on Divine Subjects I therefor hope you will not think it too Presuming in me to Propose won, Viz Discourses on Personal Religion in two Volumes by Samuel Stnnett D D Printed in London by R Hett in 1769 I borrowed them and Read them with a grat deal of Pleasure and I think you yourself would if you could find time tho there may be many things in them not altogether Agreable to your Sentiments, which I sopose may be the case with Every Volume you Read on any Subject."

Stillman, Samuel. *A Sermon Preached before the Honorable Council.* Boston, 1779.
Jane sent a copy of this sermon to her brother on October 29, 1781: "I have at length found the Sermon you were desierous to see among Mr Stillmans & now send it."

Swift, Jonathan. Unidentified work.
Jane referred to Swift in her letters on various occasions. For instance: "I am often Afflected with grat Dizenes & Expect or fear if I live much Longer to be in such Circumstances as Dean Swift was."[23] These references don't prove that she read Swift's work, only that she was aware of him. But she mentioned him often enough that I suspect she knew him in the way a reader knows an author.

Trenck, Friedrich. *The Life of Baron Frederic Trenck.* Philadelphia, 1789.
Jane referred to this book in a letter to her brother in 1789, to which he replied in a letter dated December 17, 1789. She might well have borrowed Trenck's life from John Lathrop; it is listed in the catalog of Lathrop's library, printed after his death in 1816.[24]

Weld, Ezra. *A Sermon on Sacred Musick.* Springfield, 1789.
In a letter dated November 24, 1789, Jane wondered about whether or not to send her brother a copy of this sermon: "I have a strong Inclination to send you a Sermon on Sacred musick tho my Friend Dr Lathrop & his wife tell me the Dr has been ust to Read composition on the subject so much beter it may not appear to him as I Expect, it Pleasd me & I know you will give it a Reading & tell me if it is not a Pritty Discorse from a country minester who has Every circumstance to Depres him." She did eventually send him the sermon. Franklin replied, in a letter dated December 17, 1789, "I thank you for the Sermon on sacred Music; I have read it with Pleasure—I think it a very ingenious Composition."

Willard, Samuel. *The Complete Body of Divinity.* Boston, 1726.
This work was in Jane's father's library when she was growing up. Franklin mentions it in his autobiography.

Wollstonecraft, Mary. *A Vindication of the Rights of Woman.* 1792.
It seems not altogether likely that Jane read Wollstonecraft's treatise, but it is listed in Lathrop's catalog.[25]

Works printed by Benjamin Mecom in Boston, 1757–62.
Because it seems likely that Jane had a chance to read books printed by her son during his years in Boston, below is a list of Benjamin Mecom's Boston output.

1757
COTTON MATHER. *God's Call to His People.*

1758
BENJAMIN FRANKLIN. *Father Abraham's Speech.*

JOHN MAYLEM. *The Conquest of Louisburg.*
———. *Gallic Perfidy.*
New-England Magazine.
New-England Psalter.
The Prodigal Daughter.
JOSEPH STEWARD. *Poor Joseph.*

1759

JAMES BURGH. *Britain's Remembrancer.*
JOHN CUSHING. *Gospel Ministers to Preach Christ.*
THOMAS JONES. *The Religious Remembrancer.*
ISAAC WATTS. *Christian Discipline.*

1760

All Canada in the Hands of the English.
WILLIAM BALCH. *Simplicity and Sincerity.*
WILLIAM BURKE. *Remarks on the Letter.*
W. H. DILWORTH. *Lord Anson's Voyage Round the World.*
Directions Concerning Inoculation.
JOHN DOUGLASS. *A Letter Addressed to Two Great Men.*
BENJAMIN FRANKLIN. *The Beauties of Poor Richard's Almanack for the Year 1760.*
———. *Father Abraham's Speech.*
———. *The Interest of Great Britain Considered.*
JAMES JANEWAY. *A Seasonable and Earnest Address.*
RICHARD LUCAS. *Rules relating to Success in Trade.*
JOHN MELLEN. *A Sermon Preached at the West Parish.*
A New Thanksgiving Song Revised.
JAMES OTIS JR. *A Dissertation on Letters.*
———. *The Rudiments of Latin Prosody.*
THOMAS WALTER. *The Grounds and Rules of Musick Explained.*
SAMUEL WOODWARD. *The Offices, Duties, and Qualifications of a Watchman of Israel.*
———. *A Sermon Preached October 9, 1760.*
FRANCIS WORCESTER. *Sabbath-Profanity.*

1761

An Account of the Voyages and Cruizes of Capt. Walker.
WILLIAM BURKE. *Remarks on the Letter.*
ALEXANDER CUMMING. *A Sermon.*
A Curious and Authentic Account of the Remarkable Behaviour of Francis David Stirn
W. H. DILWORTH. *Lord Anson's Voyage Round the World.*
JAMES JANEWAY. *Heaven Upon Earth.*
The New-England Psalter.
JOHN PERKINS. *An Essay on the Agitations of the Sea.*

DAVID ROWLAND. *Ministers of Christ.*
SOCIETY OF FRIENDS. *A Letter from a Meeting of the Brethren Called Quakers.*

1762
JOSEPH BUCKMINSTER. *Ministers to be Pray'd For.*
Debtor and Creditor.
BENJAMIN FRANKLIN. *Advice to a Young Tradesman.*
WILLIAM LIVINGSTON. *Philosophic Solitude.*
JOSEPH SECCOMBE. *The Ways of Pleasure.*
A Serious-comical Dialogue.

A Map of Jane's Boston

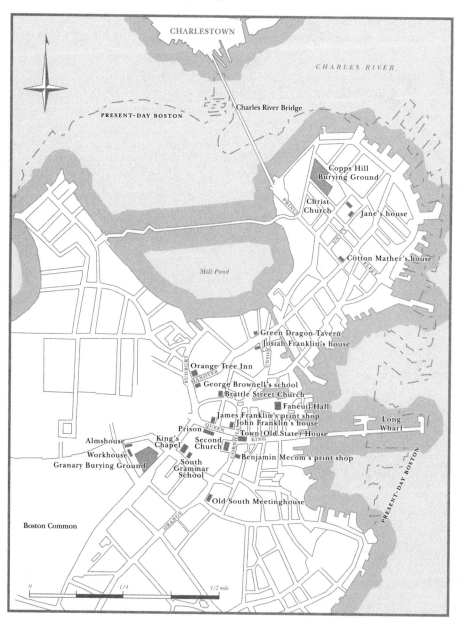

Acknowledgments

Heartfelt thanks to the generous librarians, archivists, collectors, and curators who helped me write this book. People taught me how to stitch books. People showed me how to boil soap. People pored over old pages of manuscript. People wrote me the most unbelievable letters. Thank you.

The institutions to which many of these people belong are: the American Antiquarian Society; the American Philosophical Society; the Baker Library, Harvard Business School; the Beaman Memorial Public Library, West Boylston, Massachusetts; the Beinecke Rare Book and Manuscript Library, Yale University; Firestone Library, Princeton University; the Papers of Benjamin Franklin, Yale University; the Franklin Public Library, Franklin, Massachusetts; the Historical Society of Pennsylvania; Houghton Library, Harvard University; the Library Company of Philadelphia; the Massachusetts Historical Society; the Museum of Fine Arts, Boston; the Nantucket Historical Association Research Library; the National Portrait Gallery; the New England Historic Genealogical Society; the New-York Historical Society; the New York Public Library; Old North Church; Old Sturbridge Village; the Paul Revere House; the Philadelphia Museum of Art; the Rhode Island Historical Society; the Rosenbach Museum and Library; the Thayer Memorial Library, Lancaster, Massachusetts; Widener Library, Harvard University; and the Worcester Art Museum.

Thanks as well to everyone who answered more questions and suffered through more stories about Benjamin Franklin's sister than anyone ever ought: Elise Broach, Steven Bullock, Heather Caldwell, Ellen Cohn, Nancy Cott, Amy Davidson, Roy Goodman, James Green, Charles Greifenstein, David Hall, John Hannigan, John Hench, Caitlin Hopkins, John Huffman, Julie Staples Johnson, Walter Johnson, Benjamin Kruskal, Shane

Landrum, Kelly L'Echyer, Susan Lehman, Bruce Mann, Martha McNamara, Liz and Zoe McNerney, Latif Nasser, Todd Pattison, William Reese, Charles Rosenberg, Anne Firor Scott, Gabriel Swift, Charles Van Doren, Gloria Whiting, Emily Wilkinson, Caroline Winterer, and Karin Wulf. Ellen Feldman, Maggie Hinders, and Jillian Verrillo at Knopf heroically shepherded through production a manuscript riddled with Jane's spelling errors. Julie Miller was astonishingly shrewd, always. Special thanks to the unerringly judicious Janet Hatch. Most particular thanks to Tim, and to our little rogues.

This is a book about reading. Deepest thanks, then, to the people who, very kindly, read it: Adrianna Alty, Tina Bennett, John Demos, Dan Frank, Henry Finder, Jane Kamensky, Leah Price, and Laurel Thatcher Ulrich.

This book is dedicated to the memory of my mother, who taught me how to sew, and of my father, who once wrote the story of his life. He called it "The Diary of an Unknown." On its last page, he wrote, "Everyone leaves a mark." It turns out that he was right.

Notes

ABBREVIATIONS

People

BF	Benjamin Franklin
BM	Benjamin Mecom
CRG	Catharine Ray Greene
DRF	Deborah Read Franklin
JFM	Jane Franklin Mecom
WF	William Franklin
WTF	William Temple Franklin

Archives

AAS	American Antiquarian Society
APS	American Philosophical Society
HSP	Historical Society of Pennsylvania
LCP	Library Company of Philadelphia
LC	Library of Congress
Mass. Arch.	Massachusetts Archives
MFA	Museum of Fine Arts, Boston
MHS	Massachusetts Historical Society
NEHGS	New England Historic Genealogical Society
NHARL	Nantucket Historical Association Research Library
Princeton	Firestone Library, Princeton University
Rosenbach	Rosenbach Museum and Library
SCHS	South Carolina Historical Society
Thayer	Thayer Memorial Library, Lancaster, Massachusetts
Yale	Manuscripts and Archives, Yale University

Editions of Franklin's Writings

BF, *Autobiography*	Benjamin Franklin, *The Autobiography of Benjamin Franklin: An Authoritative Text,* ed. J. A. Leo Lemay and P. M. Zall (New York: Norton, 1986).

Duane, *Letters* William Duane, ed., *Letters to Benjamin Franklin from his Family and Friends, 1750–1790* (New York: Richardson, 1859).

Duane, *Works* William Duane, ed., *The Works of Dr. Benjamin Franklin* (Philadelphia: W. Duane, 1808–18).

PBF *The Papers of Benjamin Franklin,* ed. Leonard Labaree et al., 40 vols. (New Haven: Yale University Press, 1959–2011).

Roelker, *BR and CRG* William Greene Roelker, ed., *Benjamin Franklin and Catharine Ray Greene: Their Correspondence: 1755–1790* (Philadelphia: American Philosophical Society, 1949).

Smyth, *Writings* Albert Henry Smyth, ed., *The Writings of Benjamin Franklin.* New York: Macmillan, 1905.

Sparks, *Familiar Letters* Jared Sparks, ed., *A Collection of the Familiar Letters and Miscellaneous Papers of Benjamin Franklin* (Boston: C. Bowen, 1833).

Sparks, *Works* Jared Sparks, ed., *The Works of Benjamin Franklin* (Boston: Tappan and Whittemore, 1836–40).

Van Doren, *Letters* Carl Van Doren, ed., *The Letters of Benjamin Franklin and Jane Mecom* (Princeton, NJ: Princeton University Press, 1950).

PREFACE

1. JFM thinking of her brother as her "Second Self" is mentioned in CRG to BF, Warwick, RI, June 24, 1781. Similarly, in a letter to JFM, CRG referred to Franklin as "your other Self." CRG to JFM, June 21, 1776. The likeness between Jane and Benjamin Franklin has not gone unobserved. Jared Sparks, one of Franklin's earliest biographers, wrote of Jane, "She was remarkable for her strength of mind and character, her good sense and practical views of life, resembling in these respects, more than any others of the family, her brother Benjamin" (editorial comment in Sparks, *Works,* 7:515). Or as JFM's biographer Carl Van Doren put it, "She was the only one of the many Franklins who can be compared with him" (*Letters,* 3). The sole biography of JFM is Carl Van Doren, *Jane Mecom, the Favorite Sister of Benjamin Franklin: Her Life Here First Fully Narrated from Their Entire Surviving Correspondence* (New York: Viking, 1950). But see also a brilliant and landmark essay by Anne Firor Scott in *Making the Invisible Woman Visible* (Urbana: University of Illinois Press, 1984), 3–13. And see Jeremy A. Stern, "Jane Franklin Mecom: A Boston Woman in Revolutionary Times," *Early American Studies* 4 (2006): 147–91. JFM is sometimes included in biographical encyclopedias—e.g., *American National Biography, Notable American Women,* and Carole Chandler Waldrup, *More Colonial Women: Twenty-five Pioneers of Early America* (Jefferson, NC: McFarland, 2004).

2. There is a substantial amount of scholarly literature on women and autobiography. Some scholars have argued that autobiography, a genre that took its recognizably modern form in the eighteenth century, was a masculine form of writing. Others insist that to see autobiography this way is to recapitulate the canon's own bias;

these scholars generally argue that other forms of women's "life writing," including diaries, letters, conversion narratives, and even family records like JFM's "Book of Ages," need to be counted as "autobiography." See especially Estelle C. Jelinek, ed., *Women's Autobiography: Essays in Criticism* (Bloomington: Indiana University Press, 1980), and Estelle C. Jelinek, *The Tradition of Women's Autobiography: From Antiquity to the Present* (Boston: Twayne, 1986). A useful overview of the field in its heyday can be found in the editors' introduction to Sidonie Smith and Julia Watson, eds., *Women, Autobiography, Theory: A Reader* (Madison: University of Wisconsin Press, 1998). Much of the work in this field is poststructuralist in its orientation—e.g., Leigh Gilmore, *Autobiographics: A Feminist Theory of Women's Self-Representation* (Ithaca: Cornell University Press, 1994)—or heavily indebted to Michel Foucault—e.g., Felicity A. Nussbaum, *The Autobiographical Subject: Gender and Ideology in Eighteenth-Century England* (Baltimore: Johns Hopkins University Press, 1989). Nussbaum, like Foucault, sees autobiography as a "technology of the self" (46): "I read the autobiographical texts as crucial to the formulation of a gendered bourgeois subjectivity that learns to recognize itself" (xiii).

3. JFM, "Book of Ages," NEHGS. Transcribed in "Letters of Dr. Franklin, Mrs. Jane Mecom, Josiah Flagg, Richard Bache, &c.," *New England Historical and Genealogical Register* 27 (1873): 253–54; and in Van Doren, ed., *Letters*, 100–101. All of my quotations and descriptions refer to the original manuscript. Henceforward, when quoting from the Book of Ages, no endnotes will be provided, as the source is clearly identified in the text. An interesting contrast with JFM's "Book of Ages" is "The Family Book" of Hester Salusbury Thrale, reprinted in Mary Hyde, *The Thrales of Streatham Park* (Cambridge, MA: Harvard University Press, 1977). Thrale, who also had twelve children, began her "Family Book" in 1764. It begins, formulaically, much like JFM's "Book of Ages": "Hester Maria Thrale born on the 17: Septr 1764 at her Father's House, Southwark" (21). But Thrale, a well-educated and wealthy Englishwoman, friend to Samuel Johnson, turned her "Family Book" into a detailed chronicle of her family's lives and especially of her children's emotional, intellectual, and physical development. It runs to nearly two hundred pages. Thrale's notion of a self has more in common with Benjamin Franklin's than with his sister's.

4. Virginia Woolf, *A Room of One's Own* (London: Hogarth, 1929), 64–67.

5. JFM to BF, June 13, 1781.

PART ONE · JANE, 1537–1727

Chapter I   Lady Jane

1. Roger Ascham, *The Scholemaster* (London: John Daye, 1570), 11–12.

2. Transcribed in John Gough Nichols, ed., *Literary Remains of King Edward the Sixth* (London: J. B. Nichols and Sons, 1857), 2:209.

3. Derek Wilson, *The People's Bible: The Remarkable History of the King James Version* (Oxford: Lion Hudson, 2010), 8.

4. John Foxe, *Actes and Monuments* (London: John Daye, 1563), 514, 519.

5. "Instructions given by the Kinges hieghnes unto his trusty and welbiloved servauntes," in *Literary Remains of King Edward the Sixth*, 1:xxviii.

6. Arthur Meredythe Burke, *Key to the Ancient Parish Registers of England and Wales* (London: Sackville, 1908), 7, 11; J. Charles Cox, *The Parish Registers of England* (London: Methuen, 1910), 1–24.

7. Roger Ascham to Johannes (Jean) Sturm, December 14, 1550, in *The Scholemaster,* ed. John E. B. Mayor (London: Bell and Daldy, 1863), 213.

8. Foxe, *Actes and Monuments,* 918–19.

9. Josiah Franklin to BF, Boston, May 26, 1739.

10. T. P. Taswell-Langmead, *Parochial Registers: A Plea for Their Preservation* (London: Samuel Palmer, 1872), 68.

Chapter II   The Franklin's Tale

1. BF to DRF, New York, June 6, 1758; BF to Mary Franklin Fisher, London, July 31, 1758; and BF, *Autobiography,* 3. The first entry for the Franklin family is the record of the birth of Thomas Francklyne's son Robert, in 1563, the year the register begins; the entry for Jane Francklyne is the second appearance of the family name. See also John W. Jordan, "Franklin as a Genealogist," *Pennsylvania Magazine of History and Biography* 23 (1899): 1–22. And on the genealogical impulse in early America, see the essays in *The Art of Family: Genealogical Artifacts in New England,* ed. D. Brenton Simons and Peter Benes (Boston: Northeastern University Press, 2002), especially Laurel Thatcher Ulrich, "Creating Lineages," pp. 5–11.

2. Thomas Gray, *An Elegy wrote in a Country Church Yard* (London, 1751), 6, 8.

3. Among ordinary people, gravestones were rare in sixteenth-century England. Even for the nobility and the gentry, monuments to the dead did not usually last long, as was decried by John Weever in his *Ancient Funeral Monuments within the United Monarchie of Great Britaine, Ireland, and the Islands adjacent* (London: Thomas Harper, 1631). Weever was involved in the project of turning what was carved in stone into ink pressed on pages. For a history of ancient burial practices, see Weever's chapter 2.

4. Josiah Franklin to BF, Boston, May 26, 1739.

5. BF, *Autobiography,* 3–4.

6. Benjamin Franklin the Elder, "A short account of the Family of Thomas Franklin / of Ecton in Northampton Shire," 1717, Franklin Manuscripts, Uncatalogued Manuscript Vault, "Materials by, to, and about Franklin, 1699–1750," Beinecke Rare Book and Manuscript Library, Yale University. It is reprinted in Nian-Sheng Huang, "Franklin's Father Josiah: Life of a Colonial Boston Tallow Chandler, 1657–1745," *Transactions of the American Philosophical Society* 90 (2000): 106–13. On the keeping of this sort of account, see Karin Wulf, "Bible, King, and Common Law: Genealogical Literacies and Family History Practices in British America," unpublished manuscript, 2011.

7. BF the Elder, "A short account," 107–8.

8. BF the Elder, Notebooks, vol. 1, p. 7, American Antiquarian Society. See Huang, "Franklin's Father Josiah," 3.

9. Arthur Bernon Tourtellot, *Benjamin Franklin: The Shaping of Genius; The Boston Years* (Garden City, NY: Doubleday, 1977), 27.

10. "Dyeing and Coloring," in "Common-place Book of Benjamin Franklin (1650–1727)," *Publications of the Colonial Society of Massachusetts* 10 (1907): 214, 212, 208.

BF the Elder copied many of his recipes from *The Secretes of the Reverend Maister Alexis of Piedmont,* an English translation of a recipe book originally published in Italian under the pseudonym Alessio Piedmontese (206).

11. Gravestone inscriptions at Ecton and Banbury, in *PBF,* 8:119.

12. BF, *Autobiography,* 3. Thomas Franklin and BF had the same birthday. BF then apparently became quite interested in birthdays. See BF, "List of Franklin Birthdays," 1759, *PBF,* 8:454.

13. BF, *Autobiography,* 1.

14. Ibid.

15. Ibid., 4.

16. Geoffrey Chaucer, *Canterbury Tales* (Westminster: William Caxton, 1477). William Shakespeare, *King Lear* (London: Nicholas Okes, 1608), act 3, scene 4; *Henry V* (London: Thomas Creede, 1600), act 1, scene 2.

17. Josiah Franklin to BF, Boston, May 26, 1739. See also Tourtellot, *Benjamin Franklin,* 13.

18. Thomas Carlyle to Henry Thomas Wake, Chelsea, England, November 24, 1853; Thomas Carlyle to Edward Everett, Chelsea, December 2, 1853; and Thomas Carlyle to H. T. Wake, Chelsea, December 19, 1854, in *The Collected Letters of Thomas and Jane Welsh Carlyle,* Duke-Edinburgh edition, ed. Kenneth J. Fielding (Durham, NC: Duke University Press, 2000), 28:322–23, 330–31; 29:218–19. The bound volume is stamped on the spine: "Small Tithes: Ecton Parish Northamptonshire, 1646–1700." A frontispiece reads, "Presented to the Massachusetts Historical Society at the Dedication of the Douse Library, April 9th, 1857, by the Hon. Edward Everett." Everett's correspondence with Carlyle is copied out, by hand, in the first pages of the volume. Wake's letters, in which he advertised the importance of the tithe book and its interest to Carlyle, are bound within the pages of the tithe book. Henry Thomas Wake to unknown, November 23, 1853, and Henry Thomas Wake to Thomas Carlyle, November 26, 1853. On the title page of the tithe book, Wake has written, "Henry Thomas Wake purchased this Account Book of Mr. J. R. Smith, Bookseller, 4 Oed. Compton Street, Soho, 8/6 price. Saturday, October 4th, 1851." Parish of Ecton Tithe Book, MHS.

19. BF, *Poor Richard's Almanack . . . 1751,* in *PBF,* 4:88.

20. BF to Mary Franklin Fisher, London, July 31, 1758.

Chapter III   The Tender Wombe

1. On Folger, see Babette May Levy, "Life and Work of Peter Folger, An 'Able Godly Englishman'" (MA thesis, Columbia University, 1929), and Florence Bennett Anderson, *A Grandfather for Benjamin Franklin: The True Story of a Nantucket Pioneer and His Mates* (Boston: Meador, 1940). See also Peter Foulger (1618–1690), Folder 34, Folger Family Papers, NHARL.

2. *Records of the Governor and Company of the Massachusetts Bay in New England* (Boston: William White, 1853; rep., New York: AMS Press, 1968), 1:281. Alex L. ter Braake, ed., *The Posted Letter in Colonial and Revolutionary America* (State College, PA: American Philatelic Research Library, 1975), 13. On letter writing in early New England, see also Katherine A. Grandjean, "Reckoning: The Communications Frontier in Early New England" (PhD diss., Harvard University, 2008).

3. Psalm 22:10, *The Whole Booke of Psalmes* (Cambridge, MA, 1640), unpaginated.

4. Cited in David Hall, "Readers and Writers in Early New England," in *The Colonial Book in the Atlantic World,* eds. Hugh Amory and David Hall, vol. 1 of *A History of the Book in America* (Chapel Hill: University of North Carolina Press, 2007), 120. On printing, literacy, and education in Puritan Boston, see also Samuel Eliot Morison, *The Intellectual Life of Colonial New England* (New York: New York University Press, 1956); Robert Middlekauff, *Ancients and Axioms: Secondary Education in Eighteenth-Century New England* (New Haven: Yale University Press, 1963); Jill Lepore, "A Bookish Faith," in *Perspectives on American Book History,* ed. Scott E. Casper et al. (Amherst: University of Massachusetts Press, 2002), 38–45; and E. Jennifer Monaghan, "Literacy Instruction and Gender in Colonial New England," *American Quarterly* 40 (1988): 18–41.

5. John Cotton's *Milk for Babes* was printed in London in 1646, the same year as Robert Abbot's *Milk for Babes; or, A Mother's Catechism for her Children.* "When children begin to read, let them read the holy Scripture," urged William Gouge in *Of Domesticall Duties.* "Thus will children sucke in Religion with learning." William Gouge, *Of Domesticall Duties* (London: George Miller, 1634), 548. Cotton Mather, *The A, B, C of Religion* (Boston: Timothy Green, 1713).

6. Peter Folger to Governor Andros, March 27, 1677, reprinted in Anderson, *A Grandfather for Benjamin Franklin,* 348. On the fluency in Algonquian of Peter's son Eleazar, see Anderson, *A Grandfather for Benjamin Franklin,* 138. On Folger's work as an Indian schoolteacher, see also E. Jennifer Monaghan, " 'She Loved to Read in Good Books': Literacy and the Indians of Martha's Vineyard, 1643–1725," *History of Education Quarterly* 30 (1990): 493–521.

7. John Eliot, trans., *Mamusse Wunneetupanatamwe Up-Biblum God* (Cambridge, MA: Samuel Green, 1663).

8. Roger Williams, *Key into the Language* (London: Gregory Dexter, 1643), 194. On Gibbs, see Jill Lepore, *The Name of War: King Philip's War and the Origins of American Identity* (New York: Knopf, 1998), xx, 39. Peter Folger, "Petition of Peter Foulger about Proceedings at the General Court of Martha's Vineyard, 1677," *New York Colonial Manuscripts,* XXIV, 69.

9. Edward Wharton, *New England's Present Sufferings Under Their Cruel Neighbouring Indians* (London, 1675), 7; Philip Walker, "Captain Perse & his coragios Company" in *Proceedings of the American Antiquarian Society* 83 (1973): 91; Increase Mather, *An Earnest Exhortation To the Inhabitants of New-England* (Boston: John Foster, 1676), 3; Increase Mather, *A Brief History of the Warr With the Indians* (Boston: John Foster, 1676). And see Lepore, *The Name of War,* 30, 43, 104–5, 47, 177.

10. Levy, "Life and Work of Peter Folger," 78. And see Folger, "Petition of Peter Foulger," 64–71.

11. Peter Folger, *A Looking Glass for the Times* (Boston: James Franklin, 1725), 10, 11. Folger's poem, like much written in seventeenth-century New England, might have circulated in manuscript. On scribal publication, see David D. Hall, *Ways of Writing: The Practice and Politics of Text-Making in Seventeenth-Century New England* (Philadelphia: University of Pennsylvania Press, 2008), chapter 1.

Chapter IV   A Tub of Suds

1. Late in life, Franklin met a man named Pope, from Boston, and sent a letter to Jane by way of him: "His name is Pope, and he tells me his Family is originally from Salem, where I remember we formerly had an Aunt Pope. I heard her spoken of when I was a Child, but do not recollect having ever seen her. Do you know whether she left any Children? For if she did the Bearer is probably our Relation." BF to JFM, April 12, 1788. JFM replied on May 5, 1788, but her reply is lost.

2. BF, *Autobiography*, 7. The best account of Josiah Franklin is Huang, "Franklin's Father Josiah."

3. Samuel Willard, *The Character of a Good Ruler* (Boston: Benjamin Harris, 1694), 8, 13.

4. M. Halsey Thomas, ed., *The Diary of Samuel Sewall* (New York: Farrar, Straus and Giroux, 1973), September 7, 1708, at 1:603, and December 17, 1717, at 2:874.

5. Anderson, *A Grandfather for Benjamin Franklin*, 155.

6. Peter Folger to Joseph Pratt, Nantucket, March 6, 1678, in Peter Foulger (1618–1690), Folder 34, Folger Family Papers, Nantucket Historical Association Research Library; also printed in Anderson, *A Grandfather for Benjamin Franklin*, 386.

7. Anne Bradstreet, *Several Poems, Compiled with great variety of Wit and Learning, full of Delight* (Boston: John Foster, 1678), 239.

8. On average, an eighteenth-century white woman could expect to become pregnant between five and ten times, to give birth to between five and seven live children. Mary Beth Norton, *Liberty's Daughters: The Revolutionary Experience of American Women, 1750–1800* (Boston: Little, Brown, 1980), 72.

9. Genealogical information about Josiah Franklin's descendants can be found in *PBF*, 1:lvi–lxii. Thomas, ed., *The Diary of Samuel Sewall*, February 6, 1703, at 1:482.

10. BF, *Autobiography*, 8.

11. On the nature of women's work in seventeenth- and early-eighteenth-century New England, see Laurel Thatcher Ulrich, *Good Wives: Images and Reality in the Lives of Women in Northern New England, 1650–1750* (1982; New York: Vintage, 1991), especially part 1; and Norton, *Liberty's Daughters*, chapter 1.

12. Thomas, ed., *The Diary of Samuel Sewall*, April 7, 1677, at 1:41. Cotton Mather, *Elizabeth in Her Holy Retirement* (Boston: B. Green, 1710), 35.

13. James Axtell, *The School upon a Hill: Education and Society in Colonial New England* (New Haven: Yale University Press, 1974), 87. Norton, *Liberty's Daughters*, 91–92. Ulrich, *Good Wives*, 138–44.

14. Thomas, ed., *The Diary of Samuel Sewall*, January 6, 1702, and January 16, 1702, at 1:450. And see also Judith Walzer Leavitt, *Brought to Bed: Childbearing in America, 1750–1950* (New York: Oxford University Press, 1986), and Laurel Thatcher Ulrich, *A Midwife's Tale: The Life of Martha Ballard, Based on Her Diary, 1785–1812* (New York: Knopf, 1990).

15. "Sensible of the reiterated strokes of God upon himself and family," he said, he desired to acknowledge the wrong he had done, "to take the Blame and Shame of it, Asking pardon of Men, And especially desiring prayers that God, who has an Unlimited Authority, would pardon that Sin and all other his Sins." On Sewall's regret of his part in the witchcraft trials, and its relation to his grief over the deaths

of several of his children, see Thomas, ed., *The Diary of Samuel Sewall*, January 14, 1697, at 1:397; and Judith S. Graham, *Puritan Family Life: The Diary of Samuel Sewall* (Boston: Northeastern University Press, 2000), 43–46.

16. Huang, "Franklin's Father Josiah," 52.

17. "Jane daughter of Josiah Franklin and Abiah his Wife" is recorded as March 27, 1712, in *Boston Births from A.D. 1700 to A.D. 1800* (Boston: Rockwell & Churchill, 1894), 82. She would have been baptized at Old South, as were her brothers and sisters. The baptisms of eight of Abiah and Josiah's ten children appear in the church's record book: John (1690), Peter (1692), Mary (1694), James (1697), Sarah (1699), Ebenezer (1701), Thomas (1703), and Benjamin (1706). But after the page on which Benjamin's baptism is recorded, there follow several blank pages, and the records don't begin again until 1715. Jane's baptismal record is therefore missing, as is that of her sister Lydia, who was born on August 8, 1708. Both Jane and Lydia were, however, surely baptized at Old South. Benjamin Franklin's baptismal record, dated January 6, 1706, reads, "Benjamin, of Josiah & Abiah Franklin." In a later hand, the entry is marked with an *X*, to which is added this notation: "The celebrated Benj. Franklin." Bound volume of Baptismal Records, Old South Church Records, Box 7, Congregational Library, Boston.

Chapter V   Benny and Jenny

1. BF, "Petition of the Left Hand," 1785, in *PBF,* unpublished. The essay is not a recollection but a satire, in which the left hand rails at the right.

2. There is little scholarship on siblings in early America, but see C. Dallett Hemphill, "Sibling Relations in Early American Childhoods: A Cross-Cultural Analysis," in *Children in Colonial America,* ed. James Marten (New York: New York University Press, 2007), 77–89. Hemphill mentions Franklin's relationships with James and with Jane, in passing. And, for a provocative study of siblings in Victorian Britain, see Leonore Davidoff, *Thicker Than Water: Siblings and Their Relations* (Oxford: Oxford University Press, 2012).

3. JFM to BF, August 16, 1787.

4. BF to JFM, August 3, 1789.

5. JFM to BF, August 29, 1789.

6. Women often nursed to prevent pregnancy. One colonial woman wrote of her thirty-nine-year-old daughter, who had just survived childbirth, "This might possibly be the last trial of this sort, if she could suckle her baby for two years to come." Quoted in Paula A. Treckel, "Breastfeeding and Maternal Sexuality in Colonial America," *Journal of Interdisciplinary History* 20 (1989): 38.

7. Acrostic from Benjamin Franklin the Elder in *PBF,* 1:4–5.

8. BF, *Poor Richard's Almanack . . . 1739,* in *PBF,* 2:217.

9. Cotton Mather, *A Family Well-Ordered* (Boston: B. Green, 1699), 3. William Gouge, *Of Domesticall Duties* (London: John Haviland, 1622), 17. See also Edmund S. Morgan, *The Puritan Family: Religion and Domestic Relations in Seventeenth-Century New England* (New York: Harper and Row, 1966); John Demos, *A Little Commonwealth: Family Life in Plymouth Colony* (New York: Oxford University Press, 1970); and Helena M. Wall, *Fierce Communion: Family and Community in Early America* (Cambridge, MA: Harvard University Press, 1990).

10. Ezra Stiles met JFM on September 28, 1779, and recorded the conversation in his diary. *The Literary Diary of Ezra Stiles*, ed. Franklin Bowditch Dexter (New York: Scribners, 1901), 2:375–76.

11. J. A. Leo Lemay, *The Life of Benjamin Franklin* (Philadelphia: University of Pennsylvania Press, 2006–08), 1:57.

12. Hugh Amory, "Printing and Bookselling in New England, 1636–1713," in *The Colonial Book in the Atlantic World*, ed. Hugh Amory and David Hall, vol. 1 of *A History of the Book in America* (Chapel Hill: University of North Carolina Press, 2007), 83–116. Cotton Mather, *Diary of Cotton Mather, 1681–1724* (Boston: Massachusetts Historical Society, 1911), 548.

13. BF, *Autobiography*, 9. "Inventory of Josiah Franklin's Estate," October 24, 1752, *Suffolk Probate Records* 47:437–38; reprinted in Huang, "Franklin's Father Josiah," 127–28.

14. "Breeching Little Frank," in *Childhood in America*, ed. Paul S. Fass and Mary Ann Mason (New York: New York University Press, 2000), 82. On the hanging sleeve, see Alice Morse Earle, *Child Life in Colonial Days* (Williamstown, MA: Corner House, 1989), 43–44. On the persistence of breeching and its consequences, see Davidoff, *Thicker Than Water*, 65–67.

15. BF, "The Whistle," November 10, 1779, *PBF*, 31:74.

16. BF, *Autobiography*, 10. On the verses BF wrote at the age of seven, see Van Doren, *Letters*, 27.

17. *PBF*, 1:5. On the boxing and throwing Collins into the Charles, see Lemay, *Life of BF*, 1:210. On Collins as BF's best friend, see Lemay, *Life of BF*, 1:253.

18. BF, *Autobiography*, 6. On Franklin's schooling, see Tourtellot, *Benjamin Franklin*, chapters 7 and 8.

19. JFM to BF, November 8, 1766. BF to JFM, September 16, 1758. BF, *Poor Richard's Almanack . . . 1736, PBF*, 2:137.

20. Lemay, *Life of BF*, 1:42.

21. BF, *Autobiography*, 5. LeMay, *Life of BF*, 1:43.

22. Lemay, *Life of BF*, 1:94.

23. BF, *Autobiography*, 6. BF, *Poor Richard's Almanack . . . 1753*, in *PBF*, 4:406.

24. Benjamin Colman, *Early Piety again Inculcated* (Boston: S. Kneeland, 1720), 33.

25. BF, *Autobiography*, 9.

26. BF the Elder says the Blue Ball is "the place where this briefe account was writen on the 1.2. 3. Of July 1717." BF the Elder, "Short Account," 106–8, 111, 113.

Chapter VI   The Ladies' Library

1. *The American Magazine, or General Repository*, August 1769, 243–44.

2. Joseph Addison, Essay No. 37, *Spectator*, vol. 1, no. 37, April 12, 1711.

3. Berkeley's *Ladies Library* is a hodgepodge. Berkeley never acknowledged his sources, and Steele never really even acknowledged that his "library" *was* a compilation of other people's writing. The identity of the compiler of *The Ladies Library* was the subject of some dispute but was established to have been Berkeley in Stephen Parks, "George Berkeley, Sir Richard Steele, and *The Ladies Library*," *Scriblerian* 13 (Autumn 1980): 1–2. On the sources for the compilation, see Richard H. Dammers, "Richard Steele and *The Ladies Library*," *Philological Quarterly* 62 (1983): 530–36;

and especially Raymond Francis McCoy, "A Critical Examination of *The Ladies Library* and Inquiry into Its Authorship" (MA thesis, University of Cincinnati, 1935), and Greg Holhgshead, "Sources for *The Ladies Library*," *Berkeley Newsletter* [Dublin] 11 (1989–90): 1–19. The "Ignorance" chapter draws from *A Serious Proposal to the Ladies*, part 1, as well as from part 2, chapter 3.

4. Mary Astell, *A Serious Proposal to the Ladies* [part 1] (London, 1694), 30, 37–38; part 2 (London, 1697), 27; part 1, 27. On proposals for women's academies, see Patricia Springborg's introduction to Mary Astell, *A Serious Proposal to the Ladies. Parts I and II* (London: Pickering & Chatto, 1997). On Astell, see Ruth Perry, *The Celebrated Mary Astell: An Early English Feminist* (Chicago: University of Chicago Press, 1986).

5. *Boston News-Letter*, September 9, 1706.

6. *Boston News-Letter*, March 9, 1712.

7. E. Jennifer Monaghan, "Literacy Instruction and Gender in Colonial New England," *American Quarterly* 40 (1988): 27.

8. In one Massachusetts town in 1709, for instance, there were sixteen girls in a class of sixty-four. On schooling for girls in colonial New England, see Thomas Woody, *A History of Women's Education in the United States* (1929; repr. New York: Octagon Books, 1974), chapter 4. A study of two hundred colonial towns found that only seven admitted girls (Cathy N. Davidson, *Revolution and the Word: The Rise of the Novel in America* [New York: Oxford University Press, 1986], 62). A more recent assessment of literacy rates is David Hall, "Readers and Writers in Early New England," in *A History of the Book in America*, 1:119–30.

9. For example, Samuel Sewall taught his sons to write; he had his five-year-old daughter, Mary, taught "to Read and Knit." See Graham, *Puritan Family Life*, chapter 6; quotation is from 119.

10. Anne Bradstreet, "The Prologue," in *Several Poems*, 4. See also Jane Kamensky, *Governing the Tongue: The Politics of Speech in Early New England* (New York: Oxford University Press, 1997), especially 24–27 and 71–98.

11. Abiah Folger Franklin to BF, Boston, October 14, 1751. Some and maybe all of Abiah's other daughters could write, too, maybe about as well as their mother. Jane seems to have been alone among Abiah's daughters in learning to write with any facility. Sarah Franklin Davenport did write at least one letter, but it does not survive. Nor does any reference to any letter ever written by Mary or Lydia. "Your kind and affectionate Letter of May the 15th, was extreamly agreeable to me," Franklin wrote to Sarah in 1730, "and the more so, because I had not for two Years before, receiv'd a Line from any Relation, my Father and Mother only excepted." BF to Sarah Franklin Davenport, Philadelphia, [June?] 1730.

12. According to Kenneth Lockridge, 70 percent of men and 42 percent of women could sign their names in 1710. Lockridge cited in Hall, "Readers and Writers in Early New England," 120. Gloria L. Main, "An Inquiry into When and Why Women Learned to Write in Colonial New England," *Journal of Social History* 24 (Spring 1991): 579–89. See also Joel Perlmann and Dennis Shirley, "When Did New England Women Acquire Literacy?" *William and Mary Quarterly* 48 (1991): 50–67.

13. Sarah Silsbe, sampler, Boston, 1748, Theodore H. Kapnek Collection of American samplers, reproduced in Ulrich, "Creating Lineages," 10.

14. John Langdon Sibley, *Biographical Sketches of Those Who Attended Harvard College* (Cambridge, MA: Harvard University Press, 1933), ed. Clifford Shipton, 4:120–37. On Colman's preaching as genteel and urbane and lacking the stridency of the Mathers, see, for instance, Charles W. Akers, *The Divine Politician: Samuel Cooper and the American Revolution* (Boston: Northeastern University Press, 1982), 6. BF the Elder made note of Colman's sermons in his commonplace book. See "Common-place Book of Benjamin Franklin (1650–1727)," *Publications of the Colonial Society of Massachusetts* 10 (1907): 191.

15. For Jane Colman Turell's life, and what is left of her writing, see Ebenezer Turell, *Memoirs of the Life and Death of the Pious and Ingenious Mrs. Jane Turell* (London, 1741), 8, 24, 11. In *Memoirs*, see also Jane Colman, "To My Muse, December 29, 1725." For Benjamin Colman's writing advice, see pp. 81–83.

16. On the novelty and power of this epistolary culture, see Konstantin Dierks, *In My Power: Letter Writing and Communications in Early America* (Philadelphia: University of Pennsylvania Press, 2009).

17. Ebenezer Turell, *Memoirs of the Life and Death of . . . Mrs. Jane Turell*, 82, 15.

18. JFM to BF, November 8, 1766.

19. JFM to BF, July 21, 1786.

20. JFM to BF, December 30, 1765.

21. BF to JFM, July 7, 1773.

Chapter VII   Book'ry, Cook'ry

1. "With all my own art & good old unkle Benjamins memorandoms I cant make them good colors," JFM wrote to her brother in 1766, suggesting that, at least at that point, she had his book of memorandums, or recipes. JFM to BF, November 8, 1766. (And she certainly owned his books of poetry, one of which is inscribed with her name.) The original of the recipe book is either lost or in private hands; all that survives is a transcription. See "Dyeing and Coloring" in "Commonplace-Book of Benjamin Franklin (1650–1727)," *Publications of the Colonial Society of Massachusetts* 10 (1907): 206–25.

2. BF, *Autobiography*, 6.

3. "A Dialogue between a thriving Tradesman and his Wife about the Education of Their Daughter," *Boston Evening-Post*, December 10, 1744.

4. She wrote the recipe down twice. (BF lost it; see Van Doren, *Letters*, 129.) JFM, "For Making Crown Soap," 1772, in *Letters*, 130–32. And JFM, "Recipe for Crown Soap," 1786, *PBF*, unpublished. I'm not certain that the dates assigned to these recipes are especially plausible. The first seems to have been written down after the death of John Franklin, to whom JFM must have been referring when she wrote, "My Brother in His Life time tould me it could not be conveyd by Recipt" (that is, that you couldn't write down this recipe; you needed to learn by doing). The original is Jane Franklin Mecom, Recipe for Crown Soap, n.d., Hays Calendar IV, 376, Franklin Papers, vol. 58, folio 19. Van Doren credited the invention of crown soap to John Franklin, without any substantiation. But as Huang has remarked, there is every reason to believe that Josiah, who trained his son, was involved in perfecting the soap ("Franklin's Father Josiah," 43–45). And as Lemay argues, Abiah must have been involved (*Life of BF*, 1:56) and it's highly probable that Jane was

intimately involved as well, which would also account for her subsequent frustration at her sons' being kept out of the soap business. Jane herself gave some credit to her brother John. In one letter to Franklin, she refers to their brother John as "the Inventor" of crown soap, but in the same letter she explains that he had nearly as much difficulty getting it right as she did. "The Labour is Grate, & the operation critical, the Exact knolidg not to be attained without Expearance, my Brother Him self tould me it workd some times not to his mind in a way he could not account for" (JFM to BF, December 29, 1780). When sending her own soap to Franklin in 1786, and apologizing that it wasn't exactly as fine as she had hoped, she wrote, "I beleve my Brother John Perfectly understood the Exact proportion that would do best" (JFM to BF, May 29, 1786). Yet this letter does not place John so far above herself, as a soap boiler; instead, it substantiates an argument that she and her brother knew very well how to make soap even if, at the age of sixty-four, she was having a hard time remembering the exact proportions to use.

5. JFM to BF, September 12, 1779.

6. Keziah Folger was born on Nantucket on October 9, 1723, when Jane was eleven. Keziah's father, Daniel Folger, was Abiah Folger Franklin's cousin, and her mother, Abigail Folger, was actually another cousin of Abiah Folger Franklin's. Useful information about Keziah Folger Coffin was gathered by Jared Sparks in the 1830s. In 1838, William Folger of Nantucket wrote to Sparks, about Franklin, that "her parents being so nearly related to each other the Doctor used to say, that he considered Kezia as an own cousin." Jared Sparks, "Papers sent to me by William C. Folger, of Nantucket. Relating to Franklin" in "Papers relating chiefly to Franklin. Used in writing his Life, 1839," Sparks Papers, MS Sparks 19, Houghton Library, Harvard University. (The papers are filed by manuscript number; all further references to the Sparks Papers in Houghton Library supply this reference number.) Sparks also visited Nantucket, in 1826; see his diary entry for October 10, 1826, in MS Sparks 141c. Keziah Folger married John Coffin in 1746. She and Jane remained close until the American Revolution. Franklin also corresponded with Keziah, though much less frequently, it appears, than Jane did. On Keziah Folger Coffin, see Nathaniel Philbrick, *Away Off Shore: Nantucket Island and Its People, 1602–1890* (Nantucket: Mill Hill Press, 1994), 123–33, and Betsy Tyler, *Sometimes Think of Me: Notable Nantucket Women Through the Centuries* (Nantucket: Nantucket Historical Association, 2010), 11–17. No scholar has yet investigated the ties between the Coffins and the Mecoms. William C. Folger's notes from which he compiled the information he sent to Sparks can be found in William C. Folger, "Minutes from which my letter to Jared Sparks was Compiled and from which the account of the Folgers in Spark's [*sic*] Life of Franklin is derived," Peter Foulger (1618–1690), Folder 34, Folger Family Papers, Nantucket Historical Association Research Library.

7. Grace Harris was born on August 3, 1718, the daughter of Jane's sister Anne and her husband William Harris of Ipswich (*PBF*, 1:lvii). In 1746, Grace Harris married Jonathan Williams of Boston. Jane's friendship with Grace lasted until Grace's death in March 1790, and Jane was close to all of the Williams children.

8. Lemay, *Life of BF*, 1:56. On James Franklin as a dyer, see Lemay, *Life of BF*, 1:56–57.

9. BF, *Autobiography*, 9, 10.

10. Ebenezer Turell, *Memoirs of the Life and Death of . . . Mrs. Jane Turell*, 25.

11. BF, *Autobiography*, 11, and BF, "Idea of the English School," January 1751, *PBF*, 4:101. BF, "On Literary Style," August 2, 1733, *PBF*, 1:328. BF, *Autobiography*, 10.

12. BF, *Autobiography*, 45, 11.

13. Daniel Defoe, *Essay on Projects* (London: R.R., 1697), 282–83, 293.

14. BF, *Autobiography*, 11.

15. JFM to BF, October 21, 1784. This was when she was sixty-two.

Chapter VIII   Silence Dogood

1. John Perkins, Medical Notebook Number 2, n.p., and Medical Notebook Number 3 ("Curiosa Miscellania"), 7, AAS.

2. On the early history of newsletters, newsbooks, and newspapers in England, see Joad Raymond, *The Invention of the Newspaper: English Newsbooks, 1641–1649* (Oxford: Oxford University Press, 2005); Charles E. Clark, *The Public Prints: The Newspaper in Anglo-American Culture, 1665–1740* (New York: Oxford University Press, 1994); and James Raven, *The Business of Books: Booksellers and the English Book Trade, 1450–1850* (New Haven: Yale University Press, 2007), especially chapter 9. On the early history of American newspapers, see John Hench, ed., *Three Hundred Years of the American Newspaper* (Worcester: American Antiquarian Society, 1991); Isaiah Thomas, *The History of Printing in America*, 2 vols. (Albany: Joel Munsell, 1874); Clarence S. Brigham, *A History and Bibliography of American Newspapers* (Worcester: American Antiquarian Society, 1947); David A. Copeland, *Colonial American Newspapers: Character and Content* (Newark: University of Delaware Press, 1997); John Tebbel, *The Compact History of the American Newspaper*, rev. ed. (New York: Hawthorn Books, 1969); Richard D. Brown, *Knowledge Is Power: The Diffusion of Information in Early America, 1700–1865* (New York: Oxford University Press, 1989); and David Paul Nord, *Communities of Journalism: A History of American Newspapers and Their Readers* (Urbana: University of Illinois Press, 2001).

3. On this early history, see Ruth Lapham Butler, *Doctor Franklin, Postmaster General* (Garden City, NY: Doubleday, Doran, 1928).

4. David S. Shields, *Civil Tongues and Polite Letters in British America* (Chapel Hill: University of North Carolina Press, 1997), 266. See also Perry Miller, introduction to *The New-England Courant: A Selection* (Boston: American Academy of Arts and Sciences, 1956); he writes that James Franklin "really desired to recreate in Boston that standard of wit, elegance, and satire he had learned in the printing houses of London" (6).

5. See Lawrence C. Wroth, *The Colonial Printer*, 2nd ed., rev. and enl. (Charlottesville, VA: Dominion Books, 1964). For more on the time required to set the type see Jeffrey L. Pasley, *"The Tyranny of Printers": Newspaper Politics in the Early American Republic* (Charlottesville: University Press of Virginia, 2001), 25.

6. Nord, *Communities of Journalism*, calls the *New-England Courant* "the first overtly heretical newspaper in America" (52). Thomas C. Leonard, *The Power of the Press: The Birth of American Political Reporting* (New York: Oxford University Press, 1986), begins chapter 1 with James Franklin. Michael Schudson also credits James Franklin with being "the first journalist in the world to report the vote count on a bill in the legislature" (Schudson in Hench, *Three Hundred Years*, 424).

7. *New-England Courant*, December 4, 1721.

8. Benjamin Franklin the Elder became a member of the Brattle Street Church on April 7, 1717. James Franklin followed on July 7, 1717. *The Manifesto Church: Records of the Church in Brattle Square, Boston With Lists of Communicants, Baptisms, Marriages, and Funerals, 1699–1872* (Boston: Benevolent Fraternity of Churches, 1902), 97.

9. Quoted in Lemay, *Life of BF,* 1:114. See also James Franklin's account of this encounter, *New-England Courant,* December 4, 1721.

10. Quoted in Lemay, *Life of BF,* 1:119. More broadly, see Shields, *Civil Tongues,* and Lemay's chapter on James Franklin in *Life of BF,* vol. 1, ch. 6.

11. Quoted in Lemay, *Life of BF,* 1:131–32.

12. For example, eleven months after a series of essays about liberty called *Cato's Letters* began appearing in London, Franklin extracted them in the *Courant.* Bernard Bailyn, *The Ideological Origins of the American Revolution* (Cambridge, MA: Harvard University Press, 1967), 43.

13. *New-England Courant,* December 4, 1721.

14. That same year, one of Josiah Franklin's apprentices, a twenty-year-old Irishman named William Tinsley, ran away. "Black hair lately cut off, somewhat fresh-coloured Countenance, a large lower Lip, of a mean Aspect," Josiah wrote, describing Tinsley in a newspaper ad he placed in his son's paper. *New-England Courant,* July 9, 1722.

15. BF, *Autobiography,* 15. And, on Franklin's early printed writing, see also James N. Green and Peter Stallybrass, *Benjamin Franklin: Writer and Printer* (New Castle, DE: Oak Knoll Press, 2006), chapter 1. Franklin, as Green and Stallybrass point out, not only wrote *for* print but also *about* print (vii).

16. Silence Dogood, "No. 2," *New-England Courant,* April 16, 1722; *PBF,* 1:13.

17. Cotton Mather, *Bonifacius: An Essay Upon the Good* (Boston: B. Green, 1710) and *Silentarius* (Boston: S. Kneeland, 1721). See also Lemay, *Life of BF,* 1:145.

18. Silence Dogood, "No. 1," *New-England Courant,* April 2, 1722; *PBF,* 1:9–11. Emphasis in original.

19. Silence Dogood, "No. 3," *New-England Courant,* April 30, 1722; *PBF,* 1:14. Silence Dogood, "No. 2," *New-England Courant,* April 16, 1722; *PBF,* 1:13.

20. Silence Dogood, "No. 4," *New-England Courant,* May 14, 1722; *PBF,* 1:14–21.

21. While his brother was in jail, from June 12 to July 7, 1722, Benjamin also printed a list of books in the *Courant*'s library. See Lemay, *Life of BF,* 1:162–63.

22. Silence Dogood, "No. 8," *New-England Courant,* July 9, 1722; *PBF,* 1:27–30.

23. *New-England Courant,* December 3, 1722. On BF's authorship of Hugo Grim's letter, see J. A. Leo Lemay, *The Canon of Benjamin Franklin, 1722–1776* (Newark: University of Delaware Press, 1986), 27–28.

24. Quoted in Miller, introduction to *The New-England Courant: A Selection,* 5–9.

25. On the subterfuge, see BF, *Autobiography,* 16, and Lemay, *Life of BF,* 1:193–95. BF took charge of the paper twice as a teenager: for the first time while James was in jail, in the summer of 1722, and for the second time while James was in hiding, from mid-January to mid-February 1723. On the latter occasion, BF published his "rubs" against the authorities. See Lemay, *Life of BF,* 1:187–88, and BF's essay in the *New-England Courant,* January 28, 1723.

26. BF, *Autobiography*, 15–17.

27. Ibid., 17.

28. *New-England Courant*, September 30, 1723.

Chapter IX   Dear Sister

1. BF to Jane Franklin, January 6, 1727. Only one letter known to have been written by Franklin before this date survives. BF's birthday is now rendered as January 17, but his baptismal record reads, "Benjamen Son of Josiah Frankling & Abiah his Wife born 6 Janry 1706" ("Record of Birth," *PBF*, 1:3). As the editors of the Franklin papers explain, "The clerk used the year dates of the New Style calendar (adopted by Great Britain in 1752), recording the year of BF's birth as a simple 1706 instead of the technically more correct 1705/6. He did not, however, adjust the days of the month but retained the Old Style January 6, not adding eleven days as the New Style calendar would require to make BF's birthday January 17. The clerk thus followed a not uncommon practice." See *PBF*, 1:3n1. Even in his 1728 epitaph, "BF himself gives his birthday as January 6, 1706" (*PBF*, 1:3). More important, from the vantage of understanding how Jane received this letter: she knew it was his birthday because her uncle, in his "Short Account" of the Franklin family history, had given it as January 6, 1706.

2. JFM to BF, May 29, 1786.

3. JFM to BF, April 22, 1786.

4. JFM to BF, July 27, 1779.

5. JFM to Jane Mecom Collas, April 1778.

6. BF to JFM, December 30, 1770.

7. Silence Dogood, "No. 6," *New-England Courant*, June 11, 1722.

8. BF to Jane Franklin, Philadelphia, January 6, 1727.

9. For an astute reading of Franklin's dealings with Keimer, and on the printing business more broadly, see James N. Green, "English Books and Printing in the Age of Franklin," in *A History of the Book in America*, 1:248–98.

10. BF, *Autobiography*, 22–23.

11. Ibid., 24.

12. BF to Samuel Mather, London, July 7, 1773.

13. Lemay, *Life of BF*, 1:253–54.

14. BF, *Autobiography*, 24, 31, 33–34.

15. Ibid., 56.

16. BF, *Autobiography*, 34. BF, *Dissertations on Liberty and Necessity, Pleasure and Pain* (London, 1725).

17. BF, "Plain of Conduct," 1726, *PBF*, 1:99–100.

18. Thomas Hill, *The Young Secretary's Guide*, 6th ed. (Boston, 1727), 8. Letter-writing manuals became popular in England beginning at the end of the seventeenth century; their influence in the colonies began a few decades later.

19. *The Young Man's Companion*, 3rd ed. (Philadelphia: Andrew Bradford, 1718), 160–61.

20. For a similar reading of the tea table, see Lemay, *Life of BF*, 1:319.

21. Nor is there any record that she ever owned one. There wasn't one in her father's

house when she was living there when the estate was probated, in 1752. There wasn't one in her house when her husband died, in 1765. There wasn't one in her house when she died, in 1794. For more on spinning wheels and their symbolic weight, see Laurel Thatcher Ulrich, *The Age of Homespun: Objects and Stories in the Creation of an American Myth* (New York: Knopf, 2001), especially 86–95; Norton, *Liberty's Daughters,* 15–20 (Norton mistakenly describes Franklin as giving Jane a spinning wheel as a wedding present); and Marla R. Miller, *The Needle's Eye: Women and Work in the Age of Revolution* (Amherst: University of Massachusetts Press, 2006). Ulrich has argued for abandoning the spinning wheel as the icon of women's history (*Good Wives,* 34). And see also Laurel Thatcher Ulrich, "Wheels, Looms, and the Gender Division of Labor in Eighteenth-Century New England," *William and Mary Quarterly* 55 (January 1998): 3–38.

22. *Report of the Record Commissioners of the City of Boston Containing the Boston Records From 1700 to 1728* (Boston: Rockwell and Churchill, 1883), 8:147. See also Rolla Milton Tryon, *Household Manufactures in the United States, 1640–1860: A Study in Industrial History* (Chicago: University of Chicago Press, 1917), 86, and Gary B. Nash, "The Failure of Female Factory Labor in Colonial Boston," *Labor History* 20 (1979): 165–88. At a meeting of the selectmen on April 13, 1721, members voted "for Letting out" £300 for a Spinning School. See *A Report of the Record Commissioners of the City of Boston Containing the Records of Boston Selectmen, 1716 to 1736* (Boston: Rockwell and Churchill, 1885), 13:80. On Josiah Franklin supplying the candles for the almshouse, see Huang, "Franklin's Father Josiah," 38, 92.

23. Homespun Jack, "To the venerable Doctor Janus," *New-England Courant,* January 18, 1725. And on a spinning factory operating in Boston in the 1750s, see Ulrich, *Age of Homespun,* chapter 4.

24. Edward Ward, *The City Madam, and the Country Maid; or, Opposite Characters of a Virtuous Housewifely Damsel, and a Mechanick's Town-Bred Daughter* (London, 1702).

25. *Adam and Eve Stript of their Furbellows; or, The Fashionable Virtues and Vices of both SEXES expos'd to publick View* (London, 1714), 65. On my claim that BF clearly read this, compare "Raree-Show" (*Adam and Eve,* 66), and "Country Joan" (*Adam and Eve,* 70), to BF's poem for Deborah, "Sing My Plain Country Joan," 1742, *PBF,* 2:352.

26. Anthony Afterwit, *Pennsylvania Gazette,* July 10, 1732; *PBF,* 1:239–40. To this, James wrote a reply, in the voice of "Patience Teacraft": "an honest Tradesman's only Daughter," who, inheriting a great deal of money from her father, marries a tradesman "something addicted to Drinking & Gaming." He sells everything she owns. At last, she devises a plan: "I bought a Wheel of Fortune, a Snake-Board, a Back-Gammon Table, a Set of NinePins, and had a good Alley made in the Garden." And then she buys him a tea table and a tea set and pours him so much tea that, eventually, he gives up gambling. Patience Teacraft appeared in the *Rhode-Island Gazette* but was reprinted in the *Pennsylvania Gazette,* June 7, 1733.

27. JFM to BF, July 27, 1779.

PART TWO · HER BOOK, 1727–1757

Chapter X   Book of Ages

1. Van Doren (*Letters*, 6) speculates that JFM began writing the Book of Ages only in 1762, but I am convinced she undertook it in 1731, the year of her son Edward's birth, although it's possible that the surviving "Book of Ages" is a copy made at a later time from an earlier and now lost manuscript. Quite exactly how to classify the Book of Ages is difficult. It is essentially a family register. But people kept all sorts of notebooks in the eighteenth century, a practice that has been the subject of considerable study. For a fascinating example, see Anthony Grafton, "The Republic of Letters in the American Colonies: Francis Daniel Pastorius Makes a Notebook," *American Historical Review* 117 (2012): 1–39.
2. *A very Useful Manual; or, The Young Mans Companion* (London: T. Snowden, 1681). On the history of these early copybooks and manuals, see Virginia Elsie Radatz Stewart, "The Intercourse of Letters: Familiar Correspondence and the Transformation of American Identity in the Eighteenth Century" (PhD diss., Northwestern University, 1997), chapter 1.
3. George Fischer, *The American Instructor; or, Young Man's Best Companion* (Philadelphia: B. Franklin and D. Hall, 1748), 27, 29, 28, 1, 30. On the significance and variety of hands used in the seventeenth and eighteenth centuries, see Tamara Plakins Thornton, *Handwriting in America: A Cultural History* (New Haven: Yale University Press, 1996), chapter 1, and Susan M. Stabile, *Memory's Daughters: The Material Culture of Remembrance in Eighteenth-Century America* (Ithaca: Cornell University Press, 2004), especially chapter 2. Franklin's shop included stationery supplies beginning in 1729 (Green and Stallybrass, *Benjamin Franklin*, 48). For the stationery supplies BF sold, see his advertisement in the *Pennsylvania Gazette*, May 20, 1742.
4. Ambrose Serle, *The Christian Parent; or, Short and Plain Discourses concerning God* (New York: Samuel Loudon, 1791), 96. The only other reference to a book of ages that I have seen is to an ancient record book from Ireland, which was discussed, in print, only in a scholarly context. See Geoffrey Keating, *The General History of Ireland* (London, 1723), xxi ("The particular Titles and Contents of many ancient Books are as follow: . . . *Reim Riogradh*, otherwise call'd the *Roll of the Kings*, the *Book of Ages*"). Keating's remarks are referred to in James Parsons, *Remains of Japhet* (London, 1767), 160 ("The books of greatest authority, with Dr. *Keating*, are . . . The Book of *Provincialists*, or the *Roll of Kings*; the Book of *Ages*; an Account of the *People* who lived in the same Age . . .").
5. "Dies Irae," trans. Philip Schaff, in *Hours at Home: A Popular Monthly, of Instruction and Recreation*, ed. J. M. Sherwood, vol. 7 (New York: Charles Scribner, May to October 1868), 39.
6. Thomas Walter, *The Grounds and Rules of Musick Explained; or, An Introduction to the Art of Singing by Note* (Boston: J. Franklin, 1721). Curiously, Jane's son Benjamin printed an edition of this same volume in Boston in 1760. See Thomas Walter, *The Grounds and Rules of Musick Explained; or, An Introduction to the Art of Singing by Note* (Boston: Benjamin Mecom, 1760).

7. *New-England Courant,* February 24, 1724.
8. Wulf, "Bible, King, and Common Law." Wulf writes of "genealogical literacy" and argues that "genealogical consciousness was a bedrock of British American culture." See also Karin Wulf, "Ancestry as Social Practice in Eighteenth-Century New England: The Origins of Early Republic Genealogical Vogue," Boston Area Early American Seminar, March 6, 2012, unpublished manuscript.
9. It was in the pages of his Bible that John Robison of Connecticut kept a "Book of Reckords." It begins, "A. Dom. 1744 January the 22th Day which was the Time when I transcribed the Ages and Deaths of those of My family yt were born & Dead before this Time." "John Robinson Book of Reckords 1746" transcript, Silliman Family Papers Box 49, Folder 29, Sterling Library, Yale University, as cited in Wulf, "Ancestry as a Social Practice." Sometimes keeping records was a way to own people: slave owners needed to know their slaves' ages in order to establish their market value. The Tucker family of Virginia kept, within the family Bible, a "Register of Negroes," viz.:

> Phillis was born April ye 13th in 1777
> Batt was born, July 1785
> Siliom was born August ye 26th 1790.

Family records were so much more reliable than those of the town clerk or the parish book that they were admissible in court. See Shane Landrum, "The State's 'Big Family Bible,'" unpublished manuscript. And see Robert Gutman, "Birth and Death Registration in Massachusetts. I. The Colonial Background, 1639–1800," *Millbank Memorial Fund Quarterly* 36 (1958): 58–74.
10. Ross W. Beales Jr., "In Search of the Historical Child: Miniature Adulthood and Youth in Colonial New England," *American Quarterly* 27 (1975): 392. Daniel Scott Smith, "Parental Power and Marriage Patterns: An Analysis of Historical Trends in Hingham, Massachusetts," *Journal of Marriage and the Family* 35 (1973): 426, at Table 4; the numbers are for marriages between 1721 and 1780.
11. Elizabeth born March 2, 1678, married January 8, 1707, age 28; Hannah born May 25, 1683, year of first marriage unknown, age at first marriage unknown (married for the second time on June 22, 1710, at the age of 27); Anne born January 5, 1687, married July 10, 1712, age 25; Mary born September 26, 1694, married April 3, 1716, age 21; Sarah born July 9, 1699, married May 23, 1722, age 22; Lydia born August 8, 1708, married 1731, age 22 or 23; average age at first marriage among sisters, excepting Hannah and Jane: 23.8 (if Lydia was 23) and 23.6 (if Lydia was 22). Samuel born May 16, 1681, married May 16, 1705, age 24; John born December 7, 1690, year of first marriage unknown, age at first marriage unknown; Peter born November 22, 1692, married September 2, 1714, age 21; James born February 4, 1697, married February 4, 1723, age 26; Benjamin born January 6, 1706, entered common law marriage September 1, 1730, age 24; average age at first marriage among brothers, excepting John: 23.75. For dates see "Descendants of Josiah Franklin," *PBF,* 1:lvi–lxii.
12. See, especially, Norton, *Liberty's Daughters,* chapter 2.
13. JFM to BF, December 30, 1765.

14. BF the Elder, "Since I came into New England," commonplace book, volume 2, AAS.

15. *New England Weekly Journal,* March 27, 1727.

16. This stone was still visible in 1856, when Thomas Bridgman reported that it stood "about four feet west of the Franklin monument" (erected in 1827), but it can no longer be seen. Thomas Bridgman, *The Pilgrims of Boston and Their Descendants . . . Also Inscriptions from the Monuments in the Granary Burial Ground* (New York: D. Appleton, 1856), 334. Bridgman reported that the wife of Jane and Benjamin's cousin Samuel Franklin was buried in the same place in 1749; Bridgman transcribed the epitaph on Hannah Franklin's tombstone (335).

17. BF the Elder joined the church on April 7, 1717, a few months before he wrote his family history. Jane's brother James Franklin had joined the church on July 7, 1717, exactly three months after Benjamin the Elder (*Manifesto Church,* 97) and his wife, Ann Smith Franklin, joined on April 4, 1725 (*Manifesto Church,* 107—if the "Ann Franklin" listed is James's wife). Jane's sister Sarah had been married at Brattle Street, too (*Manifesto Church,* 238), and two of James's children, Abia and James Jr., had been baptized there (*Manifesto Church,* 146, 148).

18. Jane told the story of the funeral sermon to Ezra Stiles in 1779. That is, she remembered, in 1779, the text of a sermon she'd heard in 1727. See Stiles, *Literary Diary of Ezra Stiles,* 2:376.

19. "Edward Son of Duncan Maycom and Mary his Wife, Born 15 December 1704" is the entry in *A Report of the Record Commissioners of the City of Boston, Containing Boston Births from A.D. 1700 to A.D. 1800* (Boston: Rockwell & Churchill, 1894), 30 (hereafter *Boston Births*). See also Van Doren, *Jane Mecom,* 24.

20. "Mary Daughter of Dunkin and Mary Maycom . . . 5 April 1700" (*Boston Births,* 3). "Hezekiah Son of Duncan Maicum and Mary his Wife, Born 10 October 1701" (9). "Ebenezar Son of Duncan Maycome and Mary his Wife . . . 4 September 1703" (22). "Eliza. daughter of Duncan Maycome and Mary his Wife . . . 13 October 1707" (53). "Rebecca daughter of Duncan Maycome and Mary his Wife, Born 23 November 1709" (63). "Ann daughter of Duncan Maycom and Mary his Wife, Born 27 September 1711" (77).

21. Edward Mecom's obscurity was a running joke between Carl Van Doren and his research assistant. She once wrote him, "If I found Edward Mecom's name in a newspaper, the Rare Book Room staff would have to revive me with spirits of ammonia." Jane Mecom Research Notebook, Carl Van Doren Papers, Princeton, Box 11, Folder 11. (Edward Mecom's name appeared at least twice, in the *Boston Gazette,* but—working in an age before digital newspapers—Van Doren's research assistant never found it.)

22. The hat and wig appear in an inventory of his estate, taken at his death in 1765. "An Inventory of the Estate of Edward Mecom deceased," Edward Mecom 13744 (October 25, 1765), Regist certif. 64, 546, Suffolk County Register, Mass. Arch.

23. JFM to CRG, Philadelphia, November 24, 1775. Jane meant this in jest: Caty had told her a secret, and Jane was absolving her for it. But it does display her sense of the vulnerability of wives.

24. Edward Mecom appears to have been admitted to membership in 1721 (*Manifesto Church,* 98).

25. A notation made in the church record book on September 10, 1739, while Colman was minister, reports that a "Committee appointed to consider of a Change of Version of the Psalms" had "met & applied to our good Brethren Mr Macom & Mr Johnson, & prevailed with "em to sit together & lead us in the Ordinance of Singing" (*Manifesto Church*, 27–28).

26. "Abia Holbrook, Writing Master, and Edward Macom, purpose to open a singing School to instruct Children in the Rules of Psalmody, at 20 s. a Quarter, old Tenor; the first Quarter to be paid at Entrance, to begin Wednesday next . . . The utmost Care will be taken of the Children, of either Sex; and the Place appointed is the South Writing School in the Common." *Boston Evening-Post*, June 25, 1744. And on this subject, see Allen P. Britton, "The How and Why of Teaching Singing Schools in Eighteenth-Century America," *Bulletin of the Council for Research in Music Education* 99 (1989): 23–41.

27. "Magistrates in all the New England colonies were obliged to refuse marriage to underage couples who could not provide evidence of [parental consent]" (Gloria L. Main, *Peoples of a Spacious Land: Families and Cultures in Colonial New England* [Cambridge, MA: Harvard University Press, 2001], 72).

28. BF, *Poor Richard's Almanack . . . 1734*, in *PBF*, 1:354.

29. Quoted in Axtell, *School on a Hill*, 57.

30. *Manifesto Church*, 151. There is no evidence that Jane had been raped, though it's not beyond the realm of possibility. Tradition, and in some places the law, held that a woman who had been raped could not get pregnant; conception, most people thought at the time, required female orgasm. If Jane Franklin had found herself pregnant after having been raped, she would have been very hesitant to accuse Edward Mecom of the crime. Her pregnancy would have been taken as proof against the charge. In the words of a New Haven magistrate's court, "No woman can be gotten with child without some knowledg, consent and delight in the acting thereof." Charles J. Hoadly, ed., *Records of the Colony or Jurisdiction of New Haven, From May, 1653, to the Union* (Hartford: Case, Lockwood, 1858), 123; case from October 18, 1654. Quoted in Main, *Peoples of a Spacious Land*, 64.

31. The man who became Jane's doctor recommended, after a miscarriage, that a woman not sleep with her husband for a twelvemonth: "not cohabit with sd Husband for a 12 Month Keep their beds wholey when first with Child till the time of her Miscarrying is over." John Perkins, second medical notebook, AAS.

32. Edward carried the baby to Brattle Street to be baptized four days later. Josiah Mecom (listed as "Mecum") was baptized on June 8, 1729, by Samuel Cooper (*Manifesto Church*, 151). "Jane Mecom" does not appear in *The Manifesto Church* as a communicant, but a "Jane Masum" does, on January 7, 1728, the January after her marriage (*Manifesto Church*, 107).

33. "Before the Birth of one of her Children" in Anne Bradstreet, *Several Poems, Compiled with great variety of Wit and Learning*, 239.

34. Birth and death dates, and a family history, can be found in the handwritten notes in the blank pages of a copy of Ebenezer Turell, *The Life and Character of the Reverend Benjamin Colman* (Boston, 1749), inscribed by Samuel Turell Armstrong, and preserved at the MHS. Jane Colman married Ebenezer Turell at the Brattle Street

Church on August 11, 1726, and died on March 26, 1735. The only one of her children to survive her, Samuel Turell, died on October 8, 1736.

35. Turell, *Memoir* (London, 1741), 58–59. Her father delivered a sermon at her funeral. Benjamin Colman, *Reliquiae Turellae, et Lachrymae Paternae. The Father's Tears over his Daughter's Remains* (Boston: S. Kneeland and T. Green, 1735).

36. BF, *Autobiography*, 1.

37. "The Author to her Book," in Bradstreet, *Several Poems*, 236.

38. "Before the Birth of one of her Children" in Bradstreet, *Several Poems*, 239. On Bradstreet's children and her manuscripts, see Hall, *Ways of Writing*, 36.

39. On the giving of gloves and rings, see Steven C. Bullock, "'Often concerned in funerals': Ritual, Material Culture, and the Large Funeral in the Age of Samuel Sewall," in *New Views of New England: Studies in Material and Visual Culture, 1680–1830* (Boston: Colonial Society of Massachusetts, forthcoming), 181–211, and Steven C. Bullock and Sheila McIntyre, "The Handsome Tokens of a Funeral: Glove-Giving and the Large Funeral in Eighteenth-Century New England," *William and Mary Quarterly* 69 (2012): 305–46, in which Turell's funeral is discussed. After 1742, gifts other than gloves to the pallbearers and ministers were outlawed; the ban, however, was frequently ignored.

40. Turell, *Memoir*, 33.

41. Benjamin Colman's own papers are preserved at the MHS, in several collections: Benjamin Colman Papers, Letters to Benjamin Colman, and Benjamin Colman Letters. Letters from Benjamin Colman to Jane Colman Turell can be found in the Benjamin Colman Papers, Box 1. "You are always in my heart & mind," Colman wrote his daughter when she was melancholy. He sent her two oranges and promised to visit as soon as the weather improved. (Benjamin Colman to Jane Colman Turell, March 6, 1729, Benjamin Colman Papers, Box 1.) He and his wife were greatly concerned for their daughter's health. "We beg of you . . . that if you be going with child again, that you keep your self hid, & don't ride about, no not down to us, & if you have a fancy for any thing speak or write." (Benjamin Colman to Jane Colman Turell, January 16, 1730, Benjamin Colman Papers, Box 1.) Colman's correspondence with Ebenezer Turell, after Jane Colman's Turell's death in 1735, can also be found in Box 1; it concerns matters relating to her funeral.

42. On women's writing as a "domestic archive" (as distinct from national history or national memory), see Stabile, *Memory's Daughters,* especially the introduction, "The Genealogy of Memory," and the conclusion, "The Ruins of Time"; on mourning and remains, see chapter 4, "In Memoriam."

43. Cotton Mather, *Right Thoughts in Sad Hours* (London: James Astwood, 1689), 49. On Puritan death and burial, see David E. Stannard, *The Puritan Way of Death: A Study in Religion, Culture, and Social Change* (New York: Oxford University Press, 1977), especially chapters 3 and 5; Gordon E. Geddes, *Welcome Joy: Death in Puritan New England* (Ann Arbor: UMI, 1976, 1981), especially chapters 5 and 6; and Laurel K. Gabel, "Death, Burial, and Memorialization in Colonial New England: The Diary of Samuel Sewall," *Markers: Annual Journal of the Association for Gravestone Studies* 25 (2008): 8–43.

44. John Flavel, *A Token for Mourners; or, The Advice of Christ to a Distressed Mother,*

bewailing the Death of her Dear and Only Son (Boston: S. Kneeland and T. Green, 1730). This late-seventeenth-century mourning advice book was written in England and printed in Boston in various editions, beginning in 1707. Editions appeared in Boston in 1725, 1729, and 1730. Flavel ignores how, at the death of Lazarus, "Jesus wept" (John 11:35).

Chapter XI Poor Jane's Almanac

1. BF to Sarah Franklin Davenport, Philadelphia, [June?], 1730. Sarah Franklin Davenport had evidently written to Franklin in May of that year.
2. JFM to BF, December 30, 1765.
3. BF to Sarah Franklin Davenport, Philadelphia, [June?], 1730.
4. BF, "Old Mistresses Apologue," June 25, 1745, *PBF*, 3:30–31.
5. BF, *Autobiography*, 56.
6. Green and Stallybrass, *Benjamin Franklin*, chapter 2.
7. BF, *Autobiography*, 55.
8. BF, "Apology for Printers," June 10, 1731, *PBF*, 1:194–95.
9. BF to JFM, June 19, 1731.
10. Jane's son Edward Mecom was baptized at the Brattle Street Church on April 4, 1731, by Samuel Cooper. Only Edward Mecom is listed as parent. *Manifesto Church*, 153.
11. BF to JFM, June 19, 1731.
12. Benjamin Mecom (listed as "Mecum") was baptized at the Brattle Street Church on December 31, 1732, by Samuel Cooper. Only "Edward Mecum" is listed as parent. *Manifesto Church*, 155.
13. JFM to DRF, March 17, 1760.
14. JFM to Jane Mecom Collas, May 16, 1778. Calling children "little rogues" appears to have been commonplace. See the remarks quoted in Norton, *Liberty's Daughters*, 93.
15. JFM to BF, June 25, 1782.
16. BF, *Autobiography*, 79.
17. Green and Stallybrass, *Benjamin Franklin*, 104.
18. Editorial comment in *PBF*, 2:127.
19. BF, *Poor Richard Improved, 1758*, *PBF*, 7:350.
20. Robert Newcomb, "The Sources of Benjamin Franklin's Sayings of Poor Richard" (PhD diss., University of Maryland, 1957), 65, 77, 32. Thomas Fuller, *Gnomologia* (London, 1732), 11. BF, *Poor Richard Improved, 1749*, *PBF*, 3:348. Titan Leeds, *The American Almanack* . . . . BF, *Poor Richard, 1736*, *PBF*, 2:142. And see also Green and Stallybrass, *Benjamin Franklin*, chapter 6.
21. John Adams to Thomas Jefferson, May 15, 1811.
22. BF, *Poor Richard, 1733*, *PBF*, 1:311.
23. BF, *Poor Richard, 1736*, *PBF*, 2:136.

Chapter XII Bookkeeping

1. Richard Steele, comp., *The Ladies Library*, 4th ed., 3 vols. (London, 1732). JFM's copy of volume 3 of the 1732 edition of *The Ladies Library* is at the AAS.
2. "Notes for a History of the Library Company of Philadelphia," in Samuel Hazard, ed., *Hazard's Register of Pennsylvania* 16 (September 26, 1835), 202.

3. In 1733, BF printed a catalog of the holdings of the Library Company, but no copy survives. What that catalog must have listed has, however, been carefully reconstructed. See Edwin Wolf, "The First Books and Printed Catalogues of the Library Company of Philadelphia, *Pennsylvania Magazine of History and Biography* 78 (1954): 45–70. Wolf lists neither *The Ladies Library* nor *Gnomologia.*

4. [London] *Monthly Catalogue,* October 1732, 375. *The Ladies Library* (1732) appears in *A Catalogue of Books Belonging to the Library Company of Philadelphia* (Philadelphia: B. Franklin, 1741), 46. By 1734, the 1732 duodecimo edition of *The Ladies Library* was among the holdings of the Library Company. That copy was ordered November 13, 1734, and received on April 18, 1735 (James N. Green, e-mail to the author, March 8, 2012). By 1738, Franklin was selling imported editions of *The Ladies Library* in his shop; see the ad in the *Pennsylvania Gazette,* May 25, 1738. On sending it to readers, see BF to John Ladd, June 12, 1738. Later, BF also recommended the book to his daughter, writing to his wife, "Sally's last Letter to her Brother is the best wrote that of late I have seen of hers. I only wish she was a little more careful of her Spelling. I hope she continues to love going to Church, and would have her read over and over again the whole Duty of Man and the Lady's Library." BF to DRF, London, February 19, 1758. Sally was fourteen when Franklin wrote this letter.

5. BF, *Autobiography,* 63.

6. James N. Green believes that while in New England in the summer and fall of 1733 Franklin visited Thomas Cox's Boston shop (Green, e-mail to the author, March 8, 2012). On April 30, 1733, Cox placed an ad in the Boston *Weekly Rehearsal:* "Just arrived (*per* Capt. *Shepardson*) a very curious *Collection* of the best and most valuable *Books,* in all Arts and Sciences, to be sold at the Shop of *T. Cox,* Bookseller, at the *Lamb* on the South side of the Town-House in *Boston,* at the very lowest Prices for *ready Money.*" *The Ladies Library* does not appear among the titles Cox listed as being for sale, but at the end of that list, he added, "The abovesaid Shop will be constantly supplied with the newest and most valuable Books as soon as possible, a considerable Quantity besides the above-mentioned being shortly expected in the *London* Ships." Franklin later urged the Library Company to send to Boston for books imported from London, arguing that they could be purchased more cheaply there than in London. If Cox stocked *The Ladies Library,* Franklin could have bought the book for Jane during his visit. The book does not appear in Thomas Cox, *A Catalogue of Books, In all Arts and Sciences, To be Sold at the Shop of T. Cox, Bookseller* (Boston, 1734), although it is possible that, in 1734, Cox was simply out of stock of this title. See also James N. Green, "Franklin's Bookshop," unpublished manuscript, 2012.

7. JFM to DRF, November 24, 1766.

8. BF, "Observations on my Reading History in Library," May 9, 1731, in *PBF,* 1:193.

9. Mary Astell, *The Christian Religion, As Profess'd by a Daughter of the Church of England* (London: S.H., 1705), 292. And also quoted in Perry, *The Celebrated Mary Astell,* 9.

10. David Hume, "Of the Study of History," in *Essays, Moral, Political, and Literary,* part 3, essay 6.

11. And see, by way of comparison, *The Gentleman's Library, Containing Rules for Con-*

duct in all Parts of Life (London: E.P., 1715), published a year after the first edition of *The Ladies Library* (London, 1714).

12. BF, *Autobiography,* 64.

13. Steele, *The Ladies Library* (London, 1732), 1:1.

14. Ebenezer Mecom (listed as "Mecum") was baptized at the Brattle Street Church on May 4, 1735. Only "Edward Mecum" is listed as parent. *Manifesto Church,* 157.

15. Only a handful of letters written by her children survive. All are written by either her son Benny or her daughter Jenny. They both wrote better than their mother. For letters written by Jane Mecom Collas, see Jane Mecom Collas to BF, Boston, July 9, 1773; Boston, January 9, 1778; Cambridge, June 6, 1781; Boston, November 11, 1787; and Boston, July 16, 1788. We know that Benjamin Mecom wrote to BF. For BF's references to those letters, see BF to JFM, [June? 1748]; BF to Edward Mecom and JFM, September 14, 1756, February 12, 1756, and June 28, 1756.

16. JFM to DRF, January 29, 1758. Ideas about filth were changing as, over the course of the eighteenth century, dirtiness came to be especially associated with the poor. See Alain Corbin, *The Foul and the Fragrant: Odor and the French Social Imagination* (Cambridge, MA: Harvard University Press, 1986), especially chapter 9. On laundry and the growing demand for whiter and whiter linens, see Kathleen M. Brown, *Foul Bodies: Cleanliness in Early America* (New Haven: Yale University Press, 2009), chapter 4.

17. *Pennsylvania Gazette,* April 18, 1734.

18. BF, *Autobiography,* 65.

19. Green and Stallybrass, *Benjamin Franklin,* 40.

20. For Josiah Franklin's estate inventory of 1752, including pots, pans, irons, kettles, and tubs—evidence of Jane's labor—see "Inventory of Josiah Franklin's Estate, October 24, 1752" in Huang, "Franklin's Father Josiah," 127.

21. See Charles Coleman Sellers, *Benjamin Franklin in Portraiture* (New Haven: Yale University Press, 1962), chapter 2.

22. BF to JFM, January 13, 1772.

23. Sarah Mecom was baptized at the Brattle Street Church on July 3, 1737, by Benjamin Colman. Only Edward Mecom is listed as parent. *Manifesto Church,* 160.

24. The signed promissory note is included in the case file: Massachusetts Judicial Archives, Suffolk Files Collection, Reel 163, vol. 301, no. 45414. Collson & Mecom. Jan 1737–8 (that is, January 1738).

25. On this, in fiction, see, e.g., Mary Poovey, *Genres of the Credit Economy: Mediating Value in Eighteenth- and Nineteenth-Century Britain* (Chicago: University of Chicago Press, 2008), chapter 1, "The Paper Age."

26. "It would strangely Cramp the *Trade* of a People, if it might be no more than the *Cash* that is running among them." Cotton Mather, *Fair Dealing between Debtor and Creditor: A very brief Essay upon The Caution to be used, about coming in to DEBT, And getting out of it* (Boston: B. Green, 1716), 8.

27. For the order concerning the issue of paper bills, see *At The General Court of their Majesties Colony of the Massachusetts BAY in New-England, Sitting in Boston by Adjournment. December 10th, 1690* (Cambridge, MA: Samuel Green, 1690). See also Gary B. Nash, *The Urban Crucible: The Northern Seaports and the Origins of the*

American Revolution (Cambridge, MA: Harvard University Press, 1986), 2–3. BF, *A Modest Enquiry into the Nature and Necessity of a Paper-Currency* (Philadelphia, 1729), in *PBF*, 1:139–57. And see Green and Stallybrass, *Benjamin Franklin*, 52–57.

28. Advertisement, *Pennsylvania Gazette*, October 9, 1729. And Green and Stallybrass, *Benjamin Franklin*, chapter 3.

29. Nash, *Urban Crucible*, 72.

30. Jabez Warner, a Connecticut shoemaker, wrote his own record on a page of his account book: *Anne Warner daughter to Jabez and hannah Warner was born Jan.-the 24th 1757.* And then: *Departed this Life Novbr-24th 1760 four years old wanting 2 months.* Jabez Warner Account Book, 1754–70 and 1783–1837, Connecticut Historical Society, as cited in Wulf, "Bible, King, and Common Law." And, for more on family registers, which became commonplace only at the end of the eighteenth century, see Georgia Brady Barnhill, "'Keep Sacred the Memory of Your Ancestors': Family Registers and Memorial Prints," in Simons and Benes, *The Art of Family*, 60–74.

31. For instructions on the keeping of accounts at the time, see Robert Lundin, *Reason of Accompting by Debitor and Creditor* (Edinburgh, 1718). Franklin's account books are included in *The Papers of Benjamin Franklin*, but see also *Account Books Kept by Benjamin Franklin*, ed. George Simpson Eddy, 2 vols. (New York, 1928–29).

32. Bruce H. Mann, *Republic of Debtors: Bankruptcy in the Age of American Independence* (Cambridge, MA: Harvard University Press, 2002), 286n8.

33. George Philip Bauer, "The Movement Against Imprisonment for Debt in the United States" (PhD diss., Harvard University, 1935), 37. See also Christine Daniels, "'Without Any Limitacon of Time': Debt Servitude in Colonial America," *Labor History* 36 (1995): 232–50.

34. Defoe once wrote, allegorically, about his coy mistress, Lady Credit, whose hand was hard to win: "If you court her, you lose her." See Paula R. Backscheider, "Defoe's Lady Credit," *Huntington Library Quarterly* 44 (1981): 89–100.

35. Bauer, "Imprisonment for Debt," 37. See also Daniels, "'Without Any Limitacon of Time.'"

36. Bauer, "Imprisonment for Debt," 23–24, 31–32.

37. "The Liberties of the Massachusets Colonie in New England," in *The Colonial Laws of Massachusetts. Reprinted From the Edition of 1660, With the Supplements to 1672. Containing Also, The Body of Liberties of 1641* (Boston: Rockwell and Churchill, 1889), 41.

38. JFM to BF, January 8, 1788. This remark concerns not her husband, in the 1730s, but her son-in-law Peter Collas, in the 1780s.

39. Massachusetts Judicial Archives, Suffolk Files Collection, Reel 163, vol. 301, no. 45414 (3 papers f. 43–44). Collson & Mecom. Jan 1737-8 (that is, January 1738).

40. BF, *Poor Richard Improved, 1758, PBF*, 7:348.

41. BF, *Poor Richard, 1736, PBF*, 2:141.

42. BF, "The Drinker's Dictionary," January 13, 1736–37, *PBF*, 2:173–78. Accounts between Mecom and his creditors can be found in the Massachusetts Judicial Archives, Suffolk Files Collection, Reel 162, vol. 300, no. 45226, Account of Price and Mecom, 27 Dec. 1737; Reel 163, vol. 301, no. 45414 (3 papers f. 43–44). Coll-

son & Mecom. Jan 1737–8; Reel 167, v. 309, no. 46904 (3 papers). Banister &c. v. Mecom or Corbet & Mecom. July 1738; Reel 175, v. 322, no. 49481. Perkins v. Mecom. July 1739.

43. The records of Edward Mecom's debts are in the Massachusetts Judicial Archives, Court of Common Pleas, Suffolk County, Record Books, as follows: v. 1737, p. 22, Green vs. Mecom./ [October 1737]; v. 1737, p. 78, Price vs. Mecom./ Exn 10 ffeby 1737; v. 1737, p. 117, Mecom vs. Bisco. "Exn. 4 ffeby. 1737./"; v. 1737, p. 120, Colson vs. Mecom./ "Exn. 4 ffeby. 1737"; v. 1737, p. 342, Banister &c. vs. Mecom. "Excon issued Sept.20.1738"; v. 1738, p. 45, Kneeland v. Macom./ "Excon issued Decr. 22.d 173[8]/ All. Septr. 6. 1739"; v. 1738, p. 151, Carter v. Macom, "Excon issued Feb. 1. 1738/[39]"; v. 1738, p. 361, Perkins v. Macom, [no date, probably August or September 1739].

44. John Perkins, "Memoirs of the life writings and opinions of John Perkins physician lately of Boston, begun March 1777, and continued to 1778," unpublished manuscript, AAS, 2.

45. John Perkins, Notebook, AAS, "Medical, Political, & Religious &c.," 32. Little is known about how Jane cared for her children when they were sick, but for a related account, see Helena M. Wall, " 'My Constant Attension on My Sick Child': The Fragility of Family Life in the World of Elizabeth Drinker," in *Children in Colonial America*, 155–67.

46. Peter Franklin Mecom was baptized at the Brattle Street Church on May 13, 1739. Which minister officiated is not listed, but at this point Colman had ceased conducting baptisms: "Hence forward I take ye fore-noon exurcise, & leave ye Baptisms (as at times of late I have done) to Mr. Cooper," 161. Only Edward Mecom is listed as parent. *Manifesto Church*, 162.

47. The records of Edward Mecom's indebtedness in these years can be found in the Mass. Arch., Suffolk Files, as follows: 1737 (Document 45414, Reel 163); 1737 (Document 4519, Reel 162); 1738 (Document 46904, Reel 167); 1739 (Document 49481, Reel 175).

48. JFM to BF, January 8, 1788; here again concerning the debts of JFM's son-in-law Peter Collas.

49. See Martha J. McNamara, *From Tavern to Courthouse: Architecture and Ritual in American Law, 1658–1860* (Baltimore: Johns Hopkins University Press, 2004), 47.

50. There are very few reliable numbers for colonial American debtors' prisons, and there is some debate about how prevalent they were. Bauer admits that it's hard to get real figures, but he estimates "that the number of instances of imprisonment for debt, while fluctuating widely, increased on the whole during the latter part of the seventeenth century and all of the eighteenth at a somewhat faster rate than the population, though not so much faster as one might be led to suppose from a casual survey of the evidence" ("Imprisonment for Debt," 45–46). But see the dissenting view of Edwin T. Randall, "Imprisonment for Debt in America: Fact and Fiction," *Mississippi Valley Historical Review* 39 (June 1952): 89–102.

51. As Innes points out, married women could not own property, and so could neither contract nor default on debts ("King's Bench," 263).

52. James Ciment, "In Light of Failure: Bankruptcy, Insolvency and Financial Failure

in New York City, 1790–1860" (PhD diss., City University of New York, 1992), 136–44; Mann, *Republic of Debtors,* chapter 5; the William Duer Papers, Box 6, New-York Historical Society; and Jill Lepore, *The Story of America: Essays on Origins* (Princeton: Princeton University Press, 2012), 91–110.

53. On where Jane lived, see Van Doren, *Jane Mecom,* 24–25. Captain Hugh Ledlie boarded with Jane from 1742 to 1772, first at the Blue Ball, and later at the Mecoms' house near the Orange Tree. Hugh Ledlie to BF, Hartford, May 22, 1787.

54. For record books, see "Philadelphia Post Office Record Books, 1737–53," *PBF,* 2:178–83; "Philadelphia Post Office Record Book, 1757–1764," *PBF,* 7:158–60. "Philadelphia Post Office Accounts, 1757–1764," *PBF,* 7:160–62; "Receipt Book, 1742–64," *PBF,* 2:351–52.

55. Editorial comment, *PBF,* 2:178. And see Green and Stallybrass, *Benjamin Franklin,* chapter 2.

56. BF, *Autobiography,* 91.

57. John Mecom was baptized at the Brattle Street Church on April 5, 1741. Both Edward Mecom and JFM are listed as parents. *Manifesto Church,* 163.

58. *New England Weekly Journal,* July 17, 1739.

59. William Blackstone, *Commentaries on the Laws of England, A Facsimile of the First Edition 1765–1769* (Chicago: University of Chicago Press, 1979), 1:430.

60. Hugh Ledlie to BF, Hartford, May 22, 1787. On women in Boston taking in boarders at a much higher rate than in either New York or Philadelphia, see Nash, "The Failure of Female Factory Labor in Colonial Boston," 182–83.

61. JFM to BF, December 17, 1786.

62. CRG to JFM, February 20, 1776. (Jane was, at the time, in Philadelphia.)

63. JFM to DRF, April 6, 1765. This was when she was a grandmother, caring for her grandchildren after their mother, Jane's daughter Sarah Mecom Flagg, died.

64. JFM to BF, June 17, 1782. This was while she was a great-grandmother, caring for her great-grandchildren after their mother, Jane's granddaughter Jane Flagg Greene, died.

Chapter XIII Useful Knowledge

1. Josiah Mecom was baptized at the Brattle Street Church on March 27, 1743 (Jane's thirty-first birthday). Only Edward Mecom is listed as parent. *Manifesto Church,* 166.

2. BF to Josiah and Abiah Folger Franklin, April 13, 1738, *PBF,* 2:202–4. Abiah, who had been even more worried than her husband, was, by this letter, mollified. As Franklin wrote to his father a month or so later, "It gave me great Pleasure when she declar'd in her next to me that she approv'd of my Letter and was now satisfy'd with me." BF to Josiah Franklin, Philadelphia, [May?] 1738.

3. BF, *A Proposal for Promoting Useful Knowledge,* May 14, 1743, *PBF,* 2:380–83.

4. Thomas Jefferson to Roger Weightman, June 24, 1826, in *Memoirs, Correspondence, and Private Papers of Thomas Jefferson,* ed. Thomas Jefferson Randolph (London: H. Colburn and R. Bentley, 1829), 4:452. And see Robert A. Ferguson, *The American Enlightenment, 1750–1820* (Cambridge, MA: Harvard University Press, 1994).

5. Lemay, *Life of BF,* 2:311.

6. BF, *Autobiography,* 130. BF met Spencer in Boston in June 1743. BF misremembers this as having taken place in 1746. See also N. H. de V. Heathcote, "Franklin's Introduction to Electricity, *Isis* 46 (1955): 29–35. On Franklin as a scientist and on the world of early modern scientific inquiry in which he participated, see I. Bernard Cohen, *Benjamin Franklin's Science* (Cambridge, MA: Harvard University Press, 1990), and especially Joyce Chaplin, *The First Scientific American: Benjamin Franklin and the Pursuit of Genius* (New York: Basic Books, 2007). For his work on electricity in particular, see pp. 103–17.
7. BF, *Poor Richard, 1751, PBF,* 4:96.
8. BF to JFM, July 28, 1743.
9. BF, "Articles of Belief and Acts of Religion," November 20, 1728, *PBF,* 1:109.
10. BF, *Autobiography,* 70, 68, 71, 73. And see also Green and Stallybrass, *Benjamin Franklin,* 12–17.
11. JFM to BF, December 29, 1780.
12. BF, *Autobiography,* 65: "I had been religiously educated as a Presbyterian; and tho' some of the Dogmas of that Persuasion, such as the Eternal Decrees of God, Election, Reprobation, etc. appear'd to me unintelligible, others doubtful, and I early absented myself from the Public Assemblies of the Sect, Sunday being my Studying-Day, I never was without some religious Principles; I never doubted, for instance, the Existence of the Deity, that he made the World, and govern'd it by his Providence; that the most acceptable Service of God was the doing Good to Man; that our Souls are immortal; and that all Crime will be punished and Virtue rewarded either here or hereafter." And see Ferguson, *American Enlightenment,* 76–77.
13. The influence of Whitefield and the New Lights on the Brattle Street Church, and excerpts from Cooper's sermons, can be found in Akers, *Divine Politician,* 11, 15, 17, 21, 23.
14. Jonathan Edwards, *Some Thoughts Concerning the present Revival of Religion in New-England* (Boston: S. Kneeland and T. Green, 1742), 359, 104, 101. See also Ferguson, *American Enlightenment,* 50–51.
15. Edwards, *Some Thoughts Concerning the present Revival,* 367, 372.
16. In his Book of Virtues, Franklin proposed beginning each day with the question, "What Good shall I do this Day?" and ending the evening by asking, "What Good have I done to day?" BF, *Autobiography,* 72.

Chapter XIV   Dear Reader
1. BF to Edward Mecom and JFM, [1744–45]; BF to Josiah Franklin and Abiah Folger Franklin, Philadelphia, September 6, 1744.
2. On changing funeral practices over the course of the eighteenth century, see Bullock, "'Often concerned in funerals,'" 181–211, and Bullock and McIntyre, "The Handsome Tokens of a Funeral," 305–46.
3. See editorial comment, Van Doren, *Letters,* 40, and "Executor's Account of Josiah Franklin's Estate, February 12, 1753" in Huang, "Franklin's Father Josiah," 129.
4. Josiah Franklin's will is reprinted in Huang, "Franklin's Father Josiah," 123–24. BF

gives his share of his inheritance and the additional £30 to Jane in his (that is, BF's) will, written in April 1757. *PBF*, 7:200.

5. Jane Mecom was baptized at the Brattle Street Church on April 14, 1745. Only Edward Mecom is listed as parent. *Manifesto Church*, 168.

6. James Mecom was baptized at the Brattle Street Church on August 3, 1746, by Benjamin Colman. Only Edward is listed as parent. *Manifesto Church*, 169. *New England Weekly Journal*, July 17, 1739.

7. Flavel, *A Token for Mourners*, 68–69.

8. Benjamin Colman, *A Devout Contemplation on the Meaning of Divine Providence, in the Early Death of Pious and Lovely Children* (Boston: John Allen, 1714), 4, 26.

9. *The New-England Primer Enlarged* (Boston: S. Kneeland and T. Green, 1727), n.p. Various editions of the *New-England Primer* were published regularly, and frequently, during the years Jane was raising her children.

10. Josiah Williams was born on December 31, 1747. *PBF*, 1:lviii. An obituary refers to him as "Blind from his Infancy." *Boston Evening-Post*, August 17, 1772.

11. Mary Mecom was baptized at the Brattle Street Church on March 6, 1748, by Samuel Cooper. Both Edward Mecom and JFM are listed as parents. *Manifesto Church*, 171.

12. On March 27, 1748, Jane turned thirty-six. Her first child was born on June 4, 1729, when she was seventeen. She conceived around September 4, 1728, when she was sixteen.

13. The portrait is now owned by Harvard. Henry Wilder Foote, *Robert Feke: Colonial Portrait Painter* (Cambridge, MA: Harvard University Press, 1930), 67–68, 151–54. And Sellers, *Benjamin Franklin in Portraiture*, 24–45.

14. JFM to BF, August 16, 1787.

15. See Chaplin, *The First Scientific American*, 103–17.

16. BF, "On the Internal State of America," 1785. *PBF*, unpublished. On the use of this metaphor among American writers, see Ferguson, *American Enlightenment*, chapter 2.

17. Turgot is cited in Ferguson, *American Enlightenment*, 36, and Lemay, *The Life of BF*, 3:135. See also *Oeuvres de Mr. Turgot* (Paris: de l'Imprimerie de A. Belin, 1808–11), 9:140.

18. BF to Abiah Folger Franklin, Philadelphia, April 12, 1750.

19. Jane owned the 1769 London edition (the fourth edition); it is now at Princeton. BF sent her six copies, for distribution; BF to JFM, February 23, 1769.

20. JFM to BF, August 25, 1786.

21. BF to Peter Collinson, Philadelphia, May 21, 1751.

22. In the 1740s, Williams's advertisements ran regularly in the *Boston Evening-Post*.

23. BF to Abiah Folger Franklin, Philadelphia, October 16, 1747.

24. BF, "Observations concerning the Increase of Mankind, Peopling of Countries, &c." *PBF*, 4:228.

25. His reckoning was not far wrong. Five grew up to have children of their own: three of Jane's children, Edward, Benjamin, and Sarah, all lived long enough to marry and have children, as did two of Franklin's children, William and Sarah.

26. Abiah Franklin to BF and DRF, Boston, October 14, 1751.

27. BF to JFM, October 24, 1751; "I beg'd your *Plain Truth* of Mrs. Mecom," Perkins

wrote Franklin. John Perkins to BF, Boston, February 17, 1752. Some of Perkins's case notes from the 1752 smallpox epidemic can be found in Perkins, "Medical, Political, & Religious &c.," 32.

28. BF to Abiah Folger Franklin, Philadelphia, April 1752.

29. Perkins reported on the smallpox epidemic in a letter to Franklin dated August 3, 1752, Boston.

30. BF to Edward Mecom and JFM, May 21, 1752.

31. Of Josiah Franklin's seven children by his first wife, Ann, five lived to adulthood. Of those five, two had children. Samuel Franklin had only one child, a daughter named Elizabeth, which was his wife's name. Anne Franklin Harris had both daughters and sons, including a daughter named Ann and a son named Josiah. Of Josiah Franklin's ten children by his second wife, Abiah, eight may have had children. John had only one son, whom he named John. Peter's issue is uncertain; Lydia had perhaps a daughter. Mary Franklin Homes had three children, two sons and a daughter named Abiah. James had six children, including a daughter named Abiah and another named Ann, which was his wife's name. Sarah Franklin Davenport had five children, including a son named Josiah and a daughter named Abiah. (See "Descendants of Josiah Franklin," *PBF*, 1:lvi–lxiii.) In short, Benjamin Franklin was the only one of Josiah Franklin's children not to name any of his children after either his parents, himself, or his spouse. And he was the only one of Josiah and Abiah Franklin's children not to name a child after his parents.

32. "The stone placed over their graves by their youngest son," Carl Van Doren observed, "perpetuated also the special gratitude of their youngest daughter." (*Jane Mecom,* 49.) Van Doren counts a different seven than I do. He counted all of Jane's children still alive at the time of Abiah Franklin's death: nine. Then he discounted Benny and Peter, because they were no longer living at the Blue Ball but were, instead, apprenticed. BF includes the entire text of the epitaph in his *Autobiography,* but it first appeared in print in the August 1, 1758, issue of the *New-England Magazine,* printed by Benjamin Mecom.

Chapter XV   *The Way to Wealth*

1. BF, "Articles of Agreement with James Parker," February 20, 1741–42, *PBF*, 2:341–45. See also, Worthington C. Ford, "Letters from James Parker to Franklin," *Proceedings of the Massachusetts Historical Society* 16 (1902): 186–89.

2. BF to Edward Mecom and JFM, undated but ca. 1745. On Parker, see Alan Dyer, *A Biography of James Parker, Colonial Printer* (Troy, NY: Whitston, 1982), and, for more on Franklin and Parker, as well as similar arrangements, including the financial underpinnings of Franklin's partnerships with Benjamin Mecom, see Ralph Frasca, *Benjamin Franklin's Printing Network: Disseminating Virtue in Early America* (Columbia: University of Missouri Press, 2006).

3. BF, "Advice to a Young Tradesman," was published in George Fisher, *The American Instructor; or, Young Man's Best Companion* (Philadelphia: B. Franklin and D. Hall, 1748). See *PBF*, 3:306–8.

4. BF to JFM, undated but ca. June 1748.

5. BF to Edward Mecom and JFM, September 14, 1752.

6. BF to JFM, September 20, 1750.

7. See Lemay, *Life of BF,* 2:398.

8. On Franklin sending Smith to Antigua, see Wilberforce Eames, *The Antigua Press and Benjamin Mecom, 1748-8–1765* (Worcester: American Antiquarian Society, 1929), 3-3–4. Smith died in June or July 1752. Eames, *The Antigua Press,* 8.

9. BF to Edward Mecom and JFM, September 14, 1752.

10. David Barry Gaspar, *Bondsmen and Rebels: A Study of Master-Slave Relations in Antigua* (Durham: Duke University Press, 1985), and Brian Dyde, *A History of Antigua: The Unsuspected Isle* (London: Macmillan, 2000).

11. BF to Edward Mecom and JFM, November 30, 1752.

12. Fragment of a letter from WF to JFM, undated but probably 1752.

13. *Boston Evening-Post,* October 10, 1752. This ad, about the real estate, ran again in the same paper on November 6, 1752. A new ad appeared on July 23, 1753, during BF's visit to Boston. John Franklin and William Homes were named as the persons handling the sale. The sale was announced for August 21.

14. On William Homes, see "William Homes, Sr.," in Patricia E. Kane, *Colonial Massachusetts Silversmiths and Jewelers* (New Haven: Yale University Art Gallery, 1998), 559–66.

15. Jane's brother John suffered from an excruciatingly painful bladder stone. In December 1752, Benjamin Franklin sent to his brother a catheter he'd drawn up the plans for and had a silversmith build out of silver pipes and wire. BF also sent along directions for use and care, including, kindly, tips on how to "preserve it against Putrefaction." BF to John Franklin, Philadelphia, December 8, 1752.

16. On the rent owed by the Mecoms, see Van Doren, *Jane Mecom,* 44.

17. JFM to Sarah Franklin Bache, May 29, 1786. This letter is a corrected copy; the original is missing.

18. JFM to BF, August 29, 1789. Abiah Folger Franklin writes about a visit from Keziah Folger Coffin in 1751, when Abiah was dying. Like Jane, Keziah also seems to have been an avid reader of the writings of Benjamin Franklin. "My Cozen Kesiah Coffin was hear last week and she was Sorroy that the werkes and letter was not yet printed. She bid me tell you that She Shold be glad how soone you coold do them for She wants to have a few of them very much." (Abiah Franklin to BF and DRF, October 14, 1751.) Van Doren (*Letters,* 45) was not able to identify the "werkes and letter" referred to here; nor have I. For another visit, see JFM to DRF, November 24, 1766: "Kezia Coffin . . . has been in town this fall & Desiered me to Remember Her to you when I wrot." Jane apparently wrote to Coffin frequently. "I Receiv'd all your Letters," Coffin wrote back (these letters do not survive). Keziah Folger Coffin to JFM, August 6, 1768.

19. BF to John Franklin, Philadelphia, January 2, 1753. See also Lemay, *Life of BF,* 3:319.

20. Draft of a letter from John Franklin to BF, [January 1753], *PBF,* 4:422. At this point, the household goods had sold; the house and land had not.

21. *PBF,* 2:368.

22. *Boston Gazette,* July 31, 1753. BF received an honorary master's degree from Yale on September 12, 1753; see *PBF,* 5:58 and Lemay, *Life of BF,* 3:321. This was done in absentia, but in 1755 BF stopped in New Haven, and Ezra Stiles delivered a Latin oration about him on February 5, 1755. *PBF,* 5:492–500. On November 30, 1753, BF received the Copley Medal of the Royal Society, see *PBF,* 5:126–33.

23. BF took a mortgage out on the Douse house in 1748, as security on a £60 loan to the Douses. Lemay says that sometime during BF's 1753 visit, he took out a new mortgage on the house, and the deed was recorded on September 27, with Thomas Hubbart as witness. Lemay, *Life of BF,* 3:319. *PBF* (5:66) says that after Captain Douse's death, Elizabeth Franklin Douse renewed the mortgage in her own name, acknowledging a debt of £100 rather than £60. The mortgage deed is transcribed in *PBF,* 5:67. Some more about the history of the house can be gleaned in Frank Chocteau Brown, "The Clough-Langdon House, 21 Unity Street, Boston," *Old-Time New England* 37 (1947): 79–85. Brown supposes that Jane Franklin Mecom and her family began living at the house at 19 Unity Street in about 1753, but this supposition is incorrect.

24. Franklin's surviving correspondence with Jonathan Williams Sr. is extensive. It begins in March 1755. Williams handled a range of Franklin's business affairs, including distributing gifts and cash to Elizabeth Franklin Douse and Jane Franklin Mecom and taking care of the Douse house. Franklin also shipped Williams reams and reams of paper, to be sold to tradesmen, for packing, and to printers, for printing. See, e.g., BF to Jonathan Williams Sr., Philadelphia, October 16, 1755.

25. *Boston Gazette,* November 13, 1753. On taverns and tavern culture, see Sharon V. Salinger, *Taverns and Drinking in Early America* (Baltimore: Johns Hopkins University Press, 2002); on the location of taverns in Boston, see 191–94. Salinger calculates that between 1736–37 and 1764–65, women received 41 percent of all tavern licenses (163). These women, however, were heads of household.

26. BF to JFM, June 28, 1756.

27. Benjamin Mecom to DRF, September 21, 1754.

28. BF to William Strahan, Philadelphia, April 18, 1754.

29. See Roelker, *BF and CRG,* 1–2. JFM wrote CRG, "Believe me to be be yr most faithfull & obliged frind," JFM to CRG, Philadelphia, November 24, 1775.

30. The earliest correspondence between JFM and CRG to survive is from 1775, but it seems likely that they corresponded before this time, probably beginning around 1755.

31. BF to JFM, February 12, 1756. BF knew that Benny wanted to leave the island in February. In June, BF wrote to JFM on Benny's resolve. BF had received several letters from Benny expressing "the inflexibility of his Determination to leave the Island; but without saying where he propos'd to go . . ." BF to JFM, June 28, 1756. On December 30, BF sent a letter to Jane and Edward Mecom, carried by Benny. This means that Benny sailed from Antigua to Philadelphia sometime between June and December 1756 and left for Boston around December 30. (See BF to Edward Mecom and JFM, December 30, 1756.) Benny had arrived in Boston by February 21, 1757. (See BF to JFM, February 21, 1757: "I am glad to hear your son is got well home.")

32. BF to JFM, June 28, 1756.

33. The horse is mentioned in BF to JFM, May 21, 1757. Benny insisted on leaving Antigua, and then BF told Jane that Benny "purposes to set up his Business together with Bookselling" (December 30, 1756). BF did much to help Benny set up, helping him secure books, type, and paper (BF to Edward Mecom and JFM, December 30, 1756).

34. BF to JFM, February 21, 1757.

35. Lemay, *Life of BF*, 3:563.

36. On the delayed London voyage, see *PBF*, 7:234, 174, 219.

37. BF to JFM, April 19, 1757.

38. BF to JFM, May 30, 1757.

39. BF to JFM, May 21, 1757.

40. Ebenezer Mecom is listed in the *PBF* (1:lxi) as unmarried, but he married Susannah Hiller in the Brattle Street Church on July 21, 1757. *Manifesto Church*, 249. She appears to have been a widow, as she is listed as "Mrs. Susan. Hiller."

41. BF to JFM, May 30, 1757.

42. Ibid.

43. "This is to notify the Publick," advertisement, *Boston News-Letter*, October 28, 1756.

44. BF to JFM, May 30, 1757.

45. BF to JFM, May 21, 1757.

46. William Homes Sr. employed several apprentices in these years, including his son William Homes Jr., who, in 1763, when he turned twenty-one, took over his father's shop. John Mecom, born in 1741, was a year older than Homes's son and was apparently unhappy in his apprenticeship, which he did not complete; instead he tagged after his older brother Benjamin and attempted to become a printer. Kane, *Colonial Silversmiths*, 553–59.

47. BF to JFM, May 30, 1757. Entries for dealings with a John Mecom, dated 1759, appear in a ledger book kept by Jane's brother Peter, in Newport. It's unlikely that this is Jane's son, who was still an apprentice in Boston at that point. Peter Franklin, Ledger Begun November the 6th, 1741, Franklin Papers, APS.

48. BF, "Last Will and Testament," *PBF*, 7:199–200.

49. BF, *Poor Richard Improved . . . 1758*, *PBF*, 7:341–42.

50. BF, *Father Abraham's Speech* (Boston: Benjamin Mecom, 1758).

51. On the quite different publishing history of *The Way to Wealth* in England, see Green and Stallybrass, *Benjamin Franklin*, chapter 7.

52. JFM to BF, July 4, 1784.

53. BF to JFM, April 19, 1757.

PART THREE · LETTERS, 1758–1775

Chapter XVI   Bad Writing

1. JFM to DRF, January 29, 1758. Looking at the physical letters, it's clear that Jane's capacity to write improved greatly between the writing of this first letter and the letters she wrote, at a furious clip, in the last decade of her life. Compare this letter, for instance, to JFM to BF, July 4, 1784.

2. See, e.g., JFM to BF, December 30, 1765, or November 8, 1766.

3. BF, "On Titles of Honor," *New-England Courant*, February 18, 1723.

4. JFM to DRF, February 27, 1766.

5. DRF to JFM, [May 1772?].

6. JFM to DRF, February 27, 1766. JFM was gossiping about Grace Harris Williams

here. According to *The Manifesto Church* (183), Sarah, daughter of Jonathan Williams, was baptized in the Brattle Street Church by Samuel Cooper on March 30, 1766.

7. JFM to DRF, February 27, 1766.
8. JFM to DRF, [before August 1770?].
9. JFM to DRF, November 24, 1766.
10. Ibid.
11. CRG to JFM, February 7, 1776.
12. JFM to Sarah Franklin Bache, [October 1780].
13. JFM to DRF, [before August 1770?].
14. JFM to BF, February 14, 1779.
15. JFM to BF, July 4, 1784.
16. JFM to Jonathan Williams Jr., Boston, August 11, 1792.
17. JFM to BF, August 29, 1789.
18. JFM to BF, August 16, 1784.
19. JFM to BF, September 26, 1788.
20. George Fischer, *The American Instructor; or, Young Man's Best Companion,* 9th ed., rev. and corr. (Philadelphia: B. Franklin and D. Hall, 1748), 45.
21. Samuel Richardson, *Letters Written to and for Particular Friends, on the most Important Occasions* (London, 1741; 4th ed., 1750), letters 138 (p. 181) and 139 (p. 182).
22. Thomas Keymer, introduction to Samuel Richardson, *Pamela; or, Virtue Rewarded* (New York: Oxford University Press, 2001), xiv.
23. Richardson, *Pamela* (New York: Oxford University Press, 2001), letter 1 (p. 1); letter 2 (p. 13).
24. BF to Jane Franklin, January 6, 1727.
25. Richardson, *Pamela* (New York: Oxford University Press, 2001), letter 5 (p. 17); letter 1 (pp. 12–13).
26. Green and Stallybrass, *Benjamin Franklin,* 63–64; 68–69. In *Poor Richard* for 1752, Green and Stallybrass point out, Franklin "quoted no fewer than twenty-one sayings from Samuel Richardson's *Clarissa,* a novel that Franklin and his partner, David Hall, had imported from England and advertised for sale in seven volumes in 1751" (113).
27. Samuel Richardson, *Pamela; or, Virtue Rewarded. In a Series of Familiar Letters from a Beautiful Young Damsel, To her Parents,* 5th ed. (London; repr., Philadelphia: B. Franklin, 1742). BF's copy text was the fourth London edition and printing, not completed until the summer of 1744. BF to DRF, London, November 22, 1757.
28. BF, *Autobiography,* 18.
29. On BF's printing of *Pamela,* see Green and Stallybrass, *Benjamin Franklin,* 68–70; and BF, "Observations on Mr. Parker's State of the Account," 1766, in *PBF,* 13:110–16.

Chapter XVII By the Post
1. JFM to BF, March 3, 1781.
2. BF to JFM, August 29, 1765. Also BF to JFM, July 7, 1773: "I believe it is long since I have written any Letters to you. I hope you will excuse it. I am oppress'd with too much Writing."

3. JFM to BF, December 30, 1765.
4. JFM to Sarah Franklin Bache, May 29, 1786.
5. JFM to DRF, [August?] 1770.
6. JFM to Sarah Franklin Bache, October 1780. Van Doren, *Jane Mecom,* 75.
7. Stewart, "Intercourse of Letters," chapter 2.
8. BF to JFM, July 10 and July 24, 1764.
9. BF to JFM, August 3, 1789.
10. BF to JFM, April 27, 1789.
11. JFM to BF, November 7, 1768.
12. JFM to DRF, [August 1770?].
13. JFM to BF, November 21, 1774.
14. JFM to BF, July 27, 1779.
15. JFM to DRF, [August?] 1770.
16. JFM to BF, February 21, 1786.
17. JFM to BF, November 3–21, 1774.
18. JFM to BF, October 21, 1784. BF to JFM, July 28, 1774.
19. BF to JFM, September 26, 1774.
20. JFM to BF, November 3–21, 1774.
21. David Hume to BF, Edinburgh, May 10, 1762.
22. Mather Byles to BF, 1765–66. See BF to Elizabeth Hubbart, February 22, 1756, concerning the letter of condolence Franklin wrote to John Franklin's widow, Elizabeth Hubbart Franklin (the woman Jane would have a beef with concerning the family soap), which circulated in manuscript in the 1760s and was published in *Massachusetts Magazine* in 1789.
23. Hannah Callender Sansom, *The Diary of Hannah Callender Sansom: Sense and Sensibility in the Age of the American Revolution,* ed. Susan E. Klepp and Karin Wulf (Ithaca: Cornell University Press, 2010), 86. At the beginning of 1759, Sansom cited passages from BF to JFM, September 16, 1758. The diarist was a friend of Elizabeth Ross Mecom, the wife of Jane's son Benjamin, which suggests the route a copy of the letter might have taken: from Jane to Betsy, from Betsy to Hannah. Emerging evidence suggests that a great deal of women's writing circulated only in manuscript. See *Milcah Martha Moore's Book: A Commonplace Book from Revolutionary America,* ed. Catherine LaCourreye Blecki and Karin A. Wulf (University Park: Pennsylvania State University Press, 1997). Moore (1740–1829), who lived most of her life in Philadelphia, wrote three commonplace books, including one she titled "Martha Moore's Book"; in it, she transcribed the writings of many of her female friends. Moore also copied out a letter from BF to Joseph Huey, June 6, 1753; BF's epitaph; and the inscription BF placed over his parents' graves (217–20). The last two of these items she might have come across in Benjamin Mecom's *New-England Magazine.*
24. Envelope, Richard Bache to JFM, April 19, 1790, NEHGS.
25. JFM to BF, October 23, 1781. Nor did she keep any kind of summary of letters she had written, as suggested by JFM to BF, March 3, 1781, explaining that she had written to him before but couldn't remember what about: "I wrot a Sheet full on Every thing concerning my self that I thought you would wish to know but have no coppy & can now Recolect but litle of it."
26. BF to JFM, July 7 and November 1, 1773; February 17, 1774.

Chapter XVIII   You and I Only

1. BF to DRF, January 21, 1758. And see Charles Coleman Sellers, "Jane Mecom's Little Picture," *Proceedings of the American Philosophical Society* 99 (1955): 433–35, and Sellers, *Benjamin Franklin in Portraiture,* 236–37. The miniature is now at the Museum of Fine Arts, accession no. 43.1318. Sellers's account of its provenance, in *Benjamin Franklin in Portraiture,* appears to be in error. He believes that the miniature descended through Jane's granddaughter Sally Flagg and then somehow, at Sally Flagg's death in 1881, to the descendants of Jane's great-grandson Franklin Greene. I believe the Franklin miniature in Sally Flagg's possession in 1858 was different from the miniature that descended through the family of Franklin Greene.
2. BF to JFM, September 16, 1758.
3. Benjamin Franklin the Elder, Commonplace books, AAS. Volume 1. Flyleaf.
4. BF to JFM, July 14, 1759.
5. BF to JFM, January 9, 1760.
6. BF to JFM, November 11, 1758.
7. On Keziah Folger Coffin visiting Jane, see Abiah Folger Franklin and JFM to BF and DRF, October 14, 1751.
8. JFM to BF, November 8, 1766.

Chapter XIX   The Book of Nature

1. I don't think Ebenezer Mecom and his wife, Susanna Hiller, had any children, but I do think Susanna Hiller Mecom might be the Susanna Mecom who married Benjamin Somes of Gloucester on October 28, 1762—that is, nine months after Eben's death—and with whom she had five children.
2. JFM to BF, August 18, 1777.
3. JFM to DRF, March 17, 1760.
4. BF to John Perkins, Philadelphia, February 4, 1753.
5. John Perkins, *The True Nature and Cause of the Tails of Comets* (Boston: Edes and Gill, 1772). Perkins was elected in January 1774: "Early Proceedings of the American Philosophical Society for the Promotion of Useful Knowledge, Compiled by One of the Secretaries, from the Manuscript Minutes of Its Meetings from 1744–1838," *Proceedings of the American Philosophical Society* 22 (July 1885): 87.
6. John Perkins, *Thoughts on Agency* (New Haven: B. Mecom, 1765), 7–8. And see also John Perkins, *Theory of Agency; or, An Essay on the Nature, Source and Extent of Moral Freedom* (Boston: printed for and sold by John Perkins, 1771). And see Gordon Wood, *The Radicalism of the American Revolution* (New York: Knopf, 1992), 239–40 and note 22.
7. Perkins mentions sending the essay in John Perkins to BF, Boston, March 12, 1770, but the treatise itself is among Perkins's papers at the American Antiquarian Society and is dated 1768: "A Few Thoughts on Epidemic Colds or Catarrh Fevers. Inscribed to B.F. Esq. L.L.D. with the following Epistle." It begins, "Some time since, in conversation, you was pleas'd to introduce the Subject of Catarrh Fever, commonly call'd epidemic Colds, & did me the honour of recommending them to my consideration, particularly with effect to the causes of them, which seem to have been too little enquir'd into."
8. Perkins, "Of the Diseases & casualtys incident to Mankind," in the volume of his

notebooks titled "Memoirs of the life writings and opinions of John Perkins physician lately of Boston, begun March 1777, and continued to 1778," AAS. Perkins did not trust his patients to diagnose their own ailments. "People often mistake a beginning Fever for a cold," he warned, "& immediately give such things as they use for this, either a Sweat or some Spiritous Draught, either of which in a good constitution often fires the distemper." Franklin's medical library is discussed in Edwin Wolf II, "Frustration and Benjamin Franklin's Medical Books," *Science and Society in Early America,* ed. Randolph Shipley Klein (1986), 57–91.

9. BF to Jonathan Williams Sr., Philadelphia, November 25, 1762. And on the harpsichord, see BF to Jonathan Williams Sr., New York, June 26, 1763.

10. As Eric H. Christianson has warned, "Any attempt to classify the diseases of the 17th and 18th centuries involves hazards for the historian because diagnosis was often imprecise. As one medical historian has noted, it is difficult, if not impossible, even to distinguish between such diseases as diphtheria and scarlet fever 'when eighteenth century doctors themselves made no attempt to separate them.'" "Medicine in New England," in *Sickness and Health in America: Readings in the History of Medicine and Public Health,* ed. Judith Walzer Leavitt and Ronald L. Numbers, 3rd ed., rev. (Madison: University of Wisconsin Press, 1997), 47–71; quote is from 47.

11. On its later history, see Katherine Ott, *Fevered Lives: Tuberculosis in American Culture Since 1870* (Cambridge, MA: Harvard University Press, 1996).

12. JFM to DRF, February 27, 1766.

13. Mass. Arch., Mass. Arch. Collection (SC1/Series 45X), 98B, pp. 421–36, "Coll. Jno. Phillip's Acct./Mustering Men/ 23.66/[Augt. 30?] 1761"; "466 Men were Muster'd & Sworn & Many of them had the Articles of War Read to them according to the Within Dates By John Phillips Commissary of Musters" (p. 426), "Return of Men inlisted for His Majesty's Service for the Protection and Security of His Majesty's Dominions and Conquests in North-Amarica [*sic*], 1761." Peter Mecom, enlisted May 19, 1761, attested May 19, 1761, mustered May 19, 1761, resident of Boston, 22 years of age, enlisted by Lieutenant Abraham Tuckerman; v. 99A, pp. 135–36, Pay roll for Captain Simon Jeffres's Company, 1761; p. 135, "PAY-ROLL of the Company in His Majesty's Service, Under the Command of [Blank] Captain, Viz.," Boston, March 24, 1762, [signed] [Lieut.] Thaddeus Trafton, Peter McComb [read Mecom], resident of Boston, entered into service May 21, [1761], left service June 28, [1761], served 5 weeks, 4 days, deserted.

14. JFM to DRF, [August?] 1770.

15. Benjamin Franklin the Elder, "Short Account" in Huang, "Franklin's Father Josiah," 108.

16. Barbara J. Logue, "In Pursuit of Prosperity: Disease and Death in a Massachusetts Commercial Port, 1660–1850," *Journal of Social History* 25 (1991): 314.

17. For the treatment of tuberculosis in the eighteenth century, see Cecil D. Drinker, *Not So Long Ago: A Chronicle of Medicine and Doctors in Colonial Philadelphia* (New York: Oxford University Press, 1937), chapter 4, "The Tuberculosis of William Drinker." And on TB present in the colonies since Jamestown, see "Sickness and Health in America: An Overview," in Leavitt and Numbers, *Sickness and Health in America,* 5.

18. Perkins, "Of the Diseases & casualtys incident to Mankind," in the volume of his

notebooks titled "Memoirs of the life writings and opinions of John Perkins physician lately of Boston, begun March 1777, and continued to 1778," AAS.

19. JFM to CRG, Philadelphia, November 24, 1775. JFM to BF, November 24, 1789. Jane complained about suffering from asthma more later in life. See, e.g.: "Aunt mecom wrote to you the other day and of course answered all your enquiries relative to her, she appears to me in better health than from her discription in her letter to me I expected; she is troubled with a complaint of the Astmatic kind, but it does not seem to be in a degree to indicate the presence of disease, further than as a common attendant to her age. She is in good Spirits, which is the best remedy that any Physician could prescribe." Jonathan Williams Jr. to BF, Boston, September 6, 1789.

20. BF to JFM, July 7, 1773.

21. Perkins, "Of the Diseases & casualtys incident to Mankind," in the volume of his notebooks titled "Memoirs of the life writings and opinions," AAS.

22. James Carmichael Smyth, *An Account of the Effects of Swinging, employed as a Remedy in the Pulmonary Consumption and Hectic Fever* (London, 1787).

23. DRF to BF, Philadelphia, [October 13–18?], 1767. BF was in London.

24. This is from the first (untitled and unpaginated) separate volume of Perkins's case notes, AAS. There are eleven unnumbered volumes.

25. Massachusetts Judicial Archives, Suffolk Files Collection, Reel 733, v. 1272, no. 172092, Recognizance, Case of Peter Franklin Mecom. Genl. Sessions, Suffolk, Oct. 1759.

26. Benjamin Mecom, Boston, to Deborah Franklin, Philadelphia, February 9, 1761, Franklin-Bache Collection, APS.

27. BF to JFM, June 28, 1756.

28. William Franklin to BF, ca. January 2, 1769.

29. BF to Catherine Shipley, Philadelphia, May 2, 1786. JFM to BF, December 26, 1782.

30. BF to Catherine Shipley, Philadelphia, May 2, 1786. BF to JFM, October 25, 1779. See also BF to Jean-Baptiste Le Roy, June 22, 1773.

31. JFM to BF, July 27, 1779.

32. Later research would suggest that the immune cells that fight tuberculosis do so much better in the presence of vitamin D. The human body produces vitamin D in response to sunlight. Low levels of vitamin D during brain development, including prenatally, have also been related to the adult onset of some forms of mental illness, including depression and schizophrenia. See, e.g., Susan Realegeno and Robert L. Modlin, "Shedding Light on the Vitamin D–Tuberculosis–HIV Connection," *Proceedings of the National Academy of Science* 108 (2011): 18861–62; D. Itzhaky et al., "Low Serum Vitamin D Concentrations in Patients with Schizophrenia," *Israeli Medical Association Journal* 14 (2012): 88–92; B. L. Gracious et al., "Vitamin D Deficiency and Psychotic Features in Mentally Ill Adolescents: A Cross-Sectional Study," *Biomed Central Psychiatry* 9 (2012): 38; and J. P. Kesby et al., "The Effects of Vitamin D on Brain Development and Adult Brain Function," *Molecular and Cellular Endocrinology* 5 (2011): 121–27.

Chapter XX Queer Notions

1. Benjamin Mecom's own family was growing. His wife, Elizabeth, brought their baby, Sarah, to be baptized at the Brattle Street Church on October 1, 1758, probably by Samuel Cooper. *Manifesto Church,* 178.

2. "To the honourable Republic of LETTERS, in New-England," *New-England Magazine of Knowledge and Pleasure,* August 1, 1758, 6.

3. "Introduction," *Gentleman's Magazine; or, Monthly Intelligencer* (London: F. Jefferies, 1731). The best history of the magazine in early America remains Frank Luther Mott, *A History of American Magazines, 1741–1850* (Cambridge, MA: Harvard University Press, 1966).

4. "The Design, &c." *New-England Magazine,* August 1, 1758, 9–10.

5. The magazine's cover said it was written "By Urbanus Filter"; its motto was "E Pluribus Unum." Both were nods to the *Gentleman's Magazine,* whose putative author was "Sylvanus Urban," and whose motto was also "E Pluribus Unum" (a phrase Franklin would put to another use when, on July 4, 1776, he and fellow Continental Congress delegates Thomas Jefferson and John Adams served on a committee whose charge was "to prepare a device for a Seal of the United States of America"). See Monroe E. Deutsch, "E Pluribus Unum," *The Classical Journal* 18 (1923): 387–407, and Holman S. Hall, "The First New England Magazine," *New England Magazine,* n.s. 33 (January 1906): 520–25.

6. Benjamin Mecom printed "Advice to a Young Tradesman" on March 1, 1759, in the *New-England Magazine,* 27–28. He printed the gravestone inscription under "Supplement to No. 1," *New-England Magazine,* August 1, 1758, p. 58.

7. This tale is recounted in John Tebbel and Mary Ellen Zuckerman, *The Magazine in America, 1741–1990* (New York: Oxford University Press, 1991), 3–4. And see Carl Van Doren, *Benjamin Franklin* (New York: Viking, 1938), 119–20.

8. James Parker, "Proposals for Printing by Subscription, a New *American* Magazine," *New-York Gazette; or, The Weekly Post-Boy,* September 12, 1757.

9. Webster is in Mott, *History of American Magazines,* 13.

10. *New-England Magazine,* August 1, 1758.

11. Advertisement for the *New-England Magazine, Boston Evening-Post,* September 4, 1758.

12. Benjamin Mecom, "Good Wages & Accommodation for a Journeyman-Printer," *Boston Post-Boy,* March 16, 1761.

13. Benjamin Mecom, advertisement in the *Boston Evening-Post,* February 8, 1762.

14. Mecom wrote to DRF, apologizing that he was unable to pay her money he owed her. "You may depend upon it gives me no great Deal of Pain that I cannot send you any Money yet, but when the Psalter is done 'tis very likely I shall be able to send you some, which will always be very chearfuly and thankfully don." Benjamin Mecom to DRF, Boston, April 10, 1758, APS. And see Isaiah Thomas, *The History of Printing in America* (Albany, 1874), 1:142–44.

15. Benjamin Mecom to DRF, February 9, 1761, APS.

16. Thomas, *The History of Printing in America,* 1:142–44.

17. Joseph Steward, *Poor Joseph. 1759. Being An Almanack and Ephemeris of the Sun and Moon* (Boston: B. Mecom, 1758); *The Prodigal Daughter* (Boston: B. Mecom, 1758); John Perkins, *An Essay on the Agitations of the Sea* (Boston: B. Mecom, 1761); BF, *The Beauties of Poor Richard's Almanack* (Philadelphia; Boston: B. Mecom, 1760); BF, *Advice to a Young Tradesman* (Boston: B. Mecom, 1762); and BF, *The Interest of Great Britain Considered* (London; Boston: B. Mecom, 1760).

18. JFM to DRF, April 6, 1765.

19. JFM's copy of BF's *The Interest of Great Britain Considered* descended through her grandson Josiah Flagg to his daughter Sally Flagg, who gave it to the Thayer Memorial Library in Lancaster, Massachusetts, in 1862, where it remains.

20. BF to JFM, November 25, 1762.

21. The tour would take five months (June 7 to November 5, 1763) and cover some eighteen hundred miles. At its close, Franklin established continuous mail between the trading cites. Post riders left Philadelphia and Boston every day, making it possible to get a letter between the two cities in six days. Stewart, "Intercourse of Letters," chapter 2.

22. BF to JFM, June 19, 1763.

23. BF visited CRG from around July 13 to 18, 1763, and took a bad fall. See editorial comment, *PBF,* 10:278n2 and 10:338n5. For BF thanking the Greenes for their hospitality, see BF to William Greene, Providence, July 19, 1763, and BF to CRG, Boston, September 5, 1763. Writing to Caty from Jane's house in September, Franklin sent greetings. "Sally and my Sister Mecom thank you for your Remembrance of them." BF to CRG, Boston, September 5, 1763.

24. BF to Jonathan Williams Sr., Philadelphia, November 28, 1763. And see the state of the accounts relative to the house, and to BF's payments to JFM, in Jonathan Williams Sr. to BF, October 1763. On the lack of public institutions for relief of the poor, see Ruth Wallis Herndon, *Unwelcome Americans: Living on the Margin in Early New England* (Philadelphia: University of Pennsylvania Press, 2001).

25. The first issue appeared on July 11, 1763, and the last on August 22 of that year. Franklin expected to visit Mecom in the city. See BF to DRF, New York, June 16, 1763: "I have not yet seen B. Mecom, but shall to day."

26. "To be Sold at Auction," advertisement, *New-York Gazette,* April 23, 1764. (Up for grabs as well, interestingly: "a Mahogany Tea Table.") Before closing down shop, B. Mecom printed Noah Welles, *Animadversions, Critical and Candid, Some Parts of Mr. Beach's Late "Friendly Expostulation," in A Letter, From a Gentleman in New-England to his Friend in New-York* (New York: B. Mecom, 1763).

27. John Mecom sold goods in Newport, for a matter of days, in 1763; see "Lately Imported from London (Via New-York)," advertisement, *Newport Mercury,* July 18, 1763, selling earrings, necklaces, rings, buckles, watches, "Hair Sprigs," and "Heart Lockets." His shop in New Brunswick is described in "To be Sold By John Mecom," advertisement, *New-York Mercury,* June 18, 1764. This ad ran through 1765.

28. See *PBF,* 11:241n5.

29. See, e.g., Thomas Fitch, *Viro Præstantissimo* (New Haven: Excudebat B. Mecom, 1764) and *Quæstiones Pro Modulo Discutiendæ Sub Reverendo D. Thoma Clap, Collegii Yalensis* (Novo-Portu: Excudebat Benjamin Mecom, 1764).

30. James Parker to BF, Burlington, January 4, 1766; Woodbridge, March 27, 1766; and New York, May 6, 1766. Parker relates his losses in detail in a letter to BF, New York, dated June 11, 1766.

31. BF to Jonathan Williams Sr., Philadelphia, February 24, 1764.

Chapter XXI   Black Day

1. BF to JFM, July 10, 1764.

2. Jane must at this point have written to Deborah, because on January 8, 1765, Debo-

rah wrote to her husband, "I have had one letter from Sister mecom her youngest grand child is dead" (DRF to BF, Philadelphia, January 8, 1765).

3. JFM to DRF, April 6, 1765. On Josiah Flagg using crutches from the age of five until his death, see the Lancaster historian A. P. Marvin's remarks, inserted into a flyleaf of the Flagg family Bible, which is discussed in the last chapter of this book.

4. Mass. Arch., Suffolk Files, Document 85880, Reel 274. "Ruddock vs. Mecom. January 1765. Suffolk. November ye 12 1764." And on the back of the document: "I Attach a Chair of the Estate of the within named Edward Mecom and I left a summons at the place of his abode. Benjamin Cudworth Deputy Sheriff." See also Document 85846, Reel 274, Mecom v. Dalton, January 1765.

5. Lawrence Park, *Joseph Badger (1708–1765): And a Descriptive List of Some of His Works* (Boston: University Press, 1918), 3–8. Park does not mention the Flagg portraits, which were, at the time, unknown to art historians. Nor have they become much better known since. The Flagg portraits are listed, but not described, in Richard C. Nylander, "Joseph Badger, American Portrait Painter" (MA thesis, State University of New York at Oneonta, 1972), p. 54; the sitters are identified as "Flagg, Boy" and "Flagg, Girl." Nylander had evidently not seen the actual portraits, as he was unable to specify their size or to describe them in any way. (The paintings measure 31 inches by 26 inches.) He found a record of them in a magazine; the portraits are listed, and again the sitters not named, although the images are reproduced in black-and-white, in "Lancaster Anniversary," *Antiques,* September 1953, 218. In 1953, the bicentennial of Lancaster's founding, the paintings were presumably exhibited; their current location is discussed in the final chapter of this book. Badger never signed his works, but Ellen Miles of the National Portrait Gallery agrees with the attribution of the Flagg portraits to Badger (e-mail to the author, February 7, 2012).

6. Between the decline of John Smibert in 1748 and the rise of John Singleton Copley in 1756, according to Frank W. Bayley, "Badger was the only portrait painter of any consequence in Boston" (*Five Colonial Artists of New England* [Boston: Privately printed, 1929], 1). And see Ellen G. Miles, "Joseph Badger," *American National Biography Online,* February 2000.

7. In 1755, Badger charged five pounds, five shillings, altogether, for the three children of Isaac Foster. The portraits of Eleanor Foster, age nine, and Isaac Foster Jr., age nineteen, are the same size as the portraits of Josiah and Jane Flagg (31 inches by 25 inches). A portrait of William Foster is slightly larger (35 inches by 27 inches). Badger charged six pounds for a portrait of Foster (measuring 35 inches by 27 inches), and six pounds for a portrait of Foster's wife (also 35 inches by 27 inches). Badger must have painted the Flagg children between Polly's death, in March, and his own death, on May 11, 1765. On the prices Badger charged, see also Park, *Joseph Badger,* 5, and Nylander, "Joseph Badger," 23–29. In 1756, Badger charged Timothy Orne six pounds each for portraits of Orne and his wife (both 48 inches by 38 inches) and five pounds, five shillings for a set of four portraits of his children (all presumably 25 inches by 20 inches, although only two of the Orne children portraits survive). Orne was a wealthy merchant from Salem. Closer to Jane's rank was a Boston baker named George Bray, whom Badger charged twelve pounds for five pictures (the portraits have not survived, nor is their size known). He also

sometimes accepted bartered goods in payment for portraits (Nylander, "Joseph Badger," 29–31). Badger's own estate was small, and he died insolvent. His widow, Katherine, went to probate court on August 23, 1765. The inventory of the estate is reprinted in Nylander, "Joseph Badger," 10–12. She later claimed debts equal to the total value of the estate, £140 10s. Katherine Badger signed with a mark (Nylander, "Joseph Badger," 12–14).

8. Badger's portrait of Cushing is in the Peabody Essex Museum.

9. "I saw one of your letters to the Speaker." JFM to BF, December 5–15, 1774.

10. Jonathan Williams Sr. to BF, Boston, December 13, 1771.

11. Badger's church membership is discussed in Nylander, "Joseph Badger," 7–8. According to Miles, Badger had at least seven children, of whom at least four were baptized at Brattle Street. On the proximity of the Mecom and Badger baptisms in the parish register, see *The Manifesto Church:* Josiah Mecum, 151; Edward Mecom, 153; Benjamin Mecum, 155; Samuel Badger, 156; Ebenezer Mecom, 157; Joseph Badger Jr., 159; Sarah Mecom, 160; Peter Mecom, 162; John Mecom, 163; William Badger, 165; Josiah Mecom, 166; Jane Mecom 168; Elizabeth Badger, 169; James Mecom, 169; Mary Mecom, 171.

12. JFM to BF, November 11, 1788. This is Thomas Cushing Jr.; Cushing Sr. died in February 1788.

13. If this is the case, it would be difficult to prove, as most of Cushing's papers were destroyed during the siege of Boston.

14. Telling in that regard might be this: "Sister Mecom speaks very affectionately of you, and gratefully of your kindness to her in her late Troubles." BF to Jonathan Williams Sr., London, April 28, 1766.

15. Fred Anderson, *A People's Army: Massachusetts Soldiers and Society in the Seven Years' War* (Chapel Hill: University of North Carolina Press, 1984). For an overview, see chapter 1.

16. Gary Nash, "Urban Wealth and Poverty in Pre-Revolutionary America," *Journal of Interdisciplinary History* 6 (1976): 561–63. See also Carl Bridenbaugh, *Cities in the Wilderness: Urban Life in America, 1625–1742* (1955; repr., New York: Capricorn Books, 1964), 392–94.

17. BF to David Hall, London, February 14, 1765.

18. They founded more newspapers, at twice the rate the population was growing. Pasley, *Tyranny of Printers*, 33. In the wry words of David Ramsay, a South Carolina delegate to the Continental Congress who wrote, in 1789, the first American history of the Revolution, "It was fortunate for the liberties of America, that News-papers were the subject of a heavy stamp duty. Printers, when uninfluenced by government, have generally arranged themselves on the side of liberty, nor are they less remarkable for to the profits of their profession." Ramsay, *History of the American Revolution* (Philadelphia, 1789), 1:61–62.

19. JFM to BF, December 30, 1765.

20. On Edes, see Rollo G. Silver, *Benjamin Edes: Trumpeter of Sedition* ([New York?], 1953). But see also the entries for Edes in Thomas, *History of Printing*, 1:136–39 and 2:53–56. Edes's career is summarized in Tebbel, *Compact History*, 37–39. Very useful is the detailed discussion in Joseph T. Buckingham, *Specimens of Newspa-*

per Literature: With Personal Memoirs, Anecdotes, and Reminiscences (Boston, 1850), 1:165–205. Finally, Pasley discusses Edes briefly (*Tyranny of Printers*, 37–40).

21. James Parker to BF, Woodbridge, NJ, March 22, 1765. Parker corresponded with Franklin at great length, and with great frequency, on the subject of Benjamin Mecom's ailments and his indebtedness to Parker. "As to Benny *Mecom*, he and I have had abundance of Altercations in Letters," Parker reported to Franklin in 1766. "He promises fair, but performs but little. I threaten to displace him and sue him: He says he will try to pay it, but if I sue him, he must go to Goal, and that will pay none" (James Parker to BF, New York, December 15, 1766). This went on for several years.

22. Thomas Fitch, *Reasons why the British colonies, in America, should not be charged with internal taxes* (New Haven: B. Mecom, 1764).

23. Benjamin Mecom, *To the Publick of Connecticut* (New Haven: B. Mecom, 1765).

24. C, "To Mr. Mecom," *Connecticut Gazette*, July 12, 1765. On Mecom's politics, see, e.g., "Enquiries concerning the Constitution of the English Colonies in Relation to Great-Britain," *Connecticut Gazette*, January 10, 1766. Nevertheless, Benjamin Mecom was hardly solvent. "The young Gentleman is much to be pitied, as it woud appear that his Circumstances in a good measure have gone wrong thro an Act of Providence," an Edinburgh bookseller wrote to Franklin in September 1765, reporting on the scandalous state of his account with Jane's son. John Balfour, Edinburgh, to BF, London, September 2, 1765. Balfour was preparing to sue, and wrote to Franklin, "I do think indeed Sir that you have acted generously, in suffering Mr. Mecoms effects to be equally divided amongst his Creditors; most willingly I give you power to act for us as you think proper, where coud we have our Affairs in better hands. I shall be glad to know if it is necessary to send up Mr. Mecom's letters, the last I had from him settled the Account, which I admitted in his own way, after various deductions which I did not lay my Account with."

25. Thomas Hutchinson to Richard Jackson, August 30, 1765.

26. John Eliot, *Biographical Dictionary* (Salem, 1809), 191–92. Edwin Monroe Bacon, *Boston: A Guide Book* (Boston, 1903), 59. On Eliot, see Clifford K. Shipton, "Andrew Eliot," in *New England Life in the Eighteenth Century* (Cambridge, MA: Harvard University Press, 1963), 397–428.

27. JFM to DRF, February 27, 1766. And on the genealogy, see Van Doren, *Letters*, 88, and *PBF*, 1:lx–lxi.

28. A good account of BF's views, at the time, on the Stamp Act is contained in BF to WF, London, November 9, 1765.

29. JFM to DRF, February 27, 1766.

30. JFM to DRF, September 28, 1765.

31. Ibid.

32. JFM to Jane Mecom Collas, May 16, 1778. A corrected version of this letter appears in Van Doren (*Letters*, 180–82); he relied on a corrected copy in the NEHGS. The original was sold at auction in 1934; the auction catalog includes a brief excerpt, which is uncorrected, and I have therefore quoted the uncorrected version where possible. *The Library of the Late Rev. Dr. Roderick Terry of Newport, Rhode Island* (New York: American Art Association, 1934), 132, catalog 218. A manuscript note

in the margin of the copy of the catalog in the Harvard Library indicates that this letter sold for $17.50 to "Heartman," doubtless Charles F. Heartman, a rare-book dealer and the editor of the *American Book Collector.*

33. BF to JFM, March 1, 1766. Emphasis mine, to call out the unpunctuated quotations within the quotation.

34. BF, Silence Dogood, "No. 7," *New-England Courant,* June 25, 1722, *PBF,* 1:25–26. And see also Jeffrey A. Hammond, *The American Puritan Elegy: A Literary and Cultural Study* (Cambridge: Cambridge University Press, 2000). Hammond's argument is that the power of Puritan elegies lay in their conventionality, the very conventionality Franklin—and modern critics—have found so contemptible.

35. JFM to DRF, September 28, 1765.

36. Accounts of Boston in the 1760s and 1770s include Carl Bridenbaugh, *Cities in Revolt: Urban Life in America, 1743–1776* (New York: Knopf, 1955); Gary Nash, *Urban Crucible: The Northern Seaports and the Origins of the American Revolution* (Cambridge, MA: Harvard University Press, 1986); and Benjamin Carp, *Rebels Rising: Cities and the American Revolution* (Oxford: Oxford University Press, 2007). On the fire, see William Pencak, "The Social Structure of Revolutionary Boston: Evidence from the Great Fire of 1760," *Journal of Interdisciplinary History* 10 (Autumn 1979): 267–78; and on taxpayers versus women householders, see 274–75. On the effects of the French and Indian War, see Anderson, *A People's Army.*

37. Eric Nellis and Anne Decker Cecere, eds., *The Eighteenth-Century Records of the Boston Overseers of the Poor* (Boston: Colonial Society of Massachusetts, 2007), 33–35, 57, 165–66, 635.

38. "An Inventory of the Estate of Edward Mecom . . . Taken by the Subscribers," October 30, 1765, Suffolk County Probate 13744. See also Nash, "Urban Wealth," 549, 553.

39. James Parker to BF, Philadelphia, June 14, 1765.

40. *Pennsylvania Gazette,* October 31, 1765. *Maryland Gazette,* October 10, 1765. *Connecticut Courant,* July 24, 1765. *New-Hampshire Gazette,* October 31, 1765. For other newspapers in mourning, see Arthur M. Schlesinger, "The Colonial Newspapers and the Stamp Act," *New England Quarterly* 8 (March 1935): 63–83. Printers' responses to the Stamp Act are also briefly discussed in Tebbel, *Compact History,* 35–37, and in Smith, *Printers and Press Freedom,* 136–41.

41. Isaiah Thomas gives a very brief account of what happened in Halifax during the Stamp Act crisis in his outline for the autobiography he never wrote. *Three Autobiographical Fragments by Isaiah Thomas* (Worcester, 1962), 8.

42. *Boston Gazette,* November 11, 1765. See also Hannah Adams, *A Summary History of New-England* (Dedham, [MA]: H. Mann and J. H. Adams, 1799), 249–50.

43. Inventory of the Estate of Edward Mecom, October 30, 1765, with Hutchinson's additions. "Edward Mecom's Adm. Acc," December 19, 1765, Suffolk County Probate, 13744.

44. JFM to BF, December 30, 1765.

45. Jane could not have known this, and Hutchinson was never able to find copies of those letters—even though he looked, to vindicate himself—but some of the papers Hutchinson lost that night, along with others he lost when patriots seized his country home, were saved. They eventually found their way to the Massachusetts

Archives. In 1764, Hutchinson had written to England opposing Parliamentary taxation by arguing that the colonists "claim a power of making Law and a Privilege of exemption from taxes except by their own Representatives": no taxation without representation. See Edmund S. Morgan, "Thomas Hutchinson and the Stamp Act," *New England Quarterly* 21 (1948): 459–92.

46. William Franklin knew this as well, and he wrote to his father, in September, that rioters in Boston had "plundered the Effects of several even of those who were against the Stamp Act, particularly Mr. Hutchenson." WF to BF, Burlington, September 7, 1765.

47. BF to JFM, March 1, 1766. And see also Thomas Hutchinson to BF, January 1, 1766.

48. JFM to BF, December 30, 1765.

49. JFM to BF, June 25, 1782.

50. JFM to BF, April 2, 1789.

Chapter XXII   To Be Sold

1. JFM to DRF, February 27, 1766.

2. JFM to BF, December 30, 1765.

3. JFM to BF, November 8, 1766. Van Doren tried to figure out which six but did not succeed (see the page on the Massachusetts Assembly in Van Doren's Jane Mecom notebook). Nor have I.

4. On the election, see *Massachusetts Gazette Extraordinary*, May 29, 1766.

5. "The Examination of Doctor Benjamin Franklin, before an August Assembly, relating to the Repeal of the Stamp Act, &c." (Boston: Edes and Gill, 1766). "Examination of Dr. Bejamin Franklin," *Connecticut Gazette*, September 27, 1766.

6. On why the colonists objected to the Stamp Act but not to the Post Act, see Stewart, "Intercourse of Letters," 89–90.

7. "The Examination of Doctor Benjamin Franklin" (Boston: Edes and Gill, 1766), 12, 23.

8. JFM to DRF, February 27, 1766.

9. DRF to BF, Philadelphia, [October 13–18?], 1767. See "State of the Accot: between Doctor B Franklin and Jona: Williams Senr: as it should properly stand," [October 1763], *PBF*, 10:356. At the time, Jane was also receiving financial support from William Franklin, who sent her food: "six Barrils of flower," she told her brother, "which was a grat help to me & his notice of me a grat satisfaction." JFM to BF, November 8, 1766.

10. JFM to BF, December 30, 1765. On widows as shopkeepers (and innkeepers), see Norton, *Liberty's Daughters*, 142–51.

11. JFM to BF, November 8, 1766.

12. "The Prologue," in Bradstreet, *Several Poems Compiled with great variety of Wit and Learning*, 4.

13. BF to JFM, March 1, 1766.

14. JFM to BF, November 8, 1766. For Stevenson's account with Jane, see "Doctr Benjamin Franklin to Margt Stevenson Dr for Sundries Purchased for and sent to Mrs. Jane Mecom of Boston," 1765–71, in *PBF*, 12:324–26.

15. BF to JFM, March 2, 1767.

16. JFM to Margaret Stevenson, Boston, May 9, 1767.

17. "To be Sold by Jane Mecom," *Boston Evening-Post,* November 16, 1767.
18. BF to JFM, December 24, 1767.
19. JFM to BF, December 1, 1767.
20. *Connecticut Gazette,* September 27, 1766. Franklin printed it on the title page of Richard Jackson, *An Historical Review of the Constitution and Government of Pennsylvania* (Philadelphia, 1759). The attribution of the motto to Franklin, which is now generally accepted, appears to be Mecom's. Mecom, at the time, was hardly thriving. "I can't get one Penny of Mecom and begin to fear, I never shall," James Parker, Mecom's chief creditor, wrote to Franklin from New York, on June 11, 1766.
21. JFM to BF, November 8, 1766.
22. JFM to BF, December 1, 1767. Emphasis mine, to call out the echo of BF.

Chapter XXIII   Spectacles

1. J. Hector St. John de Crèvecoeur, *Letters from an American Farmer* (London, 1782), 51, 201.
2. "Kezia the daughter of Keziah Coffin at one time boarded at Jane Mecom's, and went to school in Boston." William Folger to Jared Sparks, 1838, "Papers sent to me by William C. Folger, of Nantucket. Relating to Franklin," in "Papers relating chiefly to Franklin. Used in writing his Life, 1839," Sparks Papers, MS Sparks 19. Keziah Folger Coffin's daughter Keziah Coffin, born in 1723, married in 1777. Franklin corresponded with Keziah Folger Coffin but does not appear to have visited Nantucket, at least since his childhood, if ever. He had never met Keziah's husband or daughter. In 1765, in a letter to Keziah Folger Coffin, written possibly at Jane's instigation, he asked, "Remember me kindly to your Husband and Daughter, Tho' I am unknown to them." BF to Keziah Folger Coffin, London, August 29, 1765.
3. Jonathan Williams Sr. to BF, Boston, October 19, 1767, BF Papers, APS.
4. JFM to BF, December 1, 1767.
5. Letter extract, JFM to BF, [October 23, 1767].
6. JFM to BF, December 1, 1767.
7. BF to JFM, December 24, 1767.
8. JFM to BF, August 25, 1786.
9. BF to JFM, November 7[–9], 1770. BF to JFM, December 30, 1770. BF to JFM, November 7[–9], 1770. BF to JFM, December 30, 1770.
10. BF to JFM, July 17, 1771.
11. See especially Katherine Stebbins McCaffrey, "Reading Glasses: Spectacles in the Age of Franklin," PhD diss., Boston University, 2007.
12. In 1764, when a fire destroyed all of Harvard's scientific apparatus, Franklin purchased replacements, shipping from London the best telescopes and magnifying glasses. On the fire, see *PBF,* 11:255n6. On BF agreeing to replace the scientific instruments, see BF to John Winthrop, Philadelphia, July 10, 1764.
13. BF to JFM, September 16, 1758.
14. BF to JFM, July 17, 1771. In a letter now lost, she replied that she was tempted to use lenses that made her vision better, whereupon Franklin warned her that this would weaken her eyes: "But People in chusing should only aim at remedying the Defect.

The Glasses that enable them to see *as well*, at the *same Distance* they used to hold their Book or Work, while their Eyes were good, are those they should chuse, not such as make them see *better*, for such contribute to hasten the Time when still older Glasses will become necessary." BF to JFM, January 13, 1772.

15. BF, "Causes of the American Discontents before 1768" or "To the Printer of the *London Chronicle*," January 5–7, 1768, in *PBF*, 15:13, 9, 12–13.

16. WF to Lord Hillsborough, November 23, 1768, in *Documents Relating to the Colonial History of the State of New Jersey, 1767–1776* (Newark, 1886), 10:64–96.

17. JFM to BF, November 7, 1768.

18. Richard Archer, *As If an Enemy's Country: The British Occupation of Boston and the Origins of Revolution* (New York: Oxford University Press, 2010), xvi.

19. *Boston Under Military Rule, 1768–1769, as revealed in A Journal of the Times*, compiled by Oliver Morton Dickerson (New York: Da Capo, 1970). John Adams diary entry for September 3, 1769, *The Works of John Adams* (Boston: Charles C. Little and James Brown, 1850; repr., New York: AMS, 1971), 2:219.

20. JFM to BF, November 7, 1768. Jane had also written to him about a religious controversy involving the possibility of Anglican bishops residing in America.

21. BF to JFM, February 23, 1769. About the religious controversy, he was less tolerant: "But your Squabbles about a Bishop I wish to see speedily ended. They seem to be unnecessary at present, as the Design of sending one is dropt."

22. BF to JFM, September 20, 1768.

23. BF to JFM, April 27, 1769.

24. JFM to BF, November 7, 1768.

Chapter XXIV   The Philosophy of Soap

1. She had also just been visited by a friend of her brother's, the stamp distributor John Hughes, who reported, in a letter to Deborah Franklin, that he was overcome with feeling upon making Jane's acquaintance: "It was not in my power to Refrain taking the Sister of my Good friend in my Arms & Saluting her." (He thought he might have offended her but confessed that, "was I to meet with another Sister of Dr. Franklin," he would kiss her as well.) John Hughes to DRF, Philadelphia, September 19, 1769.

2. JFM to DRF, September 14, 1769.

3. WF to BF, ca. January 2, 1769. Jane reported her son's visit differently: "My son John & wife are Hear & send there Duty," she wrote to Franklin on November 7, 1768.

4. Mecom had printed his *Connecticut Gazette* until February 1768; then it had folded, and he and his wife moved to Philadelphia. Jane had, as always, reason to be worried about him. "I muste tell thee our Nevfew B Mecom has bin hear 5 or 6 dayes he went a way yesterday," DRF wrote to her husband in January 1768. "I did not know his buisnes but he semed verey hapey and semed to think he had verey graite prospecktes before him." DRF to BF, Philadelphia, January 21–22, 1768.

5. DRF to BF, Philadelphia, May 20–23, 1768.

6. BF to DRF, London, December 21, 1768–January 26, 1769.

7. WF to BF, [ca. January 2, 1769]. In the same letter, William proposed that his

374 · NOTES TO PAGES 154–155

father, when he returned to America, might bring with him William's bastard son, Temple: "He might then take his proper Name, and be introduc'd as the Son of a poor Relation, for whom I stood God Father and intended to bring up as my own."

8. Ibid.

9. Franklin would later refuse to help another nephew, Josiah Davenport, who wanted Franklin to appoint him to the post office in Philadelphia, telling him, "I have been hurt too much by endeavouring to help Cousin Ben Mecom." BF to Josiah Davenport, London, February 14, 1773. BF continued: "I have no Opinion of the Punctuality of Cousins. They are apt to take Liberties with Relations they would not take with others, from a Confidence that a Relation will not sue them . . . Don't take this unkind."

10. Benjamin Mecom, notice of collection of debt, *Connecticut Journal*, August 18, 1769.

11. The auction is recounted in several letters from James Parker to BF, New York, February 2, February 20, April 23[–24], and May 10, 1770. In the May 10 letter, Parker reported, "The Amount of the Whole of the Sales of B. Mecom's Books came to £175 this Money."

12. I am uncertain when DRF traveled to Boston, but in 1766 Jane wrote to Deborah, speaking of a cousin, "I Remember *she was hear when you were,* & so was cousen Kezia Coffin, she has been in town this fall & Desiered me to Remember Her to you when I wrot." JFM to DRF, November 24, 1766. Emphasis mine.

13. JFM to DRF, September 14, 1769.

14. Jane met Sarah Franklin Bache and Richard Bache on August 14, 1768, when the two visited Boston and ate a meal with Jane in her home. See editorial comment, Van Doren, *Letters*, 106. Jane wrote Deborah on September 26 expressing her high opinion of Richard Bache, and Deborah forwarded that letter to Franklin. On February 23, 1769, Franklin wrote Jane, "I am glad you approve the Choice they have made." BF to JFM, February 23, 1769.

15. BF to JFM, February 23, 1769.

16. Jane wrote Deborah in the summer after she returned to Boston, "Your King Bird I Long to see I have watched Every child to find some Resemblanc but have seen but won & that was only in Good Natuer & Sweet Smell." JFM to DRF, [August?] 1770. BF to JFM, January 13, 1772: "All who have seen my Grandson, agree with you in their Accounts of his being an uncommonly fine Boy." King Bird reminded Franklin of the son he'd lost. Accounts of Benjamin Franklin Bache, says Franklin, "often afresh to my Mind the Idea of my Son Franky, tho' now dead 36 Years."

17. DRF to BF, Philadelphia, December 13, 1769.

18. BF to JFM, March 15, 1770.

19. BF to JFM, November 7–9, 1770.

20. "I am very happy that a good Understanding continues between you and the Philadelphia Folks," Franklin wrote to her. "Our Father, who was a very wise man, us'd to say, nothing was more common than for those who lov'd one another at a distance, to find many Causes of Dislike when they came together; and therefore he did not approve of Visits to Relations in distant Places, which could not well be short enough for them to part good Friends." BF to JFM, July 17, 1771.

21. JFM to DRF, [August?] 1770.

22. The date of John Mecom's death is recorded in a notice placed by his widow, Catherine Oakey Mecom, concerning the claims of creditors on his estate: "This is to give Notice to the Creditors of John Mecom," advertisement, *New-York Gazette*, October 8, 1770.
23. JFM to DRF, [August?] 1770.
24. *A Short Narrative of the horrid Massacre in Boston* (Boston: Edes and Gill, 1770).
25. JFM to DRF, [August?] 1770.
26. BF to JFM, November 7, 1770.
27. JFM to BF, September 22, 1770.
28. Jonathan Williams Sr. to BF, Boston, August 27, 1770. Jane wrote Deborah from Boston in August 1770 (or thereabouts), apologizing for not yet having responded to Deborah's letter of June 25 and explaining that she "was in a Hurry a mooving" and "Did not take the . . . to Ansur yr Leter as I ought to have Done." It is unclear what she meant by "mooving," unless she meant that she was moving back into her house after her time away in Philadelphia. It is possible, though, that she moved into another house. It is, however, certain that Jane did not at this point move into the Douse house in the North End, because Williams was still using the rent on that house to pay for Jane's support and, when he could not get the rent, simply advancing Jane the cash, without telling her that no rent was coming in. "I hope you have before this time got another Tenant for the House, and at the former Rent," Franklin wrote to Williams in his letter of March 5, 1771. "However, I would have you go on advancing to my Sister the Amount of it; as I am persuaded she cannot well do without it. She has indeed been very unfortunate in her Children." On Jonathan Williams Jr. as BF's clerk in London, see BF to Jonathan Williams Sr., London, March 5, 1771. Jane played a role in coaxing Franklin to take on Josiah and Jonathan Williams Jr. in London. See BF to JFM, July 17, 1771: "I have never seen any young Men from America that acquir'd by their Behaviour here more general Esteem than those you recommended to me."
29. JFM to DRF, [before August 1770?]. She asked, too, if Deborah could send along "a Pare of Buter Boats of chineis" Deborah had wanted to give to her as a gift: "I should be very fond of them." JFM to DRF, September 2, 1771.
30. JFM to DRF, [before August 1770?].
31. JFM to DRF, [August?] 1770. Jane was certainly back in Boston by August. "Aunt Mecom is well settled," Jonathan Williams Sr. reported to Franklin on August 27, 1770. And she was probably back in Boston by June. She wrote Deborah from Boston in August 1770 or thereabouts, "I Recved your kind Leter of June 25 some time ago . . ."
32. BF to JFM, July 17, 1771. For the chart, see *PBF*, 18:187.
33. Franklin lost the recipe she sent him sometime before January 13, 1772. He told her exactly this in a letter on October 27, 1785, and asked her to resend it. She sent it again on January 6, 1786. In the same October letter, Franklin asked more of Jane: to make "a Parcel for me of 40 or 50 pounds weight, which I want for Presents to Friends in France who very much admir'd it." And he was specific about what he wanted: "I wish it to be of the greenish Sort that is close and solid and hard like the Specimen I send; and not that which is white and curdled and crumbly."
34. JFM to BF, May 29, 1786.

35. BF to JFM, January 13, 1772.

36. BF, *Autobiography,* 1.

Chapter XXV   On Smuggling

1. Abigail Adams to Mary Smith Cranch, July 6, 1794, in *Adams Family Correspondence,* ed. L. H. Butterfield (Cambridge, MA: Harvard University Press, 1963), 5:376.

2. An account of the fire can be found in the *New-York Journal,* June 6, 1771.

3. *Essex Gazette,* September 10, 1771.

4. In January 1772, Wright was back in New York, about to sail for London; a newspaper reported that among the passengers on the packet called the *Mercury* "is the ingenious Mrs. Wright, whose Skill in taking Likenesses, expressing the Passions, and many curious Devices in Wax-Work, has deservedly recommended her to public Notice, especially among Persons of Distinction, from many of whom we hear she carries Letters to their Friends in England." She would make her way in London by delivering letters to friends of Americans of distinction. *New-York Journal,* January 30, 1772.

5. BF to JFM, March 30, 1772. For more on Wright, see Charles Coleman Sellers, *Patience Wright: American Artist and Spy in George III's London* (Middletown, CT: Wesleyan University Press, 1976), and Wendy Bellion, "Patience Wright's Transatlantic Bodies," in *Shaping the Body Politic: Art and Political Formation in Early America,* ed. Maurie D. McInnis and Louis P. Nelson (Charlottesville: University of Virginia Press, 2011), 15–46.

6. BF to JFM, April 13, 1772.

7. *Massachusetts Gazette,* November 12, 1772. She sent her wax sculpture of Franklin to Philadelphia, a gift to the APS. *Boston News-Letter,* February 25, 1773. See also Sellers, *Benjamin Franklin in Portraiture,* 84–95, 426–29. Sellers demonstrates that Wright made at least four wax figures of Franklin: a life-size bust (1772), a complete figure whose bust is a replica of the 1772 bust (1772), an undated replica of the 1772 bust, and a head (1781). None of these waxworks survive.

8. Samuel Cooper to BF, Boston, January 1, 1771.

9. On the Brattle Street Church's move, see Akers, *Divine Politician,* 128.

10. BF to Samuel Cooper, London, February 5, 1771.

11. Samuel Cooper to BF, Boston, July 10, 1771.

12. The books were carried by Jonathan Williams Jr.'s brother, Josiah, who had stayed with Franklin in London but had grown sick. "I received per him only three 2d Volumes of Doctr. Priestly Work, when the Setts Arive compleat, I will sell them for the most I can, and pay the whole Money to Aunt Mecom, who is very well, but I believe will not have Time to write by this Oppertunity." Jonathan Williams Jr. to BF, Boston, May 29, 1772. It seems that Jonathan Williams Jr. was back in Boston by September 1771. See BF to Jonathan Williams Jr., London, January 13, 1772.

13. Jonathan Williams Jr. wrote to BF, in the letter confirming receipt of the books, "I have but just Time to acknowledge the Receipt of yours per my Brother, whose Arival we had been long wishing for, but our pleasure was greatly damped by seeing him in such a state of Health; he has not been out since he first entered the House

and is at present very low, we are all fearfull he is consuming fast." Jonathan Williams Jr. to BF, Boston, May 29, 1772.

14. "My Sister, to whom I have not now time to write, acquainted me in her last Letter, that there was some Expectation her Daughter would soon be married with her Consent," Franklin wrote Williams. "If that should take Place, my Request is, that you would lay out the Sum of fifty Pounds, lawful Money, in Bedding or such other Furniture as my Sister shall think proper, to be given the new-married Couple towards Housekeeping, with my best Wishes: And charge that Sum to my Account." BF to Jonathan Williams Sr., London, November 3, 1772.

15. Jonathan Williams Jr. to BF, Boston, October 13, 1772.

16. Jonathan Williams Sr. to BF, Boston, August 27, 1770.

17. BF to Thomas Cushing, London, December 2, 1772.

18. Cushing confirmed receipt of the letters in a letter to BF from Boston on March 24, 1773.

19. Francis S. Drake, *Tea Leaves: Being a Collection of Letters and Documents* (Boston: A. O. Crane, 1884), ix.

20. BF to Thomas Cushing, London, March 9, 1773.

21. BF to JFM, March 9, 1773, and see also editorial comment, Van Doren, *Letters,* 138. Hall owed Franklin £152 1s. 6d., or £202 15s. 4d. "lawful money."

22. BF to JFM, July 7, 1773. See also Jonathan Williams Sr. to BF, Boston, February 15, 1773.

23. BF to JFM, November 1, 1773.

24. Bailyn, *Ordeal of Thomas Hutchinson,* 236–40.

25. She also seems to have been unwell that year. "I Saw your Sizter Mecom a few Days ago who was better than She had been Some time." Samuel Franklin Jr. to BF, Boston, December 17, 1773. In this same letter, Samuel Franklin Jr. reports on the dumping of the tea into the harbor, concluding, "Such Sir is the Zeal of the Body of this people against Tea that Comes with a Duty." Samuel Franklin Jr. was the grandson of Benjamin Franklin the Elder. He was a cutler in Boston. For genealogy, see *PBF,* 1:lii.

26. BF to Jonathan Williams Sr., London, July 7, 1773. The Williams family had more ties to the Wheatleys. Williams had had a falling-out with John and Susannah Wheatley, who owned Phillis. "The Black Poetess master and mistress prevaild on me to mention her in my Letter but as its turnd out I am Sorry I Did," Williams wrote Franklin. (Jonathan Williams Sr. to BF, Boston, October 17, 1773.)

27. Here, Franklin echoed a poem their grandfather had written from his hog shed of a prison on Nantucket, more than a hundred years before. Franklin, in recounting the first part of the story of his life, said he'd been able to recall only the last six lines of Peter Folger's "Looking-Glass for the Times." (See BF, *Autobiography,* 5.) Maybe Jane had since sent him a copy, because in this letter from 1773—in which he described his own looking glass—he echoed other verses: "Tis true, there are some times indeed / of Silence to the Meek." But, sometimes, "There is a time to speak."

28. BF to JFM, November 1, 1773.

29. "I Bilive She in futer Will Supply herself with every sort of Good from our Desprate

378 · NOTES TO PAGES 164–169

Merchants on better Terms then Can be Imported from England," Williams told
Franklin. Jonathan Williams Sr. to BF, Boston, October 17, 1773.

30. The dumping of the tea wasn't referred to as a "tea party" until the 1830s. See Alfred F.
Young, *The Shoemaker and the Tea Party: Memory and the American Revolution*
(Boston: Beacon, 1999).

31. BF, "To the Massachusets House of Representatives," July 7, 1773, *PBF,* 20:282.

32. BF to JFM, February 17, 1774.

33. John Morgan to Isaac Jamieux, November 24, 1773, in *Letters and Papers of John
Singleton Copley and Henry Pelham, 1739–1776* (Boston: Massachusetts Historical
Society, 1914), 210.

34. BF to JFM, July 28, 1774.

35. BF to JFM, September 26, 1774.

36. Jane Mecom married Peter Collas on March 23, 1773, at the Brattle Street Church.
Manifesto Church, 254.

37. JFM to BF, November 3–21, 1774. JFM to BF, December 5–15, 1774.

38. *Works of Adams,* 2:367.

39. JFM to BF, November 3–21, 1774.

40. Wright's espionage is detailed in Sellers, *Patience Wright,* chapter 6. See also Rachel
Wells to BF, December 16, 1785, in which Wells, Wright's sister, writes, "It has bin
often Asked me and others of our older members if aney thing has bin don for Mrs.
Wright Mr. Pain has bin Considrd why not Mrs. Wright. Mr. Hancock and others
of our oldest members allways alowe that her intiligence was the best we Recivd
them by the hand of her sister Wells who found them in the wax heads She then
Sent to her."

Chapter XXVI   Exodus

1. "Doctor George Weed," advertisement, *Pennsylvania Packet,* August 1, 1774. Weed
was the apothecary of the Pennsylvania Hospital. He ran an apothecary shop in
Philadelphia. His advertisement contains this postscript: "N.B. He hath to sell,
at the same place, fine Crown Soap, for the washing of fine linens, muslins, laces,
silks, shirts, calicoes, and for the use of Barbers. The above Soap made and also
sold by Benjamin Mecom, of Burlington, in West New Jersey.—Some that have
made use of the above Soap, think it is the best they ever made use of for washing
or shaving."

2. JFM to BF, November 3–21, 1774.

3. BF to WF, London, September 7, 1774.

4. On Richard Bache sending the express to Amboy, see Richard Bache to BF, Philadelphia, December 24, 1774. William Franklin to BF, Philadelphia, December 24,
1774.

5. WF to BF, Philadelphia, December 24, 1774.

6. WF, address to the New Jersey General Assembly, January 13, 1775, in *Votes and
Proceedings of the General Assembly of the Colony of New Jersey* (Burlington, 1775),
5–7.

7. BF to WF, on board the Pennsylvania Packet bound to Philadelphia, March 22,
1775.

8. Patience Wright to John Dickinson, London, April 6, 1775, in Sellers, *Patience Wright*, 81–82.

9. Fischer, *Paul Revere's Ride*, 76–77.

10. Samuel Lane Boardman, ed., *Peter Edes: A Biography, with His Diary* (Bangor, 1901), 8. Silver, "Benjamin Edes," 262.

11. Gross, *Minutemen and Their World*, chapter 5.

12. JFM to BF, May 14, 1775.

13. Andrew Eliot to Thomas Hollis, April 25, 1775; Andrew Eliot to John Eliot, May 4, 1775, *Proceedings of the Massachusetts Historical Society* 16 (1878): 281–82.

14. Jonathan Williams Sr. to BF, Worcester, June 19, 1775.

15. Henry Pelham to John Singleton, May 16, 1775, in *Letters of Copley and Pelham*, 318. Boardman, *Peter Edes*, 99.

16. JFM to BF, May 14, 1775, and July 14, 1775.

17. As CRG explained to BF, JFM was a mother "whose Heart is So Divided between So good a Brother and a Distrest Daughter." But, as usual, she "keeps all to her Self." CRG to BF, Warwick, October 1, 1776.

18. JFM to BF, May 14, 1775, and July 14, 1775.

19. Ibid.

20. JFM to BF, July 14, 1775.

PART FOUR · HISTORY, 1775–1793

Chapter XXVII   Saif Back

1. BF to WF: "Journal of Negotiations in London," on board the Pennsylvania Packet bound to Philadelphia, March 22, 1775, *PBF*, 21:540–99.

2. JFM to BF, July 14, 1775; CRG to JFM, March 12, 1776; JFM to CRG, November 24, 1775.

3. Roelker, *BF and CRG*, 49.

4. JFM to BF, May 14, 1775; CRG to BF, May 14, 1775.

5. For the letter, see BF to JFM, May 26, 1775; on Jane finally receiving it, see JFM to BF, July 14, 1775. A letter Franklin had mailed to Jane from London on February 20 ended up being returned to him in Philadelphia after stopping at New England. "Let me know however if I can render you any Service; and in what way. You know it will give me Pleasure. I hear the Cousin Williams is at last got out with his Family: I shall be glad to hear from them, and would write if I knew where they were. I receiv'd the other Day here, a Letter I wrote to you from London the 20th of February. It has been to New England, and I suppose your being not found there, occasion'd its being forwarded to me." BF to JFM, June 17, 1775.

6. BF to JFM, May 26, 1775.

7. Ibid.

8. JFM to BF, July 14, 1775.

9. BF to JFM, May 26, 1775.

10. Benjamin H. Irvin, "Benjamin Franklin's '*Enriching Virtues*,'" *Common-place* 6 (April 2006), and Benjamin H. Irvin, *Clothed in Robes of Sovereignty: The Conti-*

nental Congress and the People Out of Doors (New York: Oxford University Press, 2011).

11. BF to JFM, June 17, 1775.

12. BF to CRG, Philadelphia, June 17, 1775.

13. National Archives, Microfilm Publication M804, Revolutionary War Pension and Bounty-Land-Warrant Application Files, Simeon Furbush, Pension W17895. Mass. Arch., Muster Rolls of the Revolutionary War (SC1/Series 57X), vol. 35, p. 44, Captain Charles Furbush's Company, receipt for advance pay, Cambridge, June 30, 1775, "Rec.d of Colo. Asa Whetcomb Pay Master for the Army at Cambridge by the hand of Capt. Furbush our months advanec pay as ordred [*sic*] by Congress" vol. 14, p. 95.

14. Jane received the news of Josiah's death in Philadelphia. She told Caty, "I have heard of the Death of Poor Josiah since I came hear but by what means I am not Informed. God grant I may make a proper Use of all His Dealings with me." JFM to CRG, Philadelphia, November 24, 1775.

15. Josiah Mecom died sometime between August and November 1775. On October 29, 1775, a search for him seems to have been under way. On that day, Colonial William Henshaw, who commanded a regiment of minutemen, wrote in his orderly book from Cambridge: "Josiah Mecom Soldier in this Army but in what Regiment or Company is not known may hear of some thing much to his Advantage by applying in Person to the Adjutant General at Head Quarters." "The Orderly Books of Colonial William Henshaw," *Proceedings of the American Antiquarian Society* 57 (1947): 38. By November 21, 1775, he was not listed on a muster for his company: Mass. Arch., Muster Rolls of the Revolutionary War (SC1/Series 57X), vol. 56, file 19, p. 27, Return of men in Captain Charles Furbush's Company for bounty coats or equivalent in money, Cambridge, November 21, 1775.

16. Howard Peckham, *The Toll of Independence: Engagements and Battle Casualties of the American Revolution* (Chicago: University of Chicago Press, 1975).

17. JFM to CRG, November 24, 1775.

18. Ibid.

19. Jonathan Williams Sr. to BF, Worcester, June 19, 1775. In August, Jane and Caty went to Worcester to visit the Williamses and other refugees. Roelker, *BF and CRG,* 57.

20. JFM to BF, July 14, 1775.

21. CRG to BF, July 14, 1775.

22. Stewart, "Intercourse," 164.

23. BF to JFM, August 2, 1775.

24. BF to JFM, October 16, 1775.

25. JFM to CRG, November 24, 1775.

26. Skemp, *William Temple,* 186–89.

Chapter XXVIII A Survey of Ages

1. Thomas Paine, *The Complete Writings of Thomas Paine,* ed. Philip Foner (New York: Citadel, 1945), 1:3, 17.

2. John Adams, *Papers of John Adams,* ed. Robert J. Taylor (Cambridge, MA: Harvard University Press, 1977), 4:37, 41, 53, 29.

3. Nelson, *Thomas Paine,* 49.

4. Thomas Paine, "An Occasional Letter on the Female Sex," in *The Writings of Thomas Paine*, ed. Moncure David Conway (New York: G. P. Putnam's Sons, 1894), 1:59–64 (quote on p. 59), and in Foner, *The Complete Writings of Thomas Paine*, 2:34, 36.

5. Thomas Paine, *"Common Sense,"* in Conway, *The Writings of Paine*, 1:84, 92, 85, and Foner, *The Complete Writings of Thomas Paine*, 1:17, 24, 18.

6. Thomas Paine, "To the Public on Mr. Deane's Affair," in Foner, *The Complete Writings of Thomas Paine*, 2:111.

7. Van Doren, *Jane Mecom*, 128.

8. JFM to CRG, May 8, 1776.

9. Abigail Adams to John Adams, March 31, 1776, *Familiar Letters of John Adams and His Wife Abigail Adams, During the Revolution* (Boston: Houghton, Mifflin, 1875), 149–50.

10. John Adams to Abigail Adams, April 14, 1776, *Familiar Letters*, 155.

11. Pauline Maier, *American Scripture: Making the Declaration of Independence* (New York: Knopf, 1997), 100–103.

12. Ibid., 136.

13. John Lawrence and William Smith to BF, Burlington, NJ, July 19, 1776.

14. BF, *Some Account of the Pennsylvania Hospital* (Philadelphia: B. Franklin and D. Hall, 1754), 5. See also *PBF*, 5:283–330 (range), 287 (quote). On the early history of the hospital, see William H. Williams, *America's First Hospital: The Pennsylvania Hospital, 1751–1841* (Wayne, PA: Haverford House, 1976); on the crisis during the war, see chapter 4. On the rising numbers of lunatics, see pp. 81–82. See also Michael Meranze, *Laboratories of Virtue: Punishment, Revolution, and Authority in Philadelphia, 1760–1835* (Chapel Hill: University of North Carolina Press, 1996).

15. Van Doren, *Jane Mecom*, 130.

16. Jane remained in touch with her nephew's wife, Elizabeth. See, e.g., Elizabeth Downes Franklin to WTF, in Philadelphia, July 16, 1776 ("Pray present my Duty to my Father, & Aunt Mecom"), Franklin Papers, Film 54–58 Frame 164, APS.

17. At one point, he was held in solitary confinement for 250 consecutive days. Skemp, *William Franklin*, 202–8; and on the orders to deny him pen and paper, while confined in Connecticut, see p. 221.

Chapter XXIX   A Vagrant

1. On Franklin in France, see, especially, Stacy Schiff, *A Great Improvisation: Franklin, France, and the Birth of America* (New York: Holt, 2005).

2. BF to JFM, November 4, 1787.

3. In August, she asked Temple Franklin to visit a friend of hers, to see if she knew what had become of Catherine Oakey Mecom, the widow of Jane's son John, who had married a British office named Turner. "If it is not too much Trouble," Temple reported to his grandfather, "let Aunt Mecome know, that according to her desire I waited on Mrs. Van Voredice, who being indisposed I had not the pleasure of seeing, but I saw her Son, who told me that last they heard of Mrs. Turner and her husband, was, that they were both in London and that he was to have a Commission in the Guards." JFM to Richard Bache, April 11, 1783.

4. WTF to BF, Philadelphia, August 17, 1776.

5. JFM to BF, December 15, 1776. *PBF* provides December 16 for this letter.

6. JFM to BF, February 14 [–27], 1779.

7. JFM to BF, August 15, 1778.

8. JFM to BF, August 18, 1777.

9. Skemp, *William Franklin,* chapter 12.

10. CRG to BF, Warwick, January 13, 1776.

11. JFM to BF, August 18, 1777. It is in this letter that she wrote, "I have had some children that seemed to be doing well till they were taken off by Death."

12. CRG to JFM, February 20, 1776.

13. CRG to JFM, March 12, 1776.

14. CRG to JFM, June 21, 1776.

15. CRG to JFM, June 21, 1776. Caty hinted at a marriage for Jenny Flagg in a letter to BF on July 3, 1776, from Warwick: "I dont know but think Jenny is like to get one of our best Matches you are So good a friend to Matrimony that you will be Glad to hear of it." Jane at some point during the war met Nathanael Greene; in 1778, she passed along her respects to him, in the only surviving letter from Elihu Greene to Nathanael Greene, Coventry, Rhode Island, April 12, 1778, in Richard K. Showman, ed., *The Papers of General Nathanael Greene* (Chapel Hill: University of North Carolina Press, 1980), 2:337. The editors of Nathanael Greene's papers speculate that he burned his correspondence with Elihu Greene, which contained "family secrets" (2:337n1).

16. Nathanael Greene to Elihu Greene, Prospect Hill, Massachusetts, January 28, 1776, in *Papers of General Nathanael Greene,* 1:187. This was at the beginning of Elihu Greene and Jenny Flagg's courtship.

17. BF to CRG, Paris, February 28, 1778.

18. JFM to BF, May 5, 1778.

19. JFM to Jane Mecom Collas, April 1778. (Note that this letter has been corrected and the original is missing.) According to Van Doren (*Letters,* 174), Elihu Greene and his brothers had a forge in Coventry, Rhode Island. Jane Mecom Collas had written JFM about Jenny Flagg Greene and Josiah Flagg, and JFM responded, "You mistook me about the word Genteel; what you wrote on that head was that Jenny ought to take her brother and put him in a way to get a genteel living. Now I thought it would be a hard injunction on him, her husband, who was obliged to do the meanest drudgery himself, by reason help is not to be had."

20. JFM to BF, May 5, 1778.

21. JFM to Jane Mecom Collas, May 16, 1778.

22. JFM to Sarah Franklin Bache, [October 1780].

23. JFM to BF, August 15, 1778.

24. Ibid.

25. Jane was either present at his deathbed or received an account of his passing from someone who was. She wrote BF in the February 14[–27], 1779, letter, "His mouth was opened Just before His Death to comit himself to the mercy of God & wish a blesing on those about him & sunk in to Eternity without a Groan." See also Jonathan Williams Sr. to BF, Boston, July 29, 1779.

26. Jonathan Williams Sr. to BF, Boston, August 8, 1779.

27. BF to Jonathan Williams Sr., Passy, October 25, 1779.

28. JFM to BF, February 14, 1779.
29. Ibid.
30. Jonathan Williams Sr. to BF, Boston, July 29, 1779.
31. BF to JFM, October 5, 1777.
32. BF to JFM, October 25, 1779.

Chapter XXX   Publick Affairs

1. BF entertained this idea in 1778: "I have after a long year recved yr kind leter of nov 26—1778 wherin you like yr self do all for me that the most Affectionat Brother can be desiered or Expected to do, & tho I feel my self full of gratitude for yr Generousity, the conclution of yr leter Affectes me more; where you say you wish we may spend our last days together." Years later, when Jane wrote something about the two living together, BF responded, "Your Project of taking a House for us to spend the Remainder of our Days in, is a pleasing one; but it is a Project of the Heart rather than of the Head. You forget, as I sometimes do, that we are grown old, and that before we can have furnish'd our House, and put things in order, we shall probably be call'd away from it, to a Home more lasting, and I hope more agreeable than any this World can afford us." BF to JFM, September 13, 1783.
2. JFM to BF, July 27, 1779. See also JFM to Richard Bache, July 21, 1779. This letter was auctioned in 1892: S. V. Henkels, *Revolutionary Manuscripts and Portrait . . . To be sold April 5th and 6th, 1892* (Philadelphia, 1892), 61, item 468. Jane's spirits at Warwick seem often to have been very high. A friend reported to Franklin after a visit to Warwick, "I had the pleasure of seeing, your Sister Mrs Mecom, in perfect health, gay as the Young Ladies, with whom she was incircled" (William Vernon Sr. to BF, Boston, April 3, 1779).
3. JFM to BF, June 13, 1781.
4. JFM to BF, June 23, 1779.
5. BF to JFM, October 25, 1779.
6. JFM to BF, March 27, 1780 (her sixty-eighth birthday).
7. BF to JFM, October 25, 1779. JFM to BF, March 27, 1780. Franklin sent Jane a series of likenesses. "Supposing it may be agreeable to you, I send you a Head they make here and sell at the China Shops," he, at that time in London, wrote to her in 1775 (BF to JFM, February 26, 1775). A Wedgwood medallion of Franklin's head in profile was made in London that year, and the one Franklin sent Jane is supposed to have been one of those. See Sellers, *Benjamin Franklin in Portraiture,* 74, as well as the illustration on p. 11 of the plates. A Wedgwood medallion from this year is among the collections of the Fogg Museum at Harvard (Harvard Art Museums/Fogg Museum, bequest of Grenville L. Winthrop, 1943.1217).
8. BF to JFM, October 25, 1779.
9. Jonathan Williams Sr. to BF, Boston, July 14, 1780.
10. Peter Collas to BF, Boston, October 12, 1779. She decided to try to teach Peter Collas the art of making soap but found that he had no talent for it.
11. On sending soap by way of Collas, see JFM to BF, September 12, 1779. On sending soap by way of John Adams, see JFM to BF, March 27, 1780.
12. Sending subpar soap, she asked BF not to distribute it to his friends but to wait for a batch that met her exacting standards. See JFM to BF, September 12, 1779.

13. JFM to BF, September 12, 1779.

14. JFM to BF, June 25, 1782.

15. JFM to BF, June 13, 1781.

16. JFM to BF, January 4, 1779.

17. JFM to BF, July 27, 1779.

18. See JFM to BF, June 13, 1781: "It is a year the 16th of last march since the last I receved from you was Dated & that was about Eight months coming to hand."

19. JFM to BF, January 4, 1779.

20. E.g., see BF to JFM, October 5, 1777: "I suppose some of your kind Letters to me have miscarried."

21. BF to JFM, April 22, 1779.

22. JFM to BF, January 4, 1779.

23. CRG to BF, Warwick, September 19, 1779.

24. CRG to BF, Warwick, December 28, 1780.

25. JFM to Sarah Franklin Bache, [October 1780].

26. JFM to BF, December 29, 1780. *PBF* gives December 24.

27. JFM to BF, March 3, 1781.

28. JFM to BF, January 4, 1779.

29. JFM to Sarah Franklin Bache, [October 1780].

30. Jonathan Williams Jr., in Nantes, to WTF, in Passy, April 10, 1781, Hays Calendar IV, 53, APS. Two weeks later, Williams wrote again (this time in French): "Les affairs pour madame Mecom sont achetés & soisant mises abord l'actif demain." Jonathan Williams Jr., in Nantes, to WTF, in Passy, April 23, 1781, Hays Calendar IV, 54, APS.

31. CRG to BF, Warwick, June 24, 1781.

32. CRG to BF, Warwick, October 7, 1781: "Yr good Sister has been Very unhappy in not Receiving a line from you in So long a time but She is now gone to Boston to get a little Comfort for She thinks Mr Willms has heard from you." On Caty's perturbation at the infrequent letters from BF, see the same letter: "Will you believe I grow Very Jealous of you. I fear the french Ladies have taken you intirely from us for we dont have a Single line from you this long Very long time."

33. JFM to BF, October 23, 1781.

34. "List of Letters remaining in the Post-Office," *Independent Ledger,* October 22, 1781.

35. Jonathan Williams Jr., in Nantes, to WTF, in Passy, March 2, 1782, Hays Calendar IV, 75, APS.

36. "Aunt Mecom has been Some Time in Boston, on a Vissett to her Friends, I hear She is well, but have not had the pleasure of seeing her yet (as I have just Returned home, from a long Tour, that I took for my Health, which is much mended by it,) but I Expect to enjoy that Happiness to Morrow, and it will be a sweet Regail, for I Reaely Love her, for her one [own] Sake, as Well as Yours." Elizabeth Partridge to BF, Boston, October 28, 1781. Elizabeth Hubbart Partridge was Franklin's stepniece—that is, the stepdaughter of Franklin's brother John. Jane did visit Partridge, who described the visit in her next letter to Franklin: "I wrote you in my last that I Expected to see Aunt Mecom, I have had that Happiness, she was Well, and happy in hearing from you and Receiving such Generous proofs of your affec-

tion; She had not heard from you so long, that it gave her great Pain, She left us last Week to Return to her Grand Daughter, with whome, & the dear Babes, she is very happy." Elizabeth Hubbart Partridge to BF, Boston, December 6, 1781.

37. JFM to BF, October 29, 1781.

Chapter XXXI   Sweat Peace

1. CRG to BF, Warwick, May 8, 1782. JFM to BF, June 17, 1782. See also Nathanael Greene to CRG, South Carolina near Charlestown, December 5, 1782, in *Papers of General Nathanael Greene*, 12:265.

2. "She left 3 Children the yonget a bout 8 or 10 weeks old at Nurs the name Jane the other 2 fine Children at home Sally and Franklin," Caty told Franklin, when Jenny Flagg Greene died. "Poor Girl we all lovd and lament her." CRG to BF, Warwick, May 8, 1782.

3. JFM to BF, June 17, 1782. The grief this reduced Jane to is hinted at in a letter from Jonathan Williams Sr. to BF, Boston, June 11, 1782: "Aunt Mecom paid us a Visit in the Spring & was so fourtunate as to receive your present wilest she was here & indeed apear'd as happy as I ever new her, but by a Late Letter from her I find she is sadly afflicted with the Death of her most Amiable G—Daughter Mrs Green."

4. CRG to BF, Warwick, May 8, 1782.

5. JFM to BF, June 25, 1782.

6. JFM to BF, December 26, 1782.

7. Ibid.

8. Jacob Greene to Nathanael Greene, Coventry, Rhode Island, May 4, 1783, *Papers of General Nathanael Greene*, 12:643 and 644n.

9. JFM to BF, April 29, 1783. In the same letter she confessed that at other times she concluded that "it was Reasonable to Expect it & that you might with grate propriy After my Teazing you so often send me the Ansure that Nehemiah did to Tobias, & Sanbalet, who Endevered to obstruct His Rebuilding The Temple of Jerusalem, I am doing a grate work; why should the work ceace whilest I Leave it & come *Down* to you."

10. BF to JFM, September 13, 1783: "I shall by this Opportunity order some more Money into the Hands of Cousin Williams, to be dispos'd of in assisting you as you may have Occasion."

11. JFM to BF, April 29, 1783. Jane was self-deprecating: "How many Hours have I Laid a wake on nights thinking what Excruciating Pains you might then be Incountering while I a Poor Useles, and wrothless worm was Premitted to be at Ease." JFM to BF, July 4, 1784.

12. JFM to BF, April 29, 1783. And then in a P.S., concerning Temple, Franklin's amanuensis, and the Treaty of Paris: "My Love to W T F whose Hand writing in your Leter & His name in the Signing the Trety as a Secretary gives me Pleasure."

13. Skemp, *William Franklin*, 268.

14. BF to WF, Passy, August 16, 1784. See also Mary Beth Norton, *The British-Americans: The Loyalist Exiles in England, 1774–1789* (Boston: Little, Brown, 1972), 171–73, 186–87.

15. BF to WF, Passy, August 16, 1784.

16. Will and Codicil, July 17, 1788, *PBF,* unpublished.

Chapter XXXII   Dr. Franklin's Sister's House

1. What is now known as the Old North Church, or Christ Church, on Salem Street was built in 1722. Jane called Christ Church "north church." As Christ Church was (and remains) an Episcopalian church, Jane did not attend it. (See Van Doren's editorial comment, *Letters,* 323.) She did, however, live close enough to the church that parishioners could have seen her garden out its windows, and on a warm day she would have heard their psalm singing through hers. Jane's house was so close to Christ Church that she asked BF to please "add to his Super scriptions of his Leters at the back of the north Church I might git them the Redier." JFM to BF, July 23, 1789. Confusingly, the church Jane very likely did attend, a Congregational church known as the Second Church, was also sometimes referred to as "Old North." The Second Church had been pulled down by the British during the siege. In 1779, the congregation of the Second Church combined with that of the New Brick Church and moved into the latter's building, on Hanover Street, with John Lathrop as its pastor. John Nicholson Booth, *The Story of the Second Church* (Boston, 1959). Jane became quite close to Lathrop, and also to his wife, Elizabeth. What she heard at the Second Church each week can be traced: a great many of Lathrop's sermons from these years survive. See John Lathrop Sermons, Box 5 (1776–88) and Box 6 (1789–94), MHS. Jane's name does not appear on his annual entries of newly admitted members, nor does it appear on a list of "Members of the Church," which he wrote down in 1786, but she would have had membership status in the church because of her baptism at Old South. John Lathrop, "Members of the Church," 1786, in Record Book, 1650–1808, Second Church Records, Box 1, vol. 8, MHS. It seems possible that Jane would have attended the funeral for her former pastor, Samuel Cooper, held on January 2, 1784, but she makes no note of it, and her name does not appear on a list of eminent mourners found in Samuel Cooper Papers, Folder 6, MHS. Cooper's death occasioned a poem by Phillis Wheatley (whose married name was Phillis Peters, and whose owners, before she was freed, were the parents of John Lathrop's first wife, Mary Wheatley). See Phillis Peters, *An Elegy Sacred to the Memory of that Great Divine, the Reverend and Learned Dr. Samuel Cooper* (Boston: E. Russell, 1784).

2. BF to JFM, June 17, 1784. Jane had visited Boston in the summer of 1780 and had checked in on the house, through Jonathan Williams Sr. She wrote to Franklin, "He continues to take care of the House & get what Rent from time to time that He thinks Reasonable, for my Part things runs so wild & I am so out of the world, I am no Judg of what is Right" (JFM to BF, December 29, 1780). By December 1783, Williams had cleared and cleaned the house, and Jane probably moved in right after the New Year: "I have Cleard your h[o]use agreeable to your Sisters desire, I expect Aunt with her Children to town Next week to take Possession and Live there Which I Conclude will be agreeable to you." Jonathan Williams Sr. to BF, Boston, December 29, 1783. Franklin bequeathed the house to Jane in his will, written in 1788: "I give and devise to my dear sister Jane Mecom a house and lot I have in Unity Street, Boston, now or late under the care of Mr. Jonathan Williams, to her and to her heirs and assigns for ever."

3. JFM to BF, August 16, 1784.

4. Ibid. Benjamin Mecom's disappearance at the Battle of Trenton had left his wife

and children without any means of support. In 1784, Elizabeth Ross Mecom was living with her friend Hannah Callendar Sansom, outside of Philadelphia; before the year was out, she left to go live with her own mother, in Rahway, New Jersey. Sansom, *Diary of Hannah Callender Sansom,* 280–92.

5. The house stood at 19 Unity Street; it was demolished in 1939. My description of the house comes from Jane's letters, from her estate inventory, from photographs taken while the house was still standing, and from floor plans and descriptions and visits to 21 Unity Street, an adjoining row house, now owned by Old North Church and known as the Clough-Langdon House. (Jane's house was a half house: nearly identical to but only half as wide as the Clough-Langdon House.) Although purchased by the same fund as the Franklin-Mecom House (at 19 Unity Street), the Clough-Langdon House was subsequently the subject of preservation efforts, probably because of regret at the demolishing of 19 Unity Street. See Frank Chouteau Brown, "The Clough-Langdon House, 21 Unity Street, Boston," *Old-Time New England* 37 (April 1947): 79–85. Floor plans made by the Society for the Preservation of New England Antiquities were prepared in 1943, by Frank Chouteau Brown. Old North Church, Clough-Langdon House, 1943–1959, Old North Church Records, Box 21, Folder 33, MHS. See also Abbott Lowell Cummings, "The Domestic Architecture of Boston, 1660–1725," *Archives of American Art Journal* 9 (1971): 13–16; Abbott Lowell Cummings, "The Beginnings of Provincial Renaissance Architecture in Boston, 1690–1725: Current Observations and Suggestions for Further Study," *Journal of the Society of Architectural Historians* 42 (1983): 52–53; and Jill Lepore, "The Jane Franklin House," unpublished ms., 2012.

6. The room-by-room inventory of JFM's house, taken at her death, is reprinted in Van Doren, *Letters,* 354–55.

7. Jane recalled these transactions in JFM to BF, January 8, 1788, in which she closed with a thought on "the shameles Impudence of the wretch" Peter Collas.

8. JFM to BF, October 21, 1784.

9. JFM to BF, July 21, 1786.

10. JFM to BF, July 4, 1784.

11. JFM to BF, October 21, 1784.

12. Ibid.

13. Silence Dogood, "No. 2," *New-England Courant,* April 16, 1722, in *PBF,* 1:11.

14. Benjamin Vaughan to BF, Paris, January 31, 1783.

15. Jonathan Williams Sr. to BF, Boston, June 12, 1785.

16. JFM to BF, October 21, 1784.

17. BF to Richard Price, Passy, March 18, 1785.

18. Price's Boston and Cambridge correspondents included John Lathrop, John Winthrop, Josiah Quincy Jr., Edward Wigglesworth, James Bowdoin, and Charles Chauncy. A selection appears in *Letters to and from Richard Price, 1767–1790* (Cambridge, MA: John Wilson and Son, University Press, 1903).

19. The books arrived early in 1786; they did not include any works written by Franklin. Town minister Reverend Nathanael Emmons wrote to Franklin in June 1786, thanking him for the books for the "Parish Library": "This choice and valuable Collection of Books, your Excellency will permit us to say, not only flatters our Understanding and Taste, but displays the brightest feature in your great and ami-

able Character. We only regret, that Modesty should deny us the celebrated Productions of the greatest Phylosopher and Politician in America." Nathanail Emmons and Hezekiah Fisher to BF, Franklin, MA, June 22, 1786. There followed a controversy, in the town, about "who should be allowed to read the books" ("Early Books of the Franklin Library," Finding Aid, Franklin Public Library, Franklin, MA). Emmons kept the books within his church's own collection, the parish library, not allowing anyone outside his church to read them. In 1788, five townspeople wrote to BF, requesting his aid. Between 1788 and 1790, the question of who should be allowed to read the books came up at town meetings on ten separate occasions. At a town meeting held on November 26, 1790 (that is, following Franklin's death), it was voted "That the Rev. Nathanael Emmons be directed to lend the Books presented to this town by the late Dr. Franklin to the Inhabitants of this town at large, and until the town shall order other ways, they being accountable to him for the use and improvement of said Books." (John A. Peters and Nina C. Santoro, *A History of America's First Public Library at Franklin, Massachusetts, 1790–1990* [Franklin, MA, 1990].) A few titles have since disappeared. In 1997, the volumes were cleaned and conserved by the Northeast Document Conservation Center, of Andover, Massachusetts. In 2000, a ten-foot-tall bronze statue of Benjamin Franklin reading an open book was erected in front of the library. Below, a plaque reads, "Genius without Education is like Silver in a mine" (one of Poor Richard's proverbs). But inside the library, the volumes Franklin gave to the town in 1786 are displayed behind glass, in a locked cabinet, and since 2000, it has been the library's policy that no one can open the books, for any reason, ever again. Felicia Oti, e-mail to the author, February 26, 2012. Oti is the director of the library.

20. JFM to BF, October 19, 1785. Jonathan Williams Jr. collected the list of books from Price. See Jonathan Williams Jr. to WTF, London, May 3, 1785, in *PBF,* and also as reproduced in Arthur Winslow Peirce, "The History of the Town of Franklin," in *The One Hundred and Fiftieth Anniversary of the Incorporation of the Town of Franklin, Massachusetts* (Franklin, MA, 1928).

21. JFM to BF, October 19, 1785.

22. BF responded on October 27, "You shall have a Copy of the Catalogue of Books as soon as I can find it; but you will see it sooner in the Hands of Cousin Williams, to whom the Books were consigned. Those you recommended of Dr. Stennet are among them." Jane wrote BF on November 30, "I received yours [a letter] by Cousen Jonathon Williams with the Catalogue for which I thank you."

23. *A Catalogue of Those Books in Franklin Library Which Belong to the Town* (n.p., 1812). And see Richard Price to BF, Newington-Green, June 3, 1785.

24. Van Doren, ed., *Letters,* 27.

25. JFM to BF, November 7, 1785. JFM is alluding here to Alexander Pope's *Essay on Man,* Epistle IV.

26. JFM to BF, January 8, 1788.

27. JFM to BF, May 29, 1786. There may not have been many knockers. While Franklin was at the Constitutional Convention, Captain Hugh Ledlie, who had boarded with Jane from 1742 to 1772, wrote him, wondering what had become of Jane. Despite various inquiries, he had not been able to find her. "I have never heard what became of her nor where She now lives, unto this day—notwithstanding all

the inquiry I have made by our Delegates to Congress vizt. Mr. Law, Mr. Dyer and Mr. Root, to each of whom I gave particular memorandums for that purpose. I also made enquiry of sundry Gentlemen from Boston, as well the Commissioners from Boston the winter past who were at this place to settle the line between that State and New York, but all to no purpose. I now in gratitude for the many past favors and acts of kindness formerly received from your Sister, when I lodged at her house, as above, embrace this opportunity by my particular good Friend Dr. Johnson, who is appointed and going to the Convention in your City, to beg the favour of your Excellency that you would be so kind as to favour me with a line and therein let me know what is become of your Sister and where She now lives, and if in good health, and also what is become of her family &c." Hugh Ledlie to BF, Hartford, May 22, 1787.

Chapter XXXIII Thirteen Stars

1. JFM to BF, October 1, 1785.
2. JFM to BF, January 6, 1786.
3. BF to JFM, January 24, 1786.
4. BF to JFM, September 21, 1786. For more on BF's renovation project, see BF to JFM, May 30, 1787.
5. JFM to BF, August 16, 1787.
6. BF to JFM, October 27, 1785.
7. JFM to BF, November 30, 1785.
8. BF to JFM, December 3, 1786. BF had written to Anthony Somersby Stickney's father, Anthony Stickney (Dorcas Davenport's husband), from Philadelphia on June 16, 1764, wishing him congratulations on the birth of "another Daughter."
9. JFM to BF, January 6, 1787. Sparks followed the Stickney story, too. See Anonymous to Captain Anthony Stickney, Newbury Port, Massachusetts, April 29, 1838, in Franklin, Mss. Papers, p. 106, Sparks Papers, MS Sparks 18.
10. JFM to BF, March 9, 1787.
11. BF to JFM, October 27, 1785.
12. BF to Jonathan Williams Jr., Philadelphia, February 16, 1786.
13. Jonathan Williams Jr. to BF, Boston, December 26, 1785.
14. JFM to BF, November 30, 1785; see also JFM to BF, December 29, 1785.

Chapter XXXIV The Petition of the Letter J

1. BF to JFM, January 1, 1786.
2. JFM to BF, January 6, 1786.
3. BF, "The Petition of the Letter Z," *PBF*, 28:517–21. Franklin did not publicly admit being the author of this essay, which is a rebuff to the South Carolinian Ralph Izard, who, as American commissioner to Tuscany, had known Franklin in France but, after returning to the United States in 1780, accused Franklin of malfeasance for trying to promote the interests of Jonathan Williams Jr. (Jane thought of Izard as an "Infamous Fellow," warning her brother, in 1780 from Rhode Island, that "Izeard was wery Laboreous at Newport to make People beleve you had done something criminal in mony maters" and had mentioned "that you had a Nephue there you wanted to Asist in makeing a Fortune.") Jane remarked on Izard in JFM to

Sarah Franklin Bache, October 1780, and detailed her knowledge of him in JFM to BF, December 29, 1780. *PBF* gives December 24.

4. BF to JFM, January 24, 1786. BF sent the book he promised on April 25. See BF to JFM, April 25, 1786.

5. BF to JFM, April 25, 1786.

6. BF, "A Scheme for a New Alphabet," in *Political, Miscellaneous, and Philosophical Pieces* (London, 1779), 467–79.

7. Franklin's scheme was recalled to his mind, early in 1786, when he attended a lecture in Philadelphia delivered by Noah Webster. Webster to BF, New York, May 24, 1786. The two men corresponded at some length in 1786.

8. JFM to BF, [between May and July 1786?].

9. JFM to BF, May 29, 1786.

10. BF to JFM, July 4, 1786.

11. JFM to BF, July 21, 1786.

12. Josiah Flagg to BF, Petersburg, Virginia, January 24, 1786, and February 18, 1786. Josiah Flagg's account in Jane Franklin Mecom, "Book of Ages."

13. E.g., "I cant say when I shall be in town but e're Long I hope." Josiah Flagg to Jane Mecom (that is, not Benjamin Franklin's sister but Benjamin Mecom's daughter), August 23, 1783.

14. Josiah Flagg to Jane Mecom, March 14, 1786.

15. Josiah Flagg to JFM, Philadelphia, April 17, 1786. Josiah Flagg to BF, Petersburg, January 24, 1786.

16. BF to Josiah Flagg, Philadelphia, February 9, 1786. And see Josiah Flagg's reply, Josiah Flagg to BF, Petersburg, February 18, 1786.

17. Jonathan Williams Jr. visited his grandaunt in February 1786 and reported to Franklin: "I thought it best to get my Information about Aunt Mecom from its proper source, and the affectionate Terms on which we are justifys my Frankness. She lives with great apparent Comfort and Neatness, and seems very happy and contented except when she feels a Dispair of seeing you again: If you once came together I am sure you would never part while living" (Jonathan Williams Jr. to BF, Boston, February 26, 1786). In April, Jane and Jonathan Williams Jr. inspected the soap they had made together during the winter, puzzling over its brittleness. "Aunt Mecom having spent the Day with us we have reconsidered the Cause of the Soaps appearing so brittle," Williams reported to Franklin on April 25, a letter in which he offered a full report on the process of making soap. On April 9, BF had written Jonathan Williams Jr. from Philadelphia, "As you are desirous of perfecting yourself in the Crown-soap-making Art, I give you the Opportunity of seeing by the enclos'd what has happened to that lately sent me, at the same time saving for my Sister a little Postage." When Franklin offered to pay Jane for the soap, she was hurt. "My Dear good Gentileman how could you mention my Drawing on you for the cost of a Litle Soap when all I Injoy is of yr Bounty," she wrote. "I could not help crying" (JFM to BF, April 22, 1786).

18. JFM to BF, February 21, 1786.

19. Josiah Flagg to JFM, August 18, 1786, Houghton Library, Harvard.

20. JFM to BF, May 3, 1786.

21. "I was Candid with him in telling of my indigent Circumstances," Flagg explained,

"but I never told him I spun out three Years under the patronage of St Crispin and I humbly beg you'd omit that in your Letter to him." Josiah Flagg to JFM, Philadelphia, April 17, 1786. JFM to BF, May 3, 1786.

22. And Jane sent Flagg an apology directly. Flagg was hurt and apparently wrote Jane a letter to this effect. Jane responded, "I have recd yr Long leter & read it many times & never without Tears, by which you may see that I am not without Affectionat feelings wards You . . . hope what I wrot to you has not been of any Reale Prejudice to you." JFM to Josiah Flagg, July 21, 1786.

23. JFM to BF, May 3, 1786. JFM to BF, [between May and June 1786]. Flagg used crutches from the age of five. Whether he was lame or whether he had had a leg amputated is unclear.

24. BF to JFM, June 3, 1786; JFM to BF, July 21, 1786.

25. BF to JFM, July 4, 1786. On the early celebration of the Fourth of July, see David Waldstreicher, *In the Midst of Perpetual Fetes: The Making of American Nationalism, 1776–1820* (Chapel Hill: University of North Carolina Press, 1997).

26. See John Lathrop to Richard Price, Boston, March 1786, in Richard Price Papers, APS. In the inventory of Lathrop's library, taken at his death, only "Price's Sermons" are listed. *Catalogue of rare, curious and valuable books, theological, classical, philosophical and literary [microform] to be sold by public auction at Francis Amory's auction room . . . February 22, 1816 being the library of the late reverend John Lathrop* (Boston, 1816), 3.

27. JFM to Josiah Flagg, July 21, 1786. I am fairly certain this is a misreading and that "first" must be "fourth."

28. Richard Price, *Four Dissertations on Providence*, 2nd ed., with additions (London, 1768), 5–6.

29. Price, *Four Dissertations*, 144, 145, 147, 150, 151.

30. Price knew of Jane's existence, from Franklin's earlier letter, and when Benjamin Rush wrote to Price to tell him of Franklin's death, he mentioned, in summarizing Franklin's will, "a legacy to his sister in Boston," but I can find no evidence of an exchange between them. Benjamin Rush to Richard Price, Philadelphia, April 24, 1790, in Richard Price, *Letters to and from Richard Price, 1767–1790* (Cambridge, 1903), 111.

31. On Price and slavery, see Richard Price, "Of the Negro Trade and Slavery" in *Observations on the Importance of the American Revolution* (London: Powars and Willis, 1784), 68–69. Jane also owned a book written by the British abolitionist Granville Sharp.

32. JFM to BF, July 21, 1786.

Chapter XXXV   Swords Beat into Plow-shares

1. BF to Whom It May Concern, September 4, 1786, NEHGS.

2. JFM to BF, October 12, 1786. She had written to BF on August 25, before Josiah left Philadelphia, "I will accept your thanks for the soap and thank you for recveing so kindly, it has not altogether Pleasd me yet. that Art I all ways meant to Instruct Josiah Flagg in when he shuld be in a Sittuation to Observe it, I have keept a Recipe by me for that Porpose, & now He is with you you will in some discorce with him some time if you think on it Inform him somthing about the Nature of the working

of such Ingredients togather which may help him more Easely to comprehend the Instructions he may after Recive, & it may be of some service to him some time or other."

3. BF to JFM, September 21, 1786.

4. Josiah Flagg to Jane Mecom (that is, Benjamin Mecom's daughter), Petersburg, March 14, 1786, NEHGS.

5. Josiah Flagg to BF, Boston, September 12, 1786.

6. JFM to BF, October 12, 1786.

7. "Fine Crown Soap," *New Jersey Journal,* August 29, 1787. This ad ran several times, in August and September of that year. She used, in her advertisement, almost the same language Benjamin Mecom had used when he sold the soap he described as "fine Crown Soap, for the washing of fine linens, muslins, laces, silks, shirts, calicoes, and for the use of Barbers." "Doctor George Weed," advertisement, *Pennsylvania Packet,* August 1, 1774.

8. "Fine Crown Soap," advertisement, *New York Packet,* August 11, 1789.

9. Communication between JFM and Elizabeth Ross Mecom seems to have been somehow strained. Jane sent Jenny's pocketbook, a gift for Elizabeth Ross Mecom, to Sarah Franklin Bache, writing, "My Dear Niece Will Excuse my giving her the care of the Inclosed it is no Easy mater to Convey even a leter to my Daughter or her children & Jenny has workd a Pockett book for her mother which she is desirous should go Saif your Sending them to my Grandaughter Smith will much oblige us." JFM to Sarah Franklin Bache, May 23, 1787. "My Grandaughter Smith" was another of Benjamin Mecom's daughters.

10. JFM to Sarah Franklin Bache, May 23, 1787.

11. JFM to BF, March 9, 1787.

12. JFM to BF, December 17, 1786; BF to JFM, November 4, 1787. And on BF providing JFM with wood for the winters, see JFM to BF, November 5, 1786, and BF to JFM, December 3, 1786 (a barrel of flour as well).

13. "By the President and the Supreme Executive Council of the Commonwealth of Pennsylvania, A Proclamation," March 10, 1787, *PBF,* unpublished.

14. JFM to BF, May 22, 1787; JFM to Sarah Franklin Bache, Boston, May 23, 1787.

15. Abigail Adams to John Adams, Braintree, March 31, 1776, in *Familiar Letters of John Adams and His Wife Abigail Adams,* 149–50.

16. JFM to BF, May 22, 1787.

17. BF to JFM, September 20, 1787.

18. James Madison, *The Debates in the Federal Convention of 1787, Which Framed the Constitution of the United States of America,* ed. Gaillard Hunt and James Brown Scott (New York: Oxford University Press, 1920), 577, 579, 578. And on the Constitution as an artifact, see Lepore, *The Story of America,* 72–90.

19. Madison's notes on the Constitutional Convention for September 17, 1787, in *The Debates in the Federal Convention of 1787,* p. 583.

20. BF to JFM, September 20, 1787.

21. Akhil Reed Amar, *America's Constitution: A Biography* (New York: Random House, 2005), 8.

22. James Madison, "Federalist No. 40: The Powers of the Convention to Form a Mixed Government Examined and Sustained," *New York Packet,* January 18, 1788.

23. *The Complete Anti-Federalist*, ed. Herbert J. Storing, with the assistance of Murray Dry, vol. 1, *What the Anti-Federalists Were For* (Chicago: University of Chicago Press, 1981), 54.

24. JFM to BF, November 9, 1787. CRG was visiting JFM.

25. BF to JFM, September 20, 1787.

Chapter XXXVI   Crooked Lines

1. JFM to BF, January 17, 1790.

2. JFM to BF, January 17, 1790; BF to JFM, December 11, 1787.

3. JFM to BF, January 8, 1788.

4. CRG to BF, Boston, November 8, 1787. See also: "we had each of us a feast talking of you." CRG to BF, Warwick, December 10, 1787.

5. BF to John Lathrop, Philadelphia, May 31, 1788.

6. JFM to BF, January 17, 1790. For an account of BF's writing, see "Introduction," in BF, *Autobiography*, xiii–xv.

7. Benjamin Vaughan to BF, Paris, January 31, 1783.

8. BF to Benjamin Vaughan, Philadelphia, October 24, 1788.

9. He also left a legacy to her descendants: "To the children, grandchildren, and great-grandchildren of my sister Jane Mecom that may be living at the time of my decease, I give fifty pounds sterling, to be equally divided among them."

10. BF to JFM, May 31, 1788. BF, Will and Codicil, July 17, 1788, *PBF*, unpublished.

11. JFM to BF, June 25, 1788.

12. BF to JFM, November 26, 1788.

13. JFM to BF, September 5, 1788. To this she added a prayer: "O my God I never did Distrust thy Kind Provedence & thou art continuealy conferming me in that Dependance upon Thee." Jane incurred a sizable debt in taking care of Jenny Mecom: "I was carefull to Live very frugaly & have not ben much straitned till the very Instant her mony came, but I had unavoidably contracted a large Debpt for my Grandaughters Sicknes a year ago which I have not been able to Pay. She was Extreemly sick I had very nearly lost her & it is a valuable Life to me the Docter was Exeding atentive for two months & she Recovered but has never been so strong & hardey since, on this acount & to Indulg my self in a few litle things I will thankfull accept the Forty Dolars as I see no Proble Prospect of Paying this Dept without it & Debpt is a Burden I cannot bare I owe no won Els a Farthing Exept a litle back Rates for my Pue at meteing which I have not been askd for it." JFM to BF, July 23, 1789. (Lathrop appears to have waived Jane's pew fee.)

14. JFM to BF, April 2, 1789.

15. JFM to BF, September 26, 1788.

16. JFM to BF, August 29, 1789.

17. Anna Letitia Barbauld, *Lessons for Children, From Two to Four Years Old; Lessons for Children of Four Years Old; Lessons for Children, From Four to Five Years Old; Lessons for Children of Five Years Old. All With Alterations, suited to the American climate* (Philadelphia: B. F. Bache, 1788).

18. BF to JFM, February 22, 1789; JFM to BF, July 23, 1789.

19. JFM to BF, September 26, 1788.

20. BF to JFM, August 3, 1789.

21. JFM to BF, August 29, 1789.

22. Jane's account of Keziah's trial is especially canny and informed. "She was Brought up to Boston to stand tryal, but I think there was no final condemnation at Court, she says they could not find Evedence. they [her prosecutors] say the Evedence was so strong that had they suffered them to come in to court it would have hangd her & so they supresd it not being willing it should Proceed so far." JFM to BF, August 29, 1789.

23. Keziah Folger Coffin's daughter Keziah Coffin Fanning recorded her mother's trials in her diary. See Keziah Coffin Fanning Diary, Kezia Coffin Fanning Papers, 1775–1820, typewritten copy, Folder 4, NHARL. And see also Philbrick, *Away Off Shore*, 123–33.

24. "I sopose you may have heard couzen Kezia Coffin is gone to Live at Halafax & so did not Send the Pockettbook to my care, there has been a Grate Revolution in that Famely but I hear of her Frequently tho She does not write to me." JFM to Sarah Franklin Bache, May 23, 1787.

25. Its author, Joseph C. Hart, got his account of the Folger family from Benjamin Franklin Folger, a Nantucket hermit, whom Hart described as "a walking genealogical tree, whose leaves and branches, so to speak, would unfold the birth, parentage and education of every resident of the island, from the days of the first settlers downwards to the time present." Joseph C. Hart, *Miriam Coffin; or, The Whale-Fishermen: A Tale*, 2 vols. (New York: G. & C. & H. Carvill, 1834). On the tie to *Moby-Dick*, see Leon Howard, "A Predecessor of *Moby-Dick*," *Modern Language Notes* 49 (1934): 310–11. Benjamin Franklin Folger was a descendant of Jane's maternal grandfather, Peter Folger. For more on Benjamin Franklin Folger, see Benjamin Franklin Folger (1777–1859), Folder 7, Folger Family Papers, Nantucket Historical Association Research Library. Folger left his papers and books to Nathaniel and Eliza Barney (see Benjamin Franklin Folger, January 3, 1856, Siasconset, in Folder 7, Folger Family Papers). In 1853, William Barney attempted to transcribe the genealogical information Folger kept in his head. See William J. Barney, "Sundry Items Obtained from Benjamin Franklin Folger of Nantucket in Relation to the First Settlers of Nantucket Massachusetts," 1853, in William J. Barney, Folder 9, Barney Family Papers, 1728–1860, Nantucket Historical Association Research Library. See also Nathaniel Philbrick, "Benjamin Franklin Folger: A Sconset Eccentric and Nantucket's First Genealogist," in Betsy Tyler, *Sconset: A History*, ed. Ben Simons (Nantucket: Nantucket Historical Association, 2008), 16–17.

26. JFM to BF, August 29, 1789.

27. BF to JFM, December 17, 1789.

28. BF, *Autobiography*, 28.

29. JFM to BF, January 17, 1790; February 6, 1790; January 17, 1790.

30. Judith Sargent Murray, "On the Equality of the Sexes," *Massachusetts Magazine* 2 (March 1790): 132–35 and (April 1790): 223–24. Quoted passages from March 1790, 133, 134, 133. On Murray, and especially regarding her extraordinary archiving of her own letters, in what she called her "Repository," see Sheila L. Skemp, *First Lady of Letters: Judith Sargent Murray and the Struggle for Female Independence* (Philadelphia: University of Pennsylvania Press, 2009). "On the Equality of the Sexes" was a revision of an essay titled "The Sexes" that Murray had written in 1779 (Skemp,

First Lady, 214–17). And on the postwar political critique of women's status more broadly, see Norton, *Liberty's Daughters,* chapter 8.

31. Presumably, she did find out for him, because in the papers of Franklin's executors, payments are made to Lydia Franklin Scott's descendants. "Rec'd Nov. 27th 1792 of H. Hill Seventy five pounds 11/172 or Two hundred one dollars 48/100 in full of 8/9th shares of the £50 of a 170 c. Exch. The Legacy of the late Doctor Franklin to the descendants of his Sister Lydia Scott of whom there were nine living at the time of his decease." Henry Hill, bound account book, Benjamin Franklin Estate Papers, APS.

32. BF to JFM, March 24, 1790.

33. One to Francis Childs, a printer, on March 30, and one to Thomas Jefferson on April 8.

34. Richard Bache to JFM, April 19, 1790.

35. JFM to Sarah Franklin Bache, September 6, 1790. This letter is a corrected copy. The original is in private hands.

Chapter XXXVII *Private Life*

1. "History of the Life and Character of Benjamin Franklin," *Universal Asylum and Columbian Magazine,* May 1790, pp. 268–72. On the early editions, see Benjamin Franklin, *The Autobiography of Benjamin Franklin: A Genetic Text,* ed. J. A. Leo Lemay and P. M. Zall (Knoxville: University of Tennessee Press, 1981), xlviii–lviii. And see also Green and Stallybrass, *Benjamin Franklin,* chapter 8.

2. "Self-biography," a writer for London's *Monthly Review* mused in 1797, was probably not a legitimate word. "It is not very usual in English to employ hybrid words partly Saxon and partly Greek: yet *autobiography* would have seemed pedantic." W. Taylor, *Monthly Review,* 2nd ser., vol. 24, p. 375; quoted in the *Oxford English Dictionary.*

3. As the editors of the *American Museum* explained, what they printed was "taken from his own private memoirs." "Memoirs of the late Dr. Franklin," *American Museum, or Universal Magazine* (July 1790): 12–20.

4. The best account of the manuscript—of which there seem to have been five copies—is *Autobiography of Benjamin Franklin: A Genetic Text,* xxxvii–xlvii.

5. BF to Louis-Alexandre de La Rochefoucauld, Philadelphia, November 13, 1789. See also BF to Louis-Guillaume Le Veillard, Philadelphia, November 13, 1789.

6. BF to Benjamin Vaughan, Philadelphia, November 15, 1789.

7. Richard Price to BF, ca. May 30, 1790. On June 6, 1790, in his journal, Price noted, "Received last Friday in a letter from Dr Rush" the news of Franklin's death, adding, "I had lately finished the perusal of his life written by himself which he had sent to Mr. Vaughan to be read by him and me . . . In consequence of reading it I had writ to him about a week ago"; Price mourned the loss of a man "whose name will live in all future *annals*" (Richard Price, "Richard Price's Journal for the Period 25 March 1787 to 6 February 1791," *National Library of Wales Journal* 21 [1979–80]: 394; Price's letter to BF, which is not in *PBF,* is reproduced on pp. 397–98).

8. Le Veillard was executed by guillotine in 1794; the manuscript Franklin had sent him was kept by his widow and, upon her death, by his daughter. In 1834, it passed into the hands of M. de Senarmont, Le Veillard's grandnephew. It was bound some-

time in the 1830s. A title stamped on its spine, in gold, on a red leather label, reads, "The Life of Francklin." It remained in the Veillard family's hands until 1867, when John Bigelow, a historian and the American minister to France, purchased it and brought it back to the United States. BF, *The Autobiography of Benjamin Franklin,* ed. John Bigelow (Philadelphia: Lippincott, 1868), Introduction. It is now in the Henry E. Huntington Library.

9. Temple Franklin proved a poor editor. Benjamin Franklin had originally written:

> Having emerg'd from Poverty & Obscurity in which I was born & bred, to a State of Affluence & some Degree of Fame in the World.

This Franklin himself had revised to read:

> Having emerg'd from the Poverty & Obscurity in which I was born & bred, to a State of Affluence & some Degree of Reputation in the World.

Temple Franklin made it fussy:

> From the poverty and obscurity in which I was born, and in which I passed my earliest years, I have raised myself to a state of affluence and some degree of celebrity in the world.

Franklin thought fame went too far and demoted his achievement to reputation; Temple promoted him to celebrity. *Autobiography of Benjamin Franklin: A Genetic Text,* liii–lviii.

10. WTF to the printer of the [London] *Star,* June 16, 1793, *General Advertiser* (Philadelphia), November 28, 1793.

11. A proposal for printing the first edition by subscription appeared in Portsmouth, New Hampshire, in 1793: "Proposal for Printing by Subscription," *Oracle of the Day,* November 13, 1793. An edition was offered for sale in New Jersey in June 1794 (*New-Jersey Journal,* June 25, 1794), but this was likely the London edition, as the New York printer announced that the American edition was "In the Press and speedily will be Published" only in September: *New-York Daily Gazette,* September 16, 1794.

12. In 1790, JFM had written to Sally Franklin Bache, congratulating her on the news that Benny had started a newspaper and adding, "I hope he will remember his old aunt, with a present of some of his papers, when convenient by a vessel." JFM to Sarah Franklin Bache, September 6, 1790. This letter is a corrected copy.

13. Jonathan Williams Sr. to BF, Boston, April 1, 1790.

14. Jonathan Williams Jr. to BF, Boston, November 7, 1789.

15. JFM to Sarah Franklin Bache, October 20, 1790.

16. JFM to BF, August 29, 1789.

17. JFM to Jonathan Williams Jr., Boston, August 11, 1792. Four documents signed by JFM after BF's death concern his bequest: a conveyance, dated June 23, 1791; JFM to Henry Hill (one of BF's executors), August 6, 1791; JFM to Henry Hill, August 2, 1792; and JFM to Henry Hill, July 29, 1793. All four of these documents are written

in a hand other than Jane's; she merely signed them. A letter by JFM to Edward Duffield (another of Franklin's executors), dated September 24, 1791, was auctioned in 1895. *Catalogue of the extraordinary collection of rare and valuable American history belonging to M. Polock, Esq., of Philadelphia . . . and an unique collection of Franklin imprints . . .* (Philadelphia: S. V. Henkels, 1895). I have not been able to find the original.

18. Benjamin Mecom, "Fine Crown Soap," *General Advertiser,* February 12, 1793. The notice also appeared twice in March and once in May, and then never again. The advertisement claimed that Mecom had apprenticed with Jane's brother John Franklin in 1751, which Benjamin Mecom never did; it was Jane's son Peter who apprenticed with John Franklin.

19. Mary Wollstonecraft, *A Vindication of the Rights of Woman* (Boston: Peter Edes, 1792). On the serialization in Boston, see Skemp, *First Lady of Letters,* 217. "Extracts from the Rights of Woman," *Massachusetts Magazine* 4 (October 1792): 598–99.

20. Wollstonecraft, *A Vindication of the Rights of Woman,* chapter 13, pp. 321–22.

21. Adams quoted in Norton, *Liberty's Daughters,* 251.

22. Richard Price to Benjamin Rush, Hackney, June 19, 1790, in BF, *Works of the late Dr. Franklin* (New York: Tiebout and Obrian, 1794), 1:6–7.

Chapter XXXVIII   Partial, Prejudiced, and Ignorant

1. Jane Austen, "The History of England from the Reign of Henry the 4th to the Death of Charles the 1st [1791]" is transcribed in Jane Austen, *The History of England,* with an introduction by A. S. Byatt (Chapel Hill, NC: Algonquin, 1993). On women as historians, see Natalie Zemon Davis, "Gender and Genre: Women as Historical Writers, 1400–1820," in *Beyond Their Sex: Learned Women of the European Past,* ed. Patricia H. Labalme (New York: New York University Press, 1980), 153–82; Bonnie G. Smith, *The Gender of History: Men, Women, and Historical Practice* (Cambridge, MA: Harvard University Press, 2000); Laurel Thatcher Ulrich, *Well-Behaved Women Seldom Make History* (New York: Knopf, 2007); and D. R. Woolf, "A Feminine Past? Gender, Genre, and Historical Knowledge in England, 1500–1800," *American Historical Review* 102 (1997): 645–79. A related discussion about the "body" of historical knowledge can be found in Natalie Zemon Davis, "History's Two Bodies," *American Historical Review* 93 (1988): 1–30. On women as eighteenth-century readers of history, see Mark Salber Phillips, " 'If Mrs. Mure Be Not Sorry for Poor King Charles': History, the Novel, and the Sentimental Reader," *History Workshop Journal* 43 (1997): 111–31. For a related discussion of the relationship between fiction and history, see Jill Lepore, "Just the Facts, Ma'am," *New Yorker,* March 24, 2008.

2. This, like Austen's title—"by a Partial, Prejudiced, & Ignorant Historian"— parodied Hume, who had written, "The first quality of an historian is to be true and impartial; the next to be interesting" (*Letters of David Hume,* 1:210 [Hume to Mure, October 1754]).

3. Jane Austen, "The History of England."

4. Jane Austen, *Northanger Abbey* (written in 1798 but published only posthumously, in 1818), chapter 14.

5. Jane Austen, *Persuasion* (1818).

6. BF, *Poor Richard 1734*, *PBF*, 1:355; JFM to BF, May 29, 1786.

7. Regarding the genre in America, Davidson writes, "Until well into the nineteenth century, virtually every American novel somewhere in its preface or its plot defended itself against the charge that it *was* a novel, either by defining itself differently ("Founded In *Truth*") or by redefining the genre tautologically, as all those things it was presumed not to be—moral, truthful, educational, and so forth" (*Revolution and the Word*, 40). Beck argues that the heyday of the "pseudo-historical novel" in England was 1740–1780. It lagged longer in the United States, into the first decade of the nineteenth century. See Beck, "The Novel," 409.

8. Charles Gildon, *An Epistle to Daniel Defoe* (1719), reprinted in Williams, *Novel and Romance*, 57–63.

9. See Mayer, *History and the Early English Novel*, 3.

10. Henry Fielding, *The History of Tom Jones, A Foundling* (London, 1748). Laurence Sterne, *The Life and Opinions of Tristram Shandy, Gentleman* (London, 1759–67).

11. William Owen, "An Essay on the New Species of Writing founded by Mr. Fielding" (1751); reprinted in Williams, *Novel and Romance*, 150.

12. William Godwin, "Of History and Romance" (unpublished essay, written in 1797); reprinted in *Caleb Williams*, ed. Gary Handwerk and A. A. Markley (Toronto: Broadview, 2000).

13. On Brown's philosophy of history, see Mark L. Kamrath, "Charles Brockden Brown and the 'Art of the Historian': An Essay Concerning (Post)Modern Historical Understanding," *Journal of the Early Republic* 21 (2001): 231–60, and Peter Kafer, "Charles Brockden Brown and the Pleasures of 'Unsanctified Imagination,' 1787–1793," *William and Mary Quarterly* 57 (2000): 543–68.

14. Charles Brockden Brown, "The Difference Between History and Romance," *Monthly Magazine and American Review* (April 1800): 251–53.

15. Charles Brockden Brown, "Historical Characters Are False Representations of Nature," *Literary Magazine and American Register* (February 1806): 32–36.

16. John Adams to Thomas Jefferson, May 5, 1811.

17. Brown, "Historical Characters Are False Representations of Nature."

PART FIVE · REMAINS, 1794–

Chapter XXXIX   A New and More Beautiful Edition

1. JFM, Last Will and Testament, February 17, 1794, Suffolk County Probate files, Mass. Arch. It begins, "The time must arrive when I shall be called upon to resign this decaying frame to its parent dust and my spirit to the God who gave it." It is reproduced in Van Doren, *Letters*, 350–54. The day Jane signed her will, CRG's obituary appeared in the *Boston Gazette*. "Deaths," *Boston Gazette*, February 17, 1794: "At Warwick, Mrs. Catharine Green, consort of Gov. Green of Rhode Island." It might have been Greene's death that spurred Jane to finalize her will.

2. Monaghan, "Literacy Instruction and Gender," 27. John Eliot to Jeremy Belknap, 1782; quoted in Woody, *History of Women's Education*, 146. In 1789, Boston public schools began admitting girls, but they were allowed to attend for only half the year. Discussions of girls' education in the late eighteenth century include Keith

Pacholl, " 'Let Both Sexes Be Carefully Instructed': Educating Youth in Colonial Philadelphia," in *Children in Colonial America*, 191–203. Literacy rates for both men and women rose considerably in the last decades of the eighteenth century, and the gap between male and female literacy narrowed, although just how high they rose, how much the gap closed, and how reliable the measures are remain the subjects of considerable debate. A useful summary of the debate up to 1986 is in Davidson, *Revolution and the Word*, chapter 4. Ross W. Beales and E. Jennifer Monaghan present more recent data in "Literacy and Schoolbooks," in *The History of the Book in America*, 1:380–87.

3. Jane described it as "my Silver Porringer mark'd P^{F}M." A silver porringer marked S^{F}H, belonging to Jane's cousin Samuel Franklin and his wife Hannah, and dated 1742, can be found in the collections of the Museum of Fine Arts, Boston, accession no. RES.34.6, a gift of the Franklin family. In the inscription, the *S* is for Samuel, the *H* for Hannah, and the joint *F* for Franklin. Peter Franklin's wife was named Mary Harman. The inscription on his porringer reads: *P* for Peter, *M* for Mary, and joint *F* for Franklin. I have therefore concluded that this porringer must have come to Jane from her brother. Van Doren mistakenly thought the porringer belonged to Jane's son Peter Franklin Mecom. See editorial comment, Van Doren, *Letters*, 350. My thanks to Caitlin Hopkins and Kelly L'Ecuyer.

4. The ring is now at the Museum of Fine Arts, Boston.

5. This seems to have been the Wedgwood medallion Franklin sent to Jane from London in 1775. See BF to JFM, February 26, 1775, and Sellers, *Benjamin Franklin in Portraiture*, 62.

6. Benjamin Franklin, "The Folly of Making War," *Boston Gazette*, March 3, 1794.

7. JFM to BF, May 22, 1787. Lathrop might have been involved in this. Before his death in 1816, he founded the Massachusetts Peace Society.

8. Susanna Rowson, *Charlotte: A Tale of Truth* (Philadelphia: D. Humphreys, 1794). *Charlotte* was the first best-selling novel written by an American. The only other novels, in the eighteenth century, to qualify as bestsellers were English: *Pamela*, *Clarissa*, and *Gulliver's Travels*. Frank Luther Mott, *Golden Multitudes: The Story of Best-Sellers in the United States* (New York: 1947), 303–5.

9. On the academy, see Ellen B. Brandt, *Susanna Haswell Rowson: America's First Best-Selling Novelist* (Chicago: Serbra, 1975), chapter 8. Rowson also wrote a notable history textbook, *Exercises in History, Chronology and Biography* (Boston, 1822).

10. Readers had so much sympathy with the novel's heroine that they made pilgrimages, for decades, to Trinity Churchyard in New York—where Charlotte, in the story, is buried—to weep and place flowers over a grave. The best discussion of both the author and the text is to be found in the introduction by Cathy N. Davidson in Susannah Haswell Rowson, *Charlotte Temple* (New York: Oxford University Press, 1986). And on the expansion of the republic of letters in the new nation, see *A History of the Book in America*, vol. 2: *An Extensive Republic: Print, Culture, and Society in the New Nation, 1790–1840*, ed. Robert A. Gross and Mary Kelley (Chapel Hill: University of North Carolina Press, 2010), 54–171.

11. I have found no gravestone, and no obituary lists the day on which she died, but the date of her death is mentioned in a letter from her minister: John Lathrop to unknown, Philadelphia, June 10, 1794, Smith Family Papers, 1678–1937, vol. 11

(1792–97), LCP. The letter appears to be a draft. It might have been addressed to Benjamin Smith, the husband of Jane's granddaughter Sarah Mecom, or, far more likely, to Henry Hill, one of the executors of Franklin's estate. The letter survives at the LCP in a collection of papers handed down through the Philadelphia family of John Smith, who was a trustee of the LCP in the 1750s and whose grandson was the librarian from 1829 to 1851. Benjamin Smith might possibly have belonged to this family, but the Smith family married into the family of Henry Hill. Jane corresponded with Hill regularly, regarding her annuity. (John Smith's son John Smith Jr. married Guliema Maria Morris in 1784; Henry Hill was Morris's grandmother's brother.) As Lathrop's letter concerns Franklin's bequest, and because the majority of the letters in this volume of the Smith papers are either to or from Henry Hill, it seems extremely likely that Lathrop addressed this letter to Hill.

12. John Lathrop, Record Book, 1768–1815, Second Church Records, Box 1, vol. 7, MHS. In this entry, Lathrop gives the date of death as May 10, 1794, but May 7, supplied in the Lathrop letter to Henry Hill, cited above, must be right, given that an obituary appeared in a newspaper dated May 9. Also, in the Record Book, it appears that Lathrop initially wrote "7" and then crossed it out and wrote "10." Why is uncertain. May 10 was the date of the funeral.

13. For Edes's report, see "Deaths," *Boston Gazette*, May 12, 1794. The obituary with the notice of the funeral ran in the *Massachusetts Mercury*, May 9, 1794, and in the *Columbian Centinel*, May 10, 1794. A briefer obituary appeared in the *Massachusetts Spy*, May 15, 1794.

14. John Lathrop, *Consolation for Mourners* (Boston: White and Adams, 1779), 15. On Lathrop, see Chandler Robbins, *A History of the Second Church, or Old North, in Boston* (Boston, 1852), 125–30, and Sibley, *Biographical Sketches*, 15:428–36. Two sermons Lathrop preached in May 1794 do survive. One is on charity and one is on false prophecy. John Lathrop Sermons, Box 6 (1789–94), MHS.

15. The record of the administration of her estate is reprinted in Van Doren, *Letters*, 354–59.

16. Franklin probably wrote this epitaph in 1728, when he was twenty-two. Three texts are known, all different. See editorial comment, *PBF*, 1:109–10; for a transcription, see 111. At some point, he wrote out a copy for Jane. She must have kept it with her, all her life, because when she packed her things to flee Boston in 1775, she brought it with her. When Ezra Stiles met her in Rhode Island in 1779, he recorded, in his diary, that she "shewed me his Epitaph in his own hand." Stiles, *Literary Diary*, 2:375.

17. JFM to BF, February 21, 1786.

18. JFM to BF, May 29, 1786. She closed this letter with "but oh may I not Live to hear of the Departure of My Dear Brother."

19. Benjamin Franklin the Elder's "The Chiding" is an undated poem, and Jane's copy of it ("this is won of my Good old Unkl Franklins Poims") is in the Jane [Franklin] Mecom Collection at the APS. It, too, is undated. Van Doren writes that Jane made the copy "presumably in her later life" (*Letters*, 348–50). There is no evidence on the paper itself to suggest that, except for the wobbliness of Jane's hand, suggesting that she was fairly old at the time.

20. This is usually supposed. E.g., Charles Chauncey Wells and Suzanne Austin Wells,

in *Preachers, Patriots and Plain Folks: Boston's Burying Ground Guide* (Oak Park, IL: Chauncey Park, 2004), report, "She was probably buried in Granary because she was born 2 blocks away and her boarding house was near the State House" (130). Copp's Hill, the burial ground closest to Jane's house, would have seemed another likely place for her to be buried. But in 1851, when Thomas Bridgman inventoried the epitaphs on gravestones there, he did not record one for Jane. See Thomas Bridgman, *Epitaphs from Copp's Hill Burial Ground* (Boston: James Munroe, 1851). Nor does Bridgman record any stone for Jane in his inventory of the Granary Burying Ground, published in 1856, but chances are good that, if Jane had been buried in the Granary, near her parents, her grave would have been disturbed by the erection of the Franklin monument in 1827. This fate, however, did not befall Jane's uncle's gravestone, because in 1856 Bridgman did find, "about four feet west of the Franklin monument," stones for Benjamin Franklin the Elder (Jane's uncle) and for Mrs. Hannah Franklin (the wife of Jane's cousin Samuel). See Bridgman, *The Pilgrims of Boston* (New York: D. Appleton, 1856), 332–35.

21. That the original inscription was "nearly obliterated" is asserted on the inscription that replaced it in 1827, the text of which is reproduced in *Historical Sketch and Matters Appertaining to the Granary Burial-Ground* (Boston: Municipal Printing Office, 1902), 14–15.

22. Daniel Webster, "The Bunker Hill Monument, an Address Delivered . . . on the Seventeenth of June, 1825," in *Daniel Webster's First Bunker Hill Oration*, ed. Fred Newton Scott (New York: Longmans, Green, 1902), 25.

23. The proposal to rename the Granary Burying Ground "Franklin Cemetery" was made in 1830, three years after the erection of the monument. *Historical Sketch and Matters Appertaining to the Granary Burial-Ground*, 4.

24. Ibid., 14–15. The graves of Jane and Benjamin's parents were found, during excavation; they were not moved. The original tablet, said to have been "defaced," was enclosed within the obelisk. Boston *Centinel*, June 23, 1827, reprinted as "Franklin Monument," *Pittsfield Sun*, July 12, 1827.

Chapter XL *The Librarian*

1. This annotation can be read on the reverse of BF to Abiah Folger Franklin, Philadelphia, September 17, 1749. (*PBF* dates this letter September [7], 1749.) It may be that Jane saved it because it mentions her: Franklin signed off, "My Love to Brother & Sister Macom, & to all enquiring Friends."

2. Envelope, Richard Bache to JFM, April 19, 1790.

3. Lathrop had read some of Franklin's letters to his sister before. In 1788, pressing himself and his sermons upon Franklin, he had written to him: "You will allow me to consider myself in some sort acquainted by the way of your worthy sister Mrs Mecom, who is our neighbour and particular friend, and who allows me the pleasure of reading the very improving and entertaining Letters which she has recievd from you." John Lathrop to BF, Boston, May 6, 1788.

4. The election of officers is reported in "American Academy of Arts and Sciences," *Independent Chronicle*, June 9, 1791. Lathrop had been elected a member of the academy in 1790. The keeper of the cabinet was, by statute, both the librarian and the curator. "Statues of the American Academy of Arts and Sciences," *Memoirs*

of the American Academy of Arts and Sciences 1 (1783): chapter 6, clause 1, p. xvi. Although Lathrop donated some of his sermons to the academy's archives, none of JFM's papers ended up there (Michele M. Lavoie, archivist, American Academy of Arts and Sciences, e-mail to the author, March 14, 2012).

5. "Caleb Loring, Esq. to Miss Jane Tyler Lathrop, daughter of the late Rev. Dr. Lathrop," *Salem Gazette,* May 29, 1821. Under marriages "At Boston." And see also the notice in the *Independent Chronicle,* May 30, 1821.

6. The founding of the public library, later the Thayer Memorial Library, is related in Abijah Perkins Marvin, *History of the Town of Lancaster from the First Settlement to the Present Time, 1643–1879* (Lancaster, MA: The Town, 1879), 552–62. Leslie Perrin Wilson, *Thayer Memorial Library: Celebrating 150 Years of Public Library Service, 1862–2012* (Lancaster, MA: Thayer Memorial Library, 1985, 2012), 20.

7. Flagg's notations in JFM, "Book of Ages," NEHGS.

8. On Flagg's various town offices, see Henry S. Nourse, *The Birth Marriage and Death Register, Church Records and Epitaphs of Lancaster, Massachusetts, 1643–1850* (Lancaster, MA: W. J. Coulter, 1890), 6, 9, 121, 130, 232.

9. On the popularity of family trees and family records in family Bibles in the nineteenth century, see Maureen A. Taylor, "Tall Oaks from Little Acorns Grow: The Family Tree Lithograph in America," in Simons and Benes, *The Art of Family,* 75–89.

10. *The Holy Bible, containing the Old and New Testaments, with the Apocrypha* (Charlestown, MA, 1803), annotated by Josiah Flagg and Sally Flagg, Special Collections Room, Thayer. In his Bible's Family Record, Flagg recorded, too, the survival of a family name: one of Josiah Flagg's daughters named a daughter of hers Jane Green.

11. BF, *Experiments and Observations on Electricity* (London, 1774), at the AAS. In 1827, Flagg also gave to the Society some Indian relics. On the AAS's role in collecting Indian artifacts, see Judith Kertesz, "Skeletons in the American Attic: Curiosity, Science, and the Appropriation of the American Indian Past," PhD diss., Harvard University, 2012.

12. *Columbian Centinel,* August 17, 1816.

13. Marvin, *History of Lancaster,* 327, 373, 400, 429, 431, 540–44. "The records, accurately kept and legibly written, are his best monument," noted one town historian. That monument remains in a locked cabinet in the basement of Lancaster Town Hall. His handwriting really is beautiful. It can be seen in Lancaster Town Records, vol. 3, 1800–20, Town Clerk's Office, Town Hall, Lancaster, Massachusetts. The manuscript records are kept in the basement of the town hall. I consulted this record book to be certain that Flagg had not written the words "Book of Age's" on the cover of JFM's book; he had not. His handwriting, both informal and clerical, is remarkably different from hers, and even from the "flourishing hand" with which she wrote on the cover of her book.

14. *The Holy Bible, containing the Old and New,* annotated by Josiah Flagg and Sally Flagg.

15. Norman Gershom Flagg and Lucius C. S. Flagg, *Family Records of the Descendants of Gershom Flagg* (n.p., 1907), 30. Flagg and Flagg refer to Josiah Flagg as "a voluminous letter-writer" (155), although I have not been able to find any of his letters aside from those deposited in the NEHGS.

16. John M. Dodd, Boston, October 23, 1858. R. Stanton Avery Special Collections, NEHGS.

17. BF, *The Interest of Great Britain Considered* (Boston: Benjamin Mecom, 1760). Records of the bequests by Sally Flagg can be found in the acquisition books in the Special Collections Room of the Thayer Memorial Library.

18. According to the Flagg family Bible, Samuel Ward Flagg died on June 24, 1871. Benjamin A. G. Fuller, "Letters of Dr. Franklin, Mrs. Jane Mecom, Josiah Flagg, Richard Bache, &c," *New England Historical and Genealogical Register* 27 (1873): 246–54. Fuller was a descendant of Gershom Flagg, and therefore shared a common ancestor with Josiah Flagg. The bequest was presented on February 6, 1872, and is listed in the Society's acquisition book in an entry dated September 4, 1872, where the Book of Ages is described as "Memo. book, containing family records by Mrs. Mecom and Josiah Flagg." NEHGS, Accession Book. A brief biography of Fuller appears in the *New England Historical and Genealogical Register* 39 (1885): 399. The provenance of the bequest is detailed in Benjamin A. G. Fuller to Marshall Pinckney Wilder, February 7, 1872, NEHGS, Mss. C 641.

Chapter XLI   The Editor

1. The most comprehensive account of Sparks's life and work is Herbert Baxter Adams, *The Life and Writings of Jared Sparks*, 2 vols. (Boston: Houghton Mifflin, 1893), but see also George E. Ellis, *Memoir of Jared Sparks* (Cambridge, MA: John Wilson, 1869). On the *North American Review*, see Van Wyck Brooks, *The Flowering of New England, 1815–1865* (New York: E. P. Dutton & Co., 1936), chapter 6.

2. Jared Sparks, "Materials for American History," *North American Review* 23 (October 1826): 276, 277, 292.

3. Adams, *Life of Sparks*, 2:521.

4. Sparks, "Materials for American History," 294.

5. Sparks had written to Mount Vernon in 1816, a year after he graduated from Harvard, begging for "a scrap of General Washington's handwriting." Not long after, he made his first application to Washington's nephew and literary executor, Bushrod Washington, to see the whole collection and was turned down. Adams, *Life of Sparks*, 1:389. For more on Sparks's editing of Washington's papers, as well as the controversy surrounding that work, see Lepore, *The Story of America*, 130–45.

6. Galen Broeker, "Jared Sparks, Robert Peel and the State Paper Office," *American Quarterly* 13 (1961): 140–52.

7. In London, Temple Franklin had had an affair and an illegitimate child with Ellen D'Evelyn, the sister of his father's wife. This had led to a falling-out with his father, after which Temple abandoned both mother and child and moved to Paris. Skemp, *William Franklin*, 273–74.

8. Temple proposed visiting his father in London, to consult his memory, but he never turned up.

9. *Memoirs of the Life and Writings of Benjamin Franklin, LL.D.*, ed. William Temple Franklin (Philadelphia, 1808–18). Bache died in 1798, of yellow fever, at the age of twenty-nine, his health weakened by his having been arrested and imprisoned, under the terms of the Sedition Act, for opposing John Adams's imperious and failed presidential administration.

10. For more on these letters, see appendix A.
11. Possibly, Jane Lathrop Loring already knew Sparks even before he knocked on her door, because in 1827 she had served on the ladies' committee of the Bunker Hill Monument Association, with which he was also involved. George Washington Warren, *The History of the Bunker Hill Monument Association* (Boston, 1827), 292, 305.
12. "Called on Mrs. Bache, the wife of Mr. Richd Bache, who is the great grandson of Dr Franklin," he wrote in his diary on March 9. (This Richard Bache was one of Benjamin Franklin Bache's sons.) "A few letters and other papers are in the hands of the present Mrs. Bache, which are originals of Dr. Franklin, and which I am to have." March 10: "[Went"] to see Mr. Williams, the son of the late Jonathan Williams, a nephew of Dr. Franklin. He has the original picture of Franklin painted by Martin, in England, when Franklin was about 60 years old. It is the picture in a wig, of Franklin reading papers through Spectacles." Then he went to see Franklin's grave. He was disappointed: "a plain marble covers the spot." Sparks, Diary 1829–31, March 9–10, 1831, Sparks Papers, MS Sparks 141g, part 1, pp. 263–65. Note that Sparks's diaries can be confusing because he appears to have copied them. Some entries are also reproduced in Baxter, *Life of Sparks*. The original diaries, at Houghton Library at Harvard, are bound in volumes. The volumes are unnumbered but are cataloged together as part of a series referred to as MS Sparks 141. The volumes on which I relied are:

1. MS Sparks 141g, part 1: a volume, with no title or spine stamp, with a date range of 1829–31;
2. MS Sparks 141g, part 2: a volume, stamped on the spine "Letters"; it contains no letters but is, instead, a diary, titled, on the first page, "Tour for Historical Research" and running from 1830 through 1831;
3. MS Sparks 141h: a volume on whose spine is stamped "Journal, 1831–39";
4. MS Sparks 141i: a volume with no title or spine stamp and whose date range is 1832–41.

Most of these volumes have numbered pages. For ease of reference, I have supplied the date of the diary entry, the volume's date range, and the page number, if available.

13. Sparks, Diary 1829–31, March 11, 1831, Sparks Papers, MS Sparks 141g, part 1, p. 266.
14. Sparks wrote:

I found several trunks and boxes, which contained papers & books formerly belonging to Dr. Franklin. These together with various parts of electrical machines, drawings, and a great variety of things, occupy a room, which has been appropriated to them for many years in Mr. Fox's house, seven miles from Philadelphia. On examining the papers they proved to be the correspondence and other papers of Dr Franklin during his residence in France and afterwards. They are voluminous & curious, consisting chiefly of letters sent to Dr F from persons in all parts of Europe, & of memoirs presented to him on different subjects relating to the American Revolution. The whole mass is in perfect disorder.

Mr. Fox will permit me to examine them, and make such use of them as I may think proper.

Ibid. And for more on Fox's collection, see *PBF*, 1:xxi–xxii.

15. On this visit, Sparks met William Duane, who had some leads about some papers once in the possession of BF's son William Franklin. "He tells me that Govr. Franklin corresponded with him from London till the time of his death & promised to send him many of his father's letters. But his death prevented & Mr. Duane does not know what became of his papers." Sparks, Diary 1831–39, March 22, 1832, Sparks Papers, MS Sparks 141h, pp. 63–64. "He has a curious letter from him to his father and mother in 1738 on the subject of religion," Sparks wrote—this is a letter that Franklin responded to, on April 13, 1738—but the letter from Josiah and Abiah that Duane had in 1832 is now lost. Duane's edition of BF's writing is BF, *The Works of Dr. Benjamin Franklin* (Philadelphia: W. Duane, 1808–18).

16. *PBF*, 1:xxii.

17. Sparks, Diary 1831–39, March 22, 1832, Sparks Papers, MS Sparks 141h, p. 64.

18. He received Bache's volume the following winter, acknowledging receipt in a letter to Bache dated February 11, 1833. Jared Sparks to Franklin Bache, Boston, February 11, 1833, Misc. Ms. Collection, APS.

19. Jared Sparks to Franklin Bache, December 26, 1832, Misc. Ms. Collection, APS. Sparks also wrote in his journal for March 1833, "During the progress of my historical researches I have obtained original letters of Franklin amounting to more than one hundred, mostly to his relations and intimate friends. These are curious and interesting" (Misc. Ms. Collection, APS). While preparing the *Works*, Sparks had these originals in his possession and copied them into his notebooks. On the title page of a two-volume notebook filled with copies of letters, Sparks wrote, "Copied from the originals while they were in my hands for writing the Life of Franklin, Jared Sparks, 1843." "Franklin, Benjamin. Letters from various correspondents," Sparks Papers, MS Sparks 16.

20. Thomas Motley to Jared Sparks, January 24, 1833, Sparks Papers, MS Sparks 153. Motley's relationship to Mrs. Loring is discussed in appendix A.

21. Jared Sparks to Franklin Bache, Boston, February 27, 1833, Misc. Ms. Collection, APS. In the original, Sparks wrote "forty or 50"; he then crossed that out and wrote, above it, "20 or 30."

22. Sparks lived there from April 2 to August 26, 1833: "This day I began to occupy Mrs Craigie's house in Cambridge. It is a singular circumstance, that while I am engaged in preparing for the press the letters of Genl Washington, which he wrote at Cambridge, after taking command of the American Army, I should occupy the same rooms that he did at that time. Mrs. Craigie's house is the one in which he resided, & which he made his Head Quarters during his residence in Cambridge. We propose to remain here during the summer, as well as account of its being a charming summer residence, as that my presence near the printing office is now very convenient. Washingtons Writings and the little volume of Franklins letters are now to the press at Mr. Folson's office in Cambridge." Sparks, Diary 1831–39, April 2, 1833, Sparks Papers, MS Sparks 141h, p. 108.

23. Green and Stallybrass, *Benjamin Franklin*, 168.

24. Jared Sparks to Franklin Bache, Boston, April 13, 1833, Misc. Ms. Collection, APS.
25. It was reviewed in literary journals and in ladies' journals. See, e.g., "Familiar Letters of Dr. Franklin," *Philadelphia Album and Ladies' Literary Portfolio* 7 (June 8 1833): 180, and "[Review of] Franklin's Familiar Letters," *American Monthly Review* 4 (August 1833): 124–33.
26. A reviewer in Sparks's *North American Review* called special attention to Franklin's correspondence with his sister as the most remarkable element of the collection and proof against a prevailing suspicion—promoted by Franklin's political enemies and, most especially, by John Adams—that Franklin was selfish and ambitious; his letters to Jane were taken as evidence that he was, instead, generous and loyal. "His correspondence with his sister," this reviewer remarked, "was affectionate and unremitted till the last moment of his life." The reviewer reproduces three of Franklin's letters to Jane, beginning with the letter Franklin wrote to her on his twenty-first birthday, January 6, 1727, warning her to watch out for her virginity. The reviewer concludes, "Mr. Sparks, its editor, has placed the public under new obligations to himself, for the ability and diligence with which he is laboring to preserve from oblivion the facts and documents that may serve to illustrate our history, and of the characters of our distinguished men." "Franklin's Familiar Letters," *North American Review* 80 (July 1833): 249–62.
27. BF, *A Collection of the Familiar Letters and Miscellaneous Papers of Benjamin Franklin*, ed. Jared Sparks (Boston: C. Bowen, 1833). Not all, however, are identified as having been sent to JFM. Some letters to Jane Franklin Mecom Sparks refers to as "to a Friend in America" or "to a Relation in Boston."
28. Adams, *Life of Sparks*, 2:39–40. George Washington, *The Writings of George Washington*, ed. Jared Sparks, 12 vols. (Boston: American Stationers', 1834–37). Also: George Washington, *The Writings of George Washington*, ed. Jared Sparks, 12 vols. (Boston, 1833–39); vols. 2 and 3 were published by Russell, Odiorne, and Metcalf (vol. 2) and Hilliard, Gray (vol. 3), and vols. 1 and 4–12 by Fedinand and Andrews. Sparks invested his small fortune in the American Stationers' Company, which went bankrupt in the Panic of 1837, bankrupting Sparks.
29. Sparks's defense against this last pair of charges is especially interesting. See Jared Sparks, *Letter to Lord Mahon* (Boston, 1852), 18–19.
30. These changes are recounted in many places, but the easiest place to find the ones Mahon cited is John Spencer Bassett, *The Middle Group of American Historians* (New York: Macmillan, 1917), chapter 2.
31. Jared Sparks to Franklin Bache, December 26, 1832, in Baxter, *Life of Sparks*, 2:337.
32. BF to Noah Webster, Philadelphia, December 26, 1789.
33. Jared Sparks to Franklin Bache, Cambridge, August 6, 1833, Misc. Ms. Collection, APS, and reprinted in Van Doren, *Letters*, vi.
34. I believe that by 1833, four of Benjamin Mecom's children had died. His son John Ross and his daughter Deborah died in childhood. His daughter Mary Mecom, who married a man named Carr, had been living in New York at the time of Franklin's death. She was dead by 1833. Elizabeth, single at the time of Franklin's death, married a man named Daniel Britt in 1798, but it appears that she was dead by 1833. See *A Calendar of Delaware Wills, New Castle County, 1682–1800* (New York: Frederick H. Hitchcock, 1911), 144. For more on Jane's descendants, see appendix C.

35. Sarah Mecom seems to have married Benjamin Smith sometime after 1773, as the name "Sarah Mecom" appears on a list of people for whom mail is waiting at the Philadelphia post office that year. "List of Letters remaining in the Post Office, Philadelphia, July 5, 1773," *Pennsylvania Packet*, July 26, 1773.

36. "Abia Mecom, storekeeper, 63 Mulberry" is listed in James Robinson, *The Philadelphia Directory for 1807* (Philadelphia, 1806); the pages are not numbered but the listing is alphabetical. In the 1809 directory, her address is listed as 44 South Third (Robinson, *The Philadelphia Directory for 1809*).

37. By 1796 Jane Mecom Collas had started renting the house out and gone to live with Jenny Mecom, who was renting a house on Bridges Lane. Collas lived with her niece until her death in 1802, at the age of fifty-seven, whereupon the house on Unity Street was sold. Van Doren, *Letters*, 357–59.

38. "Capt. Simon Kinsman & Miss Jane Mecom," Lathrop wrote in his record of marriages, under the date February 13, 1800. John Lathrop, Record book, 1768–1815, Second Church Records, Box 1, vol. 7, MHS. The marriage of Jane Mecom and Simon Kinsman is also recorded in *A Volume of Records Relating to the Early History of Boston, Containing Boston Marriages, 1752 to 1809* (Boston: Municipal Printing Office, 1903), 256. Simon Kinsman's death and the lack of issue is noted in Lucy W. Stickney, *The Kinsman Family: Genealogical Record* (Boston, 1876), 69. In some instances, Simon Kinsman is rendered "Simeon Kinsman."

39. Sparks's notes from his undated interview with Jane Mecom Kinsman are bound in "Franklin, Benjamin. Notes and memoranda, 1836–1840," Sparks Papers, MS Sparks 18, p. 78. Curiously, on pp. 75–76 of this volume, Sparks has transcribed JFM to BF, Boston, December 5, 1774. Sparks did not extract this letter in his *Works*, which suggests that he did not see it until near the end of his research. In May 1839, the letter was printed in a magazine, the editors stating, "The various editions of Franklin's works contain numerous letters from him to his youngest and favorite sister, Jane, married to Mr. Mecom of Boston. The following from her to him, although a fragment, will, it is believed, be interesting. It is copied from the original and has been hitherto unpublished." "Letter from Mrs. Jane Mecom," *Southern Literary Messenger* 5 (May 1839): 304. Duane did not include it in his *Letters*. The original seems to have disappeared soon after Sparks made this copy. Its proximity, in his notebook, to his interview with Jane Mecom Kinsman suggests that she likely showed it to him.

40. Jared Sparks to Hilliard Gray, April 25, 1837, Henry Wadsworth Longfellow Dana Papers, Henry Wadsworth Longfellow House, Cambridge, MA, Box 140, Folder 60.

41. He began lecturing in March 1839, having decided to confine his lectures to the subject of "the history of the American Revolution from 1763 to 1783." Sparks recounts the invitation, from President Quincy, in his diary entry for July 10, 1838: "He represented the matter in a very favorable light, saying that I should have the organization of the department, and that there was a disposition to make it in all respects agreeable to me." He also includes his inclination to accept: "As the subjects to be taught in this department accord entirely with my tastes and pursuits, and as I have certain projects of a historical nature, which I hope to execute, particularly relating to American history, and which the duties of the office, would rather facilitate than obstruct, I have been led to think favorably of the proposal."

Sparks, Diary 1831–39, July 10, 1838, Sparks Papers, MS Sparks 141h, pp. 211–12. That October, he was urged to run for Congress, as he had been in 1834. He declined and instead accepted the professorship at Harvard (October 1, 1838, pp. 218–19). On the lectures beginning in March, see his diary entry for March 12, 1839 (March 12, 1839, p. 227).

42. Jared Sparks, ed., *The Library of American Biography* (Boston: Hilliard, Gray, 1834), 1:iv.

43. In 1849, a woman named Sarah Pellet wrote to Sparks, asking to be admitted to the college. "I am not aware that any law exists touching this point," he answered. Still, he was against it. "I should doubt whether a solitary female, mingling as she must do promiscuously with so large a number of the other sex, would find her situation either agreeable or advantageous. Indeed, I should be unwilling to advise any one to make such an experiment, and upon reflection I believe you will be convinced of its inexpediency." Jared Sparks to Sarah Pellet, Cambridge, April 25, 1849, in *The Harvard Book: Selections from Three Centuries,* ed. William Bentinck-Smith (Cambridge, MA: Harvard University Press, 1953), 62. He concluded his letter by expressing regret that "an enlightened public opinion has not led to the establishment of Colleges of the higher order for the education of females." ("Harvard Annex" was created for women students in 1879; Radcliffe College was annexed 1894.) Sparks's presidency did not last long, as might have been predicted by the terms he set in 1838 when he accepted a professorship of history: "I shall not be required to take any part whatever in the government and discipline of the College, nor to reside in Cambridge" (Sparks, Diary 1831–39, December 17, 1838, Sparks Papers, MS Sparks 141h, p. 223).

44. Jared Sparks, *The Life of John Ledyard* (Cambridge, MA: Hilliard and Brown, 1828), vi. This is not to say that Sparks had an interest in hiding what he would have considered defects of character. "The character and turn of events more frequently take their coloring from the foibles and waywardness of the actors than from their merits or elevated qualities . . . The causes of evils must rest on somebody, and justice requires that they should fall on the right head. History which keeps men's defects out of sight tells but half the tale, and that half imperfectly" (Adams, *Life of Sparks,* 1:571).

45. Jared Sparks, review of William Wirt, *Sketches in the Life and Character of Patrick Henry, North American Review* 6 (March 1818): 294.

46. In 1839, for instance, Charles Sumner sent him a letter of Franklin's he found at an auction in Vienna. Charles Sumner to Jared Sparks, November 26, 1839, in Adams, *Life of Sparks,* 2:348.

47. Adams, *Life of Sparks,* 2:357.

48. JFM to BF, August 29, 1789.

49. Sparks, *Works,* 10:395n.

50. For more on Sparks's editorial methods, see appendix E.

51. Brooks, *Flowering of New England,* 527; "Lord Mahon and Mr. Sparks," *Living Age* 35 (October 23, 1852): 189; Ellis, *Memoir,* 57. See also J. Franklin Jameson, *The History of Historical Writing in America* (1891; repr., New York: Greenwood, 1969), 110–11, and Scott E. Casper, *Constructing American Lives: Biography and Culture*

in Nineteenth-Century America (Chapel Hill: University of North Carolina Press, 1999), chapter 3.

52. "Lord Mahon and Mr. Sparks," *Living Age* 35 (October 23, 1852): 189.

53. "Hawthorne's Life of Pierce.—Perspective," *Democratic Review* 31 (September 1852), 276.

54. "Mr. Jared Sparks's Liberties with George Washington," *Literary World* 8 (March 1, 1851): 165, 170.

55. *The Papers of George Washington*, ed. W. W. Abbott et al. (Charlottesville: University Press of Virginia, 1983), 1:1.

56. George Washington, [Proposed Address to Congress? April? 1789], in *The Writings of George Washington*, ed. John C. Fitzpatrick (Washington: U.S. Government Printing Office, 1931–44), 30:296–97n81. And see John C. Fitzpatrick, *George Washington Himself: A Common-Sense Biography Written from His Manuscripts* (Indianapolis: Bobbs-Merrill, 1933), 529–30n2.

57. JFM to BF, Boston, October 30, 1767 (*PBF* dates this letter October 23), partially transcribed and corrected by Jared Sparks in *Works*, 7:515n.

58. Elizabeth Duane Gillespie was the daughter of Deborah Bache Duane and William John Duane, a son of William Duane, who married Benjamin Franklin Bache's widow.

59. Elizabeth Duane Gillespie, *A Book of Remembrance* (Philadelphia: J. B. Lippincott, 1901), 59–60. Gillespie knew Abiah Mecom as well. So did Franklin Bache, who signed Abiah Mecom's death certificate. (Death notice of Abiah Mecom, Philadelphia, August 6, 1841, "Pennsylvania, Philadelphia City Death Certificates, 1803–1915," FamilySearch [https://www.familysearch.org], accessed January 2, 2012, citing Death Records, FHL microfilm 4,001,153; Philadelphia City Archives, Philadelphia, Pennsylvania). There is something especially poignant about Franklin's great-grandson Franklin Bache, taking care of Jane's granddaughter Abiah Mecom, whom Jane's son Benjamin had named after his grandmother, Abiah Folger Franklin. Elizabeth Duane Gillespie used to visit Abiah Mecom when she was a little girl. Gillespie's mother was Deborah Bache, a daughter of Sally Franklin Bache; her father was William John Duane, whose father, William Duane, married the widow of Deborah's brother Benjamin Franklin Bache. When she was a little girl, Elizabeth Duane Gillespie used to visit two dotty old ladies, relatives of her mother's: Jane Franklin Mecom's granddaughters Abiah Mecom and Jane Mecom Kinsman. "Why they drifted to Philadelphia I never understood," Gillespie wrote. Of her "Cousin Abiah": "I remember her when she was at the head of a boardinghouse in Sixth Street near Prune." When one of her boarders died, leaving behind a closetful of medicine, Abiah drank it all. "It tastes just like 'vanilla,'" she liked to say. Abiah Mecom died of dropsy in Philadelphia in 1841. Her obituary reads, "Abiah Mecom died on August 6, 1841, in Philadelphia, in the 81st year of her age." It appeared in the *National Gazette*, August 7, 1841.

60. *Charlestown Mercury*, September 27, 1856. On discovering such relics, see Alfred Young, *The Shoemaker and the Tea Party*.

61. Adams, *Life of Sparks*, 2:357n1.

62. Robert C. Winthrop, *Oration at the Inauguration of the Statue of Benjamin Frank-*

lin, in His Native City, September 17, 1856 (Boston: Press of T. R. Marvin, 1856), 5, 6, 24. Winthrop actually quotes one of Franklin's letters to JFM, from November 4, 1787 (p. 22). Sparks had printed this letter in the *Works* (10:325–27), after which it went to private hands.

63. Winthrop, *Oration at the Inauguration*, 28. Revere's obituary appeared in the *Boston Gazette*, May 15, 1818. The Massachusetts Charitable Mechanic Association wanted to celebrate Revere as the "patriot Mechanic of the Revolution." Sparks had often lectured to the association. George B. Emerson, Committee of Instruction of the Boston Mechanicks' Institution, to Jared Sparks, Boston, July 16, 1827, MS Sparks 153, Sparks Papers. Revere had no place in Sparks's *Library of American Biography*.

64. Ellis, *Memoir of Jared Sparks*, 43.

65. Robert C. Winthrop, in Adams, *Life of Sparks*, 2:586.

66. "Paul Revere's Ride," *Atlantic Monthly* 7 (January 1861): 27–30. On how Longfellow came to write the poem, see Lepore, *The Story of America*, 220–39. In a census taken earlier that year, Jane Mecom Kinsman's occupation was listed as, simply, "niece of Dr. Franklin." Eighth Census of the United States, 1860 (National Archives Microfilm Publication M653), Records of the Bureau of the Census, Record Group 29, National Archives, Washington, DC, Roll 1158, p. 408, Schedule 1—Free Inhabitants, Eighth Ward, Philadelphia, Pennsylvania, dated June 1860, Dwelling no. 220, Family no. 257. Her estate was announced in the *Philadelphia Inquirer*, December 29, 1860. John Clayton was listed as her executor. "Her last years were made most comfortable by relatives of hers, the Misses Baldwin" (Gillespie, *Book of Remembrance*, 60). By the 1850 federal census, she was listed as living with Walter Colton, Catherine Baldwin, and Sarah Baldwin, relatives of her mother's sister, Mary Ross Baldwin. She had been living with them at the time of her death. Seventh Census of the United States, 1850 (National Archives Microfilm Publication M432), Records of the Bureau of the Census, Record Group 29, National Archives, Washington, DC, Roll 812, p. 117, Schedule for the South Ward of Philadelphia, Pennsylvania, dated August 14, 1850, Dwelling no. 71, Family no. 71.

Chapter XLII   The Biographer

1. *Catalogue of Important Autograph Letters, Literary, Historical & Medieval Manuscripts... Which will be Sold by Auction, by Messrs. Sotheby and Col... On Monday, 17th of December, 1928, and Four following Days* (London: J. Davy and Sons, 1928), 75–84, Lots 414–70.

2. For more on the history of this set of papers, see appendix A.

3. Woolf wrote *Orlando* between October 1927 and March 1928. Virginia Woolf, *The Diary of Virginia Woolf*, ed. Anne Olivier Bell (New York: Harcourt Brace Jovanovich, 1980), 3:viii.

4. Virginia Woolf, "The Lives of the Obscure," in *The Common Reader* (Leonard & Virginia Woolf at the Hogarth Press, 1925), 146.

5. On Woolf's ideas about biography, see, e.g., Juliette Atkinson, *Victorian Biography Reconsidered: A Study of Nineteenth-Century Hidden Lives* (Oxford: Oxford University Press, 2010), 252–64.

6. Van Doren, *Benjamin Franklin*, ix.

7. Virginia Woolf, "The Art of Biography [1939]," in *The Death of the Moth and Other Essays* (London: Hogarth Press, 1942), 125.

8. "Jane Mecom," *Boston Globe*, March 12, 1917. This article refers to an 1882 series called "Street Saunterings" that appeared in "a Boston paper" and was written by William T. W. Ball; he says that on September 17, 1856, the day of the dedication of the statue to Franklin, the house on Unity Street "was decorated to mark it as the house in which Franklin's sister, Jane Mecom, lived." But the writer of this article disputed that Jane Mecom ever lived there because he found "Jane Mecom" in the 1798 directory as at Bridges Lane. That "Jane Mecom," of course, was Jane's granddaughter. The demolition of the house is discussed in Van Doren, *Letters*, 359.

9. Roelker, *BF and CRG*, 7, 29n2.

10. The site is now a brick-paved park, a walkway leading tourists from the Paul Revere Mall to Old North Church. Eight locust trees line the path. In 2012, a small memorial garden honored "the men and women in the Armed Forces and the civilians who have lost their lives in the Afghanistan and Iraq Wars."

11. Charles Van Doren to the author, n.d. but postmarked June 13, 2011.

12. Some letters written by Jane, rather than by Franklin, were already known. In 1859, Franklin's great-grandson (Deborah Bache Duane's son) William Duane privately published *Letters to Benjamin Franklin, from his Family and Friends, 1751–1790*. It included thirty-seven letters from Jane. Duane called her "the youngest and favorite sister of Dr. Franklin." William Duane, ed., *Letters to Benjamin Franklin, from his Family and Friends, 1751–1790* (New York, 1859), 3–4.

13. *PBF*, 1:xxii. The Bache descendants' bequest includes Benjamin Mecom's letters to his aunt—the only letters written by Benjamin Mecom that weren't destroyed.

14. The Rosenbach Company, *Catalogue Thirty-four: For Librarians, Collectors and Scholars* (Philadelphia: Rosenbach Company, 1943), item 181: "FRANKLIN, BENJAMIN. A Series of Fifty-nine Autograph Letters Signed to his Sister, Jane Mecom of Boston."

15. Van Doren, *Letters*, v.

16. Van Doren had intended to include, as an illustration, a photograph of the Book of Ages, but it does not appear. Carl Van Doren Papers, Special Collections, Princeton University, Box 11, Folder 10.

17. Van Doren, *Jane Mecom*, v.

18. Esther Forbes, "Carl Van Doren's Final Study of Our Revolutionary Past," *New York Herald Tribune Book Review*, October 15, 1950.

Chapter XLIII   The End

1. For more on the ring, see appendix A.

2. A list of books described as "Donated by Sally Flagg," dated July 20, 1881, and a second list, described as "Rev. A. P. Marvin from the bequest of Miss Sally Flagg," dated April 27, 1882, both appear in Lancaster's library: Accession Catalogue, 1311-22591, Special Collections, Thayer. Sally Flagg's bequests are also marked by the presence of a bookplate on the endpapers of books from her bequest. Not all of the books she donated remain in the library.

3. That these portraits were a gift from Sally Flagg is noted on a slip of paper stapled

to the back of the frame of the portrait of Josiah Flagg. The sitters have, before now, been misidentified as Sally and Samuel Flagg.

4. Sally Flagg, stitched sampler, embroidered silk on linen, 1802, Thayer. The verse is not original and was common. The very same lines appear on other samplers, including one owned by the Huntington Library and another (stitched ca. 1791 in Providence, Rhode Island, by Rebekah S. Munro, age eleven) at the Metropolitan Museum of Art. For a reproduction of a sampler with these lines, stitched by Anne Kimball of Newburyport, Massachusetts, in 1803, see Betsy Krieg Salm, *Women's Painted Furniture, 1790–1830: American Schoolgirl Art* (Hanover, NH: University Press of New England, 2010), 200.

APPENDICES

Appendix A   Methods and Sources

1. Quoted in Leo Braudy, *Narrative Form in History and Fiction: Hume, Fielding & Gibbon* (Princeton: Princeton University Press, 1970), 13.
2. BF, *Autobiography*, 18.
3. JFM to BF, June 17, 1782.
4. Published collections of Franklin's writings referred to in Appendix D are Sparks's *Familiar Letters*, Sparks's *Works*, Duane's *Letters*, Duane's *Works*, and *The Writings of Benjamin Franklin*, ed. Albert Henry Smyth, 10 vols. (New York: Macmillan, 1905).
5. BF to Edward Mecom and JFM, Philadelphia, November 30, 1752.
6. Sparks, *Familiar Letters*, 27. Van Doren wrote, "All of Benjamin Mecom's letters to his mother and to his uncle are missing, without much doubt deliberately destroyed" (*Letters*, 10).
7. Mather Byles to BF, Boston, 1765–66.
8. Sparks, Diary 1829–31, December 1830, Sparks Papers, MS Sparks 141g, part 1, p. 236.
9. Grace Harris Williams to BF, Boston, December 13, 1771, and BF to Grace Harris Williams, London, March 5, 1771.
10. Van Doren, *Letters*, vii.
11. On how Van Doren fell down this rabbit hole, see the pages about the Lorings in his research notebooks, in Box 11, Folder 11, Van Doren Papers, Princeton University.
12. Jared Sparks to Franklin Bache, August 6, 1833.
13. Franklin Bache to Jared Sparks, August 14, 1833, Jared Sparks Papers, Houghton Library, Harvard, MS Sparks 153.
14. Oliver Wendell Holmes, *John Lothrop Motley: A Memoir* (Boston: Houghton, Osgood, 1879). See also *John Lothrop Motley and His Family*, ed. Susan and Herbert St. John Mildmay (London, 1910). This volume contains a series of letters written by Elizabeth ("Lily") Motley, including some of her correspondence with Holmes.
15. George William Curtis, ed., *The Correspondence of John Lothrop Motley* (London: John Murray, 1889), 1:26.
16. Thomas Motley to Jared Sparks, January 24, 1833, Sparks Papers, MS Sparks 153.

17. John Lothrop Motley to Jared Sparks, Boston, October 29, 1837, Sparks Papers, MS 153.
18. "[Review of] *The Rise of the Dutch Republic. A History by John Lothrop Motley,*" *North American Review* 83 (1856): 186.
19. "Lady Harcourt," *Boston Evening Transcript,* October 24, 1896.
20. Holmes corresponded with Lady Harcourt. See Holmes, *John Lothrop Motley,* 83–84.
21. Van Doren conducted his research under the auspices of the American Philosophical Society. He served on the society's Library Committee, beginning in 1946, and was named a library research associate and provided with a stipend and an assistant, both for an edition of Franklin's letters to Richard Jackson and for his edition of the Mecom-Franklin correspondence. For Van Doren's involvement with the APS concerning the purchase of Frankliniana and the preparation of an edition of the Mecom-Franklin papers, see Van Doren Papers, Box 37, Folder 4; Box 11, Folder 13; and Box 14, Folder 3.
22. Minutes, APS, Committee on Library, December 19, 1946, Box 37, Folder 7, Van Doren Papers.
23. Frederic R. Kirkland and Jane Franklin Mecom, "Three Mecom-Franklin Letters," *Pennsylvania Magazine of History and Biography* 72 (1948): 264–72.
24. Roelker, *BF and CG,* v.
25. C. Dixon, *Benjamin Franklin,* miniature, 1774, gift of Dr. Franklin G. Balch, November 10, 1943, Museum of Fine Arts, Boston, accession no. 43.1318. "Acquisitions, April 16 through December 9, 1943," *Bulletin of the Museum of Fine Arts* 42 (1944): 22. Franklin G. Balch to W. G. Constable, October 19, 1943. Franklin G. Balch to G. Harold Edgell, November 13, 1943 (this is the letter I have quoted). G. Harold Edgell to Franklin G. Balch, November 29, 1943. Constable was the curator of paintings. Edgell was the director of the museum. Carbon copies of these letters, along with all correspondence cited here relating to the miniature and the ring, are housed in the accession files of the Decorative Arts Department, Museum of Fine Arts, Boston.
26. "DIED. Last Saturday, Mr. Josiah Williams, AE 25, eldest Son to JONATHAN WILLIAMS, Esq., of this Town, Merchant. By his Sentimental Conversation and amiable Disposition, he render'd himself an instructive as well as a pleasing Companion. He was remarkably fond of Musick, and tho' Blind from his Infancy, promised to excel in that Science. All who *knew* him, *lov'd* him." *Boston Gazette,* August 17, 1772.
27. Franklin G. Balch to W. G. Constable, October 19, 1943.
28. W. G. Constable to Franklin G. Balch, October 20, 1943.
29. In his 1943 letter concerning the ring and the Mecom letters, Balch also mentioned a daguerreotype. The museum suggested that he give all of these items to the MHS. The society accepted the daguerreotype in 1949. See *Proceedings of the Massachusetts Historical Society* 69 (1949): 469. It would not have been unusual for the society to decline these letters. Tracy Potter, the society's reference librarian, e-mail to the author, January 13, 2012.
30. R. Baldwin, Memorandum for G. Harold Edgell, Re: Estate of Katherine T. Balch,

October 28, 1946. "Perhaps your records at the Museum will show whether any of the Balch family has had a particular interest in any of our departments," Baldwin urged.

31. Mourning ring, 1772, accession no. 49.60, gift of Dr. Franklin G. Balch, February 10, 1949, MFA. "Accessions, November 19, 1948 through March 23, 1949," *Bulletin of the Museum of Fine Arts* 47 (1949): 34. "Traditionally owned by Benjamin Franklin" appeared on the item's card in the museum's card catalog and, in January 2012, in the provenance field of the item's listing in the online catalog. A letter from the museum acknowledges the gift as simply an "eighteenth century American mourning ring." C. Harold Edgell to Franklin Greene Balch, February 11, 1949.

32. Charles Coleman Sellers, *Exhibition of Portraits Marking the 250th Anniversary of the Birth of the Society's Founder, Benjamin Franklin* (Philadelphia, 1956). Charles Coleman Sellers, "Jane Mecom's Little Picture," *Proceedings of the American Philosophical Society* 99 (1955): 433–35. In Mrs. Haven Parker to Charles Coleman Sellers, August 5, 1955, Parker mentions that she intends to send an offprint of the article to Balch. Parker was the museum's assistant in American Paintings. Balch, a physician, lived in Jamaica Plain and had retired from his private practice, which had been taken over by his son, Dr. Franklin Balch III. The family summered in Chocorua, New Hampshire. Parker summered in Chocorua as well.

33. Franklin G. Balch, to Mrs. Haven Parker, August 9, 1955.

34. Ibid.

35. The letters were JFM to Sarah Franklin Bache, May 23, 1787, and JFM to Sarah Franklin Bache, October 20, 1790. Notes on the acquisition can be found in the Card Catalogue, Editorial Offices of the Benjamin Franklin Papers, Yale University.

36. All of these elements are conventional. On mourning rings, see Robin Jaffee Frank, *Love and Loss: American Portrait and Mourning Miniatures* (New Haven: Yale University Art Gallery, 2000).

37. William E. Lingelbach, "Notable Letters and Papers: Relating to (1) Early American Diplomacy and Winning the Peace, (2) Darwinism and the Great Revolution in Science, (3) A New Franklin Letter to Jane Mecom and (4) Dr. Rush to Patrick Henry," *Proceedings of the American Philosophical Society* 95 (1951), 218–19.

38. Helen Cripe and Diane Campbell, *American Manuscripts, 1763–1815: An Index to Documents Described in Auction Records and Dealers' Catalogues* (Wilmington, DE: Scholarly Resources, 1977); the Mecom items are listed on p. 603.

39. *Fine Printed and Manuscript Americana: Including the Library of Lindley Eberstadt* ([New York?]: Sotheby's, 1985), lots 12, 13, and 14. Lot 12 was purchased by John Fleming of the Rosenbach Company. Lot 13, BF to JFM, November 4, 1787, was sold for $7,500 to a dealer named Joe Rubinfine. He sold it to Donald Platten of New York, then the chairman of Chemical Bank. Platten died in 1991, and I don't know what became of the letter. (William Reese, e-mail to the author, January 18, 2012.) I have been unable to discover who purchased lot 14.

40. James N. Green, "Other Gifts: A Very Good Year," *Annual Report of the Library Company of Philadelphia* (2006), 34–35. And "Copies of Letters of Dr. Franklin," 1825, LCP.

41. George Washington, [Proposed Address to Congress?, April? 1789], in *The Writings of George Washington*, ed. John C. Fitzpatrick (Washington: U.S. Government Printing Office, 1931–44), 30: 296–97n81.

Appendix C A Jane Genealogy

1. Jane Mecom Collas, Josiah Flagg, JFM, and Jane Mecom to BF's Executors, Boston, July 2, 1790, can be found in the larger of two bound volumes housed in a box called Benjamin Franklin Estate Papers, at the APS.

2. JFM to Henry Hill, August 6, 1791. Authorization from the father of Franklin and Sarah Greene for an arrangement whereby Jane Collas would receive and disburse their portions, came in a deposition. "I Elihu Greene of Warwick . . . Guardian to my Children Franklin Greene & Sarah Greene hereby authorize & empower Jane Collas of Boston . . . To collect & receive for me & in my Acct as Guardian as aforesaid all such Legacies." Elihu Greene, Warwick, July 2, 1790. Franklin Estate Papers, Folder 3, APS. The reply, from Henry Hill, is copied into the estate papers and is dated October 31, 1791, complying with the request.

3. An entry on the back page of the larger of the two bound volumes boxed with BF's Estate Papers at the APS is dated August 12, 1790, and reads as follows:

Memorand of Doctor Franklin's descendants as they came to the knowledge of the Executors, taken with a view to the payment of the £50 Stg. Legacies—
　Mrs Jane Mecom's Son Benja. Said to be deceased. His children & Grand children entitled to shares alike one of the L50 Stg vizt.

Sarah Smith	Philadelphia
Do.[ditto] 6 Children	Do
Abiah Mecom	Amboy
Jane Do	Boston
Elizabeth Do	Philadelphia
Mary Carr	New York
Do 1 Child	Do

　16 Descendants of Jane Mecom Do's eldest daughter Sarah Flagg deceas'd her children

Josiah Flagg	Lancaster now in Boston
Jane Flagg	deceased—her children viz.t
Franklin Green }	Rhode Island
Sarah Green	
Dos 2d Daughter Jane Collas	

4. Benjamin Franklin Estate Papers, B/F85h, Folder 2, APS.

5. "The Estate of Dr. Franklin," B/F85h.3, Folder 2, Franklin Papers, APS. The bequests from the estate to the family of Benjamin Mecom's daughters Sarah Smith and Elizabeth Britt can be traced in a small bound volume kept by Henry Hill and stored in a box at the APS called "Benjamin Franklin's Estate Papers."

Appendix E   The Editorial Hand of Jared Sparks

1. Sparks's heavy hand as a magazine editor is abundantly illustrated by his correspondence with the historian George Bancroft, which is transcribed in "Correspondence of George Bancroft and Jared Sparks, 1823–1832," ed. John Spencer Bassett, *Smith College Studies in History* 2 (1917): 67–143. For instance, Sparks all but dictated to Bancroft what he could and could not say in a book review, as when he wrote, "I should like to have the author dealt gently with, although not extravagantly praised. I think you can let some parts of the book speak well for themselves; You can make a sort of analysis of things, and throw in such reflections as occur" (Sparks to Bancroft, March 31, 1824, p. 77).

2. Bancroft to Sparks, July 10, 1824, p. 80.

3. Bancroft to Sparks, July 12, 1824, pp. 80–81.

4. Bancroft to Sparks, June 31 [*sic*], 1824, p. 78.

5. Sparks to Bancroft, June 21, 1824, p. 79. Asking Bancroft to review a *Journal of a Tour in Italy by an American*, Sparks urged, "Take it in hand and do it justice; but do not get into any tantrums talking about Italian arts, scenery, and associations. Tell us of plain, entertaining, and good things" (Sparks to Bancroft, September 16, 1824, p. 86). This irritated Bancroft, who wrote back, "There must be no mind at work but my own" (Bancroft to Sparks, November 13, 1824, p. 87). In 1826, Bancroft was so exasperated with what Sparks had done to his writing that he threatened legal action, telling him, "I cannot as a man of honor, take part in this or permit it, without forfeiting my claim to self-respect." Sparks replied that he wondered at Bancroft's "strange notions of an editor's task." This exchange concerned Bancroft's unfavorable review of John Pickering's *Vocabulary*; see pp. 113–27.

6. Joseph Story to Jared Sparks, October 19, 1833, in Adams, *Life of Sparks*, 2:283–84. Twentieth-century standards for modernizing prose can be found in Samuel Eliot Morison, "Care and Editing of Manuscripts," in *The Harvard Guide to American History* (Cambridge, MA: Harvard University Press, 1974), 31–33.

7. Benjamin Waterhouse to Jared Sparks, June 6, 1833, in Baxter, *Life of Sparks*, 2:339.

Appendix F   Jane's Library

1. See BF to Abiah Folger Franklin, Philadelphia, October 16, 1747.

2. JFM to BF, December 1, 1767, and BF to JFM, December 24, 1767.

3. For her request, see JFM to BF, October 19, 1785. For what seems to be a confirmation that she received the catalog of books, see JFM to BF, November 30, 1785.

4. *A Catalogue of Those Books in Franklin Library Which Belong to the Town* (n.p., 1812).

5. BF to JFM, February 22, 1789.

6. JFM to DRF, September 28, 1765.

7. JFM to BF, June 13, 1781. Van Doren, *Letters*, 209.

8. I have not been able to discover where or how he acquired it, but one possibility is that it was from the private collection of Howard Corning, who, at least between 1927 and 1932, was a librarian at the Baker Library at Harvard Business School and who also had in his collection at least one item belonging to Josiah Flagg. In 1933, Corning became the secretary of the Essex Institute, now the Peabody Essex Museum. Tim Mahoney, manuscripts librarian, Baker Library, Harvard Business School, e-mail to the author, January 9, 2012.

9. BF to Jonathan Williams Sr., London, April 3, 1773.

10. BF to JFM, December 24, 1767.

11. JFM to BF, October 23, 1781.

12. JFM to BF, October 29, 1781.

13. BF to JFM, January 24, 1786, and BF to JFM, April 25, 1786.

14. BF to JFM, July 28, 1774. Van Doren, *Letters*, 145.

15. Van Doren, *Letters*, 145.

16. JFM to BF, January 6, 1786. BF to JFM, January 24, 1786. *Life of Chesterfield*, 386.

17. Van Doren, *Letters*, 209.

18. BF to JFM, October 25, 1779, and JFM to BF, March 27, 1780.

19. For instance, Benjamin Colman, who was Jane's minister at the Brattle Street Church, once wrote a reply, called "The Transport. To Mr. Pope, on looking again into his Essay on Man," February 14, 1740. Benjamin Colman Papers, Box 1, MHS.

20. Van Doren, *Letters*, 145.

21. JFM to BF, May 22, 1787. Van Doren, *Letters*, 293.

22. Van Doren, *Letters*, 145.

23. JFM to BF, July 4, 1784.

24. *Catalogue of rare, curious and valuable books, theological, classical, philosophical and literary to be sold by public auction at Francis Amory's auction room . . . February 22, 1816 being the library of the late reverend John Lathrop* (Boston, 1816), 2.

25. Ibid., 6.

Index

Page numbers in *italics* refer to illustrations.

ILLUSTRATION CREDITS

iii Jane Franklin Mecom, Book of Ages, 1731–67, detail. New England Historic Genealogical Society.

xii Jane Franklin Mecom, Book of Ages, 1731–67, detail. New England Historic Genealogical Society.

24 Benjamin Franklin the Elder, "A short account of the Family of Thomas Franklin of Ecton," 1717. Beinecke Rare Book and Manuscript Library, Yale University.

36 Silence Dogood, "No. 2," *New-England Courant*, April 16, 1722. Massachusetts Historical Society.

47 Detail of inscription by Jane Franklin Mecom in Richard Steele, comp., *The Ladies Library*, 4th ed. (London, 1732). American Antiquarian Society.

49 Jane Franklin Mecom, Book of Ages, 1731–67, detail. New England Historic Genealogical Society.

50 The Flourishing Alphabet. George Fischer, *The American Instructor* (Philadelphia: Benjamin Franklin and David Hall, 1748). American Antiquarian Society.

55 Title page from Benjamin Colman, *The Father's Tears over his Daughter's Remains* (Boston, 1735). American Antiquarian Society.

61 Title page from Benjamin Franklin, *Poor Richard, 1733. An Almanack*, third impression (Philadelphia, 1732). Historical Society of Pennsylvania.

64 Inscription by Jane Franklin Mecom in Richard Steele, comp., *The Ladies Library*, 4th ed. (London: 1732). American Antiquarian Society.

69 Fifteen-shilling note (Philadelphia: Printed by Benjamin Franklin and David Hall, 1756). Colonial Williamsburg.

71 Edward Mecom, sheriff's writ, 1739. Massachusetts State Archives.

85 Benjamin Franklin, *Experiments and Observations on Electricity* (London, 1769). Inscribed by Jane Franklin Mecom. Princeton University Library.

103 A letter from Jane Franklin Mecom to Deborah Read Franklin, January 29, 1758. American Philosophical Society.

A NOTE ABOUT THE AUTHOR

Jill Lepore is the David Woods Kemper '41 Professor of American History at Harvard University. She
is also a staff writer at *The New Yorker*.

A NOTE ON THE TYPE

This book was set in Adobe Garamond, designed
by Robert Slimbach (born 1956), and named for
Claude Garamond (c. 1480–1561).

Composed by North Market Street Graphics,
Lancaster, Pennsylvania

Printed and bound by Berryville Graphics,
Berryville, Virginia

Designed by Maggie Hinders